THE S. MARK TAPER FOUNDATION

IMPRINT IN JEWISH STUDIES

BY THIS ENDOWMENT

THE S. MARK TAPER FOUNDATION SUPPORTS

THE APPRECIATION AND UNDERSTANDING

OF THE RICHNESS AND DIVERSITY OF

JEWISH LIFE AND CULTURE

THE JEWS OF THE UNITED STATES, 1654 TO 2000

JEWISH COMMUNITIES IN THE MODERN WORLD

DAVID SORKIN, EDITOR

THE JEWS OF THE UNITED STATES

1654 TO 2000

HASIA R. DINER

UNIVERSITY OF CALIFORNIA PRESS

BERKELEY · LOS ANGELES · LONDON

University of California Press
Berkeley and Los Angeles, California

University of California Press, Ltd.
London, England

© 2004 by The Regents of the University of California

Library of Congress Cataloging-in-Publication Data

Diner, Hasia R.
  The Jews of the United States, 1654 to 2000 / Hasia
R. Diner.
      p.   cm. — (Jewish communities in the modern
world ; 4)
  Includes bibliographical references and index.
  ISBN 0–520–22773–5 (cloth : alk. paper)
    1. Jews—United States—History.   2. United
States—Ethnic relations.   I. Title. II. Series.
E184.35.D55   2004
973'.04924—dc21   2003012766

Manufactured in the United States of America

12   11   10   09   08   07   06   05   04
10   9   8   7   6   5   4   3   2   1

To the memory of Dave and Helen Diner, whose lives in Europe and America demonstrate the many different versions of Jewish history

CONTENTS

ACKNOWLEDGMENTS

My warmest thanks go out to a number of people who made this book possible. They all made a real difference, and I am indebted to them for what they have taught me. Their help and encouragement at each stage of the process sustained me and helped me to tell a complicated story about a group of people who prided themselves on their contentiousness and diversity.

It goes without saying that one volume hardly does justice to the narrative of this group. Synthesis, by definition, leaves out, collapses, and generalizes. The individuals whose names I cite here pointed out to me the implications of my decisions about what I would, and, more important, what I would not, include. They indicated that I needed to broaden and complicate what I had written and showed me how and where to do that. Even when I could not fully follow their words of counsel, owing to the limitations of space, I learned much from their admonitions.

I would like to thank David Sorkin first. I was thrilled that he, as the editor of this series published by the University of California Press, chose me to write this book. I am proud that he asked me to join Paula Hyman, who wrote on the Jews of modern France, and Todd Endelman, whose book about England's Jews provided me with models. That David offered me this project would have been an honor in and of itself. But I am particularly grateful that he gave me the opportunity to try my hand at crafting a unique overview of American Jewish history. In my teaching at New York University I have played with some of the concepts and ideas that emerge in these pages. Putting them into written words proved to be a very different and more difficult matter, and I thank David for giving me this chance. Likewise, I have found working with Stan Holwitz of the University of California Press a delight, and our meetings in New York and Los Angeles have always stimulated me to keep at this project.

I asked a number of colleagues—or better, dear friends—to read this manuscript and to give me their comments. Eric Goldstein, Marion Kaplan, Tony Michaels, Walter Nugent, Beth Wenger, and Stephen Whitfield gave me much of their time and wisdom. They each insisted, despite the nature of this type of book, that I go further, tell alternative stories, and provide examples counter to the dominant paradigm.

Several of my students read an early draft of the manuscript. They used it to prepare for their doctoral examinations in American Jewish history, and their critical reading of my words helped me to focus on the places that needed more clarity, more documentation, and more depth. Rebecca Boim Wolf and Joshua Perelman will become part of the next generation of historians of the American Jewish experience; they will no doubt go on to rewrite this book when their time comes.

Avinoam Pat provided wonderful help in researching the photographs, and Lynn Slome of the American Jewish Historical Society sped up the process of making the illustrations available to me. Additionally, the staff at the American Jewish Archives responded to my requests with courtesy. Various librarians at New York University's Bobst Library helped in a multitude of ways.

Last but not least, my family—Steve, Shira, Eli, and Matan—always and forever gives meaning to my life and work.

INTRODUCTION

The major developments of American Jewish history grew out of both a Jewish and an American context. The chronology of American Jewish life, the structure of its communal network, and the inner dynamism that propelled it demand explanations from both American and Jewish sources and cannot be divorced from either of these historics. Yet by itself neither one can explain how American Jews lived and what the patterns of their lives meant to them.

A constant process of negotiation shaped the history of Jews in America. Many—probably most—ordinary Jews wanted both to be good Jews and to be full Americans. They looked inward to Jewish tradition to shape the patterns of their lives, while looking outward to their American neighbors as they decided how to live and how to present themselves. They thought about the Jewish past and the American present, trying to determine what each demanded of them.

But American Jews did not just react to the actions of non-Jews, the dictates of communal leaders, the sanctity of authoritative texts, or the tumultuous political events at home and beyond their borders. Rather, they actively fashioned their communities, both locally and nationally, according to their understanding of what their Jewish and American identities demanded of them. At times the process of negotiation set them apart from other diaspora Jewish communities, while at other times putting them at odds with the behaviors and attitudes of other Americans.

Negotiating between American and Jewish identities, they operated with a sense of empowerment. They did not believe that they had to ac-

1

cept America as it was, nor did they see Judaism as a fixed entity that they could not mold to fit their needs. They could put their impress on both to ease the traumas of accommodation and to bring the two into harmony.

The Jewish women and men of America tested the boundaries of Judaism as they understood it, searching for ways to render the traditional system acceptable to their American sensibilities. In matters of religious practice, American Jews looked less often either to canonical works or to authoritative leaders. Rather, they fashioned their religious lives in their own image. American Jewry thus took on a character distinctive from that of other Jewries. The mere fact that they created a derivative society, made up of immigrants, rendered the construction of American Jewish identity fluid, negotiable, and highly voluntary. Jews who emigrated from Poland to Germany, for example, stood out dramatically from the German population because of their foreign origins. They were expected, both by non-Jews and Jews, to subsume their former identities under a German Jewish rubric. By contrast, Polish Jews who immigrated to America came to a country where almost all residents traced their roots to someplace else, and Jews did not stand out as unusual for being immigrants or the descendants of immigrants. They rarely had to hide their Jewishness completely or to erase where they had come from.

Yet at times some did conceal or abandon their Jewish identity altogether. For many the demands of America and the burden of Jewishness led to discontinuity, discomfort, and disjunction. For some, the lure of America proved stronger than allegiance to Jewishness. Some left Jewishness behind, dropping out completely from the Jewish world. Their stories, of the occasional great-grandparent in a Christian family who had been born Jewish, the Jewish-sounding surname in a non-Jewish household, and so on, emerged through family histories. Other Jews, from the most observant to the most politically radical, had little interest in America, its values, institutions, and practices. They expressed disdain for what they saw as the shallowness of American culture, the cruelties of its economic system, and the seductive power of its popular culture. But most, from the days of the earliest Jewish communities in America, self-consciously sought to be part of American society, first in the local community and then, after independence, in the national milieu. Their professions of loyalty to America and their actions in the name of the American common good won them friends and allies among their non-Jewish neighbors. American Jews found themselves notable in the history of the Jewish diaspora in that they never functioned as their nation's most stigmatized group. By virtue of their skin color, and through the middle of the nineteenth century by virtue of the fact that they were not Catholics (Irish Catholics in particular) in a fervently Protestant society, they enjoyed a degree of acceptance, however attenuated. That acceptance, as they saw it, existed relative to the tremendous persecution that Jews experienced elsewhere and that some non-Jews experienced in America. From the end of the eighteenth century, at the beginning of the era of Jewish Emancipation in western Europe, American Jews enjoyed relatively full political and civil rights. They also functioned in a political system in which the state eschewed any interest in the religious lives of its people.

And yet anti-Semitism reared its head in America too and left its mark on the Jews. While racist talk did not translate into direct political action against the Jews as it did in Europe, a series of social and governmental policies, culminating in the 1920s in the immigration quota system written into the National Origins Act and the quota systems in colleges and universities, hospitals, and law firms, limited—or eliminated—Jewish entry. This meant that Jews shaped their life choices in part around a set of options informed by the fact that they were Jews.

This book describes how the Jews came to America in the seventeenth century and lived in general obscurity, making a point of attracting little attention to themselves and to their differentness. For almost all of their history in America, after Peter Stuyvesant greeted with enmity the first group of Jews on the docks of New Amsterdam in 1654, Jews lived in Jewish communities, which functioned as structures of support. These highly regulated, self-governing, hierarchical Jewish communities were built around a single synagogue in each of five Atlantic coast seaports and in Richmond, Virginia, which sat at the head of the internal waterways that served the Appalachian frontier.

These small Jewish communities functioned as American outposts of the Jewish communities of Amsterdam, London, and several others scattered around the Caribbean. They centered on Jewish traditions such as respecting, if not observing, the Sabbath, eating kosher food, and preparing Jewish children for life in a Jewish world. At a more profound level, Jews differed from other Americans by virtue of their identification with a worldwide people. They derived a sense of themselves from their participation in a set of practices whose origins went back millennia, from their reverence—even when not observed—for inherited texts viewed as sacred, and from their identification with people around the world in whom they discerned a commonality of history and fate.

After the ratification of the Constitution, although the United States may have operated on the principles of separation of church and state and the nonestablishment of any one religion, many still considered it a Christian country. The basic tone of the society was set by Christian idioms, and the Christian calendar reflected the seasons. But Jews had their own idioms and their own calendars. How they negotiated between the Christian character of America and their own Jewishness provides one of the leitmotifs of their history.

From the second decade of the nineteenth century until the second decade of the twentieth, America functioned as a magnet for Jews leaving Europe. The great era of European Jewish immigration to America spanned a century from 1820 through 1924. That successively larger waves of immigrants crested on the shores of the United States meant that Jewish communities always existed in a state of flux. Newcomers intersected with old-timers, who a decade or two earlier had been newcomers themselves. Jewish communities both welcomed and sought to remake the immigrants, who both retained some familiar practices and identities and created new ones as they found a place in their new homes.

The era of immigration coincided with two crucial moments in the economic history of the nation. When in the early nineteenth century white America pushed westward and into the hinterlands beyond the Atlantic seaboard to exploit the natural resources of the continent, Jews, as peddlers, small-town merchants, and wholesalers in regional entrepôts, outfitted this westward expansion. When the American economy shifted its focus to the production of nondurable consumer goods in the last quarter of the nineteenth century, Jews, with a long history in the needle trades, came to America in part to operate the sewing machines that helped clothe the American public.

The lives of American Jews often deviated from those of other Americans in other ways. Throughout most of American history, until the end of the nineteenth century, most Americans made their living as farmers. The rare Jewish farmers have been noted in communal chronicles because their stories differed so much from the basic American Jewish narrative. Whereas other Americans made a living through agriculture, Jews made theirs through commerce, and by the end of the nineteenth century many worked in industry. Not until the early twentieth century, as revealed in the 1920 census, did a majority of Americans live in cities. Jews, however, all through their history in America, had opted for cities over small towns, especially large cities. The communal histories of small-town Jews in the South, the Southwest, and the Pacific Northwest stood apart from those of most Jews. Likewise, by the middle decades of the twentieth century, Jews acquired university educations and entered into the professions far out of their proportion to the population as a whole.

The nineteenth century saw not only the triumph of national independence but also the growth of cities beyond their colonial borders and the expansion of the white population into the trans-Appalachian west, the Great Lakes, the Pacific Rim, and then the filling in of the vast prairie regions. Americans liberated themselves not just from Britain but also from many (although not all) of the hierarchies and restraints of the eighteenth century. Likewise, Jews in the older cities, and then in all the new places in which they settled, broke out of the strict structure of a synagogue governing the entire life of the local Jewish community. Clusters of Jews built a variety of synagogues as well as various kinds of extra-synagogal institutions. They experimented with new forms of worship. American Judaism, like America, came to be increasingly pluralistic and accepting of the idea that in matters religious, groups of women and men had the right to create their own institutions as they saw fit.

By the end of the nineteenth century, individual Americans issued a call for the creation of new structures to tame the unsettled and disorderly life of the nation, culminating in the Progressive Era and the New Deal of the 1930s. Likewise, individuals in Jewish communities sought to impose order on what they saw as a bewildering welter of Jewish charities, schools, organizations, prayer books, and synagogues. Reform Judaism achieved its institutional form in the late 1860s and 1870s. Conservative Judaism evolved slowly from the Jewish Theological Seminary founded in 1886. Starting in the 1890s Orthodoxy in America began to search for ways to centralize the practice of traditional Judaism. All conformed to the organizational and managerial model of the society as a whole. The rise of federations of Jewish philanthropies beginning in the 1890s and the local Jewish community councils in the 1920s fit with the progressive passion for order as well.

If the history of the Jews in the United States paralleled the history of the nation, it also flowed along the course of modern Jewish history in general. As in Europe, Jews in America formed communities that provided a wide array of services to their members, although in America the members always affiliated because they chose to. All the great political and intellectual streams coursing through Jewish life in the modern age traveled in a transnational Jewish path, linking Europe, America, and Palestine (and, after 1948, Israel): Reform, secularization, modern Orthodoxy, Socialism, Zionism, the flowering of Yiddish and Hebrew literature and letters, and the expression of Jewish idioms in new art forms such as theater and film. For much of its history American Jewry functioned as a kind of outpost of Europe. It was in the great Jewish population centers in Poland, Russia, and Germany that Jewish high culture was created. Warsaw, Berlin, Vienna, Odessa, Vilna, and other cities of Europe were the cradles of Jewish political and artistic inspiration, while America was a kind of sideshow. Although these ideas and movements also flourished in New York, Chicago, Los Angeles, and Philadelphia, the basic flow went from east to west.

The pivotal moment in the history of American Jewry took place in the crucial years between the middle of the 1920s and the end of World War II. In that two-decade period, a population of Jewish immigrants transformed itself into a population of native-born American Jews. By the eve of World War II, a majority of American Jews had been born in America. By the 1960s most Jews in America no longer had a direct link to Europe—particularly Eastern Europe—and to the legacy of anti-Semitism and of densely organized, highly structured Jewish communities. Therefore, it should not be surprising that American Jews articulated, albeit in Americanized forms, similar ideas, sensibilities, fears, hopes, and beliefs as did Jewish people elsewhere. Likewise, regardless of what many Americans liked to believe, American ideas, technological sophistication, and economic fortunes operated in concert with developments in Europe.

World War II proved to be the tragic turning point. Not only did it witness the destruction of Jewish lives and communities, but it also heralded the passing of the baton, by default, to American Jewry. By the war's end America became the largest, most significant, and most powerful Jewish community in the world. American Jews played a key role in the reconstruction of Jewish life around the globe, attempting to remake it in their image. They framed that image around the fact that American Jews lived with a high level of physical comfort. Yet, both before and after the Holocaust, the specter of violence and persecution that hung over the heads of their sisters and brothers elsewhere not only shaped their political behavior, it also haunted them. The bonds of shared identity influenced American Jews, causing them to wonder about and fret over their own fate in a non-Jewish land. Indeed, the moments when anti-Jewish and anti-Semitic rhetoric in America rose to audible levels coincided with the great outbreaks of anti-Semitic rhetoric and action in Europe. The kinds of defense organizations that American Jews founded reflected events and developments across the Atlantic as imagined by Jews in America.

Economically, American Jews, as compared to European Jews, had access to higher wages and greater levels of material comfort, and at almost any point in time they expected to experience some mobility. But they, like Jews elsewhere, functioned within a specific kind of Jewish economy. The kinds of jobs they pursued, the provision of credit within Jewish networks of assistance, and the ways in which new fields using technological innovations opened up to them took place in Europe as well, and immigrant Jews coming from America went from one Jewish economy to another.

When measured alongside other Jewish communities, American Jewry ought to be seen as sui generis up to World War II. Yet since the end of the war and the tectonic shifts in Jewish life that resulted from it, American Jewry has become paradigmatic of the diaspora communities almost everywhere else. Before the war, American Jewry stood out among Jewish communities for its freedom to shape its internal institutions, with no interference from the state, and for its high level of integration into the larger society. The relative absence of anti-Semitism, which manifested itself in organized political action, also shaped the contours of American Jewish life, rendering it different from other Jewish communities. American Jewry emerged as distinctive because of its own internal tolerance and pluralistic views about Judaism and Jewish practice. With the end of World War II American Jewry emerged as the dominant center of diaspora Jewish life. It began to function as a model for the older communities, which had been shaped by long histories of anti-Semitism, political struggles over emancipation and the problematic status of the Jews, and the state's meddling in the inner life of the Jewish community. By the end of the twentieth century the older Jewish centers pursued strategies, allowed for pluralism, and engaged in debates that mirrored what American Jews had been doing for decades, indeed centuries.

The era from the 1930s through the 1960s thus might be seen as both the golden age of American liberalism and as the enshrinement of the legacy of the New Deal and the high point of Jewish institutional orderliness, which followed the move of American Jews out of the central cities and into the new suburbs of the postwar era. The late 1960s, however, brought about severe internal criticism of that quest for order and the triumph of bureaucracy. Many, especially students, took America to task for its continuing racism and sexism. Likewise, a Jewish counter-culture, embodied in the *havurah* movement, chided the suburban synagogues for what young people saw as their parents' shallow compromises with American bourgeois civility. The issue of women's rights within Judaism challenged the denominations and the community institutions, and the specter of the Holocaust and the charge that American Jews had failed to react in the face of its horrors left their mark on the Jewish communities. The rise of a new kind of Orthodox Judaism that questioned the kinds of adjustments Jews and Judaism had made to America took place in the context of late-twentieth-century America, which became more tolerant of displayed differences.

American Jews faced the beginning of the twenty-first century with a sense both of comfort and concern. Before them lay seemingly limitless choices in their personal lives and in the kinds of Jewish practices and idioms they could fashion for themselves. Yet they also saw a dwindling of numbers and a weakening of group loyalties. Much of their communal time went into discussions and debates over these two, possibly irreconcilable, trends. How they will play out surely cannot be hazarded by anyone, a historian in particular.

The year 2000 offers a convenient ending point to this narrative. On the one hand, the fact that the Democratic party nominated for vice president an observant Jew, Joseph Lieberman, deserves to serve as the terminal point of this history of nearly 350 years of Jewish life in America. In the days and months following Lieberman's nomination the American public became quite familiar and, by all accounts, comfortable with the fact that on Saturdays the candidate took a rest from the frenetic pace of campaigning to observe the Jewish Sabbath. In the early fall, the high point of the campaign, he observed a cycle of holidays that set him apart from the vast majority of Americans, the electorate who would in November decide his political fate. Press accounts and opinion polling demonstrated not only that Americans did not harbor negative feelings about Lieberman's Jewishness, but indeed that they respected and admired his faith and commitment. They did not see him as somehow less than fully American.

That same autumn witnessed the start of a new and deadly cycle of violence in Israel. The outbreak of bloodshed in the region, the spread of anti-Israel rhetoric around the world—including on some American college campuses—caused American Jews grave consternation. They were torn and tormented by the grim news coming out of the Middle

East. The fact that criticism of Israel had melded with frightening ease in parts of western Europe into familiar, old-style anti-Semitism shocked the American Jewish public.

While American Jews debated, with great intensity, about what role they, Israel, and the United States government ought to play, they could not but be struck by the contrast between France, for example, and the United States, where with a few isolated exceptions, public support for Israel remained high and where mobs did not attack Jewish communal institutions. Whatever their political opinion about Israel, or indeed about any subject, they saw graphically how America and its Jews had created a very special relationship.

PART ONE

THE EARLIEST JEWISH COMMUNITIES

1

AMERICAN JEWISH ORIGINS

1654–1776

In September 1654, twenty-three Jewish refugees from Brazil stepped ashore in the Dutch colony of New Amsterdam. They had not journeyed there intentionally. They simply knew they had to get out of Brazil, which had recently been snatched by the Portuguese from the Dutch, who allowed Jews religious and economic freedom. Memories of past Iberian inquisitions and massacres compelled these Jews to flee, and the captain of the *Sainte Catherine,* which happened to be heading for the Dutch colony at the mouth of the Hudson River, agreed to take them.

Two other Jews, Solomon Pieterson and Jacob Barsimon, actually had preceded them to New Amsterdam. But they had stayed there only briefly, and more important, they sojourned there as solitary individuals who took no steps to live as Jews in a community.

Those who made the journey on the *Sainte Catherine* did so as the nucleus of what would become the first Jewish community in the New World. To live as Jews in a Jewish community and in such large numbers required the approval of the local authorities, namely, the governor of the colony, Peter Stuyvesant, a devout member of the Dutch Reformed Church, and his superiors in Amsterdam, the Dutch West India Company. Stuyvesant had no desire to let the Jews stay. They would, he believed, engage in "their customary usury and deceitful trading with the Christians." They would destroy the Christian character of the colony by practicing their religion, since Jews were "hateful enemies and blasphemers of the name of Christ," and their poverty, he claimed, would make them a burden to the community.[1] Stuyvesant conveyed these sentiments in a letter to Amsterdam. While he awaited an answer, the Jews sent their own communiqué across the ocean. They addressed theirs to the Jews of Amsterdam, who enjoyed a relatively high level of religious tolerance. The Jews stranded in New Amsterdam begged the Jews in old Amsterdam to intercede for them with the Dutch West India Company.

The Jews in Amsterdam agreed. They submitted a petition to the directors of the company, pointing out that for decades the Jews had been loyal to the Netherlands and had served Dutch interests. They had been economically useful at home as well as in the far-flung Dutch colonies. In the worldwide competition for colonies and resources raging between the Dutch and the Spanish, Portuguese, British, and French, the Jews and their trade connections had been, and could continue to be, very helpful to the Netherlands. The Jewish petitioners pointed out that actually "many of the Jewish nation are principal shareholders in the Company." The Amsterdam Jews' argument proved stronger than that of their nemesis, Peter Stuyvesant. In April 1655 the directors in Amsterdam communicated to Stuyvesant that "these people may travel and trade . . . and live and remain there."[2]

The Jews who settled in New Amsterdam used that letter to argue for rights and cited it as the basis of their entitlement to the considerable resources of the Dutch holdings in the North America. When in 1655 Stuyvesant and the council governing the colony barred Jews from participating in the lucrative Indian trade, Abraham De Lucena, Salvador Dandara, and Jacob Cohen, writing in the name of "others of the Jewish nation, residing in this city," reminded them that "the Honorable Lords Directors of the chartered West India Company, masters and patrons of this province, gave permission and consent to the petitioners, like the other inhabitants, to travel, reside and trade here, and enjoy the same liberties, as appears by the document here annexed."[3]

Despite the intervention from Amsterdam, the Jews had not scored a total victory in their initial encounter with the colony. A number of conditions set the Jews apart from the Dutch Reformed population that represented the colony's mainstream. Permission to live in New Amsterdam did not mean that Jews could now function in complete freedom. The authorities initially barred them from training with the guard and participating in the defense of the colony from an impending attack from the Swedes. The law required the Jews to pay a special tax in lieu of military service. Stuyvesant also issued orders banning Jews from trading outside the city limits and from building houses, symbols of a permanent presence. The Dutch West India Company placed one further condition on them that revealed much about the status of the Jews in a Christian world. The Jews could remain, the directors wrote, but they must take care of their own poor. Jews must never become public charges who would become burdens "to the company, or to the community."[4]

Yet despite the force with which the governor imposed these restrictions, the Company did see fit, with notable frequency, to lift them. In the next several years, the Jews of New Amsterdam indeed demanded and won expanded rights. In 1655 Asser Levy, who would become the first prominent Jew of New Amsterdam (and then of New York), petitioned for and won the right to participate with other burghers and be part of the guard, and as such to be free of the tax. Limitations on Jewish trading up the Hudson and Delaware Valleys were dropped, giving Jews a chance to participate in the lucrative fur trade beckoning from the vast frontier extending northward along the Hudson River. In addition, the order forbidding them to construct houses lapsed, and the Jews settled in the new city, clustering together in houses along Whitehall Street. In 1657, also as a result of Asser Levy's aggressive determination, the right of citizenship was extended to them, and they could become burghers.

THE FIRST JEWISH COMMUNITIES

Yet despite the importance of these gains, they needed something more. These immigrants wanted to be able to live as Jews. They began, early on, to demand the right to establish their own communities, based on traditional religious practice and communal obligations.

The Sephardim, or Iberian Jews, among them had a particularly pressing reason for wanting to live publicly as Jews and to follow the religious obligations of their tradition. Many of them came burdened with family and with painful memories of forced conversions to Christianity. The Jews' recent history in the Iberian Peninsula had been painful. It witnessed a long age of persecution involving forced conversions, deaths, and eventually expulsions and the scattering of families over several continents. For those who chose baptism, suspicions lingered. The Inquisition served as a mechanism, in part, to weed out crypto-Jews, Catholics who in the privacy of their homes maintained some elements of Jewish practice. The specter of the Inquisition still haunted them, as did the trauma of expulsion. The colonies offered to many of them a chance to live openly as Jews, to reinvent themselves according to their ancestral identities.

The life of Aaron Lopez provides a case in point. Lopez, who would become one of the wealthiest and best connected of the colonial Jews, came to New York in 1740 and to Rhode Island in 1752. A Portuguese Catholic by birth, he had borne the name Duarte Lopez. Upon his arrival in America he and his family shed their Christian personae, and he took a new name, Aaron Lopez. He submitted himself to circumcision, and henceforth lived as a Jew, concerned with the details of observance. During the American Revolution, when Newport lay under British siege, Lopez lamented to a correspondent that months had gone by since he had eaten meat. The blockade kept out all outside goods, kosher meat included, and he would not deviate from the practice of kashrut, or keeping kosher.[5] For many Sephardic Jews like Lopez, choosing America meant choosing Judaism.

For those who had landed in New Amsterdam a century earlier, religious freedom also had to be won piecemeal. As in all the European colonies in the New World, the civil authorities established churches of various denominations, the Church of England in Virginia and the Puritan congregations in Massachusetts being notable examples. In New Amsterdam the Dutch Reformed Church worked hand in glove with the political authorities of the colony and served as the spiritual embodiment of Dutch rule. All charitable and educational activities in New Amsterdam emanated from the Dutch Reformed Church, and its powerful clergymen, like Johannes Megapolensis, who had sided with Stuyvesant against the entry of the Jews, set most colonial policy. He determined in 1655, for example, that the relatively large community of Lutherans who lived in New Amsterdam could not hold religious services, even in the privacy of their homes. In 1657 the colony forcibly deported a newly arrived German Lutheran minister, for fear that his religion, although a Reformation-era sibling of the Dutch Reformed Church, would compete for souls and influence in the colony.[6]

Ironically, despite the image of Stuyvesant in American Jewish history as an enemy of the Jews, the Jews actually had an easier time establishing the legitimacy of their religious system than did the Lutherans. In 1656, one year after the Lutherans lost their right to worship in their homes, the Jews won that very privilege. The Company in Amsterdam directed Stuyvesant to allow the Jews to hold religious services, mandating that they "exercise in all quietness their religion within their houses."[7]

It would not be until 1682 that these Jews would be permitted to mark off a special space for communal religious worship. What New

Amsterdam officials knew about Judaism is not clear. They may not have realized, for example, that Jews had no need of a designated building for religious worship. Ten Jewish men worshiping together constituted a minyan, a quorum for prayer, be it in a private house, the back of a store, or an inn. The act of praying together made it sacred, not the facade of the building. In the meantime, in anticipation of building a synagogue they did, in the spring of 1655, petition for a more fundamental Jewish right, that of consecrating a plot of land to be used as a cemetery. Again, whether or not they understood the importance in Judaism of a burial ground, the officials granted its adherents the burial ground without much ado.

Once they were granted the right, members of every community made sure they had a Jewish cemetery. Moreover, New York Jews, even before they could build a house of worship, constructed and maintained a *mikveh,* or ritual bath, used primarily by women to fulfill the duties associated with family purity laws. In one of the earliest historical accounts of New York Jewish life, based heavily on oral accounts, Naphtali Phillips wrote in the nineteenth century, "before the Synagogue was built, there was a fine run of water in Mill Street, over which a bathing house was erected, where the females of our nation performed their ablutions."[8] Apart from these spaces, Jewish life unfolded largely in private homes and places of business. But worshiping in private still required some outside assistance. New Amsterdam Jews also imported Torah scrolls from Amsterdam so that they could engage in religious worship, despite their lack of a formal worship space. Although the authorities barred them from having a synagogue, these Jews successfully transplanted to the New World the basic elements of historic Judaism.

The narrative of the Jews of New Amsterdam and their confrontation with Peter Stuyvesant offers an analogous historical lesson to that of the next group of Jews to come to America, those who arrived in Georgia almost eighty years after the first group arrived in New Amsterdam. These Jews were not very warmly welcomed when they stepped ashore in their new home. But the solidity of transnational, intra-Jewish bonds and the influence that one group of Jews wielded for the benefit of another mitigated the crisis. In early July 1733, forty-two Jewish women, men, and children landed on the shores of the Savannah River, in the British colony of Georgia, disembarking from the *William and Sarah* after a seven-month journey from London. While they constituted the single largest group of Jews to land in America up to that date, their story represented but a small moment in American and Jewish history. Yet it tes-

tified to the continuity of the Jewish people and to the particular circumstances of American life that made the development of its distinctive
Jewry possible. Jewish experience and tradition put these immigrants on
the *William and Sarah* and sent them off across the Atlantic. American
conditions provided them with a relatively benign but complicated greet-
ing and an ample vista of opportunities. This in turn produced among
them a profound loyalty to their new home that would evolve into the
forging of an American Jewish identity. The son of one of these immigrants, Mordecai Sheftall, would in three decades become a hero of the
American Revolution, captured by the British in the Battle of Savannah.

None of the Jewish passengers of the *William and Sarah* had particularly long roots in England and could by no stretch be considered "English Jews." They had sojourned there only briefly, having come recently
to England to escape the difficulties they faced as Jews in Prussia. England had earned a well-deserved reputation among Ashkenazi Jews,
Jews of northern and central European origin, as a tolerant place. These
immigrants knew that among its Jews could be found a visible elite of
well-situated wealthy Sephardim, associated with the Bevis Marks Synagogue. To the refugee Jews from the continent, moving to London to
seek out the assistance and protection of the notables of Bevis Marks
seemed a reasonable way to overcome the dire conditions of life in Prussia. The forty-two who ended up in Savannah were indeed just a small
trickle of the large flood of needy Jews who were making their way
across the English Channel.

But the influx of poor Jews into England posed a dilemma to the
Sephardic elite. On the one hand they felt an unquestioned responsibility to other Jews. They believed, as had Jews for centuries, in the Tal-
mudic dictate "All of Israel are responsible one for the other." They also
understood that England's tolerance was rooted in rather thin soil. Less
than a century had passed since 1655 when Oliver Cromwell had invited
the Jews back to England, bringing to an end an expulsion that had lasted
four hundred years. Since 1290 growing numbers of dependent Jews, visibly foreign and markedly needy, had not aided the Jews of England in
their exceedingly slow quest for acceptance and greater rights. The English Jews did not relish the influx from the continent and sought ways
to mitigate their responsibilities. This mix of intra-Jewish responsibility
and fear put the forty-two Jews, former subjects of the despotic King
William I of Prussia, on the *William and Sarah,* heading for America.

As circumstances would have it, these Jews had shown up in London
at a propitious moment. Three members of Bevis Marks, Anthony da

Costa, Alvarez Lopez Suasso, and Francis Salvador, had recently received commissions from the Trustees of the Georgia Charter to help finance and people the new colony in North America. The colony was envisioned as a place to send some of England's paupers, and Georgia's Trustees assumed that the deserving poor would naturally be Christians. Salvador, Suasso, and da Costa, however, reasoned that the Jewish poor would also benefit from removal to the colony, where they might also become self-supporting.

The other Trustees did not rejoice to learn that these three had been putting together a Jewish contingent to join the band bound for Georgia. A majority of the Trustees resolved that the Jews must give up their commissions, lest Georgia "soon become a Jewish colony." Were that to happen, Christians, who would never want to live among Jews, would "fall off and desert it as leaves from a tree in autumn."[9] At that time no more than 120 Christian colonists lived in Georgia, and its backers wanted to see a healthy upsurge in population to make it viable. The forty-two Jews would make a measurable demographic impact on the fledgling colony, and that deeply concerned the Christian London merchants who stood to gain from Georgia's growth. But they had waited too long. The *William and Sarah* had already set sail with its Jews aboard. They all (with the exception of an infant who died during the voyage) survived the journey. The colony's leader, James Oglethorpe, had to decide if they could actually disembark and join this quasi-utopian venture dedicated to the transformation of paupers into hardworking, self-reliant, and respectable men and women.

Oglethorpe consulted English attorneys in Charleston, South Carolina. They offered him the opinion that the Jews should be allowed to stay since the Georgia Charter maintained, "Forever, hereafter, there shall be a liberty of conscience allowed in the worship of God, to all persons," except Catholics. He also wrote to London for further advice, and in the long, drawn-out exchanges between London and Savannah, the Trustees stood their ground. They wanted the Jews out of the colony, even after Oglethorpe reported to them how one of the Jews aboard, Dr. Samuel Nunes, one of the few Sephardim among them, had been instrumental in ministering to the colonists in the grip of a raging epidemic and fever. The Trustees instructed Oglethorpe to pay the doctor for his services and then send him and all the other Jews packing.

In the end Oglethorpe refused to listen to the voices in London. He saw in the Jews two virtues that he intended to exploit. He had an idea that the soil and climate of Georgia could be suitable for growing grapes for wine, and one of the Jews, Abraham De Lyon, another Sephardic Jew, had been raised in Portugal and possessed viticultural skills. Additionally, young men constituted the majority of the Jews, desirable since they could serve in the colony's defense, one of Oglethorpe's greatest concerns, as he looked to the south and saw the massing of Spanish troops on the border with Florida. Furthermore, a number of the Jews actually possessed some money. Fourteen of them brought enough to buy their plots of land, thereby adding to the colony's coffers. More Jews owned land than Christians, a larger proportion of whom had been drawn from the very poorest of the pauper class. The Jews stayed.

The cloud that hung over their arrival originated in Europe; in America the authorities instead considered the usefulness of the Jews' presence. Whatever Christians might have thought of Jews and their religion, many evaluated them from a purely practical perspective. How might the arrival of Jews lead to the flourishing of the colony? How might the Jews strengthen its defenses? How could Jews, despite their religion's defects, serve the colony's needs? This more practical view prevailed. The Jews stayed and transplanted Judaism to their new soil. They had carried a Torah scroll with them, a box with circumcision tools, and "Cloaks," no doubt, tallitoth, or prayer shawls. Two years to the month that they walked off the *William and Sarah* they formed a synagogue, Kehillat Kodesh Mikva Israel, the holy congregation of the hope of Israel. Two years later a benefactor in London sent them another Torah scroll, a set of sacred books, and a Hanukkah candelabrum.[10]

A GROWING TOLERANCE

The drama that unfolded in New Amsterdam also testified to the fundamental purpose of European colonial ventures in the American colonies, the exploitation of natural resources to enhance trade. However negative Stuyvesant or Megapolensis's attitude toward Judaism and the Jews, those responsible for overseeing the colony primarily saw Jews not as adherents of a problematic religious tradition but as a people who could augment the colony's wealth. They placed commercial concerns over spiritual purity and argued that despite their religious defects, Jews would benefit the colony. American religious tolerance flowered out of the soil of necessity.

In the eyes of the colonial authorities, the Jews possessed several assets. First, they rightly saw the Jews as a commercial people with worldwide networks based on family and religion.[11] Most Jews in the colonies engaged in commercial activities. Unlike the majority of Europeans who transplanted to North America and farmed, Jews settled in a handful of port cities and made a living in trade. In 1695, for example, several decades after New Amsterdam had been captured by the British and renamed New York, of the eight Jews listed as taxpayers, seven fell into the category of merchants and retailers, and one, a kosher butcher, appeared to be a skilled artisan. In 1730 the number of Jews had grown, but they still concentrated in trade with only two—another butcher and a tallow maker—earning a living in other occupations.[12]

Jews traded with each other in the colonies and between the colonies and Europe. They relied on family and community ties when negotiating business transactions. When their business ventures necessitated travel, they sought out the Jews in the many ports cities where they did their buying and selling. A Jewish merchant from Philadelphia could depend on Jews in Newport to provide him with lodging and food. Jews from Barbados arriving in Philadelphia came with letters of introduction to local Jews who would then help the newcomers get started in a business venture or in filling an order of goods to be taken to yet another port. Esther Pinheiro, for example, lived in Charles Town, Nevis, a Caribbean British port colony. Her husband, Isaac, had also been a "freeman" in New York, and after his death she continued his business practices. She carried sugar and molasses from Nevis to New York and Boston aboard her sloop, the *Neptune*. In New York she did business with the Jewish businesspeople there and loaded up the *Neptune* with flour, cod, lumber, and finished goods made in Europe to take back to Charles Town. Together this businesswoman and the Jewish merchants in New York participated in a Jewish "triangular trade route."[13]

The kinds of connections that developed among Jewish merchants regardless of which colony they lived in went beyond just informal assistance. Jews in Newport forged business partnerships with Jews in Charleston, South Carolina, as did Jews in New York with Jews in Jamaica. These commercial connections depended on their common origins and common language, separated though they might have been by oceans. As with Jews in Venice, Livorno, Trieste, Bordeaux, as well as Amsterdam and London, liberal state policies enacted to foster trade worked to their advantage.[14] Where business ended and Jewish communal life began blurred. Jews in New York, for example, imported kosher meat from Jamaica, and Jews in Newport exported theirs to Suriname and Barbados. In 1728, when New York Jews needed financial assistance finally to build a synagogue, they turned to their brethren in Jamaica, London, and Curaçao. The Jews of New York lent a Torah scroll to the Jews of Newport; that same scroll had once belonged to the congregation in Savannah.

Business connections often spilled over into the bonds of matrimony. The sons and daughters of Jewish merchants around the Atlantic basin married each other and established branches of family businesses in new places, which in turn stitched together even more tightly a seamless cloth of Jewish trade, community, and family. Not only did these business networks work to the advantage of the Jews, but they also enriched the treasuries of the colonies and added to the general prosperity. Since trade made the colonies and Jews made trade, European antipathy toward Jews as the rejecters of the Gospel weakened. This de-emphasis on doctrinal anti-Judaism took place not just in New York but also in the other British colonies in North America where Jews settled: Pennsylvania, Rhode Island, Virginia, Georgia, and South Carolina.

This tolerance grew in the context of a society that supported much more religious diversity than did England at that time. The bitter and often bloody religious wars that raged in Europe did not carry over to America. It mattered little to most residents of the colonies if their neighbors worshiped as Anabaptists, Mennonites, Methodists, Presbyterians, or even Jews. Some colonies, however, such as Massachusetts and Connecticut, demonstrated a profound inhospitality to anyone who did not share in the religious vision of the founders. Jews, Catholics, and Quakers experienced a similar antagonism in these bastions of Calvinist conservatism. Indeed, Catholics and Quakers suffered greater antipathy than did the Jews. These militantly Protestant colonies considered Catholicism a far greater evil and a more potent threat than Judaism. These colonies, which took religious differences most seriously and linked the privileges of citizenship with religious affiliation longest, did not attract Jewish settlers in any number.

Indeed, no Jewish communities developed in these places, even by the end of the eighteenth century. Individual Jews did make their way into fervently Calvinist Connecticut as early as 1670. Yet although solo merchants lived there briefly, they created neither a Jewish community nor a longstanding commitment to the place. Not until the 1840s did the nucleus of a Jewish community grow into an organized, visible Jewish presence in Connecticut, a long-lasting legacy, no doubt, of the state's colonial charter of 1662, which declared that the propagation of the faith "is the only and principal end of this plantation."[15] So too Massachusetts of the seventeenth and eighteenth centuries saw only a handful of Jews, who dwelled there just briefly.

In contrast, Rhode Island and Pennsylvania boasted strong and early Jewish communities in part because Roger Williams and William Penn, their respective founders, set out to form colonies that allowed for greater religious difference. Williams, an exile from Massachusetts and its orthodox religious controls, envisioned his colony as "a receptacle for people of severall Sorts and Opinions."[16] The Jews who came to Rhode Island's busy town of Newport in 1658 traded throughout the Atlantic world, linking North America with Europe and the Indies. The first individual Jews arrived in Philadelphia in 1706, and during the next decades full families arrived in this colony envisioned by its Quaker founders as a haven of religious freedom.

Each colony had its own history of Jewish settlement and of granting rights to the Jews. But nowhere did the right of residence and of religious tolerance equate with full privileges of political participation for Jewish men. In Rhode Island they petitioned the legislature in 1761 for naturalization under the terms of the Naturalization Act of 1740. After the legislature turned them down, they turned to the Superior Court of the colony, which also rejected their appeal. And this took place in the tolerant Rhode Island founded by Roger Williams. One of the Jewish petitioners, Aaron Lopez, slipped over the border into Massachusetts, whose Superior Court of Judicature did grant him his request. With regard to the earning of rights and privileges, inconsistency rather than universal entitlement prevailed among the various colonies. Jews always had to remain aware of local realities and to devise strategies to live with whatever rights their jurisdiction offered them. They could never rest content with what rights they had; nor did they, however, believe that those rights could never increase.

The restrictions on Jewish male civic participation in colonial America existed in the context of a European culture in which Jews assumed that their religion set them apart from and put them at a clear disadvantage to the Christians among whom they lived. In America, however, Jews did not occupy that subordinate position alone. Others also experienced exclusion from privilege and political disabilities, and Jews sometimes made common cause with them. In 1697 four Jews signed a petition in Charles Town, South Carolina, written by some local Huguenots asking for the right of full citizenship.[17]

That the disqualifications circumscribing Jewish political participation affected all sorts of religious outsiders, with Jews not as the prime victims, represented something of a new page in Jewish history. Unlike in Europe, where Jews existed as the most obvious practitioners of a deviant religion, in America they had plenty of company. These Protestant-dominated colonies expended much more energy restricting Catholics than they did Jews. The colonial experience itself owed much more of its cultural dynamic to the aftershocks of the Reformation than to any dispute between Christianity and Judaism. In nearly all the colonies potential members of legislatures and juries had to take their oaths on the King James version of the Bible. Catholics would, no more than Jews, swear on the Protestant version of the holy scripture. The stipulation excluded Catholics, perceived by colonial Americans as the embodiment of evil, and served first and foremost to ward off Catholic influence in public life.[18]

In essence, this grudging tolerance of Jews stemmed from the novelty of the colonial enterprise. In most of the colonies no one group could claim significantly longer roots than anyone else. These colonies existed as sources of revenue for England. What outweighed religious identity involved someone's willingness and ability to produce goods and services that made a profit for the colony. Most white people, regardless of religion, enjoyed a kind of equality by default. Even Catholics enjoyed greater liberty in Pennsylvania or New York than they did in London or Dublin. Neither the colonies nor the Christians who lived in them believed in universal principles of religious liberty and freedom of expression. Rather, they believed in economic activity and commercial robustness. Religious intolerance basically interfered with the task of extracting raw materials from the land, processing them, and making them available for imperial markets.

The status of the Jews in the colonies in which they lived derived from their neighbors' willingness to allow the Jews to dwell, work, and quietly observe religious rituals. Although they did not enjoy the same rights of the Protestants, neither did the Jews seem to mind too much. Perhaps the privileges they enjoyed coincided precisely with what the Jews most wanted, or perhaps they believed they represented the outer limits of Christian tolerance and that they could ask for no more. Either way, the status they had achieved represented one of the highest that Jews anywhere in the world could claim. The convergence between the needs of the colonies and the human capital provided by the Jews played a crucial role in making a place for them in North America.

The colonies suffered from chronic labor shortages. The governors of the individual colonies and those who oversaw them in England thought up various schemes to augment the labor pool. Profits overrode piety, and in a number of cases even Catholics could come as indentured servants to help people the "plantations."[19] The colonies' concerns about economic development also outweighed strong ties of ethnicity and the stigmas of national origins. Jews of Iberian, Polish, or German background did not stand out in communities made up of women and men from Scotland, Ireland, Wales, France, Sweden, and the many German principalities and states. By the eve of the American Revolution about one-third of all residents of Pennsylvania came from German-speaking communities originating in the Palatinate and other Germanic regions. In 1740 the parliament enacted the Naturalization Act, which permitted foreigners who had lived in the colonies for seven years to become naturalized. Further, the legislation specifically exempted Jews from having to take oaths using words of Christian profession.[20]

Religious and ethnic tolerance in the North American colonies came as a welcome relief to the Jews. This open climate owed its origin to the deep divide between blacks and whites created by the slave trade. In Europe the profound divide in society had been between Christians and Jews. In the countries that had undergone the trauma of the Protestant Reformation, Catholics and Protestants had fought each other, often in bloody confrontations. But in most of those places, despite these struggles, Jews remained the most stigmatized and subordinated element of the population. Jews had been enculturated in, and carried the memories of, Europe as a place where their Jewishness had ipso facto put them outside the mainstream of society and rendered them different and defective. But in America that position came to be occupied by Africans.

The first Africans were brought to Virginia in 1619. While initially not defined as perpetual slaves whose children would share their status, by the 1660s Africans had become exactly that. The colony's legislature and the courts recognized slavery as an "appropriate" and "normal" condition for Africans. The practice soon spread to all the colonies, except for Rhode Island. African slavery became the engine that drove the economic development of British North America. It brought great riches to some. It enabled relatively poor white farmers to acquire land and wealth and to enjoy a comfortable social status. Its existence profoundly shaped American ideas about freedom. And obviously the system of slavery was predicated on skin color, with whiteness the badge of privilege.[21] Therefore, Jews in the colonies had yet another asset that served them well: they were white. They no longer bore the burden of being the stigmatized group whom others reviled and oppressed. As women and men

considered among the privileged by virtue of their whiteness, they enjoyed relative tolerance and could increasingly demand, by virtue of the
service they rendered to the colonies, and length of time in residence, the
right to live freely. By the time the Jewish communities took root in
America and increasing numbers of European Jews opted to live in
America, to be "white" meant to be free, and not being white meant enduring enslavement.

A mark both of the Jews' inclusion as whites and of their worldwide
involvement in trade was the fact that like their white neighbors in New
York, Georgia, South Carolina, and Pennsylvania, Jews owned slaves. A
1703 census in New York found that fully 75 percent of the Jewish
households contained slaves, averaging about two per family.[22] Into revolutionary times, owning slaves was an unquestioned fact of American
life. Jews of this era revealed nothing in their letters, wills, and other
writings indicating any ambivalence about the practice; indeed, following this fashion helped them to be even more like their neighbors. As
merchants linked to international trade, Jewish businessmen joined with
Christian and Muslim traders in the worldwide traffic in human beings.
Aaron Lopez, Isaac Eliezer, Jacob Rodriguez Rivera, and Samuel Moses,
notables in the Jewish community of Newport, Rhode Island, shipped
rum and hardware, spices, spermaceti candles, lumber, fur, and African
slaves. The Jews' level of material comfort and integration into American
business life came to them by virtue of the wealth such commerce
brought to them.[23]

JEWISH LIFE IN THE COLONIES

In the context of a society based on religious tolerance and in which
privileges were granted according to skin color, the earliest Jewish communities formed and flowered. Each of the five Jewish communities that
existed on the eve of the American Revolution—New York, Philadelphia, Newport, Charleston, and Savannah—has its own history. In each
the process of initial settlement, consecration of a cemetery, formation
of a congregation, and the building of a synagogue took place. In each
Jews both accepted their status in the larger society and sought to expand the rights they enjoyed. In each they forged intense bonds with
each other and tried to construct comfortable relationships with the
Christian majority.

Although the rights enjoyed by Jews and the restrictions placed on
them varied according to which colonies they inhabited, certain basic

characteristics of Jewish life prevailed. For example, nearly all Jews lived in port cities. While some showed up in relatively remote outposts in the interior of the American colonies early on, their numbers never rose to more than a mere handful. In the middle of the eighteenth century Jewish traders and shopkeepers could be found in the backwoods of New York, as far north as Albany, and in the backwoods of Pennsylvania, Virginia, and the Carolinas. Because only one or two Jews lived in each one of these isolated frontier settings, selling goods to fur trappers, buying from the Indians, and speculating in lands, they never formed communities.

Yet even in the cities of eighteenth-century America Jews lived in small numbers. New York had the distinction of hosting the largest Jewish population; by 1695 about one hundred Jews lived there. That number doubled by 1730, and from then on it remained relatively static, with about 242 Jews residing in the city in 1773. Since New York itself grew dramatically in this period, the proportion of Jews declined, although the numbers did not.[24] Jewish communities throughout North America were woven from the threads of relationships that held together Jews throughout the Atlantic world. In Newport, Rhode Island, only a small Jewish presence existed in the late 1650s. In 1677 Jews bought a plot of land for a cemetery. But when an epidemic ravaged Curaçao in the 1690s, almost a hundred Jews fled for the healthier climate of Rhode Island and joined the small Jewish merchant community. In the middle decades of the eighteenth century about twenty Jewish households could be found there, and to mark their growing presence there, the Jews dedicated their first synagogue in 1754.[25]

Their numbers did not grow dramatically or in proportion to the growth of the European-derived population of America for two reasons. Emigration from Europe to America in general took off slowly. Prospects for life in America remained shaky well into the early nineteenth century. Non-Jewish European emigration conformed to this pattern as well. But unlike non-Jews, the Jews of early America married later in life, and many never married at all. So few Jews lived in the colonies that finding a Jewish marriage partner proved difficult. Many of the single men who came to America made no mention in their wills of wives and children, indicating that they had lived as bachelors.[26] Large numbers of Jewish children born in the American colonies never married, at least if they stayed put. However, given their constant travel around the Atlantic area, many who wanted to marry had to return to Europe to find a suitable Jewish mate or to relocate to the Caribbean.

The Jews lived in close proximity to each other in the five cities, forming small enclaves. None of the American colonies mandated that their
small band of Jews live in European-style ghettoes, but Jews voluntarily
sought each other out when looking for a place to settle. In Dutch New
Amsterdam, for example, the Jews clustered around Whitehall Street,
but by the time the city switched over to British rule, New York Jews as
a group lived on or near Mill Street.[27] Yet the Jews didn't necessarily stay
put once they settled. Because nearly all made a living in trade, they
moved around a great deal among the colonial cities of North America
and elsewhere. They shifted from one community to another, resettling
in the Caribbean and Canada or moving to London and Amsterdam.[28]
They left one place for another as their fortunes ebbed and flowed and
as new markets opened up in other places.

A handful of Jewish merchants in the colonial cities rose to dazzlingly
high heights. Individuals who had amassed great fortunes in world
trade, importing and exporting goods from ports around the globe, functioned as leaders of the small Jewish communities. Most Jews, however,
experienced less dramatic success, although they too engaged in trade,
many by peddling or owning a small store. Hannah Moses, for example,
ran a kind of general store in Philadelphia in the 1750s and 1760s, a
place described as selling "cheap jewelry, knives, snuff boxes" and an assortment of other odds and ends. Others ran several small businesses at
the same time, a strategy designed to maximize options. The widow
Grace Levy, left with seven children and five stepchildren, not only operated a small shop but also turned her home into a boarding house.[29]

Most had come from Europe with small amounts of money, often just
enough to get started, and they lived as modest shopkeepers and artisans,
silversmiths, barrel makers, and tinsmiths who sold the products they
made. Yet not everyone experienced even this level of success. Throughout the colonial era, small numbers of impoverished Jews also found
their way to North America. Widows and orphans constituted a significant portion of this poor population. Occasionally merchants who had
lost everything in a disastrous business deal and ended up stranded in
some western hemisphere port joined the ranks of the Jewish poor in one
city or another. In other cases, poor Jews from Europe showed up in
New York, Philadelphia, or Charleston, and the Jewish community had
to decide what to do with them. Usually the community supported them
for a period of time, giving them room and board at common expense.
Charity Cohen ran a boarding house like this in New York. After lodging and feeding the transients, the community usually provided them

with the funds to travel on to another community, where once again local Jews would sustain the paupers for a while and hand them over to yet another community.

Ashkenazim and Sephardim Mingle

The poorer Jews in pre-Revolutionary America typically did not come from the ranks of the Sephardim but from the Ashkenazim, who by the early eighteenth century had begun to come to America as well. Generally poorer than the Iberian coreligionists, they constituted the majority of American Jews by 1720. With each passing decade Jews hailing from Germany and Poland outnumbered the Sephardic pioneers.[30] Indeed, their migration to America followed a course different from that of the Sephardim. They had not undergone the horrors of the Inquisition and expulsion, but neither did they enjoy the same complicated networks of trade that might have enabled them to prosper greatly when personal circumstances improved. The Polish Ashkenazim had come to America because the middle of the seventeenth century had been one of great hardship for the Jews of Poland. The combatants in the Thirty Years' War (1618–1648), the Catholics and Protestants, had savagely turned on the Jews, who suffered an intense period of persecution. Tens of thousands were slaughtered, and even more lost their homes.[31]

A sizable number of these refugees from Poland also ended up in Amsterdam and London. The Sephardic elite did not particularly want to share communal institutions with the newcomers, the "tedescos," but they felt a sense of responsibility toward them. The better-off offered the Poles and Germans some material aid but did not make a place for these poor Yiddish speakers in their communities and congregations. Despite the vast social distance between the two communities in Europe, charitable responsibilities linked the Ashkenazim and the Sephardic elites who played a crucial role in facilitating Ashkenazic migration to America. News of the success of the fledgling Jewish communities in America filtered back to Europe, and the Ashkenazim in England and the Netherlands learned about the burgeoning economic opportunities for young people willing to try their hand in the new world. A small number of them journeyed to America. Some of them, like those who arrived in Georgia, had been sent to America through the largesse of the Jewish communities governed by the wealthy Sephardim. Others went on their own.

The Sephardic-Ashkenazic relationship offers a unique lens through which to observe the developing differences between Europe and America. In London and Amsterdam, Sephardim and Ashkenazim inhabited

two separate worlds and spoke different languages. While both groups
acquired the dominant tongue, Dutch or English, among themselves the
former conversed in Portuguese and the latter in Yiddish. They had their
own synagogues, cemeteries, and social lives. For centuries intermarriages did not take place between these two distinct segments of the Jewish people.[32]

In America, while these differences did not erode completely and immediately, they did lose their sting quite swiftly. In every early American
Jewish community Sephardim and Ashkenazim shared one synagogue.
They lay buried next to each other in the one communal Jewish cemetery. They sat in the same classrooms in the synagogue vestry rooms, and
they shared a common status in society. Ashkenazic and Sephardic men
worked together to create the institutions of Jewish communal life. They
joined forces to build the cemeteries and synagogues, to ensure the provisioning of kosher meat, and to direct the affairs of the communities.
They married each other and gave charity to each other. The number of
Jews proved to be too small and their communities too lacking in institutions for them to maintain the divide that predominated in Europe.
More important, so few eligible Jewish marriage partners could be
found in the colonies for the young Jewish women and men to choose
from that this intra-Jewish divide had to be crossed. Had parents limited
their children to marriage only with Sephardim or Ashkenazim, Jewish
marriages would have become all but impossible.

In 1738 Isaac Mendes Seixas, newly arrived in New York, asked
Rachel Levy to be his wife. The marriage of Seixas, a Sephardic Jew, to
Levy, an Ashkenazi, caused local tongues to wag at Shearith Israel, New
York's congregation, which had been formed in 1706, and throughout
the tightly linked Jewish world of the American colonies. "The Por-
tugeuze here are in a great ferment about it. And think Very ill of him,"
wrote Abigail Franks, a relative of the bride, to her son then residing in
London. But Franks went on in her letter to note that the local Sephardic
gossipers had been enraged less because of the ethnic divide that had just
been breached and more because "he Did not invite any of them to ye
Wedding."[33] The product of this union, Gershon Mendes Seixas, born
six years later, would become Shearith Israel's cantor, the *hazzan,* and
the spiritual leader of New York Jewry in the early Republic. The marriage of his parents, which could not have taken place in London or Amsterdam, and the lack of any profound stigma beyond the censorious
gossip, demonstrated the leveling influence of American conditions.

Yet the historical animosity did not die down completely in the face of frontier conditions, as evidenced by an Ashkenazi-Sephardi squabble among the Jews who came to Georgia in the 1730s. Their struggle lasted a few years, and considerable harsh accusations flowed between them before men of the two groups could agree on the structure of the synagogue that they would have to share.[34] Rather, the same kind of equality by default that had facilitated the integration of Jews into colonial America also made possible the twining of these two Jewish branches. It took place not because of any conscious decision-making or serious discussion about the meaninglessness of such categories. Rather, their scarcity in America brought together Jews who in Europe would have lived apart.

The Sephardim clearly had the upper hand. They claimed the lion's share of social prestige, and the newcomers from Poland deferred to them and their proud Iberian legacy. All the congregations in America until the last decade of the eighteenth century functioned according to the Spanish rite, the *minhag Sepharad*. Therefore, all the *hazzanim*, those who chanted the service, followed the Sephardic tradition. Although the majority of American Jews were Ashkenazic, the services they attended resonated with the melodies and Hebrew pronunciations of Spain and Portugal. The interior architecture of the synagogue boasted decidedly Iberian accoutrements. The congregational minutes had to be recorded in Portuguese, although few of the members would have understood a word.

Despite claiming the religious rite, the Sephardim did not exercise power very long in the congregations. The two groups shared in synagogal and communal governance. Ashkenazic men served the congregations as lay leaders, *parnassim*, just as often and in the same manner as did the Sephardim. Wealth mattered more than place of origin, as together these men directed communal affairs. Because the Ashkenazim outnumbered the Sephardim, they ultimately contributed more money to building the synagogues and cemeteries than their Sephardic counterparts. They likewise expended more energy on governing the community and as such had a greater influence on its character.[35]

The Role of the Synagogue

The fact that each of the cities where Jews lived as a community supported only one synagogue further necessitated this Ashkenazic-Sephardic fusion. Those synagogues—like Mikveh Israel in Philadelphia and Mikveh Israel in Savannah—functioned as the only existing Jewish institutions. The synagogue functioned as a kind of all-purpose hub of Jewish life. It provided not only a place for religious worship but also a place where Jews could have their sons circumcised and educated. Here Jews entered into matrimony, were buried, and received aid in times of distress. The synagogue distributed kosher meat as well as matzo during Passover.

The fact that Jews needed the synagogue if they wanted to live as Jews gave a great deal of power to those who ran these institutions. Synagogue affairs lay in the hands of the *parnassim,* wealthy businessmen who also represented the Jews to the larger society. Shearith Israel's *parnassim* operated as a kind of council of elders, called a *mahamad.* In Kahal Kodesh Beth Elohim, the congregation in Charleston, South Carolina, founded in 1749, the *parnassim* formed a group of eighteen and called themselves an *adjunta.* They took up the power to issues rules "for the peace, harmony, and good government of the people."[36]

The *parnassim* assigned seats according to the pecking order of the society. The best seats for men, those nearest the eastern wall, went to the elite. In the women's section in the balcony, social status also dictated who sat where. In 1760 Shearith Israel became embroiled in a great controversy when Judah Mears went "into the womens Gallery in time of worship last Sabath & turn'd Miss Josse Hays from the seat, claimed by Miss Mears." The board fined Mr. Mears forty shillings for violating the gender barrier, but the argument originated with Miss Hays's violation of the status barrier.[37] Notably, in those years no rabbis had settled in America, a place so far removed from the centers of Jewish life, so these coteries of wealthy men, exercising their power as an oligarchy, ran the synagogues. They doled out ritual honors and controlled access to the synagogue's services. They attempted to enforce a kind of orthodoxy in practice, not just in the confines of the house of worship, but in the Jews' private homes as well.

In 1757 the *parnassim* of Shearith Israel sought to expel a number of Jews living outside the city's boundaries who, rumor stated, had been violating Jewish practice. The communal leaders declaimed that these people had been "Trading on the Sabath, Eating of forbidden Meats & other Heinous Crimes." The names and misdeeds of the guilty were to be publicly announced in the synagogue at the upcoming Yom Kippur services, when a temporary ban would be placed on them.[38] In 1774 the *parnassim* called to task Hetty Hays, an innkeeper, accusing her of serving unkosher food. They even brought a rabbi visiting from London to inspect her premises, to verify the veracity of the rumors. The *parnassim* ordered her to remove all offending pots and pans from her home and to clean them thoroughly, or they would declare her place "a Treffo [unkosher] house" for all to know.[39]

Offenders could be fined and their access to the community's services suspended for a period of time. The most potent weapon the *parnassim* wielded was that of excommunication. Not only could they deny individuals who had violated congregational rules access to communal services, but they could completely deny transgressors the company of other Jews. Such threats worked in part because much of seventeenth- and eighteenth-century American society functioned in hierarchies, which existed to reinforce the social order. Such limitations appeared appropriate and normal. Just as human beings needed to admit their subordination to God, so too did the ruled need to submit to the ruler. Children and wives had to acknowledge the authority of the husbands and fathers, and servants were to defer to their employers.[40]

A society based on individual choice and personal conscience lay in the future. Colonial society venerated stability through authority, and families and churches, headed by fathers and ministers respectively, wielded vast amounts of power over those subordinated to them.[41] The synagogues that fined and expelled, that monitored personal behavior, and that drew no distinctions between what went on in members' homes and in public sacred spaces differed little from the churches, which behaved similarly, or indeed from the other institutions, like apprenticeships, that dominated the common culture. Such threats also worked to inspire conformity because the Jews themselves understood identity as a corporate rather than as an individualistic concept. The group gave shape to the lives of its members, and the community, the *kahal*, as embodied in the congregation, functioned as the all-inclusive focus of social life. For centuries Jews had been enmeshed in communities with the legal power to exercise their authority on individual Jews and their households.

Yet by historical standards the synagogues of early America and their leaders exercised little clout over the members. The increasingly porous nature of American society, even in the middle of the eighteenth century, began to challenge the hegemony of the communal leadership. The men and women living in these Jewish communities varied in their levels of religious observance, but most did not feel obligated to follow halakah, or Jewish law, closely. Some of this relaxed attitude no doubt grew out of the *converso* legacy of the Sephardim, whose religious practices shaped the formal institutions of the communities. The lack of religious personnel and the relative absence of rigid boundaries demarcating Jews from others also contributed to the prevailing casualness toward Judaic practice.

Hints of what would become the most salient characteristic of American Judaism in the nineteenth and twentieth centuries—the ability of individual Jews to shape their own institutions independent of leaders— could actually be discerned in the congregational squabbling and the moments of defiance among the *parnassim*, decades before the Revolution and the beginnings of an internal Jewish democracy. But in the eighteenth century, since each city had only one synagogue, threats of cutting off services and excluding individual Jews from membership had real potency. Because Jews needed other Jews not only for religious reasons—marriage, burial, common prayer, circumcision—but also for business purposes, the *parnassim* as enforcers of community discipline had considerable power at their command. Dissent, by necessity, remained at bay.

Finally, the fact that no formally trained religious officials had made their way to America enhanced the power of the *parnassim*. The absence of rabbis and the dire shortage of other Jewish functionaries— slaughterers to provide kosher meat, circumcisers to usher baby boys into the covenant—had tremendous implications for the development of Jewish life in the American colonies. The lack of rabbis, however, did not get in the way of conducting services. Jews did not need rabbis to chant the service and read from the Torah scrolls. Any knowledgeable layman could fulfill these tasks, as well as officiate at funerals and even perform marriage ceremonies. Most of the early American congregations actually employed only one salaried individual, the *hazzan*.[42]

But without rabbis or other learned Jews in the colonies, no authoritative countervailing voices challenged the oligarchic *parnassim*. In 1731 a handful of members of Shearith Israel, at odds with the *parnas*, took a stand and refused to recite a prayer for his health. To retaliate, the *parnas* declared that anyone who did something like this again would be fined thirty shillings.[43] Such a prayer had no basis in halakah, and no such ruling had any binding legal precedent. But no one with influence and authority could prevent the *parnassim* from making such extralegal pronouncements.

Perhaps the presence of rabbis who could invoke Jewish law and tradition would have served to quell the high level of internal dispute. Despite their skeletal size the early congregations became rife with bickering and conflict. Given the tight ties of business and family that bound members to each other, conflict may have been inevitable. The *parnas-*

sim, merchants just like everyone else, worked on the assumption that their wealth, not their learning, gave them privilege. As for their learning, they had no more than the ordinary members of the congregation who did not perceive the elite as the bearers of tradition.

Additionally, without rabbis to serve as arbiters of Jewish law, a variety of issues could not be settled according to normative standards. The *parnassim,* who had maintained authority not by virtue of learning but by wealth, had to rule on legal matters about which they possessed no knowledge or expertise. They stepped in, for example, to decide if the child of a Jewish father and a non-Jewish mother could be buried in the Jewish cemetery. In this matter, they ruled in the affirmative. These merchants who led the congregations did not necessarily know the details of Jewish law and their decisions, like this one, derived from all sorts of extralegal considerations. Further, no one in the colonies could write a Torah scroll. When congregations needed *sifrei torah,* Torah scrolls, they had to communicate with other congregations around the Atlantic diaspora to procure them. When the first Jews in Philadelphia, for example, wanted to begin worshiping together in 1761, they wrote to Shearith Israel in New York asking if the older, more established congregation could lend them a Torah.

Because of their small number and the paucity—indeed near absence—of any individuals particularly well versed in Jewish knowledge, these Jews produced little in the way of a distinctive American Jewish culture. They did not print their own prayer books or Haggadoth, books providing the readings for the Passover seder held in Jewish homes. None among them wrote learned treatises that would become part of the corpus of Jewish knowledge. The one book of note published on a Jewish subject in this period, a Hebrew grammar, issued from the pen of Judah Monis, who had converted to Christianity and taught Hebrew at Harvard, and as such, his work added to the body of Christian, not Jewish, knowledge in America. Like Americans of this period in general, the Jews lived in a kind of Atlantic backwater, a colonial outpost, and they imported most religious items and texts from abroad.

Despite the absence of rabbis, the lack of locally produced texts, and of a community of Jews involved in learning and scholarly activities, Jewish life in America continued to take shape. Despite the incessant squabbling in the synagogues and the resentment sometimes articulated against the *parnassim,* Jewish communities in the colonial cities still functioned around the synagogues. The synagogue offered not only a place to gather for communal prayers but also a setting where the Jews could maintain their basic patterns of life, setting them apart from their non-Jewish neighbors.

At a very basic level, the synagogues maintained their centrality because they provided kosher meat. The range of religious chores needed to provision the communities with ritually acceptable meat required communal control and could not be left to individuals and the marketplace. The *parnas* typically hired a slaughterer, a *shochet*, and an inspector, a *mashgiach*. The congregation voted on the individuals and set aside a sum of money for their payment. No one but the *shochet* could perform the act of slaughtering, and he in turn had to supply the Jews with the amount of meat that had been specified by the congregation.[44] Colonial Jews cared more deeply about the ritual purity of the meat that they consumed than about the punctiliousness of Sabbath observance or many other details of Jewish law. Food embodied identity for Jews, and the connection between sanctity and diet deeply informed their lives. At various times congregations took away the license and stipend of the slaughterer when they suspected that he had not conformed to the strictures of Jewish law.

The synagogues also provided education to boys. As did Christian churches, synagogues served as schools. At Shearith Israel the *hazzan* provided instruction to the young in Hebrew, Spanish, English writing, and arithmetic. Over time other teachers came to teach, relieving the *hazzan* of the responsibility of teaching the non-Judaic subjects.[45] Some Jewish children, girls in particular, received their education at home, as did Abigail Franks's daughter, Phila Franks, in New York in the 1730s, but by and large education, both Jewish and general, however rudimentary, emanated from the synagogue, strengthening the connection between community and congregation.

Cemeteries had preceded the synagogues as communal institutions, but once the congregations came into being, they took over the elaborate set of Jewish rituals surrounding death and burial. Everyone, regardless of economic status, depended on the Jewish community to bury them and their loved ones. The monopoly the congregations had on burial rites may have been their most potent weapon in enforcing community discipline.

In addition, since care of the poor concerned everyone, the synagogue functioned as a social-service hub. In 1728 Shearith Israel issued a regulation stating that impoverished members would be given as much in the way of food, clothing, medical care, and money as the *parnas* considered necessary. In the mercurial economy of the eighteenth century, comfortable storekeepers understood that they might someday be in need of such communal support, and that knowledge fostered the bonds within the community, with the synagogue at its heart. Isaac Levy, Moses Hart, and Michael Jacobs, at one time prosperous New York merchants, by the late 1750s and 1760s found themselves debtors bound for jail. The assistance they and their families received from the congregation mattered greatly.[46] The synagogues offered protection and sustenance to widows and orphans and supplied poor brides with dowries. Congregational funds paid for medical care for the indigent, and they sometimes went toward boarding homeless Jews.

Given how much colonial Jews depended on their congregations, it is no wonder that the building of the first synagogue in each community became an important milestone in its history. This act represented a pivotal moment in their development, a point in time when Jews thought of their presence as permanent and their position in society secure enough to have a Jewish structure become part of the city's landscape. Most of these first synagogue buildings went up in the second half of the eighteenth century. Coincidence or not, Jews began building synagogues in America just as their Christian neighbors experienced an intense wave of religious fervor, the Great Awakening that swept the colonies, bringing women and men into churches in record number. Although the Jews may have been ready to put up Jewish structures, the spiritual intensity that whipped through the colonies made the Jews' decision harmonious with the emerging culture emphasizing public religiosity.

The buildings they constructed to house their congregations fit harmoniously and inconspicuously into the urban landscape. They conformed to the popular Palladian style, replete with pediments and columns, emphasizing the era's interest in elegance and symmetry. Their buildings were not adorned with any outward symbols of Jewishness. They had no Hebrew signs or words. No six-pointed Jewish stars, Ten Commandments, or any other symbols marked these spaces as visibly Jewish on the outside. Passersby would not necessarily know that the building housed a Jewish congregation, a community of worshipers who faced the east, to Jerusalem, as they prayed. They would have no idea that within its walls the language of prayer would be Hebrew or that the interior designs replicated the style of synagogues around the world.[47] Those passing by Jeshuat Israel, dedicated in 1763 in Newport, Rhode Island, would have seen an elegant public building that looked like most of the other public buildings in this bustling seaport. They could not know that inside an exact copy, although smaller, of the interior of the great Spanish-Portuguese Synagogue in Amsterdam could be found.[48]

This blend of external harmony with the outside world and internal conformity to the dictates of Jewish tradition characterized the experience of these early American Jews. They did not feel particularly secure in their enjoyment of the liberties that had been meted out to them in the colonies. They saw their good life in the colonies as fragile, and they had no interest in calling attention to their differences. Behind the closed doors of the synagogue and in the privacy of their homes, however, they lived as Jews, worrying about the details of kashrut, marking time with the Jewish calendar, and fretting over how their children would live as Jews in a future that seemed all but certain.

Given their small number and their deep connections to American trade, they made every effort to fit in, at least from the outside. They dressed very much like other Americans of their class. The wealthiest among them commissioned artists to paint their portraits, and in those pictures they do not stand out as different in appearance from other well-off eighteenth-century Americans. The men, for example, did not have beards, and married Jewish women kept their heads uncovered, conforming to current style of fashion rather than to traditional Jewish practice. The dresses they wore for their sittings, with their low-cut necklines, would have been deemed highly immodest by Jews in Poland or Lithuania.

It may have been that because Jews tried so diligently to fit in that few European restrictions survived with any force in America. American Jewish men enjoyed more rights of citizenship and a larger bundle of civic privileges than did Jews in England. A half-century before the French Revolution transformed Jewish men in France into citizens, Jews in the British colonies of North America inched toward that same status with little fanfare. The colonies where Jews lived had removed most restrictions, and those limitations on their public participation that remained proved to be mildly irritating at most and were often not enforced.

Unlike in Europe, the American colonies had no ghetto walls segregating the Jews from the rest of society that would need to be razed when circumstances changed. They had no legacy of guilds that excluded the Jews from making a living. The established churches existed in places where nonmembers constituted the majority. American Jews could cite no harrowing examples of individuals being martyred because of their religious affiliation.[49] American Jews frequently entered into business partnerships with non-Jews, further testifying to a growing level of ease between Jews and Christians.[50] At the top echelons of eighteenth-century American society, many Jews maintained friendships with non-Jews, mingling publicly and visiting each other's homes. They carved out religiously neutral spaces where they and their Gentile friends could discover common interests and concerns.[51]

Marrying outside the faith was not unknown to colonial Jews. The most notorious case of intermarriage in those years took place in the late 1730s and involved Phila Franks, whose parents were among the most active and observant of New York's Jewish families, and Oliver Delancey, the son of one of New York's leading Christian families. Phila's marriage to a Christian may have testified to the power of romance, but the fact that Phila and Oliver had met in the first place also indicated the facility with which Jews and Christians could meet and socialize.[52]

The general fluidity of American culture also helped the Jews to assimilate with little anguish or discussion. The rights they won and the comforts they enjoyed may have had less to do with their efforts and determination and more with the openness of colonial society and its high level of religious tolerance of the practitioners of numerous outsider faiths. The commercial bent of the colonies meshed neatly with the fact that Jews made a living as merchants. The stigma attached to blackness opened up for Jews, a white people, opportunities unavailable to most Jews in Europe at that time.

Despite this fairly high level of acceptance, the Jews carried with them some painful memories. Those in New York would have remembered their uneasy confrontation with Peter Stuyvesant, and those in Georgia would have recalled the unwillingness of the Trustees in London to allow them to stay. More powerfully still, they would have remembered the horrors experienced on the Iberian Peninsula and of the bloody turmoil of the Thirty Years' War. They would have known that Jews in England, the ruling power in the Jewish community, had not yet been emancipated and enjoyed few rights of citizenship. They also knew that in some of the New England colonies, Jews did not even have the right of residence, let alone the right to build synagogues and establish communities. They probably also understood that what rights they had could be rescinded. Much of their culture reflected the smallness of their communities. In 1700 about two hundred Jews lived in the British colonies of North America. They neatly bifurcated their lives into being a state "everyman," blending in and proving their value to society through their trade ties, and maintaining in private their Jewish identities and sustaining their own communities, with the synagogue playing a crucial role in their lives. Like most people in the colonies they accepted the hierarchical nature of the society and deferred to communal authority figures.

Three-quarters of a century later, on the eve of the American Revolution, their number had grown tenfold. When the Declaration of Independence was signed, about 2,500 Jews, out of a population of 2,500,000 Americans, lived in the former colonies. They had changed as America changed around them. The opening up of new land, the unleashing of democratic forces for institution building, and new ideas about individual choice profoundly influenced the Jews as it did all Americans. The Jews who lived through the tumultuous decades of revolution and nation building did so mindful of their piecemeal acceptance and relative equality and ever mindful of the restrictions that had early on been placed on them. Just as Americans were liberating themselves from British rule and creating new governmental forms, so too were Jews beginning the process of building new communities as they participated in building a new America.[53]

2

BECOMING AMERICAN

1776–1820

In January 1784, a trio of members of New York's Shearith Israel presented a letter to the state's first governor, George Clinton. They wanted to acquaint him with the "ancient congregation of Israelites" that had planted itself within the borders of the state he governed. They hoped that by introducing themselves and making him aware that "though the society [they] belong[ed] to is but small when compared with the other religious societies . . . none has manifested a more zealous attachment to the sacred cause of America in the late war with Great Britain" than it. These self-appointed leaders noted that they, and the people for whom they spoke, now expected to reap the benefits of living "under a constitution wisely framed to preserve the inestimable blessings of civil and religious liberty." Signed by Hayman Levy, Mycr Myers, and Isaac Moses, the letter represented a kind of Jewish communal calling card to the new governor of a new state in this very new nation.[1]

This document mixed hope, fear, genuine enthusiasm for the American cause, and concern that somehow the Jews, a miniscule community living in a sea of Christians, would be invisible. It embodied the deepest concerns and aspirations of Jews in America in the short but tumultuous period from the end of the 1770s through the second decade of the nineteenth century. Just as this era witnessed the emergence of the United States as an independent country, guided by a written constitution based on the ideal of individual rights, so too did American Jewish communities burst out of the constraints of the colonial past. They entered this era

as relatively inconspicuous clusters of people, living in the port cities in
small, simple communities. They ended it by ushering in a period of Jewish institution building, creating new forms for Jewish expression and
life. Just as Americans surged out of the geographic confines of the Atlantic seaboard, so too did American Jews expand into new neighborhoods, new cities, and new regions. They did this with a sense of empowerment that propelled them to experiment with new communal
structures, guided more by what these women and men wanted and less
by what past practice dictated. When they did conform to the latter, they
did so voluntarily and not because normative practices and texts dictated
that they do so.

The American Revolution made these changes—American and Jewish—possible. In liberating themselves from British rule and creating new
governmental forms, Americans rejected the colonial legacy that defined
order and hierarchy as natural and good. While it would be decades, indeed centuries, for the full promise of the Revolution to extend to all
Americans (and one could argue that even in the twenty-first century serious gaps between rhetoric and reality endure), the idea, in the words
of the Declaration of Independence, that "all men are created equal" existed from the beginning. The Constitution, adopted in 1789, began the
process of severing the bonds between religion and citizenship, between
birthplace and access to full participation in civic life. But even by the beginning of the nineteenth century religious affiliation became so far removed from the affairs of state that all forms of religiosity became matters of choice and conscience. Americans could belong or not belong, and
if they belonged, the state could not care where and how.

In the divorce between the religious matters and public life, the state
adopted a hands-off approach. It did not judge variants of faith and
practice. It rarely supervised the inner workings of churches and denominations, of synagogues and sects, in turn putting more power into
the hands of laypeople in America than European governments had at
that time. Although this process did not flower all at once, the seeds for
the rise of the religiously neutral state had been planted.

The momentous events of the revolutionary era transformed America
into a society built on individual entitlement rather than on corporate
identities. In its emphasis on freedom of expression, however imperfectly
realized, the United States became a society based on consent rather than
descent. For the first time dissent also trumped descent.[2] These changes
served to transform the Jews, whose forebears had been Europe's pariahs, whose brethren still suffered that fate, and whose religious tradition

by definition marked them as different from the Protestant mainstream of American culture.

SUPPORTING INDEPENDENCE

The Revolution and the subsequent adoption of the Constitution, which launched this new era and the United States, had a tremendous impact on the Jews, both those who already lived in the States and those on the other side of the Atlantic whose consciousness of themselves as Jews would be altered by the events unfolding in the thirteen former British colonies of North America. In this period of nation building, American Jews came to enjoy a status unlike any their people had ever known. Infused with the ideology of the Revolution, Jews restructured their own communities, enunciating their own declarations of independence, challenging the authority structure of their *kehillot,* or communities. By the 1820s news of how America's Jews were faring under the new constitutional system began to filter back to the Jews of Europe. This knowledge, along with the technological and economic revolutions of the age, set in motion a mighty and unprecedented Jewish migration from Europe to America. This short span of time played a crucial role in the emergence of modern Jewish life around the world.

This transformation of colonial consciousness took place independent of the fact that about two thousand Jews lived in the thirteen colonies whose representatives came together in July 1776 to declare their independence. Constituting less than one-tenth of 1 percent of the population, they could do little more than echo the sentiments of the people around them. The vast majority of Americans had never even encountered a Jew—other than in the pages of the Bible—and most likely had no idea that Jews and Jewish congregations could be found in the emerging nation. All the names and deeds of Jewish patriots of the revolutionary era need to be measured against the fact that no Jews signed the Declaration of Independence. None sat through the deliberations in Philadelphia in 1787 that produced the Constitution, and none helped to persuade the voters in the newly independent states to ratify it. All these events would have transpired even if two thousand Jewish women and men had not set up homes, shops, and congregations in the seaport cities of British North America.

That is not to say, however, that the Jews played no role in the events leading up to the Revolution, or that the Revolution occurred with no Jewish participation. Rather, Jews, most of whom actively supported the cause of independence, functioned as supporting players facilitating the actions of the drama's stars.

In the emerging struggle between the colonies and England, traceable to the aftermath of the imperial conflict between France and England, known variously as the Seven Years' War and the French and Indian War, in 1763, Jews had little to gain from supporting the British and their American allies, the Tories. Most supported the Revolution. But Jews have never been politically homogeneous, and a few sided with the British. Families were divided on the issue. In New York, families such as the Hays, the Myers, and the Nathans split in their political loyalties. The Hart family of Newport, however, seemed united in its loyalty to England, and Aaron Hart, like many Tories, relocated to Canada rather than face the wrath of his patriot neighbors. Ezra Stiles, a local Protestant minister who would later become president of Yale, reported that those Newport Jews who stayed on after the British had occupied the city, had been "Informing against the Inhabitants—who are one & another frequently taken up & put in Goal [sic]."[3] Isaac Touro, *hazzan* of the Newport congregation, collaborated as well, and he ultimately opted to move to Jamaica and lead the congregation there under the protection of the British authorities rather than live with the stigma of being a traitor in the United States. Levi Sheftall of Charleston fed useful information to British military commanders in his region.[4] David Franks, Jonas Phillips, and the Pollock family of Newport also aided the British in their effort to put down the rebellion.[5] At least one Jew, Alexander Zuntz, has been identified as having served in the Hessian forces that fought with the British army.

But these Jews proved to be the exception. Most found the arguments for American independence persuasive. Part of their support for the patriot cause grew out of their economic profile. American Jews, with few exceptions, made their living as merchants. Some of these merchants made a handsome profit from international trade, while others operated as small traders and craftsmen selling goods to their neighbors. But regardless of the level at which individuals functioned, as a mercantile people their livelihood depended on the free flow of goods as well as the goodwill of their neighbors.

Grievances against the British for trying to overregulate American trade in favor of the needs of imperial power therefore fell on sympathetic ears. The Proclamation of 1763, which banned Americans from engaging in trade beyond the crest of the Appalachian Mountains, stifled commerce. Numerous Jewish merchants had their eyes and hands on the fur, timber, and other seemingly boundless resources that lay beyond that boundary. A number of Jewish merchants, like the brothers Michael and Bernard Gratz, signed the Non-Importation Resolution of 1765 as well as the Agreement of 1769, both of which pledged the subscribers to refusing to deal in import, which meant British goods. In 1770 New York Jews found themselves among the ranks of those protesting the tax on tea, while Jews in the southern colonies joined even more vociferously in the demand for a relaxation of trade restrictions. Mordecai Sheftall of Savannah chaired the nonimportation committee in Georgia, while Francis Salvador, only two years in America, took a seat in the South Carolina provincial congresses, elected in 1773 and then in 1776. Shortly thereafter Salvador volunteered to serve in the militia, and after being captured in an ambush, was scalped. A few days later he died of his wounds.[6]

Few Jews in the colonies had come from England. Those who did were really German and Polish Jews, some of them former *Betteljuden,* or Jewish beggars, who had briefly sojourned in England and then decided to try their luck in America, such as those who had arrived aboard the *William and Sarah.* They harbored few positive or patriotic sentiments toward England, its institutions, or its culture. By definition no colonial Jews held any position that derived from the crown, and as such they were in no danger of jeopardizing any office or privilege by siding with the revolutionary cause. None had any reason to express loyalty to the Church of England, the religious arm of the imperial force. In short, they did not have any stake in the preservation of the status quo.

When hostilities broke out, some Jewish men expressed their support for independence by taking up arms. Francis Salvador fell in battle in August 1776, making him the first Jew and one of the first Americans to die for the cause. So many of his coreligionists in Charleston—like Solomon Bush, David Franks, and Benjamin Nones—had joined with the patriots in the military effort that they formed themselves into a "Jews' Company." This group consisted of thirty men, including the *hazzan* of Kahal Kodesh Beth Elohim, Charleston's congregation. They had the chance to prove their military mettle at the Battle of Beaufort, where Salvador fell. Nones went on to serve as the Marquis de Lafayette's aide-de-camp and in 1779 fought under the leadership of Casimir Pulaski. A Jewish doctor, Phillip Moses Russell, ministered to Washington's troops at Valley Forge. Jews could even be found in the militias of Maryland and New Jersey, where no Jewish communities existed. When the British put up a naval blockade of the port of Savannah, Mordecai Sheftall tried to break it. Caught by the British, he endured a brief incarceration on a prison ship and then went into forced exile to the colony of Antigua. Altogether about one hundred Jewish men participated in the military effort. Of this number, twenty-two, all members of New York's Shearith Israel, volunteered en masse when they fled the city as it fell into British hands.

The majority of Jews in the American colonies joined with their neighbors in May 1776, observing a day of assembly and fasting, as proclaimed by the Continental Congress. They hoped that efforts at compromise would stave off war and that England would back down from imposing harsh sanctions on Americans. At New York's Shearith Israel they intoned in unison, "O Lord; the God of Fathers . . . may it please thee, to put it in the heart of our Sovereign Lord, George the third, and in the hearts of his Councellors, Princes and Servants, to turn away their fierce Wrath from against North America. And to destroy the wicked devices of our enemies, that it may fall on their own heads." [7] They left no doubt that by "their enemies" they meant the enemies of American independence.

The willingness of some Jewish men to pick up arms for the patriot's cause meant that some Jewish women—the wives, mothers, and daughters of those in uniform—found their lives disrupted. Frances Sheftall, for example, had to take up needlework to support her family while her husband languished in a British prison. She also continued her husband's business enterprises, reporting business transactions to him in letters. She took pride in her business acumen, commenting in a letter, "I make exceedingly well out by doing a little business." Mrs. Sheftall made an arrangement with a Mr. Levy, who would go to North Carolina for her and acquire some gold coins, "as they are much cheaper thare than [they] are here." [8]

Subsequent generations of American Jews took great pride in reciting the names of the Jews who stood, and fell, in battle for the cause of American independence. They put up plaques and historic markers to prove their participation in the birth of America. They used the episodes of the revolutionary era to stake their claims against later challenges to their loyalty and integration. These historic memories gave them a role in the narrative of the country's founding, allowing them to say that they too had been present at the dawn of U.S. history. They pointed with pride to the story of Haym Salomon, a Jew from Lissa, Poland, who earned the nickname "financier of the American revolution." Salomon joined with other Jews from New York who had relocated to Philadelphia when the British occupied the city. His service to the revolutionary cause came not in the form of military participation but in fund-raising for the revolutionaries. Robert Morris, superintendent of the Office of Finance of the Continental Congress, appointed him to act as a broker for the shaky treasury of the even shakier government. Subsequently, Salomon served as paymaster for the French troops who came to fight and, without commission, he orchestrated substantial loans from France and Holland for the United States.[9]

Salomon's role represented Jewish participation in the war more fully than did that of the soldiers. Jews capitalized on their long history of trade for the benefit of the nation in its struggle for independence. Not accidentally, such service worked in their own interests as well. As suppliers of commodities and as purveyors of goods, engaging in these commercial activities, however patriotic, suited their business needs. Michael and Barnard Gratz demonstrated this combination of service to America and the expansion of Jewish mercantile interests. Born in the 1730s, in Silesia, a Polish region recently brought under Prussian rule, the Gratz brothers first migrated to London and then to Amsterdam, where they apprenticed with a number of Jewish merchants. By the 1750s the brothers had moved to Philadelphia, where they worked and lived among the city's Jews, worshiping with the small Jewish band in a private home on Sterling Alley.[10]

Their American business ventures took them in many directions. As Western men, the Gratz brothers learned an American lesson early on: they realized that fortunes could be made in the vast lands and resources beyond the urban fringe. They cast their eyes to the west and participated in numerous efforts to plant colonies in the American interior. The brothers established trading posts in what would become Pittsburgh and Louisville and maintained an active interest in the Illinois Company, which helped to develop the Midwest for white settlement. For merchants like them, British restrictions on trade west of the Appalachians would have been a disaster, and not surprisingly, they sided with the patriots supplying arms and clothing to the American army. They outfitted George Rogers Clark's expedition to defeat the British in the Northwest, while Virginia officials relied on the Gratz brothers to "act for them" in procuring the goods needed for an effective militia.[11]

Yet the American Jews' role in the Revolution extended beyond that played by a handful of Jewish heroes or the activities of a number of well-connected merchants. When the British occupied New York in 1776, the *hazzan* of Shearith Israel, Gershon Mendes Seixas, along with many members of the congregation, fled. Taking their Torah scroll and other ritual objects with them, the members of Shearith Israel relocated in Philadelphia with the help of the members of Mikveh Israel. Meanwhile, the British soldiers stationed in New York City ripped up the lead plates in the Shearith Israel's Chatham Square cemetery that bore the funeral inscriptions of deceased members, melting them down for ammunition.[12]

The flight of Shearith Israel to Philadelphia demonstrated both Jewish support for the revolutionary cause and the bonds of communal obligation linking American Jews to each other. Not only did the Jews of New York find refuge among the Jews of Philadelphia, but so too did coreligionists fleeing the British troops from Newport, Savannah, and Charleston. The story also demonstrated the tenacity of ideas of *"k'lal yisrael,"* the fellowship of all Israel, despite politics and place of origin. A handful of New York Jews remained there while the British held control of the city. Some did so under duress and, despite the war, maintained the functions of the congregation. Alexander Zuntz, the Hessian officer stationed in New York, served as the president of the congregation.[13]

A CONTINUING STRUGGLE FOR RIGHTS

In the years to come, when they felt under attack, Jews would cite the bravery of a few and the support of the majority for independence. They would indeed erase the history of the Jewish Tories and make the case that all Jews had stood with the patriots. Their exaggeration grew out of the complicated immediate aftermath of the Revolution. In the new states emerging from the old colonies, the status of the Jews remained ambiguous. It had not improved, become clarified, or been made uniform. Only New York, which adopted its first state constitution in 1777, immediately and in one stroke removed all previous disabilities. In article 38, it swept away all limitations tied to religion: "In the name and by the authority of the good people of this State, *ordain, determine, and declare*, that the free exercise and enjoyment of religious profession and worship, without discrimination or preference, shall forever hereafter be allowed, within this State, to all of mankind."[14]

The other states offered the Jews less than full rights. The remaining offered what amounted to a hodgepodge of inconsistencies and ambiguities. In Pennsylvania, for example, the constitution writers vastly expanded the meaning of democracy but mandated that only professing Christians could hold office. The oath that all office holders had to take, "I do acknowledge the Scriptures of the old and new Testament to be given by divine inspiration," remained in effect until 1790 when a new constitution removed the words *new Testament*. Each state had its own process of granting full political participation only to Christians for some period before divorcing political rights from creed.[15] Eventually all of them severed the knot. South Carolina did so in 1790, Delaware in 1792, and Georgia in 1798. But the total separation of full rights and religion involved a long, drawn-out process. Maryland, for example, passed its "Jew bill," allowing Jews to hold office, as late as 1826, and North Carolina and New Hampshire waited until the ax of the Fourteenth Amendment swung over them to remove religious language from their constitutions.[16]

The process of gaining Jewish rights in Maryland proved to be the most complicated. Of the places that maintained disabilities into the nineteenth century, only Maryland had Jews among its residents, and only there did the supporters of the Jews point out to legislators and to the public that Jews would not threaten the essentially Christian nature of the state. As early as 1797 a Baltimore Jewish merchant, Solomon Etting, petitioned the legislature to remove the disability on Jews. It denied his petition. The issue came up again in 1818, and opponents of Jewish rights frankly admitted that they feared that passage of the "Jew bill" would open the floodgates to future Jewish migration to the state, which they believed would dilute the strength of Christianity there. The debate that took place in Maryland and culminated in the 1826 bill allowing Jews to hold office focused public attention like never before on the supposed assets or defects of the Jews living there and on the state's ability to thrive despite the presence of a non-Christian group within its borders.[17]

Most of the states that wrote constitutions requiring Christian affiliation or demanding professions of belief in Christian principles as a sine qua non of earning complete political rights in fact had no Jewish communities, let alone congregations, to inspire the restrictions. Not even individual Jews resided in most of these places. North Carolina proved something of an exception, but a minor one. Scattered Jews had been present there since the late seventeenth century, taking advantage of the lucrative indigo trade. In the 1740s and 1750s the names of Jews—such as David David and Aaron Moses—showed up on official documents. Aaron Cohen of Albemarle served as a volunteer in Washington's army, and in 1809 Jacob Mordecai of Warrenton established one of the new nation's earliest private schools for girls. But no congregation existed there, and these individuals lived without the benefits of a Jewish community.[18]

Despite the paucity of Jews there, the state constitution of North Car-

olina required that all office holders accept the authority of both the Old
and New Testaments. Jacob Henry, one of the few Jews residing in the
state, had been elected to the House of Commons in 1809, but he could
not, in good conscience, take the oath. The House allowed Henry to
speak in his own defense. In his oration he invoked his commitment to
the Constitution, which he considered the only belief necessary for holding the office to which he had been elected. Swayed by his rhetoric, the
House voted to seat him. It was not until 1868, with the impetus of Reconstruction, that the House of Commons made it possible for any Jew
to sit in the legislative body.[19]

In most instances of legislative or judicial broadening of Jewish civic
rights, the merits, or demerits, of the Jews never emerged as motivations
behind the choice of political language.[20] In fact, Christian—that is,
Protestant—legislators and judicial officials worried more about
Catholics and the irreligious and the nonbelievers than they did about
Jews.[21] Indeed, Christians feared the widespread indifference to religion
much more than they sought to exclude Jews from political life. Deism
in particular, the worldview of many of the founders, Thomas Jefferson
in particular, concerned them greatly. Efforts to write religious qualifications into new state constitutions and to bring Christian rhetoric into
public life did not target Jews. The potentially pernicious and ungodly
affect of Gentile nonbelievers, defenders of secularism, worried them
much more.[22]

Whether or not the framers of the state constitution meant to target
them, the Jews found it necessary to speak up, politely, in their own defense. They did not always take on the idea that all people regardless of
their creed, or lack thereof, should be empowered. Rather, they pointed
out their own exclusion and harkened to their service to the nation at its
hour of birth. When the draft of the Pennsylvania constitution became
known, Jewish notables associated with Philadelphia's congregation—
including Gershon Mendes Seixas, then serving as *hazzan* in this place of
refuge—appealed to the convention. They made their plea "in behalf of
themselves and their brethren Jews, residing in Pennsylvania." He, along
with Barnard Gratz and Haym Salomon, indicated that the religious requirements for holding office needed to be seen as "a stigma upon their
nation and their religion" and that it flew in the face of the valuable service the Jews had rendered to the revolutionary cause, which had made
this new constitution possible.[23] Indeed, this kind of pleading for consid-
eration would be heard continuously in early American history.

The men pointed out to the state officials that if the state kept these words in place, future immigrants would shy away from Pennsylvania. They would probably migrate to New York and hasten the triumph of that state as America's premier business and shipping center. Pennsylvania in particular had been an attractive destination for Lutherans, Quakers, Anabaptists, Pietists, Catholics, Presbyterians, and even those with no religious affiliation. Linking religion and public service would send them elsewhere. And, Seixas and Salomon pointed out, Jews had been fighting for independence and laying down their lives alongside their Christian neighbors. "The Jews of Pennsylvania," they claimed, had earned the right to hold office and be full and equal citizens, since "some of them" fought in the Continental army and "some went out in the militia to fight the common enemy; all of them have cheerfully contributed to the support of the militia and of the government of this state."[24]

These public appeals for inclusion became all the more forceful as individual Jews found their fortunes greatly changed after the Revolution. Most of the Jews who had actively worked for the Revolution through financing and outfitting the military ended up with ruined careers and empty bank accounts. More serious still, their political enemies used the fact that they had handled loans and dealt in money during the war to question the sincerity of their actions. These critics accused the Jews of having served the revolutionary cause for personal gain, which they considered a Jewish trait, while others, non-Jews, had fought with purely patriotic motives. Those who attacked Jewish merchants for supporting the war for financial reasons succeeded in casting aspersions on all Jews.

In 1784 a dispute broke out in the Pennsylvania legislature over the efforts of a number of individuals, including Salomon and several other Jews, to obtain a charter for a new bank. Miles Fisher, a Quaker lawyer with a history of Tory sympathies, led the attack. He castigated not just this particular proposal but all the Jews involved in it. He aimed his charge against the "Jew Brokers" and depicted Salomon and his compatriots as the "despisers of Christianity." He and the other opponents of the new bank charter went on to employ classic anti-Jewish rhetoric: "They create nothing and are mere consumers. They will not cultivate the earth, nor work at mechanical trades, preferring to live by their wit in dealing and acting as if they had a home nowhere."

Salomon died the following year, but he did have a chance to answer his critic in print: "I am a Jew; it is my own nation and profession." But that fundamental fact did not lessen, he claimed, his American credentials. In challenging his detractors, and those of his people, he lashed out. "I exult and glory in reflecting that we have the honour to reside in a *free*

country where, as a people, we have met with the most generous coun-
tenance and protection." He noted in addition that he had served his
country, while Fisher, a Tory, had been banished from Pennsylvania for
the duration of the war.[25]

Benjamin Nones, who also participated in the revolutionary effort,
found himself similarly attacked, in his case in the pages of the *Gazette
of the United States and Daily Advertiser,* a Federalist publication. The
writer charged him with being unworthy because of his poverty and because he was a Republican. Nones penned a passionate response, but the
Gazette would not print it, so he turned to the city's Republican newspaper, the *Philadelphia Aurora,* to challenge publicly the scurrilous
charges. In his challenge he linked his Jewishness, his Republican ideology, and his poverty: "I am a Jew. I glory in belonging to that persuasion, which even its opponents, whether Christian, or Mohammedan,
allow me to be of divine origin—of that persuasion on which Christianity itself was founded," he wrote. "I am a *Republican!*" he continued. "I
have not been so proud or so prejudiced as to renounce the cause for
which I have *fought,* as an American throughout the whole of the revolutionary war." Finally, he admitted, "I am *poor* . . . but soberly and de-
cently brought up . . . not . . . taught to revile a Christian, because his religion is not *so old*" as his own Jewish faith.[26]

Jewish acquisition of rights in postrevolutionary America did not just
involve Jewish self-defense couched in language of patriotic service to the
cause. It also saw the beginnings of affirmative and bold Gentile support
for the Jews, articulated in strikingly similar language. Some non-Jews
came to the defense of their Jewish neighbors by invoking the stories of
Jews supporting the revolutionary cause. They too enunciated a feeling
of goodwill toward Jews, rejecting the historical stereotypes of Jews as
devious, rapacious, and uninterested in the common good. A letter appeared in the *South-Carolina Gazette and General Advertiser* in August
1783, written by an anonymous "WELLWISHER TO THE STATE." In this
letter the writer sounded a note that echoed throughout the new nation:
"He who hates another man for not being a Christian, is himself not a
Christian." The writer continued in this vein. "Christianity breathes
love, peace, and good-will to man. The Jews have had a considerable
share in our late Revolution. They have behaved well throughout. Let
our government invite the Jews to our State, and promise them a settlement in it. It will be a wise and politic stroke—and give a place of rest at
last to the tribe of Israel."[27]

In Maryland, in the protracted struggle for the Jewish right to hold office, legislators such as Thomas Kennedy, William Worthington, and Henry Brackenridge had to lead the assault, since Jews could not serve in the legislature and argue for themselves. This trio argued that the Jews would not undermine Christianity and that they had proved themselves at the nation's birth. The Jews, Kennedy declaimed, had "bled for liberty."[28]

THE CONSTITUTION BRINGS GREATER SECURITY

Despite these incidents in some state legislatures, the American Jewish quest for rights differed from that of their coreligionists in Germany, England, and France at that time in that Jews in America did not have to suffer through the torturous process of emancipation. Americans found themselves far more vexed by religious issues such as the status of Catholics and of nonbelievers, whose rejection of any religion violated the broad assumption of the need for America to shore up its religious infrastructure, than by the presence of Jews.[29] With the exception of the Maryland case, the Jews' defenders and detractors did not take their arguments into courts and legislative halls. In the North Carolina episode, Henry argued for the right of all white men, not of all Jews, to serve. Americans did not line up in political debates as supporters or enemies of the Jews, as occurred in the various German states during the protracted struggle over Jewish Emancipation. Jews did not have to present themselves as worthy or as having gone through some kind of reeducation that transformed them into model citizens. Finally, once legislators wiped the final disabilities off the law books, they never reappeared.

However helpful non-Jewish rhetorical support may have been in this era, the drafting and ratification of the national Constitution proved to be the most formative events in securing Jewish political rights, both in the short and long term. Although it would not be until the end of the Civil War that state constitutions had to conform to the basic principles of the national constitution, the document adopted in Philadelphia in 1787 provided the blueprint for American political rights and created a climate that made possible a Jewish comfort zone.

Until the passage of the Fourteenth Amendment, the Constitution gave states the right to determine qualifications for state and local elections. States could choose to support religious bodies and even to interfere with the practice of religion. Massachusetts and Connecticut did so into the late 1810s and early 1820s. But the federal model of severing the connection between religious sentiments and public life inspired the dominant ideology, and ultimately the principle of religious neutrality triumphed as national policy. In none of the states admitted to the union after the passage of the Constitution did any kind of religious disabilities prevail, with the exception of Vermont, the fourteenth state, which did not drop its religious disabilities until 1793. Two years later it entered the union. The language of the Constitution set the standard, while the older states, which kept their religious disabilities in place, proved to be the exceptional throwbacks to a preliberal era.

Indeed, Congress, operating under the older Articles of Confederation, which the Constitution superseded, had set the stage for this kind of religious aloofness as it made federal policy for the new territories. In 1787 Congress passed the Northwest Territory Ordinance, which carved out policy for the future states of Michigan, Ohio, Indiana, Illinois, and Wisconsin. This ordinance, which had broad implications for all future national land policies and for the development of the West, made manifest the framers' vision that religious persuasion should be no barrier to political participation. The first article of the Ordinance stipulated clearly that "no person, demeaning himself in a peaceable and orderly manner, shall ever be molested on account of his mode of worship, or religious sentiments, in the said territory."[30] The terms of the Northwest Ordinance shaped the political structure being hammered out in Philadelphia that summer.

The Federal Convention held its meetings in secrecy. But at least one Jew, Jonas Phillips, a New York Jew residing in Philadelphia, worried so much about what might emerge from the closed-door deliberations that he took it on himself to draft a letter to "those in Whom there is wisdom and understand and knowledge . . . the honourable personages appointed and Made overseers of a part of the terrestrial globe of the Earth, namely the 13 united states of america in Convention Assembled." Phillips wrote to them as "one of the people called Jews of the City of Philadelphia, a people scattered & dispersed among all nations." He called their attention to the fact that the constitution of the state where they were deliberating made it impossible for Jews to participate fully as individuals in civic life, and he urged them to craft a different kind of document. He implored the members of the "honourable convention" to "in their wisdom think fit and alter the said oath and leave out the words . . . I do not acknowledge the scripture of the new testament [sic] . . . . If that should be the case, then the Israelites will think themselves happy to live under a government where all Religious societies are on an Equal footing."[31]

No doubt the framers paid little attention to Phillips's letter, which he boldly dated "24th Ellul 5547 or Spr 7th 1787." They spent little time on matters of religion. Yet what they produced indeed conformed to his vision and proved to be transformative. The document had nothing to say about the Jews, or about religion at all. By avoiding discussion of the role religion played in the governance of the new nation, the authors made it a voluntary matter. The document never mentioned, either directly or indirectly, any divine being who served as the ultimate source of political authority. It made no invocations to God. Rather, it spoke in the name of "We, the people."

Article 5, section 3, stipulated that all office holders in the national government "shall be bound by oath or affirmation to support this Constitution; but no religious test shall ever be required as a qualification to any office or public trust under the United States." The only office that required American birth was the presidency, and parental birthplace merited no mention at all. For the Jews, all too willing to proclaim their loyalty to the nation, this proved to be a requirement they could meet without reservation. Further, since most of the Jews had been born abroad, the disassociation between birthplace and the privilege of political participation proved to be significant. Only the highest office lay beyond their reach, but not—potentially—their sons'.

The words contained in the first article of the First Amendment to the Constitution played an even greater role in shaping the lives of American Jews. Adopted immediately upon ratification of the Constitution to allay the fears of the Jeffersonians, who worried about the vast power put in the hands of the federal government, the amendment offered in a few words two complicated principles about the relationship between the state, as embodied in Congress, and religion: "Congress shall make no law respecting an establishment of religion, or prohibiting the free exercise thereof." The two concepts, that of nonestablishment and that of "free exercise," both left their mark on the Jewish life that would develop in America when immigration became a major force in the 1820s.

Historians, government officials, and constitutional scholars continue to debate the intent of the framers in their choice of words. Cases involving school prayer, state aid to parochial schools, or the tax-exempt status of religious institutions that test the limits of the amendment come up repeatedly. Practices such as naming chaplains to Congress demonstrate the cracks in the wall between church and state. The adornment of public spaces with religious symbols has also come under intense scrutiny.

These debates notwithstanding, the free exercise clause gave Jews a legal basis for protesting anytime they believed that federal policy was preventing them from practicing their religion. After the 1860s they could use similar arguments at the state level. They would point to this clause when they complained about "blue laws," which forced them to close their businesses on Sunday, the Christian Sabbath. Such laws put them at a great disadvantage, since many did not work on Saturday, the Jewish Sabbath. The free exercise clause also allowed synagogues, and later other Jewish institutions, to become incorporated. Whatever privileges the states granted to Christian institutions, such as exemption from taxes, would pertain to synagogues as well. These privileges would also extend to those participating in the U.S. military. After a Civil War incident in which two Jewish chaplains lost the right to minister to soldiers, the religious lives of Jewish soldiers received the same respect as that of their Protestant and Catholic comrades-in-arms.

The nonestablishment clause likewise made clear that although Christians constituted the vast majority of the population, and Christian words, symbols, and motifs existed as a part of everyday American life, a boundary existed between the functions of the state and the support of any religious systems. The federal census, for example, mandated by the Constitution, does not ask Americans to specify their religion. Congress, granted the right to determine standards for naturalization, had to devise "a uniform rule" (article 1, section 8, subsection 4) rather than one discriminating on the basis of religion or place of origin. No tax money collected by the federal government went toward paying the salaries of the clergy and other religious functionaries or toward the upkeep of religious buildings, whatever their denomination.

For Jews, the two clauses together, particularly that of nonestablishment, created an environment that would lead to important developments in later decades. In particular, it would make possible innovations in religious practice. Since the government took no interest in the inner workings of any religious community, and the clergy received no support or power from the state, individual members of the congregation rather than the clergy would have the power to shape religious practice. American synagogues and other kinds of Jewish communal bodies would function according to the will of the majority rather than to the rulings of the clergy. American Jewry would be governed by grassroots activism, making it unlike almost all other Jewish communities.

These changes came about gradually. In the immediate aftermath of the ratification of the Constitution, Jews in America rejoiced. "Jew and

Gentile are as one," one young woman, Rebecca Samuel, wrote to her parents in Germany.[32] Gershon Mendes Seixas marched at the head of the great parade in Philadelphia celebrating Pennsylvania's ratification of the Constitution, his arms linked with the city's notable Christian clergy. According to Benjamin Rush, a prominent resident of the city, the parade's organizers had taken "pains . . . to connect Ministers of the most dissimilar religious principles . . . thereby to show the influence of a free government in promoting christian charity." At the end of the parade route a festive common meal had been laid out, including a special kosher table. Seixas and his coreligionists could participate as Americans and dine as Jews.[33]

Further, three Jewish communities sent formal letters of greetings to George Washington, the newly elected president of the newly formed United States of America. The letters, not unlike those sent by Catholics to Washington, served to remind him that they too should be considered part of the polity and asked him to keep in mind the religious diversity of the nation he would soon guide. The letter sent to Washington by the Jews of Newport has been the most quoted and most enduring document in American Jewish history. On August 17, 1790, when Washington came to Newport, officials of the local synagogue, Jeshuat Israel, came out to greet him on behalf of the congregation. In their name and in that of all American Jews, they handed him a letter politely asking if they might express the "cordial affection and esteem for your person and merits." They called on Washington to remember that they, "the stock of Abraham," had for much of their history, been "Deprived . . . of the invaluable rights of free citizens." Therefore, they felt high hopes for "a Government erected by the majesty of the people." The New York, Philadelphia, and Savannah congregations sent similar letters to the new president.

While they made no specific requests of him or of the nation whose helm he stood ready to take, their letter implied a hope that the new government would protect them as it did all its citizens. Their letter expressed uncertainty about their future status in the nation they had helped to create. When Washington replied to the leaders of the "New Port" congregation, he echoed their words and made a promise to the Jews. This new "good government" will offer, he wrote, "to bigotry no sanction, to persecution no assistance." The "children of the Stock of Abraham, who dwell in this land" will do well so long as they "demean themselves as good citizens."[34]

Washington's Legacy

For more than two centuries American Jews have quoted this letter, focusing particularly on the phrase "to bigotry no sanction," to demonstrate
that from the beginning Jews in America have enjoyed a modicum of protection from the kind of endemic hatred that poisoned Jewish lives in Europe. Yet Washington's letter did contain that other phrase as well. The
Jews should be secure in thinking about their future in America, he wrote,
as long as they comported themselves respectably and "demean[ed] themselves as good citizens," words that implied some conditionality. As long
as the Jews do not behave deviantly they could expect "to merit and enjoy
the good will of the other inhabitants." While this part of the letter has
been less widely invoked, its legacy has also been part of the history of
American Jews.

For since they could never be completely sure what it meant to "demean themselves as good citizens," they constantly scrutinized their public behavior. They engaged in an ongoing internal debate about how
their actions, whether political or social, would be viewed by the majority population. They examined their communities, scanning for anything
that others might define as inappropriate or as evidence that the Jews
comported themselves as anything other than "good citizens." They split
themselves into public Jews, behaving one way for general approval, and
private Jews who in the comfort of their homes and communal institutions could let down their guard to express themselves more honestly and
with less circumspection.

The ambiguity expressed in Washington's letter repeated itself in various ways. Rush's description of the Philadelphia parade made clear that in
the dominant American view, Christian charity implied the highest level
of moral order. The public culture placed great emphasis on its Christian
content, which fundamentally made anything Jewish different and not
quite American. Jews understood clearly that their neighbors in the early
Republic perceived Protestantism, particularly its evangelical iteration, to
be synonymous with American culture. Jews, like Catholics, suffered constantly from being the focus of intense missionary activity. Starting in the
second decade of the nineteenth century, organized evangelical outreach
programs targeted Jews, hoping to convince them that one of the benefits
of living in America, a place of voluntary religious participation, involved
the privilege of being exposed to "divine favor and . . . [that] they shall
unite with Christians with one heart and one voice in celebrating the praise
of a common and universal Saviour."[35] Groups such as the Female Soci-

ety of Boston and Vicinity for Promoting Christianity among the Jews, the American Society for Evangelizing the Jews, and the American Society for Meliorating the Conditions of the Jews appeared in the 1810s and early 1820s. They combined benevolence and propaganda in their effort to bring Jews over to the "truth" of the Christian faith.[36]

In the early decades of the nineteenth century such evangelical groups not only reigned on street corners but also received the support of municipal governments from whom they received contracts to run schools. Schools in New York City providing education to poor children acted, for example, as aggressive arms of evangelical groups bent on converting the pupils.[37] Indeed, when in 1805 a group of New Yorkers thought of creating a state-incorporated, publicly supported nonsectarian free public school, they meant that it would not represent one single Protestant denomination; rather, nonsectarian meant that all Protestant religious viewpoints could be accommodated.[38] Orphanages existed as much to indoctrinate unfortunate children in Protestant piety as they did to feed, clothe, and shelter them.[39] Evangelicals combed the charity wards of hospitals hoping to elicit deathbed conversions from poor Jews, Catholics, and unbelievers. Such evangelical behavior carried the full endorsement of prominent Americans and tinged the relationship between Jews and others.

The thin line walked by Jews in the early decades of U.S. history between acceptance and discrimination can be illustrated in the career of Mordecai Noah, America's first politically prominent Jew. A journalist, playwright, diplomat, and politician, Noah was born in Philadelphia in 1785. During his political career he worked for New York's Tammany Hall and at different times sided with both the Jacksonians and their rivals, the Whigs. He benefited from his active service to the political parties. Noah held office as a sheriff, surveyor of the Port of New York, and judge. In 1811 he accepted appointment as the consul to Riga, Latvia, and in 1813 assumed the highest position a Jew had ever held in the fledgling Republic. President James Madison appointed Noah U.S ambassador to Tunis, a position of real substance, given how vexing America found the issue of piracy in the Barbary States.

Yet in 1815 Noah received a stunning blow from Secretary of State James Monroe. In a letter, Monroe recalled him from his post. "At the time of your appointment," read the letter from the capital, "it was not known that the Religion which you profess would form any obstacle to the exercise of your Consular function." All sorts of political considerations independent of Noah's Judaism motivated Monroe. But the fact that he couched his decision in language about religious limitations demonstrated how close to the surface lay the popular vision of America as a Christian, that is, Protestant, nation.[40]

Throughout the early period of the Republic, shaped though it was by Constitutional guarantees, Jewish men walked a fine line between feeling part of the polity and entitled to full access and knowing that their Jewishness placed them in an outsider category. From the Revolution onward, American Jews felt the need to prove themselves. They invoked their revolutionary service. They sought out neutral spaces, for example Masonic lodges, where they could gather and steer clear of matters religious.[41] They participated in common civic ventures. The children of well-off Christian North Carolina planters received their education at Jacob Mordecai's academy.

JEWS LAUNCH THEIR OWN REVOLUTION

Jews also recognized the need to prove the value and dignity of their religious traditions. In the 1780s, even before the expansive language of the Constitution had been crafted, Jewish congregations in America began inviting prominent government officials to special synagogue events. The practice of including governors, mayors, members of the judiciary, and other notables to the dedication ceremonies of new religious buildings became particularly common. The presence of important figures at such events made the events newsworthy, and the American press treated the consecration of Jewish sacred spaces as important milestones in local history. "The ceremony was witnessed by a large assemblage of Christians," reported a Richmond, Virginia, newspaper in 1820, as it commented on the dedication of that city's first congregation.[42] When Shearith Israel held the dedication ceremony for its rebuilt structure in 1818, invitations went out to the vice president of the United States, the governor of New York, the mayor of the city, and to the city's leading Christian clergymen.[43]

In the early nineteenth century synagogues took their place beside other establishments in American cities as institutions representing civic order. Non-Jews could feel good that in their democratic land, as reported in the *South-Carolina State Gazette & Timothy & Mason's Daily Advertiser* in 1794, "the shackles of religious distinctions are now no more" and that the Jews were "admitted to the full privileges of citizenship, and bid fair to flourish and be happy."[44] The presence of Jews as represented by the presence of a synagogue allowed Americans to believe that their revolution had indeed produced a nation unlike any other. It enabled them to hold up their Republic as distinct from Europe and as liberated from past prejudice. Likewise, Gershon Mendes Seixas, the closest thing American Jews had to a clergyman, found himself elevated to a public level almost equal to that of New York City's Protestant ministers. The Humane Society and Columbia College invited him to sit on their boards of trustees, and he often intoned the benediction at public gatherings as the representative of the Jewish people. New York notables addressed him as "Reverend."[45] The years between the emergence of the new nation and the opening up of mass migration from central Europe in the 1820s saw the first steps toward the transformation of Jewish communities. The Jews had launched their own American revolution, the full implications of which would become manifest only in the decades to come.

Male congregation members began to demand that their religious bodies also be governed by constitutions and that they, like the nation and the states, adopt more egalitarian procedures for congregational decision making. The laymen, through newly crafted constitutions, stripped the *parnassim* of much of their power and put the affairs of the congregations into the hands of officers democratically elected by all adult males. The constitutions contained new provisions for adding amendments, and congregational leaders became dependent on the "consent of the governed" as they managed congregational affairs. Some congregations moved away from formalized seating arrangements assigned on the basis of economic status. Shearith Israel's first constitution, adopted in 1790, included a "bill of rights," which opened with the words "We the members of K. K. Shearith Israel," obviously echoing the United States Constitution. The words of this constitution merit a close reading, since they reveal the porous relationship between the American political tradition and the Jewish life developing in tandem. The introduction to its bill of rights read:

> Whereas in free states all power originates and is derived from the people, who always retain every right necessary for their well being individually, and for the better ascertaining those rights with more precision . . . form a declaration or bill of those rights. In a like manner the individuals of every society in such state are entitled to and retain their several rights, which ought to be preserved inviolate.[46]

Notably, the members of the congregation did not allude to the Torah or Talmud as the basis of their call for rights. They cited instead the fact that they resided in a free state, and they demanded that the "holy congregation of Shearith Israel" conform to the political culture of their American home. In their view, rights came to them as individuals and derived from "the people" rather than from the covenant articulated at Sinai.

Much of congregational life became infused with the new democratic spirit. In 1786 the elite Gomez family lost its privilege of having a special bench set aside for its women in the women's gallery.[47] The space once designated for this wealthy clan was now opened up to any married woman attending services. By 1792 a majority of Shearith Israel members defeated a motion barring unmarried women from sitting in the front row of the women's gallery.[48]

Shearith Israel, even with its bold language, actually lagged behind other American congregations in its transformation. This synagogue tried to retain some of the characteristics of a compulsory institution. In 1805 it tried to tax all New York Jews, including those not involved in the congregation. Unable to collect the tax, it admitted that like all American congregations, it had to function as a purely voluntary institution. It also sought, unsuccessfully, to institute a system of indirect voting for *parnassim*. But in its 1790 constitution, it moved to a system of universal adult male suffrage.[49] Other congregations actually went further in destroying the vestiges of privilege inherited from the colonial and European models. The newly created congregation in Richmond, Virginia, Beth Shalome, anticipated the next era in American political history, the "age of the common man," when it offered full voting privileges to every man over the age of twenty-one. Its constitution thoroughly echoed the rhetoric of the Constitution, declaring in its preamble, "We the subscribers of the Israelite religion resident in this place desirous of promoting divine worship."[50]

Beth Shalome issued in its constitution an invitation to all Jewish men in Richmond to join the congregation. Like the other synagogues, it realized that in the new climate support would come from members, or potential members, who would have to be won and retained by persuasion. No one had to belong. Therefore, to attract members, Beth Shalome, like every religious institution in America, had to devise a strategy for attracting dues payers, and to do so it had to respond to the sensibilities of the masses. The implications of this democratization proved to be momentous. Because they now relied on dues, they could no longer derive revenue from fining members for violations of congregational rules or infractions of halakah. Their first priority had to be to serve their members, the dues payers. They shed their function of providing services to all Jews in the vicinity. Just as practicing Judaism, and any other religion, had become unrestricted in the new nation, so too did membership in any congregation grow out of personal choice rather than communal obligation.

Not only did this membership recruitment project, embarked on by synagogues in the late eighteenth century, grow out of the changed political context, but it also reflected the fact that they now faced internal competition. For the first time, in Philadelphia and then New York, a second congregation formed. A group of Ashkenazim in Philadelphia, newcomers to the city, resented the Sephardic control of the city's only, albeit relatively new, congregation, Mikve Israel. In 1795 the newcomers founded the German Hebrew Society and built a *mikveh* for its members and not for the entire local Jewish community. In 1802 they renamed themselves Rodeph Shalom and drafted a constitution that prohibited members from belonging to another synagogue.[51] In New York central Europeans founded B'nai Jeshurun in 1825, breaking the stranglehold the Sephardim had on Gotham's Judaism. In both cities the next decades saw the proliferation of more synagogues, all competing among themselves for members.

These second and then third and fourth congregations represented the growing will of the majority to shape the institutions to which they belonged. By the eve of the Revolution more American Jews came from the ranks of the Ashkenazim rather than the Sephardim. The Revolution had given them a psychological boost and enabled them to declare their independence from the old elite. As Americans they believed that institutions should function by the "consent of the governed." They could not give their consent to a style of prayer and an institutional language— Portuguese—that did not represent them.

The physical growth of cities after the Revolution also undermined the one-synagogue-per-city model of the earlier era. With the expansion of cities like New York and Philadelphia, Jews, like their neighbors, moved to new neighborhoods. While these walking cities seemed minuscule compared to the cities of the industrial age, they did experience steady growth in the late eighteenth and early nineteenth centuries, and with that growth came the emergence of distinct neighborhoods. When Jews took advantage of the opening up of new parts of the cities for business and residence, they moved away from the physical orbit of their original synagogues. The Jews very much wanted to move to better quarters for both trade and residence, and they wanted to have access to a synagogue. They began creating new synagogues in their new neighborhoods, bolstering competition for members.

Extra-synagogal Institutions

Competition also emanated from another source when late-eighteenth-century Jewish residents of New York, Charleston, and Philadelphia began to create Jewish institutions independent of the synagogue. The first was probably Charleston's Hebrew Benevolent Institution of 1791. Until then charity in its various forms had come from the synagogue. The congregations made available fuel, free matzo, money, and other forms of assistance to its members in distress as an entitlement of belonging.[52] But by the late eighteenth century, synagogue constitutions failed to mention such services either as a benefit of membership or as a congregational responsibility to all Jews. That these congregational constitutions did not provide for such communal needs as education and charity indicated both the stripping of functions from the congregations and the congregations' decision to curtail the range of its activities. In the early nineteenth century a number of Jewish institutions came into being that had no direct connection to any congregation. These institutions, most of which performed charitable functions, allowed Jewish women and men to act in service to the Jewish people without the need to be part of a formal congregation. Notably, they fulfilled functions that normative Judaism defined as no less religious and obligatory than the public chanting of the service or the reading of the Torah. Yet in this environment the latter came to be defined as the domain of "religion" while the social service function became translated as "charity" and only religious by association.

The activities of one of the most notable early American Jews, Rebecca Gratz, can be seen as an example of this new kind of Jewish communal organizing and of the renegotiation of the meaning of religion in the new nation. In 1819 she and a number of other Philadelphian Jewish women, most of whom had participated in general female charitable societies for a decade or more, created the Philadelphia Female Hebrew Benevolent Society. Gratz and all the other women who founded this group by definition had only a tangential connection to "the Hebrew Congregation of Philadelphia," namely Mikveh Israel. Their fathers, brothers, and, in some cases, husbands, did maintain membership. But since these women themselves did not and could not belong, they enjoyed the freedom to create institutions like this one outside the orbit of the congregation.

The Female Hebrew Benevolent Society, which provided fuel, food, and clothing to the Jewish poor of the city, did not stipulate that those joining had to be members of any synagogue, nor did they have to have a male relative who did. Any Jewish woman in Philadelphia could become a member of the FHBS. She could, through the Society, occupy a leadership position, providing direct service or administering its operations. Moreover, those "indigent sisters of the house of Israel" who received assistance from it did not need to maintain any link to Mikveh Israel. Essentially, this voluntary Jewish body had been created to protect all poor Jewish women from the twin scourges of poverty and evangelism. Its independence from any synagogue empowered these women to develop their own ideas about and styles of leadership.[53]

Jewish education also underwent a process of redefinition. Previously, all Jewish children received their education through the synagogue, which charged no fees. But now Jewish parents, such as members of Mikveh Israel in Philadelphia, as contributors to a voluntary society, had to pay for their children's education. The schools did not aim to serve all Jewish children.[54] Education, like the care for the Jewish poor in the city, no longer fell under the aegis of the one all-encompassing institution to which all Jews had to belong if they wanted to live as Jews. The new constitutions said nothing, in fact, about education or the historical obligation of the community to all those in need and who might someday be in need.

That Jewish women and men could join charitable and later literary and social groups where they could meet as Jews meant that the synagogues needed to compete with rival Jewish bodies. After the Revolution the congregations served the Jews' religious needs, while gradually other institutions served all their other needs. The development of charitable societies, schools, and eventually social institutions outside of synagogues also meant that American Jews could live as Jews without belonging to synagogues. If Jews fell on hard times, they sought the assistance of independent Jewish benevolent institutions, which essentially competed for the most generous donors with publicity campaigns and fund-raising events. When they wanted to educate their children, they sought out, or created, schools.

The mushrooming of schools, charitable societies and institutions, and eventually social clubs also meant that synagogues came to be the custodians of something called "religion." The idea that religion, a set of public ritual practices connected to divine worship, existed as distinct from communal Jewish life—education, charity, the provisioning of kosher meat—did not derive from traditional Judaism, which maintained no distinction between religion and culture, between ritual practice and community life, between social and worship services. Rather, this division between religious Judaism and Jewish communal life represented a modern, Western trend of which these Jews were the forerunners. These Jews did not set out to create something new out of discomfort with the old. Rather, they acted and thought as Americans, regardless of whether they were new immigrants or the descendants of the colonial Jews. They essentially created a system that operated around a kind of internal Jewish separation of church and state. As religion, the province of the synagogue, began to be pushed to one side, the other functions, paralleling those of the state, occupied the "secular" or "state" side.

This arrangement represented a significant shift and threatened the centrality of the synagogue to sustain and coordinate Jewish life. It opened up the possibility that some, perhaps large numbers of Jews, would derive their sense of community and fulfill many of the needs of Jewish life without joining a synagogue, paying dues, and participating in worship. It added the factor of intra-Jewish institutional competition into the equation and invested in ordinary people a vast amount of communal power. If some of them did not like the synagogue or its leadership, they could quit and join another Jewish institution. If none suited their tastes, they could create one they liked. They had the right to build institutions as they saw fit, and no authority, Jewish or Gentile, could decide for them that the institutions they designed were unauthentic or unacceptable.

These institutional innovations, along with the opening of second and third synagogues, took place in the face of the first stirring of massive geographic change. By the beginning of the 1820s, Jewish life in the port cities hugging the Atlantic experienced transformation as a by-product of growth. The influx of immigrants from central Europe altered the small, inconspicuous urban Jewish communities by vastly expanding their populations and undermining the essentially quiet, inconspicuous nature of American Jewish culture. Beginning in the 1810s individual Jews began to make their way west, journeying over the Appalachians in search of trade. Other Jews joined these lone individuals, and then more, and eventually full families lead to the creation of new communities. The vast geographic expansion that began in the 1820s, along with the launching of the mass migration of European Jews and the dramatic shake-up in religious practice in America, all pointed to the emergence of a radically new era.

The 1820s represented a turning point in the history of the Jews in the United States. In 1819 an American Christian, W. D. Robinson, issued a pamphlet in which he invited Europe's Jews, "an industrious, abstemious, and preserving race of people" to relocate to America.[55] Little did he know that "American fever" was already beginning to burn through central European Jewish towns. In 1824 the first congregation west of the Appalachians, K. K. Bene Israel, in Cincinnati, was founded. The next year a group of dissidents in South Carolina's K. K. Beth Elohim, then the single largest Jewish congregation in America, left in rebellion. They wanted to be able to pray partly in English. They wanted to hear a weekly sermon, and they thought that Jewish ritual should be performed with dignity and decorum so that it would inspire loyalty and awe in its young American adherents. Their demands for reform unmet, they seceded to create a Reformed Society of Israelites, a synagogue conforming to their vision.

These three events could not have happened a century earlier when Atlantic seaboard Jews lived in small, self-contained communities. They could not have taken place in 1776, when America launched its war for independence. Rather, they were emblematic of the century to follow, one of massive Jewish movement and profound redefinition of the nature of Jewish life in America.

PART TWO

THE PIVOTAL CENTURY

3

A CENTURY OF MIGRATION

1820–1924

In 1853 Sigmund Aron Heilner left the small town of Urspringen in Bavaria. His parents had been fretting over the declining opportunities faced by their son and by other young Jews. The Jews found themselves burdened by several special taxes levied just on them. The government restricted the number of Jews legally allowed to marry. The Heilners had few resources to expend on their son, not only because of their limited circumstances, but also because they needed to save up for a dowry for Sigmund's younger sister, Regina. To get her established in her own home, they knew they needed a sizable amount of money.

Sigmund, like thousands of other young Jewish men in the region, opted for immigrating to America as the best way both to fulfill his personal aspirations and to support his parents, who, because of their age, would never join him. He did not have to ponder the decision for long. He already had a brother in America, and he knew other relatives and townspeople, who had paved the way for his journey. Arriving in New York, he stayed with a cousin for a month until he felt ready to make the journey across the continent to reunite with his brother, Seligmann, then living in Crescent City, California. Sigmund remained in California only briefly, deciding to try his luck in an even smaller town, Brownton, Oregon, a tiny enclave of copper and gold miners. Here Sigmund opened a small dry goods shop and also tried his hand at money lending, an occupation practiced by his father in Urspringen. From Brownton he went further afield into the Oregon hinterlands, to Althouse, where he met two other young Jewish men from Bavaria, Bernard and Isaac Goldsmith.

During the next decade Sigmund lived in Portland, where he went into a partnership with Bernard Goldsmith, as well as in Bear Gulch, Montana, and Sparta, Oregon, all tiny towns with no stores to meet the basic material needs of the residents. In 1874 he felt confident enough in his economic circumstances to marry, and he sought a bride in Portland, which by then boasted a sizable Jewish community. He decided on Clara Neuberger, like him also an immigrant from Bavaria. The couple eventually made their home in Baker City, Oregon, where Sigmund rose to prominence as a banker, a hide and wool merchant, and an owner of a freight forwarding firm, an insurance company, and the Mammoth Mine in nearby Sumter. They had four children who grew up in an imposing house, described by a local magazine as "the most elegantly furnished private residence in Eastern Oregon." In this home the Jewish families of the region gathered every fall to hold services to usher in each Jewish New Year.[1]

Esther Katziv, an immigrant from eastern Europe, came to America almost seventy years later. She arrived in New York, going through the immigration inspection station at Ellis Island, on August 14, 1921. Esther came with her mother, two older brothers, one younger brother, and two older sisters on the S.S. *Lapland*. A few days earlier the S.S. *Cedric* had brought another sister, already married, and her two young daughters, as well as several cousins. A year later, on June 25, 1922, yet another sister arrived with her husband and five children, who went through the same process, making their way through the portals of the same massive building at the southern tip of Manhattan. Each contingent of this family, which hailed from the Ukraine, continued on to Chicago, where Esther's father, Eli Leib, had lived since 1913.

Leib, probably born in 1867, hailed from the town of Vladovka, Kiev Guberniya. Although an observant Jew, he found himself in the Russian Army and served during the Russo-Japanese War of 1904–1905. When Leib returned from the war, he went into the flour business with his father. In 1909 the mill burnt down, and he and his dozen children moved to Korosten, where they made a living—of sorts—cutting trees and selling them for timber. Four years later Katziv, his father, his oldest daughters, his son, and a son-in-law immigrated to America, where two of his brothers already lived and where they had established a family beachhead, in Chicago.

Here the bearded Eli Leib changed his surname to Kite, as his brothers had, and started selling an assortment of goods door-to-door in Chicago's bustling Jewish immigrant neighborhood of the Maxwell Street market. His daughters went to work in the city's garment factories. He intended to save as much money as he could, as quickly as possible, and then send for the rest of the family. Within a year he indeed had squirreled away enough money to pay their fare, but the outbreak of World War I and the ensuing Russian Revolution and civil war delayed the family reunion until 1921.

Back in Russia, upon Leib's departure for America, his wife, Chasya, had moved from the small town with her children to the larger city of Kharkov, where she had family and hoped to make a living. In a profound sense, Esther's American story began in Kharkov. With her father gone and unable to limit her educational aspirations—he was, after all, a traditional Jew who saw no reason for girls to go to school—she began to pressure her mother to allow her to enter the prestigious gymnasium, or high school. For eastern European Jews, a gymnasium education represented a high level of exposure to western European culture, and it often proved a difficult achievement, given both their poverty and the many restrictions on their matriculation imposed by Russian authorities. For a Jewish woman, it represented an embrace of secular culture and a step away from a conventional life of marriage, children, and housekeeping. Esther prevailed. Her mother let her study, and the school officials let her in. Although Esther would eventually work as a milliner, she arrived in America having studied Latin, Greek, mathematics, history, literature, and science. In 1921 she came to America exposed to the political, social, and intellectual currents of the modern world.[2]

JEWS FLOCK TO AMERICA

These two migration stories encapsulate a revolutionary period in Jewish history, an era involving tectonic shifts in the lives of Europe's and America's Jews. The nineteenth century brought about the breakdown of traditional economic relationships in central and then eastern Europe. It involved lingering disabilities on Jews, and the Jews' increasing exposure to modern ideas. The wars, revolutions, and the continuing problems associated with Jewishness in Christian Europe unsettled familiar patterns. At the same time, changes in technology, including the development and expansion of the railroad and the introduction of steamship travel, made it possible for large numbers of Europeans, Jews among them, to trans-

plant to America. They rightly perceived the new nation as a veritable
sponge, soaking up newcomers who could work. The labor they contributed, along with that provided by people with deeper roots in American soil, produced an abundance of goods and crops in particular,
which undermined the basis of European local economies, in turn further
influencing young women and men in their decision to immigrate. It was
these global changes that had sent Sigmund Aron Heilner and Esther
Katziv, their siblings and friends, and millions of other Jews like them
out of Europe and into America.

Migration represented one of the most characteristic aspects of Jewish life in the century from 1820 through the 1920s. The migration went
almost always from east to west, from places of limited Jewish rights and
restricted opportunities to places of expanded rights and greater opportunities. In that century Jews transformed themselves into an urban
people. Before the nineteenth century, most Jews had been small-town
dwellers. The transformation of Jewish residence took place on a global
scale. Jews left small communities of central and eastern Europe for
larger cities in their home countries. They moved from one European
country to another. They sought out the British Isles, South America,
South Africa. Among them, though, the largest outflow went across the
Atlantic to the United States. As Jews made their way to England,
France, Germany, Canada, and South America, as well as to the large
cities of central and eastern Europe, they changed the ways they lived
and made a living. This transition in turn informed deep changes in what
Jewishness meant to them.[3]

The massive waves of Jewish immigrants that surged westward from
1820 through the 1920s owed their origins, in large part, to the great upheavals of European Jewish life ushered in by the age of emancipation,
industrialization, population growth, and urbanization. The Jewish migrations grew out of a wrenching internal Jewish debate accompanying
the *haskalah*—the Jewish enlightenment—and the breakdown of coherent, self-governing Jewish communities. Jews embarked on their journeys as their political and legal status underwent dramatic changes. They
were not only leaving Europe, but they were also moving "out of the
ghetto."[4]

Of the massive Jewish population movements of that century, none
surpassed that which brought Jews in the millions across the Atlantic to
America. About one quarter of Europe's Jewish population came to the
Americas, most of them opting for settling in the United States. Almost
one-third of all eastern European Jews left in the latter decades of the

nineteenth century and the early decades of the twentieth. About 80 percent of them chose America.[5] By 1924 when free and open immigration ended, the United States housed one of the world's largest and most significant Jewish communities. Three million European Jews had made this westward journey to a country where in principle church and state stood separate and where religious, ethnic, and racial diversity characterized social life. Those European Jews who became American Jews experienced profound changes in their lives.

Europe had changed dramatically in this century of migration. The Jews had left small, relatively isolated villages of countries like Bavaria and Bohemia. They came with little exposure to warring political ideologies or to any wrenching debates over the nature of Jewish identity. Young people from small towns, most of the immigrants of the 1820s through the 1860s, had abandoned traditional Jewish communities. By the time the U.S. Congress brought the migration to an end, Jews came as urbanites, dwellers of cities in the Soviet Union and Poland, which had not existed as an independent state when the migration began. The later immigrants, particularly those who made their way to the United States after the 1890s, had already witnessed and indeed participated in social and political conflicts over how best to solve the seemingly insolvable problem of Jewish life in Europe. Socialists, members of various Jewish worker groups, Zionists, and those who stressed secular education all struggled against each other and against the established religious authority structure to win over the Jewish masses of eastern Europe. The later immigrants, unlike their predecessors, had consumed secular Jewish culture, particularly literature.

America too had changed. It had evolved from a rural nation in 1820, with only one state west of the Mississippi, into an urban one by 1920, which spanned the continent. Indeed, the census of 1920 demonstrated that the majority of Americans now lived in cities. In 1820 Protestants constituted the overwhelming majority, while by 1920 Roman Catholics could claim to belong to the nation's single largest denomination. In 1820 Americans were descended primarily from British stock, whereas by 1920 no single group could claim to represent the majority. For the Jews, America had begun the century of migration as a small, insignificant Atlantic outpost. In the 1820s fewer than three thousand lived in America. They produced no texts themselves and depended on Jewish communities in Europe for prayer books and Torah scrolls. They had no rabbis or institutions to teach their children about Jewish life. They drew little attention to themselves as Jews as they interacted with other Amer-

icans. The places where they lived and worshiped had no visible mark-
ings of a Jewish presence.[6]

In the ten decades from 1820 through the early 1920s the Jews went
from being a nearly invisible element in the American social mosaic to
emerging as a group that played a role in shaping America's political, cultural, and religious life. Their unmistakable presence on particular streets
and in certain neighborhoods, in New York in particular, made clear that
they represented a distinct culture. They maintained communities with
religious, political, cultural, recreational, educational, philanthropic,
and medical institutions bearing the name "Jewish" or "Hebrew." They
trained rabbis and Jewish teachers. Now instead of importing prayer
books and Torah scrolls, they exported ideas and cultural texts to Jews
in Europe. Indeed, the political actions of America's Jews helped to determine the fate of the Jews worldwide.

This shift in the locus of Jewish life took a full century to be realized, and it occurred slowly. Until the 1820s America could not have
been the target of any large-scale voluntary migration from anywhere
in Europe, Jewish or Christian. The avenues of transportation both
within the continent and across the Atlantic proved too unreliable to
facilitate a flood of westward-traveling immigrants. The sailing pack-
ets bringing individuals and goods from Europe could not be counted
on to bring about such a massive transfer of population. Before the
1820s those who relocated to North America did so as individuals, and
their removal from home communities did not transform the places
they had left.

America's economy was as weak as its transportation links to Europe.
Only with the first stirrings of industrial development in the cotton mills
of New England in the 1820s, as well as the revolution in the young nation's transportation system, which connected the Atlantic coast with the
hinterlands through the development of canals, could a mass migration
from Europe to America take place. Indeed, it was the 1825 completion
of the Erie Canal, linking New York with the Great Lakes and the Midwest, that helped make America the most coveted overseas destination
for Europeans.[7] In addition, wholesale emigration from Europe commenced only when the Napoleonic Wars had ended in 1815. Europe then
entered a century of relative peace, with skyrocketing birth rates and
profound industrial developments, upsetting local economies. New
forms of transportation shook up long-standing relationships between
peasants and markets, and both potential emigrants and policy makers

in capital cities decided that an exodus to America would improve the lot of all. About 30 million Europeans made their way to America in this period.[8]

TWO WAVES OF MIGRATION

The geographic sources of that European population flow shifted over time, and not as uniformly as American popular history has depicted it. Initially, immigrants hailed from Europe's northern and western regions, but over time, particularly after the 1880s, increasing numbers of southern and eastern Europeans began to migrate. While they outnumbered those who came from the more developed western parts of the continent, little actually separated the old and the new immigrants, other than the names of the places they had left behind. After all, the communities in Norway, Sweden, and Germany that the first wave of immigrants had left in the 1840s and 1850s experienced about the same level of economic development as did the towns in Italy, Greece, Poland, and Hungary that the second wave of immigrants abandoned later in the nineteenth century and in the early twentieth. The two groups migrated for the same reasons: the decline of the local economy as set against population growth, along with the reconstruction of family networks, since kin brought each other over. Those who arrived in the United States first set up communities reflecting traditions of their hometowns, but in the process they crafted new ethnic identities and institutions.

Each group had its own reasons for migrating, its choice of places to settle, and its way of structuring communities. Each emigration took place in stages, with different regions and classes sending its excess population, mostly young people, at different times. Some immigrant groups manifested more or less permanent patterns of settlement, while others had relatively high rates of return. In some cases women and men migrated in equal number, while in others men or women made up the majority. Each group has its own list of notable achievements.[9]

These differences notwithstanding, what differentiated the two waves of migration most was their magnitude. From 1820 through the Civil War about 5 million immigrants left Europe for America, and from the Civil War through 1890 about 10 million landed on American shores. After 1890, through the 1920s, about 20 million arrived, despite World War I and the virtual cessation of European immigration. The difference stemmed in large measure from the American need for unskilled labor as

well as technological changes in transoceanic transportation that facilitated the journey and encouraged steamship companies to bring over
larger and larger loads of human cargo. Likewise, the explosion in American agriculture in the middle of the nineteenth century, the development
of vast tracts of land for farming and grazing, and the takeoff in American industry after the Civil War dramatically altered the pace and scale
of production and prices in Europe. America produced more raw material, particularly foodstuffs, at such a low cost that it outsold the yields
of European farmers. It became cheaper to buy American-grown wheat
for baking than to buy domestic grain.[10]

How History Has Been Told

Yet although these two waves of immigrants were more similar than not,
from the 1890s on American critics of immigration created an imaginary
divide between the pre- and post-1880 immigrants. They invented a bu-
colic and benign past in which pre-1880 newcomers came from places
that reflected the United States much more than they really did. The 1911
Dillingham Commission of the U.S. Senate depicted the "old" immigrants as permanent immigrants bound for America to find freedom,
particularly in American agriculture. According to the Commission, the
immigrants had brought their whole families and eschewed the cities,
opting for the noble life of farming. They had sought to become Americans and readily had shed their "Old World" loyalties.[11]

   In contrast, the "new" immigrants were depicted by nativists as unas-
similable and less admirable. According to early-twentieth-century
American opinion, the newest immigrants had little interest in embrac-
ing the values of their new home. Rather, these immigrants from southern and eastern Europe had come primarily to find a livelihood, their
critics claimed. They would make no commitment to American ideals of
freedom, and their low level of cultural development would prevent
them from grasping American ideas. They clung together in urban enclaves, learning little about America, its language, and its values. When
they could, they went back to Europe, never having become American.

   These inaccurate renditions created categories of difference that said
little about the millions of women and men who had left Europe for
America. Nonetheless, this understanding of the history of immigration
and the supposed dichotomy between the "old" and "new" immigrants
ultimately triumphed and made its way into policy. The 1924 National
Origins Act, which severely restricted immigration, did so based on a
quota system that not only limited the number of people who could enter

the United States as immigrants, but it did so on the basis of national origin. Women and men hailing from northern and western Europe received large quotas. Essentially, this system mirrored the widely held perception that differences in birthplace mattered.

About 3 million Jews were among the 30 million Europeans who came to the United States, and the restrictions of the 1920s affected them directly. In many ways their story resembles all the other immigration stories. The birthplaces of Jewish immigrants shifted over the course of the century. The opportunities of America, as measured against the liabilities of Europe, lured young people in particular. Like other immigrants, Jews responded both to these liabilities that compelled them to leave their homes and to the opportunities that attracted them to a new place. Most emigrated with a deliberate strategy to help shore up their family's economy, and they sought places where they could work. Over time they gravitated to places where they had relatives and townspeople who had paved the way for them by sending money, providing job leads, and offering information about their new home. Once there they began to adapt, while retaining ties to their families and home communities.

Conventionally, historians and others who have written about the Jewish past have also thought in terms of a "German" and an "eastern European" immigration, positing two different eras of American Jewish history. Typically this first era lasted from 1820 through 1880. Thinking in these terms allowed the history of Jewish immigration to flow in tandem with the conventional thinking about a small "old immigration" of northern and western Europeans who experienced little conflict in becoming American and a larger "new immigration" of southern and eastern Europeans whose arrival changed America more radically. In the histories of both general European and Jewish immigration, according to the accepted historical narrative, the first group quickly assimilated to American standards of behavior. The latter group, Jews in particular, have been seen as markedly different, emerging in history and memory as more urban, more "ethnic," more "Jewish," and more resistant to change than the Jewish immigrants of the earlier decades.

These popular categorizations should not be dismissed as completely inaccurate, just overly simplistic. The two hundred and fifty thousand Jews who came to America between 1820 and 1880 tended to come heavily from those areas either that had been incorporated into a unified Germany in 1871 or that, like Austria, Hungary, Bohemia, and Moravia, had an urban elite deeply influenced by German culture. Similarly, the vast majority of the two and a half million Jews who arrived in the

United States after 1880 left lands east of the Elbe River, with those hailing from czarist Russia making up the largest chunk of the migrating Jewish population.

Complications emerge as historians look more closely at who migrated and why. Many of the "German" Jews who left for America before 1880 came from Polish provinces like Silesia and Posen, which had been annexed by Prussia and later incorporated into Germany. On paper these Jews seemed to be German, and indeed, many described themselves that way. But the term does little to convey their poverty, their religious traditionalism, and the kinds of Jewish communities they left behind. Even their language linked them to the later group of immigrants. The Bavarian Jews, at the time of their migration to the United States, spoke western Yiddish. Bavarian authorities had passed numerous pieces of legislation intending to transform them into German speakers. The Jews of Posen also spoke Yiddish, a dialect no different from that spoken in other parts of Poland. Jews from Posen indeed differed little from the Jews who by dint of circumstance lived in those areas of Poland that had been incorporated by Russia or by Austria-Hungary.

During the 1820–1880 migration, Jews from Lithuania, western Russia, and Galicia arrived in America as well. In most ways these emigrants resembled those Jews of eastern Europe who would begin their large-scale exodus to America in later years. With regard to their Yiddish speaking, their dense settlement in large Jewish enclaves, their economic profile as small-scale artisans, and the unalloyed traditional religious ideology of their home communities, little differentiated those who came early and those who came in subsequent decades from eastern Europe. Local circumstances, including epidemics, famines, and wars, as well as the general migratory trends in their towns and regions, sent them westward to America somewhat before the great exodus of the latter half of the nineteenth century. The presence of young men seeking to avoid conscription into the Russian army also created a commonality between waves of immigration.[12] By 1880 when the massive wave out of eastern Europe began to crest, one-sixth of America's Jews already had been born someplace east of Germany.[13]

Indeed, well before 1880 many congregations in America worshiped according to *minhag Polin*, the Polish rite. Enough Russian Jews lived in New York City by the early 1850s that they founded a congregation of their own in 1852, Beth Hamedrash Hagodol, and in that same decade contingents of Jews from the Lithuanian provinces of Kovno and Suwalk settled in Buffalo, Chicago, Philadelphia, San Francisco, and other

American cities. In the late 1850s Los Angeles Jews—the first Jews to come to southern California—all listed their birthplace as "Russian Poland." In 1869 a Jewish newspaper in Odessa, *Hamelitz,* reported on the large number of Polish Jewish families going to America. Even at that seemingly early date, it noted that "there is virtually no family in Poland which has no relatives in America." The first Romanian Jews came to America in the late 1860s and early 1870s.[14]

Many of these eastern European Jews made the journey to America in steps, spending some time in German states and the British Isles before continuing further west. Although the latter immigrants who came to the United States in the 1860s and 1870s arrived with a smattering of English acquired by peddling in Scotland, Ireland, Wales, or England, they still resembled in important ways the later Jewish immigrants who came directly from Lithuania, Poland, and Russia.[15]

This rigid division of American Jewish immigrants into "German" and "eastern European" also erases from history the thirty thousand Jews from the Balkans, Turkey, and Greece who came to America during the first quarter of the twentieth century. The largest group among this Sephardic contingent spoke Ladino, or Judeo-Spanish. Along with arrivals from elsewhere in the Levant, the countries bordering the eastern Mediterranean, they settled in New York, occupying a distinctive space on the Lower East Side along Allen Street. Small contingents of Levantine Jews headed for San Francisco, Seattle, Los Angeles, and Portland. Like their coreligionists from Europe's heartland, they founded ethnic synagogues, created charitable societies, and sought ways to educate their children. In 1910 Moise Gadol, a Bulgarian-born Jew, launched *La America,* a Ladino weekly publication that survived until 1925. These Jews united in practicing *minhag Sepharad,* or the Sephardic rite, but even among them deep divisions existed owing to the constant turmoil in their region of origin.[16]

While most Jews who came to America in the decades flanking the Civil War did indeed come from those states that in 1871 made up a unified Germany, in and of itself, that fact tells us little about which Jews immigrated to America and why. Nor does it validate long-standing assumptions about the "German" era of American Jewish history. Actual behavior of Jews from Bavaria, Westphalia, and Rhineland, let alone Posen and Silesia, deviated from the popular idea that these immigrants arrived relatively well-off, Germanized, minimally committed to Jewish practice, and easily integrated into America. From the 1820s through the 1840s tens of thousands of young Jewish men in particular left Bavaria for America. After the 1840s the migration continued and included more recruits from Posen, Silesia, Bohemia, Moravia, Hungary, and other communities to the east. Both the earlier and the later immigrants appear to have been among the least Germanized of their group, the poorest, the most traditional, and the least able to take advantage of the fruits of emancipation at home.

CENTRAL EUROPEAN IMMIGRANTS

Jewish emigration out of central Europe in the middle of the nineteenth century grew out of the complex economic and political changes of that era. For centuries Jews throughout central Europe had functioned as peddlers and other low-level merchants who shuttled back and forth between the peasants and the larger regional markets. They tended to live in extremely small Jewish communities with only a skeletal communal infrastructure. With the modernizing of central European economies, improvements in transportation, and the emergence of early factory production, relationships between peasants and markets changed. There was less need for the services of small-time Jewish traders. While Jewish peddling persisted in Germany, particularly in the south into the early twentieth century, by and large the Jewish peddler faded in memory as a curious relic of the past.

As they became increasingly modernized, the states of central Europe began to offer some Jews the chance to experience greater political equality, individual rights, and material prosperity. For Jews living in places like Bavaria and Prussia, the era of emancipation deeply divided them, creating classes of "winners" and "losers." For those Jews who could afford it, moving from a village or small town, with its declining economic opportunities, to a larger city meant the chance to open a more substantial shop. It meant the chance to attend a state school and qualify for a professional position. The same decades that saw Jewish emigration from central Europe to America saw the entry of some Jewish men into the fields of medicine, law, and various other white-collar occupations. In this era Jews began to function in neutral public institutions where Jewishness did not necessarily function as a barrier. They could participate in the cultural and leisure activities of the cities. But taking advantage of the bounty of emancipation also required that they adapt their dress and personal bearing. It also demanded facility in German.[17]

Bavarian sources make it clear that not all Bavarian Jews spoke German, particularly at the beginning of the migration era. Many, especially the least affluent among them, spoke Judeo-German, a variant of Yiddish. The lower their economic status, the less likely it was that they knew German, and the less German they knew, the less possibility there was that they could participate in the twin forces of transformation: political emancipation and movement into the middle class.

At the same time the states began to interfere in the lives of the Jews, attempting to regulate their names (passing laws forcing them to take German names), how they worshiped, the languages in which they kept their business records, and even how and where they lived. In 1813, just before the emigration to America began, Bavaria imposed restrictions on the number of Jews legally allowed to reside within its borders and restricted the right of marriage to eldest sons. What seemed a draconian measure to the Jews occurred at a time when the Jewish birthrate began to skyrocket but their economic circumstances had started to plummet. State officials worried that the growing number of Jews, poor ones in particular, would upset the religious status quo. These restrictions and the decline of the Jewish economy inspired many young people, those who could not move to cities and into more substantial business enterprises, to leave for America. The "winners" could stay in their home countries and develop into the urbanized German Jewish middle class, while those who did not fit into the new equation had to find another place to live.[18]

These least Germanized, least modernized young Jews opted to move to America, sparking what has been termed an "America fever" that raged through Bavaria, other parts of Germany, and much of Europe's heartland. Their exodus led not only to a depopulation of young Jewish men but also to a persistent age and gender imbalance in the small towns. The older people, unable to go either to cities or to America, stayed in their rural communities. Young Jewish women faced much more difficulty in choosing to go to America on their own. Social convention made it difficult for them to travel alone to spearhead their families' migration to America. Many found themselves left with no local work options and little chance of marriage. Observers at the time noted the motives of the migration out of central Europe. In 1839 the *Allgemeine Zeitung des Judentums,* a German Jewish newspaper keenly interested in the migration, commented that the ranks of the Jewish emigrants was composed of "many more single people than families . . . who are motivated not by greed but by the conviction that . . . they will not be able to settle and find a family."[19]

The sons of Jewish peddlers, horse traders, and semiskilled artisans and some women who had labored as domestic servants turned to America, seeing no chance of working or marrying if they stayed at home. They tended to migrate along well-articulated family chains, and they developed a distinctive migration pattern that linked the Jews of central Europe to those transplanting themselves to America. Typically a son left for America, serving as the family pioneer. He worked there, almost invariably in the occupations of his forebears, peddling and petty business. After saving money he sent passage money for one or more of his brothers to join him in America, share in his enterprise, and lay away enough money to bring over more siblings, all the while sending money back to aging parents and siblings not participating in the American migration.

Over time the brothers saved enough to fulfill the ultimate goal of the migration: one of them returned home. Here he could see his parents for the last time, and he could also find a young woman who, like him, had no real marriage prospects, and the two would wed. She might have sisters, cousins, and other female friends. The newlyweds often convinced these unmarried women, who like the new bride had few opportunities for making a living and minimal chances at matrimony, to join them on the journey to America, where a cohort of Jewish bachelors awaited them. The details of this chain migration, by which brothers brought brothers and sisters brought sisters to America, led to a class- and age-specific transfer of central European Jewish population to America. By the 1850s a Jewish teacher in Jebenhausen, a town in Wurtemberg, reported that 40 percent of his townspeople had left for the United States and "that other communities had been similarly stripped of their young men."[20] While the more affluent and educated of their peers moved to Munich, Hamburg, and Berlin, the poorest of the young Jews chose America instead.[21]

Those village Jews who successfully transplanted to America and made a tolerable living for themselves in their new home never returned to Germany, other than perhaps for a nostalgic trip to visit parents and elderly relatives or to find a suitable Jewish bride. Although as a whole the Jews understood their political prospects to be improving throughout central Europe, in Germany, Alsace-Lorraine, and Austria-Hungary, those who went to America had no interest in returning with their earnings to take part in the new possibilities. While some developed a fondness for certain elements of German culture, among them its music and literature, they did so from afar, from their new homes. In America they partook of many of the German cultural institutions that developed in key cities, such as theater, singing societies, and athletic clubs. The fact that hardly any of them returned to Germany demonstrates the immigrants' understanding that Europe provided no place for Jews, while America did.

Versions of this story could be told about the Jews in much of central Europe in the middle decades of the nineteenth century. This same drama played itself out, for example, in Bohemia, part of the Hapsburg empire and home to a substantial Jewish population. It, like Baden and Bavaria, sent its least Germanized and least modern Jews to the United States before 1880. Rather than harboring a substantial middle-class, assimilated, and comfortable Jewish community, Bohemia, in the first decades of the nineteenth century, counted among its number many impoverished, small-town Jews who spoke Yiddish and eked out a living in peddling and horse-trading. They also lived under the burden of numerous restrictive laws, which made Jewishness a serious liability. Until the 1840s Jews could own no land, and they had to pay a special Jewish tax. State officials tried many strategies to limit the number of poor and poorly Germanized Jews within their borders. Through the middle of the nineteenth century, for example, only Jews with a German-language elementary school education could obtain a marriage license. Poor young Bohemian Jews paid a very high price for their lack of German-style education. In the eyes of society, that deficit made them worthless.

For these Jews migration to America after the 1820s represented a chance to fulfill such basic goals as marriage and raising a family.[22] Even after the various states lifted the most discriminatory laws against Jews in the late 1840s, the outmigration from Bohemia continued. "It is conspicuous," observed a Jewish newspaper account in 1849, "that despite the emancipation, the desire for emigration, especially to North America, increases here from day to day. Hundreds of Bohemians emigrated even this year. The second-class cabins of the boat that is leaving Bremen on April 15 are completely taken by Jews from Prague. The captain is prepared to supply *kosher* food if desired. . . . One can see that there is little faith in the future of Austria. From Hungary, too, a large number is emigrating to America."[23]

Poor Jews also came to America in the middle of the nineteenth century from Alsace. Although part of France, Europe's most liberal country, the first, in fact, to emancipate the Jews, Alsace did not provide a comfortable home to the Jews. Unlike the small number of Jews in Paris or the Sephardim in the south, the spread of modernization and liberalization had bypassed the Jews of Alsace. Through the 1840s they had little in common with other French citizens. They spoke Yiddish rather than French, and despite the universal granting of citizenship to Jewish men, those who lived in Alsace gained little from the promises of "Liberty, Fraternity, and Equality" heralded by the Revolution of 1789. Few Jews left France for the United States, but those who did mainly included Alsatians whose poverty set them apart from the Jews of Paris who could take advantage of new economic, political, and legal realities.[24] Well-off French Jews in 1854, under the leadership of Baron Alphonse de Rothschild, created an emigration society, the Society for Promoting Migration to the New World, specifically intended to facilitate the migration of Jews from Alsace to America.[25]

This particular effort to send a group of poor Jews from a specific region of Europe, with hopes of resettling them in America, grew out of the complex dynamics of mid-nineteenth-century change. Some Jewish families had succeeded spectacularly as a result of emancipation and the new economic order. Many found ways to make modestly comfortable places for themselves in cities, and they created a new Jewish urban middle class. The Jews who had triumphed understood that some among them had not, and they believed that America offered the best solution to the vexing problem of Jewish poverty. In the 1840s emigration societies cropped up in Vienna, Budapest, Prague, and as far east as Lemberg. A Jewish novelist in Bohemia, Leopold Kompert, advised his poor coreligionists to head "On to America."[26]

Hep! Hep! Riots

The poor Jews of central Europe did not actually need Rothschild or any of the emigration societies to tell them about the bounties of America or to prove that Europe held out little promise. For they not only recognized their dimming economic prospects, but they also experienced or read about the periodic violence being waged against them. Just a year before migration to America began, in 1819, a series of mob attacks on Jews broke out in central Europe. They began in Wurzberg, in the province of Baden, quickly engulfed much of southern and western Germany, then spread northward. The violence that began in Wurzberg came to be known as the "Hep! Hep!" riots, a phrase of unknown origin or meaning shouted by the marauding mobs that destroyed Jewish property and beat up Jews on the streets. Led by students, the riots caused tens of thousands of Jews to reconsider their place in their hometowns.[27]

The initial cause of the rioting stemmed from a request by Wurzberg's small Jewish community for residential and trading rights. This petition inflamed some of Wurzberg's Christians, who launched a series of attacks on the tiny Jewish community. So frightening did the Jews of Wurzberg find the mob action that after three days all had fled the city, seeking temporary refuge in the countryside.[28] In the days that followed the violence spread to larger Jewish communities, like Frankfurt, Danzig, and Hamburg. One commentator, a French diplomat stationed in Bavaria, reported that Jews should be considered safe nowhere in Germany. He failed to mention, however, that similar anti-Jewish rioting could be witnessed at precisely that time in Alsace.[29] In the 1830s and in 1848, after the failed liberal revolutions throughout much of Europe, Jews became the victims of repeated mob violence, and while few lost their lives, many lost their confidence in the promises of emancipation.

Jewish Migration versus European Migration

The Jews' migration differed from that of other Europeans in several ways. Economic opportunities for most Jews had seriously eroded. Further, the sporadic violence visited on the Jews throughout central Europe rendered the Jews' leave-taking different from that of the non-Jews emigrating from the same places. Further, the enormous exodus of Christians out of central Europe, an emigration of approximately a million peasants and small landowners from Bavaria, Wuerttemberg, and Baden, took place between 1820 and 1860. Unlike the Jews, they tended to migrate as full families, and a sizable number returned to their German homes. Also, unlike Christians, Jews emigrated out of proportion to their total population. For example, Jews made up about 1.5 percent of the population of Bavaria but accounted for 5 percent of the emigrants to the United States. From Posen, whose Christians left later than its Jews, Jews predominated among those leaving for America. Between 1824 and 1871, 46,640 Jews left, compared to 18,790 Christians. A disproportionate number of Jews also decided to leave Alsace, Bohemia, Moravia, Western Russia, and such Lithuanian provinces as Suwalk and Kovno for America.[30] From 1820 through 1840 about fifty thousand Jews left Europe for America, and from 1840 through 1880 that number quadrupled. For these Jews America emerged as the only real alternative to life at home. The growing U.S. economy provided seemingly limitless options for immigrants.

Notably, many Jewish immigrants opted for peddling as a way to enter into that economy. The transportation revolution of the early decades of the nineteenth century only went so far. Large numbers of Americans lived on farms and in hinterland communities not served directly by the canals, roads, and railroads, which brought raw materials to the port cities. Therefore, peddlers who chose to go by foot or by horse and wagon to the many scattered farms throughout the enormous continent, or the small-time merchants willing to open general stores in small towns, could do reasonably well. Likewise, urban peddlers who traversed city neighborhoods in the years before department stores, selling off their backs and out of wheelbarrows, could also make a modest living. Americans relied on Jewish peddlers to supply them with everything from buttons and sewing needles to stoves to clothes to plates.

The emigration from central Europe continued through the last decades of the nineteenth century, despite the formal acquisition of full rights of citizenship in Germany and Austria-Hungary. Although unified Germany offered all political rights to all of its Jews after 1871, small-town Jews continued to leave Germany for America.[31] The exodus from Posen intensified after 1860, even though increasing numbers of them acquired Prussian citizenship and theoretically, anyway, enjoyed full rights.[32] They embodied the words of the German Jewish poet Heinrich Heine, who commented, "Everyone over there can find salvation his own way. . . . Even if Europe should become a single prison there is still another loophole of escape, namely America, and thank God! the loophole is after all larger than the prison itself."[33]

EASTERN EUROPEAN IMMIGRANTS

The American "loophole" grew increasingly larger during the last decades of the nineteenth century and the first two decades of the twentieth. Through it streamed substantially larger contingents of Jews, drawn from the significantly larger communities of eastern Europe. After 1880, traditionally considered the beginning date of the eastern European Jewish emigration, the number of Jews coming to America grew wildly. Between 1881 and 1924 over 2.5 million moved to America, a tenfold increase over the exodus of the previous six decades. Looking at a shorter period of time, the numbers become even more dramatic. In the years between 1899 and 1910, 750,000 Jews left Russia alone, amounting to one-seventh of that country's Jewish population. The previous wave of emigration had nowhere near as profoundly shifted Jews from one continent to another.[34]

In these years, about one-third of eastern European Jews left their countries of origin, with about 90 percent of them choosing America. Those who did not went to Germany, France, or England, creating eastern European enclaves in Berlin, Paris, and London, not unlike those created in New York, Chicago, and Philadelphia. Of those, however, a substantial number treated places like England as way stations to America.[35] A small handful cast their lot with the emerging Jewish settlements in Palestine as part of the Zionist project. Larger numbers flooded the cities of central and eastern Europe, moving to Warsaw, Lodz, Kiev, Vilna, Kharkov, Lublin, Vienna, Prague, and Budapest, where jobs in industry had emerged.[36]

Like the earlier migration, the "Russian" migration from the end of the nineteenth century through the first years of the 1920s should be analyzed in terms of how eastern European Jews calculated the balance between the problems of home and the opportunities of America. Just as the pre-1880 migration represented a selective process by which some Jews opted to move to America, so too the emigration from the East should not be viewed either merely as a desperate flight from terror or as a wholesale transfer of Jews and their communities from places of peril to a place of safety.

Yet this has not been how historians and other commentators have thought of Jewish migration. Instead, they have invested the eastern European migration, which started after 1870, rather than 1880, as is commonly thought, with unique qualities, describing it as utterly unlike the one that came before. Indeed, the traditional narrative dates the onset of that migration precisely in 1881, a date that as a result reverberates in Jewish historical memory. One historian has gone so far as to say: "[W]ith hindsight, three dates may be invested with capital importance." They were 1789, the year of the French Revolution, with its emancipation of the Jews and the eventual breaking up of the Jewish community; 1933, the year Adolf Hitler assumed office in Germany, setting in motion a train of events that culminated in the murder of 6 million Jews and the near destruction of Jewish life in Europe; and 1881.[37]

The Pogroms

In that year, on April 15, in the city of Elizabetgrad in the Kherson province of Russia, following news of the assassination of Czar Alexander II, an anti-Jewish riot broke out. Mobs, composed primarily of workers, many of them peasants transplanted to the city, attacked the local Jewish quarter, destroying property, killing innocent people, terrorizing those who witnessed the rampage, and in the process teaching the world the word *pogrom*. Local officials stood by idly. Because of the general indifference evinced by the authorities, the state shared some degree of responsibility for the rampant looting, widespread destruction of property, and bodily harm endured by the Jews.[38] About sixty Russian cities experienced pogroms that month, and by the end of the year about three hundred more such attacks had been visited on Jews in communities throughout southern and southwestern Russia.[39] The pogroms continued to erupt in this region sporadically for the next few years, coming to an end in 1884. In 1903 a second cycle of violence broke out and lasted until 1906, while in the years during and after World War I and coinciding with the Russian Revolution and the subsequent civil war, from 1917 through 1921, a third, more devastating wave washed over the Jews of Russia.[40]

The pogroms turned the Jews of Russia into a haunted people. They also shaped the Jews' political consciousness, leading many of them to embrace Marxist socialism and others to subscribe to Zionism. In the early 1880s, after the first great wave of pogroms, groups of Jewish intellectuals and workers involved themselves in projects designed to spread Socialism among Jewish laborers. In the fall of 1897 a group of Jewish women and men founded the Algemayne Bund fun Yidishe Arbeter in Rusland Poyln un Lite (General Association of Jewish Workers in Russia, Poland, and Lithuania), known as the Bund. The Bund, which throughout the early twentieth century advocated for Socialism, for Yiddish as the authentic expression of the culture of the Jewish masses, and for secular Jewish nationalism, developed out of a Jewish perception that Russian society had to be thoroughly reconstructed. By 1905, with the outbreak of the second wave of pogroms, the Bund turned to self-defense, forming a "Fighting Division," which sought to meet the pogromists head on.[41]

The seeds of Zionism, like those of the Bund's Socialism, had been planted long before the flaring up of the first pogroms. Jewish writers had been describing in polemics, imaginative literature, and poetry the advantages of a return to Zion. Yet it was the 1882 publication of Leon Pinsker's *Autoemancipation* and the arrival in Palestine of the first fourteen members of the BILU society (an acronym, derived from the Hebrew phrase "*Beth Yaakov Lechu v'nelcha,*" "house of Jacob, let us go") that opened a new chapter in the history of the Jewish people. The Zionist message, repeated for decades to come, echoed Pinsker's words, which boldly predicted that until the Jews had a homeland of their own they would function as a pariah people subject to whatever hostility and ill will others chose to inflict on them.

Both movements represented radical political breaks with the past, and both reflected the brutality of the pogroms. The imagery of the pogroms suffused Jewish literature around the world. After the first wave of massacres in 1881, the American Emma Lazarus, best known for her poem "The New Colossus" engraved on the base of the Statue of Liberty, wrote *Songs of a Semite* (1882) in which she decried the pogroms and the fate of Russian Jewry and held Christianity responsible for the tragedies visited on the Jewish people. In "The Crowing of the Red Cock," she asked with passion, "Where is the Hebrew's Fatherland?" She continued:

When the long roll of Christian guilt
    Against his sires and kin is known,
The flood of tears, the life-blood spilt,
    The agony of ages shown,
What oceans can the stain remove,
From Christian law and Christian love?[42]

After the 1903 outbreak in Kishinev the Hebrew poet Hyaim Nahman Bialik, then living in Odessa, went to that Moldavian city to interview survivors at the behest of the Jewish Historical Commission in Odessa. Out of that visit came "Al ha-Shehita" (About the slaughter) in 1903 and in 1904 "Ir ha-Harega" (The city of murder). Like Lazarus he put the blame on Russian bestiality. But unlike the American poet, Bialik pointed an accusatory finger at the victims themselves, who he saw as meekly going to their deaths.

Jewish communities around the world organized mass protests against each wave of violence. In the United States, in 1903, eighty rallies, from Boston to San Francisco, drew attention to the pogroms and the suffering of Russia's Jews. The protests raised money to help the victims and generated sympathy for the Russian Jewish immigrants then landing in America. They also drew the attention of the American press. Editorials in newspapers across the country held up the pogroms as evidence of Russia's barbarism and backwardness. The protests brought together Christian clergy and local elected officials with rabbis and leaders of American Jewish organizations. And in June 1906, the U.S. Congress passed a resolution stating that "the people of the United States are horrified by the report of the massacre of the Hebrews in Russia."[43]

Indeed, from the 1880s onward, each surge of pogroms in Russia played a key role in galvanizing American Jews politically. They provided a powerful rallying cry for Jewish organizations. The B'nai B'rith, founded in 1843, the Board of Delegates of American Israelites of 1859, the American Jewish Committee organized in 1906, and the American

Jewish Congress of 1918 all responded to the outbreaks of anti-Jewish violence in Europe. Each of these American Jewish communal organizations used depictions of the horrors of the pogroms to lobby for U.S. government involvement. In whatever civic and political movement American Jews involved themselves, they highlighted the pogroms to their non-Jewish colleagues.[44]

In 1903 Irish nationalist Michael Davitt went to Kishinev after the pogrom there, covering its aftermath for American newspapers. He compiled his observations, which included a call for a Jewish national homeland, in his book *Within the Pale*.[45] In 1909 the National Association for the Advancement of Colored People met for the first time. Jews had played a crucial role in founding the NAACP. At that inaugural meeting, delegates passed a resolution of sympathy with the victims of the Kishinev massacre and linked the pogroms in Russia with the unending physical violence visited on America's black population.[46]

BEYOND EASY CATEGORIES

The pogroms confirmed for many Jews the utter impossibility of integration and the nearly total cultural and social chasm between Jews and non-Jews in the czarist country. Memories of these brutal, senseless, and violent attacks on Jews have also figured dramatically in the construction of American Jewish history. The story of eastern European immigration to the United States by and large has been told in terms of the pogroms and the Jewish reaction to them. The pogroms, as historical thinking has it, essentially sparked the exodus to America. Many, indeed most, of the details about the east European Jewish emigration to America have been recounted in terms of the pogroms, helping to foster a broad belief in the stark contrast between the earlier "German" Jewish immigration and the later "Russian" one.

Because of the drama of the pogroms, the pre-1880 eastern European Jewish migration to America has been virtually ignored. Jews leaving Russia for any reason other than escape from the pogroms ran counter to the dominant paradigm. Likewise, the similarities between the immigrants of the two eras—their class backgrounds, the permanence of their migrations, their motives in emigrating in particular—have been gilded over in order to tell the more dramatic stories of two migrations, one "before" and one "after" the pogroms ushered in by the 1880s. Indeed, even thinking about the Jewish migration from Europe in terms of two eras reflects just how much the pogroms have shaped both popular and scholarly historical thinking.

Historians, popular writers, and American Jews generally have assumed that the two migrations differed radically from one another since the immigrants had left two very different geographic areas. Germany represented liberalism, and the Jews who left there, conventional interpretation assumes, came to America already firmly set on the road toward acculturation. Eastern Europe—often referred to in shorthand as "Russia"—stood as the polar opposite. From there Jews fled for their lives, and the place they had fled from had made few steps toward modernization.

But adhering to these binary categories of "Germany" and "eastern Europe" clouds the process of understanding Jewish migration to America and leaves out some important facts. For example, important parts of Europe that lay east of the Elbe did not suffer under czarist rule. Austria-Hungary, for example, contained some of the largest pockets of Jewish settlements. In Galicia, which constituted the part of Poland annexed by the Habsburg monarchy, Jews experienced some forms of emancipation as early as 1867, as did those of Hungary. These Jews swelled the ranks of the immigrants in the latter part of the nineteenth century, though, and the early part of the twentieth. Galician Jews were among the poorest in Europe, and by the 1880s some 60 percent of them ate and lived on Jewish communal charity. Making up approximately 10 percent of the province's population, Galicia's Jews, though they experienced no pogroms, lived under conditions "even worse than in Russia. . . . Emigration alone offered them an escape from misery."[47] While anti-Jewish sentiment existed in Galicia and acts of physical violence against Jews did occur, Galician Jews migrated out of the utter desperation of their poverty. They emigrated at the same time and in the same ways as did the Russian Jews who lived with the knowledge that pogroms could break out at any time.[48] Indeed, the proportion of Jews leaving Galicia, where no pogroms erupted, exceeded that of Russian Jews.

Additionally, many Russian and other eastern European Jews who went to England, Canada, and South and Central America did so with the ultimate goal of moving on to the United States. In the decades of mass eastern European Jewish emigration, many more Jews landed in Britain than remained there.[49] Since those places offered Jews broad political freedom and freedom from physical abuse, the desire of immigrant Jews to settle in New York, Chicago, Baltimore, or Los Angeles ultimately—as opposed to London, Montreal, or Havana—points to a much broader motivation than the flight from pogroms.[50]

Although some historical accounts would have us believe that Russia was virtually emptied out of all its Jews, in truth approximately two-thirds of the Jewish population stayed in Russia. These Jews may have listened to the stern advice of the Russian rabbis who warned that in the United States Jews would lose their Jewishness. In addition, many who did not join the groundswell of migration to America may have pinned their hopes on the opening up of industrial opportunities in the large cities of eastern Europe. Indeed, the majority of Russian Jews who migrated in this period chose Russian cities—some of which had experienced pogroms—rather than American ones. The 1905 pogrom in Odessa may have been the deadliest. Over three hundred Jews lost their lives, and thousands were wounded. Yet the Jewish population of Odessa continued to climb into the early twentieth century. In 1897, 140,000 Jews lived there. By 1926 the number had grown to over 153,000, despite the specter of the pogrom and the exodus to America.[51]

The actual demographic and class details of the post-1880 immigration shed more light on conditions in the sending society—eastern Europe—and the kinds of communities the immigrants created in America than did the simple yet dramatic pogrom narrative. Of those who went to America, able-bodied workers, young adults at the peak of their physical ability, far outnumbered children or older people. While approximately one-quarter of the eastern European Jewish immigrants to the United States fell into one of those groups, the young and the old, most came from the age group typical of nearly all immigrants—young people able to work long hours. This represents one of the few significant differences between this migration and the earlier one, in which neither children nor older people came to America in any appreciable number. It also differentiates the Jewish migration from the other great waves from Europe at the time, migrations including almost no dependent family members.

Gender patterns also differentiated both the two eras of Jewish migrations and the Jewish migration in general from other migrations of the time. In the first wave of migration, before 1880, young single men predominated. Young women migrated on their own rarely. Daughters did not accompany fathers as pioneers in the family's relocation to America. But in the second wave, after 1880, Jewish women left just as often as Jewish men. Fathers immigrating to the United States took their older children with them, daughters as well as sons. Birth order and age rather than gender determined which family members from Jewish eastern Europe spearheaded the family relocation. In contrast, women showed up rarely as solo emigrants from Italy or Greece, and men far outnumbered women among these newcomers.

Yet the two Jewish migrations, as well as the general immigrant flow into the United States, shared many similarities in that the economically disadvantaged chose to migrate to America, although as in nearly all migrations, the very poorest, like the richest, did not participate. In the eastern European, post-1880 emigration, young people with experience in certain occupations opted for America more often than those with other work backgrounds. Skilled workers, those previously employed in manufacturing, made up 64 percent of the Jewish emigrants but constituted only 40 percent of the Russian Jewish population as a whole. Those who made a living in commerce in Russia found themselves underrepresented among the immigrants across the Atlantic, and Jewish women who in Russia had spent part of their young adulthood in domestic service cast their lot with other immigrants more often than women in other occupations. Finally, although southern and southwestern Russia represented the epicenter of the pogroms, the emigrants came more often from northern and northwestern Russia, which included Lithuania.[52]

Eastern European Jews, among whom Russians made up the largest group, with Romanians and Galicians swelling their ranks, consisted mostly of young people who faced a grim and uncertain future if they remained in Europe. Jewish families with young children who could look forward only to limited prospects chose to move to America. The Jewish population of eastern Europe had skyrocketed in the decades before the 1870s and 1880s at the same time that the Jewish trades, particularly tailoring, experienced a sharp decline. In 1800, 1,250,000 Jews lived in eastern Europe. By 1900, despite the flow to America, the population mushroomed to 6,500,000, even though there had been no influx of immigrants to the area. This growth in population exacerbated the decline of Jewish occupations, since competition grew just as those trades entered the first stages of obsolescence.[53]

The number of industrial jobs opening up in the large cities of Russia and elsewhere in eastern Europe could not sustain the increasing number of Jews who clamored for them. Young people had little prospect of establishing families amid the growing impoverishment. Tailors in particular had a chance of successfully transferring their work experiences to the United States, a place that in the middle of the nineteenth century had assumed the premier place as the world's manufacturer of ready-made garments. New York in particular functioned as the heartland of that industry.[54] Economic conditions for Jews in Russia, on the other hand, worsened. The first stirrings of industrialization and the emancipation of the serfs in Russia in 1861 undermined the Jewish economy, while the introduction of the railroad brought goods into the Russian cities that had previously been conveyed by Jewish traders.

Jewish migration from eastern Europe became self-perpetuating. Family members, unmarried sons and daughters, or young married men and women traveling alone began the migration. Few ever returned to their hometowns.[55] They settled in American cities, labored, and saved to send for siblings or wives as well as young children and sometimes parents, providing them with passage money. This then brought the cost of transportation within the reach of those with less means, making it possible for an elaborate process of family and community building in the United States to take place.

To emphasize the selective nature of the eastern European Jewish emigration and the economic forces that fuelled it does not diminish the specific Jewish context in which it took shape. For instance, Jews emigrated from eastern Europe in much greater number and intensity than did non-Jews. Jews constituted about 5 percent of the population of the vast Russian Empire but made up nearly half of its emigrants. The numbers of Galician and Romanian Jews appeared even more dramatic when set against the general figures. Of all the emigrants from Galicia, Jews, who made up about 10 percent of the population, accounted for 60 percent of the emigrants, and from Romania they constituted 90 percent of those who left.[56]

In addition, Russia had long been inhospitable to the Jews. At the end of the eighteenth century Catherine the Great realized that her acquisition of vast chunks of Poland brought with it large numbers of Jews. Decisions made during her reign and during those of her successors limited the Jews to the Pale of Settlement, restricting their movement and their economic opportunities. Czarist policies beginning in the early nineteenth century focused on destroying the structure of the Jewish communities, encouraging conversion to Christianity, and dividing the Jews among themselves. The Russian Orthodox Church had long been an enemy of the Jews, and its policies went hand-in-hand with state efforts to rid Russia of its Jews by making them into Christians.

The record of the Russian government's attitudes toward the Jews fluctuated between two poles. At times the state sought to liberalize its policies. Czar Alexander II repealed some of the harshest elements of his father's regime. "Useful" Jews, merchants in particular, as well as university students, certain craftsmen, and trained medical personnel won the right to live outside the Pale. This in turned opened the door for some Jews to achieve great wealth, enter the professions, gain a general education, and participate in Russian cultural and intellectual life.[57] In the middle of the nineteenth century a handful of Jewish women, for example, enjoyed the privileges of a general education and exposure to the literary and artistic currents of Russian society. Among these educated women a cadre of writers began to produce a body of literary work that belied the idea of Russian Jews as premodern pariahs living outside the intellectual developments of the society. Hava Shapiro, who wrote under the pen name *em kol hai*—"the mother of all living things"—wrote for newspapers and wrote short stories in Hebrew. A product of the Pale, she had been raised in a wealthy Jewish home and received a doctorate from the University of Berne. She participated in a literary circle that included the great Yiddish writer Y. L. Peretz.[58]

Despite the possibilities of liberalization for some and the burgeoning opportunities for a handful to acquire either a Western education or new wealth, Jewish emigration logically flowed from places like Russia. Until 1917 and the end of the czarist regime, Jews had no inherent rights. What benefits they might enjoy at one moment could easily be rescinded at another. To spark it, the emigration that had commenced in the late 1860s needed only a predictable means of transportation, a dramatic economic downturn, and a destination where Jews could live as they chose.

Finally, the pogroms themselves took place in a particular economic setting in which issues of livelihood and issues of religion blurred, becoming indistinguishable. When the first pogroms took place, in 1881, the government put together a commission to study the causes of the violence, and it easily placed the blame on the Jews, pointing out that they had aroused the anger of the peasants by mercilessly exploiting them. That report led to the promulgation in 1882 of the May or "Temporary" Laws, which prohibited Jewish settlement in large numbers of rural villages even in the Pale of Settlement. The new laws removed Jews from the rural liquor trade and forbade them from doing business on Sunday. Even within the Pale, Jews could no longer buy land or build houses.

Ironically, these laws set in motion a dynamic that only created more tension. As a result of them, nearly half a million Jews found themselves expelled from their homes. Most of them went to the developing industrialized cities, where they joined the Jews already living there. The new

Jewish city dwellers had to compete fiercely for the limited number of jobs available to Jews. But more crucial still, upon their arrival in the cities they also had to compete directly with newly arrived, unskilled, poor Christian peasants who had been displaced owing to the emerging forces of economic modernization. In sum, economic realities as well as religious and ethnic factors intertwined to push millions of Jews onward to America.

The general condition of the Jews, their poverty, and their deviance from the national Christian norm became after the 1880s a matter of debate at the state level. Administrative authorities harassed Jews repeatedly, restricting their already limited entry into educational institutions and selectively enforcing with vigor the residence restrictions of Jews in designated cities. One government official expressed his wishes and probably those of the state when in 1891 he predicted that "one-third of the Jews will convert, one-third will die, and one-third will flee the country."[59]

The Jewish migration to the United States from eastern Europe, just like the migration out of central Europe in earlier decades, operated as a permanent social force, indicating in both cases that the Jews believed they had no home to which they could return. In both cases over time an equal number of men and women chose America as the place where they would have a reasonable chance to work, marry, raise their children, and live freely as Jews. In essence, the Jewish context of the emigrants' poverty bridged the starting and end dates of this century of migration.

To discuss economic motivations, thereby minimizing the impact of the pogroms, is not to dismiss the hostility with which Jews lived in eastern Europe and the connection between anti-Jewish hostility and emigration. The point, rather, has been to demonstrate that the cyclical outbursts of physical violence, beginning with the "Hep! Hep!" riots of Bavaria in 1819, when coupled with the Jews' much more frequent encounters with economic deprivation, sparked movements outward. The 1819 violence ushered in the great century of migration. The desperate economic plight of Jews in Poland created in the aftermath of World War I framed its terminal point. Their experience in this decidedly nationalistic and Christian country and the connections between adversity, both physical and economic, and migration brought this century to a close. A war of terror engulfed the Jews in the newly independent nation, but it was as much an economic campaign as a political one. While wartime pogroms came to an end with the emergence of the new government, an economic assault on the Jews took over. The Polish government carried on an explicit policy of removing Jews from their positions and purposefully sought to undermine Jewish livelihood. No wonder that between the end of World War I and 1924, when immigration restrictions went into effect, about sixty thousand Jews had left from the port of Danzig alone.[60]

OCCUPATIONS AND SETTLEMENT PATTERNS

Jewish immigrants to America, whether they arrived in the 1820s or the 1920s, came in search of work. Like most immigrants, they settled where they could expect to find ample prospects for making a living. The history of Jewish settlement—where Jews built their communities and how—dovetailed with the history of Jewish work patterns. As immigrants they considered geography in making their choices, since some locations offered the best opportunities for them to trade immediately on past work experiences. In those places they created ethnic niches and by doing so drew in other immigrants like them. As more Jews—friends from back home, family members, or simply other Jews who shared sensibilities and identities—joined them, those places became more comfortable settings for Jewish communal life.

Peddling

In the earliest decades of the migration, Jews relied on their long-standing history of peddling as the economic factor determining their geographic and communal choices. Peddling offered the comfort of familiarity. Indeed, the decline of peddling had pushed them out of central Europe, and the need of Americans, both manufacturers and consumers, pulled them in. Itinerant merchandising took its shape from the basic structure of the American economy and the magnitude of the developing continent. Jews, in essence, served as an "entrepreneurial proletariat" in the American system of merchandising.[61]

Equally important, this economic activity took place around a dense Jewish nexus. Jewish wholesalers in port cities, New York in particular, but also Philadelphia, Baltimore, New Orleans, and, after 1849, San Francisco, supplied new immigrants with a load of goods, which they placed on their backs and took to the farms, mining and logging camps, and railroad crews far removed from urban markets. This pattern played itself out all over America. As new interior cities such as Cincinnati, St. Louis, Chicago, Pittsburgh, Nashville, Sioux City, Omaha, Milwaukee, Kansas City, Atlanta, and Chattanooga developed, Jews arrived early.

Among the first Europeans to arrive in these places, they began as peddlers, carrying goods that traveled along Jewish trade routes. As they acquired enough capital during their stints on the road, they opened stores in town. Multipurpose stores stocking goods such as fabric, needles, and thread, as well as pots and pans, paper, and ribbons, in particular became their specialty.

Each peddler functioned in a long Jewish economic chain linking shopkeepers to Jewish wholesalers in the larger cities on whom they depended for credit. The Jewish peddler on the road served as the agent of the Jewish town shopkeeper and the big city jobber. This trading network depended on intracommunal trust. Wholesaler and peddler understood each other, spoke the same language, and knew the same people. They also shared a sacred tradition that understood assistance in the form of interest-free loans as a religious obligation.

A staggering numbers of Jews in the decades before and after the Civil War first experienced America through peddling. It could even be said that peddling functioned as the nearly universal American Jewish male experience. Of the 125 Jews who lived in Iowa in the 1850s, one hundred of them peddled for a living. Of the Jews who lived in Syracuse, New York, two-thirds peddled. In Easton, Pennsylvania, a town serving farmers and coal miners, 46 percent peddled in 1840, 70 percent in 1845, and 55 percent in 1850.[62]

The peddlers began to fan out into the hinterlands adjacent to cities. As they sought out new territories where they faced little competition, they established new Jewish beachheads in the interior. The burgeoning towns and growing farm population, which created a high demand for goods, determined Jewish settlement patterns in America. As a result of this commercial pattern, by the 1880s Jews could be found in every region and in nearly every state. New England, the Deep South, the Midwest, the Pacific Northwest, the Southwest, and the prairies, first as territories and then as states, became home to Jewish peddlers, to Jewish dry goods dealers in the small towns with Jewish enclaves, and then to Jewish merchants in the larger cities developing in tandem with the farming frontier.

Despite the thousands of miles between these places, the Jewish clusters within them functioned as part of a transcontinental Jewish economy. Jewish newspapers circulated across America, linking places through print. These newspapers, like *The Israelite* or *Jewish Messenger,* reported on the economic prospects of newly opened up regions.[63] Jewish merchants in one city supplied goods and credit to Jewish merchants in another. In the South, for example, peddlers went from plantation to plantation, selling secondhand clothes to landowners who bought these inexpensive garments for their slaves. Most of the shirts and pants had in fact been made in New York on Chatham and other adjoining streets in lower Manhattan by Jewish tailors in their "slop shops," where used clothes were made over into saleable "new" garments. When these peddlers had saved enough money, they put down roots, at least temporarily, in the numerous small towns in the Mississippi Delta or in larger communities like Nashville or Memphis.

In the middle of the nineteenth century peddling functioned not only as the centrifugal force behind Jewish dispersion across the continent but also as a centripetal force making possible Jewish migration to America and the reformation of Jewish families and communities. The young men who led their families to America came on their own and began as peddlers. They spent their Sabbaths and holidays resting in the nearest Jewish enclave, often in the company of other Jewish peddlers and townsfolk. When a peddler had saved enough money, he sent for one or more of his brothers. Together they could cover a wider territory, which allowed them to save even more money.

Those savings bought them two related items, a shop in a town and the chance to marry. The point at which Jewish peddlers became married men coincided with the point at which they became sedentary shopkeepers. The stores they constructed in towns and cities of every size and in every region depended on the labor of all family members. Wives and children played a crucial role in sustaining the Jewish economy. Jews could, in the last half of the nineteenth century and into the early twentieth, be found in Helena, Arkansas, and Helena, Montana; Portland, Maine, and Portland, Oregon; Madison, Indiana, and Madison, Wisconsin; Berkshire County, Massachusetts; Macon, Georgia; Shelbyville, Tennessee; Cheyenne, Wyoming; or Oswego, New York. In most of these places a handful or more of Jewish families settled, worked in small business enterprises, and found ways to worship together.

They maintained links to the larger Jewish communities in bigger cities through kinship networks. They often turned to those larger cities to get kosher food and matzo at Passover. They received newspapers published in these cities, which provided them with Jewish news from around the world. For many of the immigrants these small-town stores represented just a first (or often second) stage in their American lives. Many who lived in places like Tupper Lake, New York, or Elman, Wisconsin, or who peddled for some part of their lives ended up in big cities later on. Indeed, even in the middle of the nineteenth century, when Jews found themselves highly dispersed, with many living in hinterland communities, more Jews lived in cities than did Americans as a whole.

City Work

By the 1840s one-fourth of all American Jews made their homes in three big East Coast cities: New York, Philadelphia, and Baltimore. Jews flocked to other large cities as well, and their numbers grew with the growth of Cincinnati, Chicago, Cleveland, Rochester, Albany, and San Francisco. In those cities Jews clustered in particular neighborhoods and in particular sectors of the economy, trade in particular. Jews engaged in trade at every level. Some traversed the city streets as urban peddlers who sold fresh produce and finished goods. Immigrants from the west Lithuanian province of Suwalk dominated urban peddling in Chicago in the 1860s. One New York congregation was dubbed the "India Rubber shul" because so many of its members sold rubber suspenders from street stands. As early as the 1850s Russian Jewish immigrants in New York City and Brooklyn cornered the glass trade, and newly arrived peddlers, knowing little or no English, made their way through the city bellowing the one phrase they had been taught: "glass put in."[64]

Others owned stores. The concentration of Jews in small retail business, particularly the dry goods business, also influenced Jewish residential patterns. Generally, Jews lived above or behind their business establishments. They fused work and home, business and family. All family members could contribute to the enterprise. That Jews tended to operate the same kinds of businesses in the same towns led to a clustering of Jewish families in the central business districts of dozens of American cities and towns. Their businesses ran the gamut from small, shabby ones in immigrant neighborhoods to the grand department stores in the small and large cities in which Jews pioneered. Of the smaller shops owned by Jews, many blurred the line between entrepreneurship and manufacturing. In places like Rochester, New York, for example, in the back rooms of the many Jewish-owned dry goods stores, family members sewed garments to be sold in the front.

The Jewish concentration in the garment trade had begun decades before the 1880s. In 1855, 22 percent of New York City's employed Polish Jewish immigrants made a living sewing, while other Jews labored making caps, hoopskirts, cloaks, and fur goods. The secondhand clothing trade, the collecting, resewing, and then reselling of garments in New York, Chicago, Baltimore, Boston, and elsewhere, lay in Jewish hands.

Cigar making also saw a dense concentration of Jewish laborers and employers, with the line between the two not always clear. Many Jewish cigar manufacturers, from Poland and Bohemia in particular, began their careers stripping, rolling, and performing the other parts of the operation. Some workers on the shop floors eventually became factory owners, a phenomenon made possible by the low level of capital needed to ascend from employee to employer.[65] Two Jewish workers in cigar making, Adolph Strasser and, most important, Samuel Gompers, played key roles in organizing workers. The latter, who immigrated to America in 1863, founded the American Federation of Labor.

A Jewish newspaper, *The Asmonean,* reported in 1852 that Jews could be found working in America as cigar makers, glaziers, needleworkers, "bakers, paperhangers, book-binders, pocket-book makers, gold and silver smiths, jewelers, diamond cutters, tin plate workers, gold lace weavers, mechanical dentists, engravers . . . printers and compositors." Jewish "shoe and bootmakers, [and] hatters," could be found in some of the largest U.S. cities.[66] In fact, the Jews engaged with the American economy in ways atypical of most Americans at the time: almost none made a living farming, and most lived in cities. The bigger the city, the more likely Jews lived and worked there.

URBAN COMMUNITIES

The Jewish geographic dispersion fueled by peddling characterized the early decades of Jewish migration more than it did the later ones. After the 1870s and 1880s immigrants tended to venture less often outside the big cities, the ports in particular. Jewish settlement in America became decidedly lopsided and idiosyncratic. Jewish newcomers to America rarely went beyond New York, and the vast majority of those who did venture beyond this port of entry went to other big cities—Philadelphia, Chicago, and in lesser numbers, Cleveland, Pittsburgh, Baltimore, and Boston—where they maintained their distinctive economic profile and built distinctive communities.

The overwhelmingly metropolitan character of the later Jewish immigrants should not obscure the several ways in which these two eras of migration resembled each other. First, well into the early twentieth century some newly arrived eastern European Jewish immigrants did exactly what their predecessors had. Some peddled in the remote hinterlands not yet served by stores and transportation, and when they had put aside enough money from their peddling, they opened stores in small towns.

In the first decade of the twentieth century, Jews came to Tupper Lake, a town in the center of New York's Adirondack region dominated by the twin enterprises of farming and logging. All Russian, Polish, and Lithuanian Jews, they began by peddling and then settled in town. The synagogue they founded, Beth Jacob, became known throughout the region more commonly as "the peddlers' shul," demonstrating that these eastern European Jews, like the Germans of nearly a century earlier, saw their economic opportunities on America's back roads. Similarly, in the early twentieth century, eastern European Jewish immigrants peddled in New Mexico, Arizona, Colorado, Oregon, Washington, and other places where transportation had not become as well developed as it had in older areas and where farm families still had little access to the markets. They reproduced and resembled in their economic behavior the "German" immigrants of the nineteenth century.[67]

Second, although after 1880 most urban Jews concentrated overwhelmingly in a single city, eastern European Jewish immigrants went everywhere, behaving just like the Jewish immigrants of earlier decades. They functioned within a Jewish commercial niche and linked themselves to Jews in bigger cities to sustain their livelihoods. They maintained their connections to Jews in other places through family ties and other networks. Jews settled in smaller places such as Fargo, North Dakota; Kankakee, Illinois; Columbus, Ohio; Appleton, Wisconsin; Kingston, New York; and Springfield, Massachusetts, because of the commercial possibilities of the late nineteenth and early twentieth centuries. They conducted much of their trading with longtime Americans, primarily English speakers, who earned a living on farms.

Although the Jews of Johnstown, Pennsylvania, may have been atypical, their experiences reveal much about the complexities of the post-1880 migration. A small group of eastern European immigrants headed for this town because of the dominant presence of the steel industry and coal mining. The bulk of the industrial laborers, the customers of the Jewish storeowners, hailed from eastern Europe as well. Slavic immigrants provided the manpower for the mines and mills, and the Jewish merchants had no problem communicating with these workers. The Jewish shopkeepers knew Polish, Ukrainian, Hungarian, and other languages that they had had to master for the same purpose on the other side of the Atlantic. Johnstown Jews opened up their shops through internal Jewish communal credit networks and spent their leisure hours in an almost totally Jewish environment. Small-town life did not foster integration but rather solidified traditional Jewish practice and fostered cultural conservatism, despite the small number of Jews living in Johnstown.[68]

New York existed at the other end of the Jewish spectrum from Johnstown. Between 1880 and 1890 about sixty thousand Jews lived in lower Manhattan, on a twenty-block square of streets south of Houston and east of the Bowery. Indeed, more Jews resided in that one neighborhood than there were residents in many American cities. By 1910 Jews accounted for about one-quarter of the city's population. With the largest concentration of Jews in the world, New York functioned as the hub of American Jewish life. In 1880 slightly over one-third of American Jews called New York their home. By 1927 this number had climbed to 44 percent. The 1,765,000 Jews who lived in New York constituted a kind of internal Jewish metropolis. Of the other nine large cities with major Jewish populations, including, in descending order, Chicago, Philadelphia, Boston, Cleveland, Detroit, Newark, Los Angeles, Pittsburgh, and San Francisco, none even came close to New York in size. All together they accounted for 25 percent of American Jewry. Chicago came closest to New York, with a mere 8 percent of American Jews living there in 1927.[69]

In each one of these places, newly arrived immigrant Jews tended to settle in neighborhoods closest to their place of entry. In New York the newcomers clustered on Manhattan's Lower East Side, not far from the port of entry, at first located at Castle Clinton and then, after 1892, at Ellis Island, the places where the ships had docked and let off their human cargo. In Chicago, Philadelphia, Boston, and other immigrant destinations, the first Jewish settlements formed relatively close to the train stations and ports. Housing proved to be inexpensive, and the kinds of places where Jews looked for work—garment factories and small businesses—abounded in these urban spaces.

The neighborhoods where Jews settled in New York and the other cities also tended to be places where Jewish communities already had been established. Jews had been living in what was to be called the Lower East Side since the 1840s.[70] Known in the middle of the nineteenth century as *Kleindeutschland*, or "little Germany," this neighborhood supported a substantial range of Jewish establishments. In 1843 on Essex Street, a group of Bavarian Jewish immigrant men founded the B'nai B'rith, the oldest Jewish organization in the United States.[71] The neighborhood supported numerous synagogues, kosher food shops, religious schools, and other institutions that sustained Jewish life. Its distinctive residential form, the tenement building, dated to the 1850s, and German Jews spent their early years in New York as tenement dwellers, just as the eastern Europeans would.

Newly arriving eastern European immigrants inherited this German Jewish urban space and many of its buildings.[72] They, as well as immigrant Jews moving into Baltimore, Chicago, Philadelphia, and Boston, took over these Jewish neighborhoods as the Jews who had lived there for several decades began the process of moving out. The more-established and better-off Jews who had come to America earlier did not necessarily leave neighborhoods like *Kleindeutschland* because the eastern European immigrant had arrived, although they may have had little interest in living among "greenhorns," Jews much poorer than they. Rather, all American cities expanded after the Civil War, developing new neighborhoods and becoming more segmented by the development of early forms of urban transportation, such as streetcars. For the first time middle-class Americans could live in neighborhoods removed from their workplaces, and they could also enjoy more spacious dwellings, graced by lawns and trees.[73]

As these middle-class Jews left their old neighborhoods, in essence they turned them over to the newcomers, who eagerly sought out the least expensive housing, particularly that which was closest to their jobs. The neighborhoods they chose have been described as dense, throbbing with street activity, teeming with life, and crowded with people. Apartments often served as both home and workplace for large families, as well as unrelated boarders. One memoirist recalled about her Rutgers Place apartment, in New York City, that "the rooms were small, and there were ten of us altogether. So people slept on the floor and on the fire escapes."[74] Yet given the poverty these immigrants had known in Europe, the crowded streets and the small apartments with poor ventilation and primitive plumbing did not seem particularly degrading to them.

Immigrant Jews lived as a population in tremendous flux. Neighborhoods operated as sieves, with people leaving and other people coming in to take their places almost simultaneously, at least into the second decade of the twentieth century. An almost universal pattern developed, discernable in almost every city. Newcomers arrived, found places to live near their work, and when they could afford to, they moved to better neighborhoods, turning their apartments over to those who had just landed. In addition, by the early twentieth century the freshest immigrants had many more choices than did those who had come before them. By as early as 1905 the Lower East Side had lost two-thirds of its

Jewish population, as newer arrivals headed immediately for neighborhoods that had been unavailable a decade earlier, particularly Williamsburg and Brownsville, across the East River in Brooklyn, and to Harlem
in the city's upper reaches.[75]

Jewish newcomers from Galicia, Russia, Poland, or Romania inherited not only Jewish space but also Jewish trades. The streets that had
once pulsated with "German" Jewish clothing stores, bakeries, and
butcher shops now did so with eastern European establishments. Just as
they had earlier, Jewish small businesses sold both to a general public
and to a Jewish one food and shoes, watches and paper, dishes and cig-
arettes. They also purveyed items for Jews only: kosher meat, religious
objects, books on Jewish subjects, and, after the 1890s, Yiddish newspapers. The pushcart vendors who clogged the streets of American cities
after the 1880s could be seen as an updated version of the urban Jewish
peddlers from earlier in the century. In both eras Jewish immigrants who
wanted to be entrepreneurs or who could not find a place in industry sold
goods in the streets.

New York's Garment Industry

The garment trade also bridged the experiences of America's Jews from
the decades before the Civil War and those of Jews until well after World
War I. Although the industry underwent tremendous changes in that
long century, it continued to be a crucial part of the American Jewish
economy. Until the 1850s all sewing had to be done by hand. Jews in
America and in Europe sewed clothes garment by garment. They usually
did so in conjunction with the direct sale of the garments, the new ones
to well-off customers and secondhand ones to the working class and the
poor. In the pre–Civil War era and, more important, in the pre–sewing
machine era, the making and the selling of clothes went hand in hand.
Most American women sewed their own clothes, however, and most
Americans made do with a relatively small wardrobe.

Two events revolutionized the garment industry and further concentrated Jews in this trade: the invention of the sewing machine in the
1850s and the Civil War. The first dramatically increased the speed with
which garments could be sewn. A tailor of relatively modest means could
buy a few sewing machines, hire a few workers, bring them together in
his apartment, and vastly expand the number of dresses or shirts he
could sell. The *New York Tribune*, recognizing the power of the machine
to change social practice, uttered a prophecy in 1859: "The needle will
soon be consigned to oblivion, like the wheel, the loom, and the knitting-

needles. The working woman will now work fewer hours and receive greater remuneration. People will . . . dress better, change oftener, and altogether grow better looking."[76] The Civil War followed shortly after the invention of the sewing machine. The need for uniforms transformed small stores that had hand-produced garments into workshops and proto-factories churning out clothing for soldiers. Given the demand, manufacturers came up with a fixed size as a standard of production.

Another change in the industry was brought about by the fact that young women in all parts of the country, American-born daughters of immigrants as well as the daughters of long-time working-class Americans, increasingly worked outside the home before marrying. They worked in factories and department stores. Some of them taught. Others mastered that era's other new piece of technology, the typewriter, helping to create the modern office of the emerging corporate bureaucracies. And these working women needed clean and stylish clothing to bolster their respectability. [77]

New York emerged as the center of the garment industry, although Chicago, Boston, Baltimore, Rochester, Cleveland, and a number of other interior cities also produced clothing at a dizzying pace. In 1910 New York produced 70 percent of the nation's clothing for women and 40 percent for men.[78] It also functioned as the center of the American publishing industry, and the dozens of magazines published in the city and distributed around the country advertised a definitive New York style.

Much of that garment manufacturing, done either in apartment workshops, known as sweatshops, or in the more modern factories that came into being by the second decade of the twentieth century, lay in Jewish hands. Jews constituted most of the workers in the field as well. By 1897, 60 percent of employed New York Jews made a living in garment making, making up 75 percent of all its workers.[79] Initially most of the Jewish employers had come to America before the 1870s and fell into the category of "German" Jews. However, many actually had come from Posen or Lithuania.

One of the most notable characteristics of the garment trade was the fact that it took a relatively meager amount of capital to cross the line from being an employee to becoming an employer. Most of the contractors in the garment industry's sweatshops came from the ranks of relatively recent Jewish immigrants who had worked for contractors before entering that class themselves. The contractor received garments from a manufacturer. The garments had been cut but not yet sewn together. In his apartment, or in a rented loft, the contractor brought together a group of workers, both women and men, including sewing machine operators, finishers, basters, pocket makers, and pressers. The contractor worked in the same space as the workers. He, however, if lucky, turned a profit, while the immigrants who worked in these shops endured low pay and stifling, dangerous conditions.

The fluid lines between workers and employers and the low level of capital required to go into business made garment making a unique niche in the American economy. Furthermore, it was also one of the few industries in which men and women overlapped in their jobs. While certain parts of the sewing operation, such as cutting and pressing, were off-limits to women, most women and men labored at the core part of the process, operating sewing machines. While men earned more than women, had greater chances for mobility, and mostly remained at their jobs for a lifetime, the garment industry did offer young women with relatively little skill or training the chance to find work right away. As a result, many eastern European Jewish families sent daughters to America with their fathers to pave the way for the rest of the family. In addition, because of the high demand for laborers, male or female, some eastern European Jewish women migrated on their own or with female friends and relatives.

Jews dominated the industry from the top to the bottom. From the manufacturers to the contractors to the laborers to the union activists bent on organizing the workers, they shared Jewish roots, and by early in the twentieth century, most hailed from eastern Europe. Likewise, in the modern factories like the Triangle Shirtwaist Company, which women workers preferred, Jewish employers hired Jewish workers.[80] This phenomenon, which had multiple implications for the continued immigration of Jews to the United States into the 1920s and for the development of Jewish community there, represented an exquisite confluence of time and place. Eastern European Jews, already well versed in garment making, came to New York just as the industry was taking off. The revolution in the garment industry happened in part because of the vast numbers of eastern European Jews who had already moved to America and chose to remain in their port of entry. But then had the garment industry not burst out of its preindustrial mode when it did, eastern European Jewish migration to America might have looked quite different.

As it happened, of the two and a half million eastern European Jewish immigrants who had chosen to come to America after the 1870s, vast numbers of them spent some or all of their working lives in the garment industry. Here they worked primarily for and with other Jews. Unlike the other immigrants in steerage who had come to America from Italy or Poland, for example, and gone to work for people with whom they shared no birthplace and no bonds of communal responsibility, immigrant Jews went to work for Jews, with whom they shared so much. They spoke the same language. They had the same history and a common understanding of communal, familial, and personal priorities. Further, the employer provided a model of mobility. The fact that he, a fellow Jew and fellow immigrant, had not needed vast amounts of money to get his start offered workers the sense that they too could aspire to self-employment.

Yet for employers this familiarity proved to be a double-edged sword. Many workers grew resentful, seeing no reason for their employers to earn so much more than they did and to live so much better. They felt entitled to as good a life as other immigrant Jews who had perhaps preceded them to America by a decade or two.[81] Indeed, the impetus for unionization in the Jewish trades in part grew out of this internal class conflict.

Jewish employers in turn were influenced in their treatment of their employees by the Jewishness of their workforce. While initially they could view the act of giving a friend, a relative, or simply a fellow Jew a job in a sweatshop or a basement bakery as a favor, over time the demands for better wages and better working conditions made by immigrant women and men could no longer be ignored.[82] The creation of Jewish unions—the International Ladies' Garment Workers' Union in 1900 and the Amalgamated Clothing Workers' Union in 1914 in particular—took place with dramatically less strife and opposition from employers than did unionization efforts in textiles, steel, automobile manufacturing, coal mining, or other heavy industries in which employers could answer, "Nothing," to William Graham Sumner's rhetorical question of 1883, "What do the social classes owe each other?"

The dramatic strike of 1909 in the shirtwaist industry, known in labor history as "the uprising of the 20,000," referring to the masses of Jewish women shirtwaist makers who went on strike, ultimately was resolved owing to the intervention of leaders of the American Jewish community. Jacob Schiff, Louis Marshall, Louis Brandeis, Henry Moskowitz, Abraham Lincoln Filene, and Julius Cohen, all successful and prominent American Jews, pressured Jewish manufacturers to agree to mediation with the strikers. They reminded them directly that Jews, be they employers or laborers, had to contend with anti-Semitic critics who used the class warfare in the immigrant community as ammunition against all Jews. They convinced the employers to enter into an arrangement, a Protocol of Peace, with the union out of their obligation to other Jews. Essentially, they indirectly reminded them that "all of Israel are responsible one for the other."

Decades separated the Jewish migrations out of central Europe and the larger ones out of eastern Europe. A whole century, one that had witnessed great changes in economic patterns, technology, and political ideology, divided the beginning of the huge migrations to the United States from the end. But much more linked the immigrants from either end of the century than divided them. Wherever they settled, they created new communities, more diverse than the ones they had left. Once settled, they became the "old timers," the "real Americans," to the group of immigrants who followed.

Throughout this century of migration, America exerted a powerful influence on these immigrants, regardless of where they had come or when they had arrived. As newcomers who had little interest in returning to their communities of origin, they reinvented themselves in America, creating identities that combined Jewish and American mores. They greatly admired their new land and sought to be part of it. The incredible array of economic, political, and cultural options available to them in their new home had allowed them to build new institutions and new identities. What actually came to divide Jews in America was less their European origins and more the number of years they had spent in America, as well as the degree to which American realities collided with how they defined the Jewishness of their American lives.

4

A CENTURY OF JEWISH LIFE IN AMERICA

1820–1924

The huge migrations taking place between 1820 and 1924 profoundly shaped Jewish life in America. Yet great differences marked the beginning of this century and the end, which bore witness to the emergence of modern America and modern Judaism. At the beginning of this hundred-year period, most American Jews lived in a string of older East Coast cities, with a few small outposts of Jewish life starting to crop up beyond the Appalachian Mountains. By the 1920s, although one city—New York—served as the home to the largest Jewish community, housing about 45 percent of all American Jews, Jews lived in almost every one of the forty-eight states of the union. They created large enclaves in every city, particularly, Chicago, Philadelphia, Boston, Cleveland, Los Angeles, Baltimore, St. Louis, Pittsburgh, and San Francisco. They also lived in smaller Jewish communities in hundreds of towns in New England, the Midwest, the Deep South, and the West.

In the beginning of the period no rabbi lived in America. For decades young men interested in the rabbinate had to travel to Europe to be educated and ordained. By the 1920s several rabbinical seminaries in Cincinnati and New York were ordaining Jewish men as rabbis and cantors, and they certified teachers, both female and male. These seminaries represented yet another dramatic novelty, the creation of denominations within American Judaism. One could find Reform, Conservative, and Orthodox synagogues throughout American cities. These synagogues established not only schools to train rabbis but also congregational bodies and rabbinical associations, as well as magazines and other publications to spread their ideologies. The rabbis who led the congregations functioned as the leaders of American Jews, and in all but the smallest of communities, Jews could choose both their rabbi and their synagogue. At the start of this century of migration Jews maintained relationships from city to city both through personal connections and through trade. They had no organizations or nationally circulating publications. When the mass migration out of Bavaria began to take off in the early 1820s, few institutions existed to meet the Jews' political, cultural, economic, and social needs. The first American Jewish newspaper, *The Jew,* an anti-missionary tract, appeared in 1823 but was short-lived. It defined itself as providing "a defense of Judaism against all adversaries."[1] By contrast, in 1920 American Jews supported a multilingual press with newspapers and magazines in Yiddish, English, Hebrew, and Ladino to suit the tastes and interests of a diverse readership. By 1920 a single Yiddish newspaper, the *Forverts,* which first began rolling off the presses in 1897, sold almost two hundred thousand copies daily. Published in New York at an imposing building on East Broadway built in 1908, it was available in local editions to Yiddish readers in eleven cities around the country.[2]

By the 1920s nearly every major national Jewish organization that exists at the beginning of the twenty-first century had been formed: the B'nai B'rith (1843), the Workman's Circle (1892), the National Council of Jewish Women (1893), the American Jewish Committee (1905), Hadassah (1912), the Anti-Defamation League (1913), and the American Jewish Congress (1928). Various major religious bodies also had been formed: the Union of American Hebrew Congregations (1873), the Central Conference of American Rabbis (1889), the Union of Orthodox Jewish Congregations (1898), the Rabbinical Assembly (1901), and the United Synagogue (1913). A dazzling array of synagogues, hospitals, theaters, schools, labor unions, summer camps, resorts, social and family clubs, newspapers and magazines, charitable associations, and benevolent societies structured the lives of Jews and framed their encounter with society, providing them with social, cultural, and economic activities.

These establishments, along with the tens of thousands of small businesses clustered in Jewish neighborhoods, made up America's "Jewish street." The mushrooming of institutions on the local and national levels did not simply happen as a result of the growth in numbers. Rather, the increasing tendentiousness of Jewish communal life, debates between traditionalists and reformers, between Zionists and Yiddishists, between

Socialists, Communists, and those content with mainstream American politics—and all the internal splinterings within these groups—led to this proliferation. In addition, the ever-present gap between immigrant parents and their American-born children led to the creation of institutions whose goal was to resolve foreboding questions about the future of Jewish life in America. The heated discourse among Jews over what it meant to be Jewish in America catalyzed a highly engaged community life.

In 1920 American Jews lived very differently from how they had lived in 1820, in great measure because of the tectonic shifts taking place among European Jewry. In 1820, except for those in France and Holland, only the Jews in the United States could be considered fully emancipated. All Jews, with the exception of small bands in Berlin and Hamburg who in the late 1810s began to reform, adhered to traditional, rabbinic Judaism committed to the observance of halakah in matters personal and public. Conversion to Christianity offered the only way to escape both the lack of emancipation and the demands of the Jewish communal system. Most Jews lived in fully organized, self-governing communities. At that point the distinction between a secular or cultural Jewish identity and a religious one barely existed. Rather, Jewish life and matters of the spirit worked together as a whole, undisturbed by debates over the nature of Jewish identity.

In contrast, by the 1920s from the United States in the west to the newly founded Soviet Union to the east, multiple variants of Jewish culture flourished. By the 1920s the monolith of rabbinic Judaism had sustained repeated and serious challenges from reformers bent on reinterpreting Judaism. By the 1920s Zionism, in its many political iterations, and Jewish Socialism, also ideologically fragmented, offered Jews a multitude of perspectives. Since they had so many ways of being Jewish at their disposal, the *kahal*, the formally organized community, in large part existed as a voluntary entity.

A CHANGING AMERICA

The differences between life in 1820 and in 1920 reflected both revolutions in the Jewish world and the deep changes taking place in America. In 1820 Americans lived in a predominantly rural society held together by a tenuous system of roads. The Erie Canal had not yet linked the port of New York to the natural resources of the Midwest via the Hudson River. Slavery had not yet been challenged in any significant way. Women enjoyed no political rights and had no public voice. Married women could neither own property nor inherit estates from either fathers or husbands. They could not even expect to have custody of their own children.

In the 1820s most Americans had never seen, let alone interacted with, a Jew. What they know about Jews they knew from the pages of the Hebrew Bible. The handful of Americans who took note of Jews happened to be Christian evangelicals bent on converting them to Christianity and saving them from the error of their ways.[3] In some older states, such as New Hampshire, North Carolina, and Maryland, since Jews could not hold political office they remained relatively quiet and unobtrusive.[4] When they reflected on them at all, Americans mainly saw Jews as exotic others.

In some ways the 1920s heralded the beginnings of Jewish "normalcy" in America. Their dense urban concentration no longer stood out, now that a majority of Americans lived in cities, according to the 1920 census. The Jews' almost total absence from agriculture did not seem deviant in a nation where decreasing numbers of Americans made a living as farmers. Nor did their foreign origins make them particularly remarkable. Between 1820 and 1920 America had absorbed over 45 million European immigrants; Jews made up 3 million of that total.

Not only did America in the 1920s house numerous ethnic communities, Jewish included, but its political system was slowly beginning to respond to calls for greater equality among its citizens. Although it would be another half century until race, ethnicity, religion, and gender discrimination were prohibited by law, organizations—such as the NAACP, founded in 1909—representing a number of once-stigmatized groups, had begun to chip away at the edifice of discrimination, and increasingly emboldened people stepped forward to assert their rights. Labor unions, radical groups, feminist organizations, and bodies such as the American Civil Liberties Union (1917), the American Association of University Professors (1915), and the National Conference of Social Workers (1917) made criticizing the established order politically possible. Muckraking journalists exposed one flaw after another of American society. Women gained the right to vote in 1920, the culmination of "a century of struggle" to expand their educational, legal, and professional options.[5] The challenges lobbed at American society by labor unions, immigrants, African Americans, reformers, feminists, and others created a backlash. White Protestant Americans, those who identified with the older social order and who believed that they represented true "Americanism," scored what they considered significant victories in the 1920s.

Among them none had as dramatic an impact on the composition of the American population and as profound an implication for the Jews than the passage of laws restricting immigration in the 1920s.

Calls to curtail immigration severely and to ensure that immigrants represented the more "desirable" races went back to the founding of the Immigration Restriction League in 1894. The members of this league, old-stock New England patricians who banded together to call for an end to free and open immigration into the United States, expressed a vision of America in which people like them would define the culture and hold the political power. Phillip Brooks, a member of the League, stressed the gravitas of its mission: "If to this particular nation there has been given the development of a certain part of God's earth for universal purposes; if the world is going to be richer for the development of a larger type of manhood here, then for the world's sake . . . we have a right to stand guard over it. Standing guard meant locking the door to keep out those not representative of some ideal 'larger type of manhood.' "6

While in the 1920s the old guard had succeeded in restricting immigration, they failed to return cultural and political control to America's small-town, Protestant, white roots. By the end of World War I America had become increasingly unified not only by roads and railroads but also by radio and movies. These revolutions in technology and communication made challenging the white Protestant elite possible, since the creation of new media took the production of culture out of the hands of a small group who defined themselves as the custodians of the nation. While these men mostly still held sway over the most prestigious institutions, they recognized the tenuousness of their hold.

Not coincidentally, at the same time that these advances in motion pictures, transportation, photography, and radio were being made, Congress ended immigration from Europe. Ivy League institutions like Harvard and Columbia imposed quotas on Jews and other applicants from immigrant backgrounds. This curtain of exclusion fell over a number of elite colleges and universities, prestigious law firms, and recreational watering holes for the Gentile well-off. Discrimination against Jews spread to hospitals, which limited Jewish doctors' ability to see patients. It was felt in the practices of some large employers like the telephone company in both Boston and New York, numerous department stores, and other potential venues of white-collar employment for Jewish women from immigrant homes.

This exclusion taking hold in "the tribal twenties"7 to a degree not witnessed before did not, however, dampen American Jews' understanding of themselves as both Jews and Americans. In their religious, educational, social, and cultural practices they found ways to be both. They considered neither "Jewish" nor "American" as frozen in form. Rather, they felt empowered to shape their Jewish lives to fit their American ones, while feeling confident enough to press America to make room for their Jewishness. This desire of American Jews to be both Jewish and American, and to alter both identities to that end, manifested itself most dramatically in the religious realm. The history of American Judaism from 1820 to the 1920s can be understood best in this context.

RELIGIOUS DIVERSIFICATION

The history of American Judaism from 1820 through 1920 is a dramatic and complicated story of growth, diversification, institutionalization, incessant splinterings, and constant creativity. Debates raged over Jewish practice and the meaning of Judaism in the modern world, with the participants in the debates representing ever-shifting orthodoxies and endless challenges to tradition. Each iteration of Judaism saw itself as the best solution to the problems of a normative religion planting itself in a land of choice. Each movement, faction, or party, whether it stood to the left, right, or center, considered its solution to be the most potent. Each hoped to unify American Jews under a single banner, yet each played a crucial role in representing the many divisions within it.

The vast panoply of synagogues, seminaries, denominations, and other religious bodies on the American Jewish scene by the 1920s would have been unrecognizable to an American Jew of 1820. But in all the changes that took place between 1820 and 1920, American Jews, in the public and private practice of their Judaism, understood that their religion set them apart from other Americans, and, to some degree, they wanted that to be the case.[8] Yet they also understood that they had—and indeed they wanted—to accommodate to America. They realized that whether they called themselves Reform, Orthodox, Conservative, or simply Jewish, they had to find ways both to resist American ways and to adapt to them.[9]

In the 1820s ordinary Jewish men directed the synagogues, and *hazzanim* led services, functioning as lay rabbis. Wherever Jews settled, they went about the business of creating the institutions necessary for Jewish life, cemeteries and congregations in particular. They found ways to procure kosher meat and matzo for Passover. They sought the services of *mohelim* to circumcise their sons, readers to chant the prayers, and whatever other functionaries they could afford. They constructed *mikvaot,* ritual baths, to conform to Jewish family law. Sometimes the most knowledgeable among them stepped forward to serve as rabbi, despite his lack of training and the fact that he had not been ordained. Yet all congregations conformed to traditional Jewish practice, and when they splintered off from one another they did so because of their European birthplaces and often as a result of personality clashes between members.

In the 1840s rabbis began to trickle into America. The earliest, like Abraham Rice, who came to Baltimore in 1840, and Bernard Illowy, who arrived in New York in 1848, attempted to control what they saw as the anarchic state of American Judaism and to impose rabbinic restraint on the laity. They considered themselves traditionalists, operating out of a normative system encoded in the Talmud.[10] They found an ally in Isaac Leeser, the *hazzan* of Philadelphia's Mikveh Israel. Like Rice and Illowy, Leeser feared for the fate of traditional Judaism in America. These men skirmished constantly with the members of their congregations who viewed rabbis and cantors as employees to do their bidding. Key to the chasm between the traditional rabbis and the membership was the fact that few of the members observed Jewish law, particularly in matters of diet and Sabbath observance, with the kind of punctiliousness that the rabbis considered appropriate.

The Evangelical Threat

Leeser and the others fretted not only about the laxity of religious observance among their congregations and among American Jews in general but also about the degree to which democracy had insinuated itself into congregational life. They understood that to inspire members to be more observant, they had to acquiesce to the wishes and tastes of the laity. Leeser, for example, agreed to the request of Mikveh Israel's members that he give a weekly sermon facing them, rather than the ark, the repository of the Torah, as was the tradition when chanting the service, and he also accepted his congregants' request that he dress in the garb of a Protestant minister. He responded positively to the demands of congregants when he felt that their demands did not violate any key element of Jewish law. In 1830 he yielded to the wishes of several women—who, although not permitted to be members, still shaped synagogue policy— to deliver a sermon each Sabbath morning. However much he stood for tradition, he could not resist innovation.[11]

Leeser gave in on such matters because he feared the vigor of the evangelical Protestant missionaries, who launched a mighty campaign to convert the Jews. The American Society for Meliorating the Condition of the Jews had been founded in 1820, just as "America fever" had started to spread through the Jewish hamlets of Bavaria. Never particularly successful, this organization and other evangelical groups strove to bring the "truth" of the Gospels to the Jews. They set up schools and orphanages designed in particular to attract Jewish children. They roamed hospitals and sought deathbed conversions. In New York through the 1850s Protestant evangelicals ran the city's public schools, and Christian prayers, hymns, and mandatory readings of the King James version of the Bible made immigrant children a captive audience of the missionaries. Leeser worried that the missionaries would in fact win over many of the immigrants, and he felt that Jews committed to the preservation of Judaism had to combat them vigorously and creatively.

Indeed, much of Leeser's vision, which he followed from the 1830s until his death in the 1860s, derived from his fear of the missionary effort. Leeser aided his congregant Rebecca Gratz, who conceived of the idea of a Jewish Sunday school as a bulwark against the evangelical onslaught. Gratz, who herself received numerous entreaties from Christian friends to convert, believed that the school, which should be open to "all who are hungry for the bread of life," could arm Jewish children with Judaic knowledge and thereby serve as a defense against Christian evangelism. She turned to Leeser to help her organize the school and to assist her in putting together a curriculum. Leeser assisted her by putting together a booklet entitled *Catechism for Younger Children* in 1839.[12]

Gratz's inspiration as well as the widely recognized activities of the missionaries led Leeser to publish the first instructional books for Jewish children, *Instruction in the Mosaic Law* in 1830; a ten-volume set of *Discourses* about Judaism in 1837, 1841, and 1867; and a six-volume bilingual prayer book and commentary, *The Form of Prayer According to the Custom of the Spanish and Portuguese Jews,* which appeared in 1837 and 1838. He published the first American translation of the Torah in 1845 and the first American-edited prayer book, which addressed the religious sensibilities of the newest immigrants to America, those from Germany and Poland. He hoped that his efforts would stem the tide away from meaningful religious practice and keep Jews from becoming alienated from Judaism.[13]

The Reform Movement

Leeser, Rice, Illowy, and a handful of other rabbis in the 1840s and 1850s had yet another, possibly greater, threat to consider. Jews in

America, like some in central Europe, had begun to challenge the traditional core of Judaic ritual, practice, and law. In Berlin, Hamburg, and other German cities, beginning in the second decade of the nineteenth century, groups of laypeople and a growing number of university-educated rabbis launched reforms that would in time become the Reform movement. They sought greater decorum in the service. They believed that adding music to Jewish worship would enhance its aesthetic tone, heighten spirituality, and, in the process, keep Jews from converting to Christianity, a growing concern. Reform-minded Jews found themselves deeply troubled by the gap between modern, rational science and certain core principles of Judaism, such as the resurrection of the dead. They measured the distance between their emerging political and social integration, gifts of emancipation, and the dictates of Judaism, which kept them apart and different. In central Europe, Reform Judaism was surfacing to ease the discomfort brought about by a new age.[14]

Some of the rabbis who came to America starting in the 1840s had already experienced the stirring of Reform on the other side of the Atlantic. David Einhorn, Leo Merzbacher, Max Lillienthal, and Samuel Adler had been drawn into Reform in Europe and brought much of its ideology to the many American congregations they served during their careers. Einhorn, a Bavarian-born reformer, for example, came to the United States in 1855 to serve Baltimore's Har Sinai Congregation. He launched a German-language newspaper, *Sinai,* and published a reform prayer book, *Olat Tamid,* in 1856. Einhorn represented the radical wing of American Reform. He not only celebrated German as the most appropriate linguistic vehicle for achieving a loftier Judaism, but he believed that Judaism had to cleanse itself of ideas and practices antithetical to modernity and rationalism. Einhorn expressed only disdain for much of Mosaic law, the dietary restrictions, and Sabbath limitations, as well as such ideas as the truth of a messianic age in which the Jews would be restored to Palestine and the dead revived. Einhorn tried to present Judaism as a religion based on ethical principles to advance the progress of all. He wanted to rid Judaism of its tribal, or ethnic, components, which he thought only hampered the Jews' integration into the modern world.

He likewise found the role of women in Judaism abhorrent and dysfunctional. In the world around him he saw that women had begun to acquire education and expanded legal rights. By the time he arrived in the United States several women's rights conventions had already been held. In fact, in the very year that Einhorn came to America, woman's rights orator and organizer Lucy Stone made a public declaration that when she married Henry Blackwell she would retain her name and not give up her identity to become someone else's wife. To Einhorn as well as many of the other reform-minded rabbis of this era, the disjunction between the expansiveness of America and the strictures of Judaism needed to be remedied. In America women had begun to demand the vote. Yet in Judaism women, as understood by Einhorn, remained passive and mute objects rather than active participants in their religion.

Yet Einhorn did not intend his reforms to constitute a "break with the past, but to enlist the old in service of the new and to preserve it in transfigured form." Until his death in 1879 he considered the project of Reform to be the invigoration of Judaism in America, not the obliteration of the ancient tradition.[15] Upon his relocation to the United States he joined the other rabbis in America at a conference in Cleveland. That conference was dominated by his soon-to-be archrival for the leadership of American Judaism, Isaac Mayer Wise. Unlike Einhorn, Wise had not been initiated into Reform in any substantial way before coming to America from Bohemia in 1846. But he quickly fell into step with the American zeitgeist, one that saw the creation of hundreds of new denominations and that asserted the right of Americans to create the religious practices they wanted.[16] In his first congregation, Beth El, in Albany, New York, Wise began instituting such reforms as adding music performed by a mixed male-female choir to the service. When his lay board fired him in 1850, he and a group of followers founded an explicitly reformed congregation, Anshe Emeth, the first in America to do away with sex-segregated seating.

In 1854 Wise accepted the pulpit in Cincinnati's Bene Yeshurun (B'nai Jeshurun) congregation. He remained there until his death in 1900, directing nearly all the major developments of Reform Judaism in America. In Cincinnati he organized the first lasting seminary to train American rabbis, the first organized body of congregations, and the first association of rabbis. He hoped that the movement and its institutions would unite all American Jews under a single banner. Despite Wise's efforts, it did not. This became clear as early as 1855 when Wise called together the rabbinical conference in Cleveland, where he met and clashed with Einhorn, who believed that Wise had not gone far enough in advocating a thoroughgoing revision of rabbinic Judaism. But Wise also sparred with Leeser, who had hoped that Cleveland would stem the tide toward Reform. He left bitterly disappointed, returning to Philadelphia and issuing diatribes against Wise in his newspaper *The Occident*.

The years between the 1855 Cleveland Conference and the 1880s can be considered the "age of Wise" and the triumph of his vision over both Einhorn's and Leeser's. Leeser had hoped to found the first American seminary to prepare young men for the rabbinate, and to that end in 1867 he organized Maimonides College in Philadelphia. But owing to a paucity of scholars to teach and of money to fund it, the school lasted just a few years and produced no graduates.[17] In contrast, in 1875 Wise created Hebrew Union College, which by 2000 still produced graduates, women as well as men, to serve as rabbis, cantors, and teachers. Leeser wanted all American Jews to use the same liturgy and conform to a single praxis, but it was Wise who created the Union of American Hebrew Congregations in 1873. It began with thirty-four congregations, mostly from the Midwest, but by 1875 its number had jumped to seventy-two. In 1880 only twelve synagogues in America—out of two hundred—had not affiliated with the Union.

But by the 1880s the "age of Wise" was on the wane. Its decline can be attributed to forces both on its left and the right. The Einhorn faction had not been completely stilled and had survived Einhorn's death. Einhorn's son-in-law, Kaufman Kohler, became the standard-bearer for the radical faction. In 1885 he played a pivotal role in promulgating the Pittsburgh Platform, a statement of essential Reform principles. Kohler, like Einhorn, believed that the rabbis of his age needed to change Judaism in order to save it. Einhorn had taken on a simpler project than had Kohler, because unlike Kohler, Einhorn did not have to face an even more radical faction. Kohler considered the rise of Ethical Culture in 1876 a harbinger of the disaster awaiting Judaism in America. This movement had been created by Felix Adler, the son of a rabbi and an ordained Reform rabbi himself. A rationalist, Adler rejected Judaism completely, including its Reform variant, because of its continued insistence on the existence of God and its fusion of peoplehood and religion. Adler severed his connection with Judaism and Reform because, he charged, Reform had liberated itself neither from rabbinic Judaism nor from Jewish ethnicity.

A Backlash to Reform

Kohler wanted to prevent educated, affluent Jews who made up the membership of the larger Reform congregations from defecting to Ethical Culture. He wanted to provide them with a Judaism that they would find compatible with their social place in the world and with their intellectual understanding of it. Kohler also feared that another development threatened the hegemony of Reform. For one, the massive influx from eastern Europe had taken off in the 1870s, and Jewish communities across America experienced measurable growth. As more observant Jewish newcomers arrived, they made demands on their congregations, insisting that they stifle or roll back reforms. When their demands were unmet, traditionalists began seceding and creating their own institutions, which would never be part of the UAHC framework and which threatened communal unity.

To take but one example, thirty-eight members of the Washington Hebrew Congregation, many of them recent arrivals from Posen, withdrew from the city's only synagogue when it installed an organ in 1869. They objected with equal vigor to the conversion of the service to an English-only ritual and to the elimination of the kiddush, the prayer ushering in the Sabbath, on the grounds that it blessed God for having chosen the Jews "among all the nations." The dissenters believed that only Hebrew should be the language of worship and that texts like the kiddush could not—and should not—be altered. Those who seceded formed Adas Israel, the capital's second congregation. The exodus of the traditionalists empowered the more strident reformers to go even further in their re-creation of Jewish worship, but it also depleted the numbers of the original congregation.[18]

Cities like New York, Philadelphia, Boston, Baltimore, and Chicago witnessed the mushrooming of Russian, Lithuanian, and Polish congregations, some of them occupying small storefronts but all representing the demon feared by the reformers: an old-style, decidedly unmodern eastern European Judaism transplanted to America. As early as 1857 Rabbi Pesach Rosenthal opened a Talmud Torah—a school for torah study—in New York. Young Jewish boys in New York could now learn from canonical texts in Yiddish. Developments like this violated the vision of the reform minded of a future when a progressive, American-oriented, culturally dignified Judaism would triumph.

At the same time that Jewish emigration from eastern Europe was swelling, a number of rabbis who represented the "positive-historical school" in Germany, the Wissenschaft des Judenthums, also began to arrive in the United States. They considered Judaism capable of modernization, but within the parameters of the rabbinic system. Emancipation, science, modernity, and Western ideas, they believed, could enhance Judaism, which had always been an evolving religious system. Modern Jews, they believed, could continue this evolution through intense study both of its normative texts and of those produced by the best of science and scholarship. They turned to the history, philosophy, archeology, ancient languages, and other fields of inquiry to bolster Jewish learning.[19]

Chief among these new immigrant advocates of the scholarship of Judaism and this positivist approach was Alexander Kohut, a Hungarian rabbi who debated Kohler in the Jewish press and from the pulpits of their respective New York congregations in the early 1880s. Kohut had declared that "Reform is a Deformity" because it rejected Jewish law. Kohler, hoping to mediate between what had now emerged as the two extremes challenging Reform, called together a conference of Reform rabbis in Pittsburgh to commit to writing a statement of Reform beliefs.

The 1885 document could not but offend the more traditional among the American Jews, represented by Kohut and Philadelphia's congregation, Sabato Morais. It cast aside all customs "not adapted to the views and habits of modern civilization," declaring that Jews should consider themselves "no longer a nation, but a religious community." To announce how Reform differed from Ethical Culture, however, it affirmed its belief in the "God-idea" and declared Jews to be members of a "religious community" with a special mission in the world, the establishment of ethical monotheism.[20]

These statements served as a gauntlet thrown down in front of traditional American Jews, whose numbers made them a more serious threat than the individuals who had drifted over to Ethical Culture. Just three years earlier the traditionalist world in America had experienced a powerful trauma, partly symbolic, but offensive nonetheless. Members of Sabato Morais and several others from the observant camp had been invited to the first graduation of the Hebrew Union College in Cincinatti. At the celebratory dinner to mark this momentous event—the first ordination of a class of American rabbis trained in America by an American seminary—waiters brought to the tables a sumptuous feast. The meal, no doubt tasty and elegant in its presentation, however, violated every stricture of Jewish dietary law. Meat and dairy products appeared on the table at the same time, while shellfish and other forbidden foods graced the plates of the banqueters. This famous "trefah [unkosher] banquet" played a small but visible role in galvanizing the traditionalists, who in 1886, after the promulgation of the Pittsburgh Platform, established the Jewish Theological Seminary of America in New York.

They intended the seminary to be a place where traditional rabbis could be trained to serve traditional congregations, while providing them with English sermons and decorum as integral elements of Judaism. Although seminary students would partake of Western learning, they and the founders did not see themselves as planting the seed of another denomination, its founding had that unintended consequence. The seminary got off to a shaky start, plagued by poor funding and somewhat unclear ideas about what distinguished it from religious and educational developments among the eastern European masses flowing to the United States.[21]

In fact, in the same years that some of the traditionalists gathered to found and support the seminary, others coalesced around Rabbi Abraham Ash at New York's Beth Hamedrash Hagodol congregation, and yet others around Rabbi Jacob Joseph, brought in 1888 by a group of New York congregations to be the Chief Rabbi of the United States. In 1889 the short-lived Union of Orthodox Jewish Congregations of America was founded in an attempt to bring some order to the chaos experienced by Jewish immigrants who wanted to adhere to traditional practice.

Some in the eastern European community pinned their hopes for the flowering of traditional learning in America on such recently created educational institutions as the Machazikai Talmud Torah, founded in 1883 in New York, and Etz Chaim Yeshiva, established the same year as the Jewish Theological Seminary. More significant yet, in 1897 some rabbis and lay leaders banded together to create the Rabbi Yitzhak Elhanan Seminary, named for the Chief Rabbi of Kovno, Yitzhak Elhanan Spektor, who died in 1896, the year before they opened the new school. From the start tense relations developed between the Seminary group and the growing number of eastern European newcomers, despite the Seminary's understanding of itself and its public claims to be an orthodox institution. Some in the New York eastern European community considered it not much different from a Reform institution draped in the garb of traditionalism. They asserted that the Seminary taught too little Talmud and too many ancillary subjects and considered its emphasis on English elocution and bourgeois manners to be Reform masquerading as Orthodoxy.

In 1902 some of the major financial backers of the Seminary, notably Jacob Schiff and Louis Marshall, brought Solomon Schechter, a world-renowned Semiticist, from Cambridge University to guide a newly reorganized Seminary. Under Schechter's leadership the institution, which had previously taken relatively young students, many of them recent immigrants from poor eastern European homes, changed its admissions policy, limiting its student body to college graduates ready to study for the rabbinate.

In the years following Schechter's arrival in the United States the Sem-

inary moved toward establishing itself as the center of a second movement, one that would challenge Reform as the most appropriate articu-
lation of Judaism in America. In 1913 Seminary graduates serving in
congregations across the country—some of which belonged to the Union
of American Hebrew Congregations—met and created the United Synagogue of America. Shortly thereafter the rabbis who had been trained at
the Seminary banded together into the Rabbinical Assembly. Taken together, these three bodies made up the Conservative movement, which
emphasized the binding nature of Jewish law while at the same time declaring that under certain circumstances the law could change. It
claimed, however, that these changes could be wrought only after intense
study of the law and only within the parameters of halakah. In essence
the Conservative movement hoped to marry rabbinic Judaism with
Western ideas about democracy, modernity, and rationality, emphasizing the social aspect of Jewish life, built on middle-class standards of
decorum.

While the intense period of the movement's growth took place after
World War II, its founding helped galvanize those in the traditional
community who found the Seminary's project too modern and too quick
to make concessions to American values. This group, which adopted the
label "Orthodox," might be considered both the oldest and the newest
branch of Judaism in America. After all, until the rise of Reform all congregations conformed to traditional practice and as such could be considered "Orthodox," although that label did not figure into their rhetoric or their descriptions of themselves. But as a movement, with a
self-consciousness of purpose and an array of institutions, the Orthodox
organized latest and as such should be considered newer than either Reform or Conservative. Institutionally it experienced internal weakness
and the absence of any centralized bodies.

The idea of building American traditionalism around a chief rabbi,
as tried in 1885, failed miserably, and Jacob Joseph, the scholar
brought from Vilna to assume that position, quickly ended up being the
supervisor of a group of New York kosher butchers instead.[22] However, his decision to come to the United States may have facilitated the
immigration of a number of other eastern European rabbis. Jacob
Joseph indeed brought with him assistants who formed themselves into
a *beth din,* or rabbinical court. Even before Joseph's arrival with his en-
tourage, so many traditional eastern European rabbis found themselves
in the United States that in 1902, the year Schechter took over the leadership of the Seminary, they formed themselves into the Agudath Ha-

Rabbonim, the Union of Orthodox Rabbis of the United States. A century later it continues to set the standard for many Orthodox rabbis and to exert a powerful influence on the process of certifying kosher food.

Reconstructionism and Other Reforms

Even at the eastern European–style educational institutions, American influences crept in. In 1908 students at the small Rabbi Yitzhak Elhanan Theological Seminary in New York protested the narrowness of their curriculum and forcefully persuaded the school's leaders to broaden their studies to include American subjects. In 1915, with its recently augmented program, it merged with the older Etz Chaim Yeshiva under the presidency of Bernard Revel. Through a series of educational innovations and expansions in the 1910s and 1920s, the school received a charter in 1928 as Yeshiva College.

Even the very youngest of America's Jewish denominations owed its origins to this tumultuous era. While Reconstructionism did not emerge as a movement with institutions until the 1930s, its founder, Mordecai Kaplan, experimented with some of his ideas in the late 1910s and early 1920s. In 1890 Kaplan had come to America as a nine-year-old from Lithuania. His father had preceded him to New York, having come to serve with Rabbi Jacob Joseph on the rabbinic court. Kaplan received his earliest education at the Etz Hayim Yeshiva and enrolled at the Jewish Theological Seminary, receiving ordination in 1902. In the late 1910s he started publishing a series of articles in the *Menorah Journal* calling for a "renascence" of Jewish life in America and used the word *reconstruction* in describing his vision of how Judaism in America could be shored up. In 1922, having left the pulpit of an Orthodox congregation, Kaplan founded the Society for the Advancement of Judaism. He and members of SAJ started experimenting with new liturgical modes. Kaplan wanted, for example, to excise the traditional Kol Nidre text from the Yom Kippur service, believing that its words about Jews being released from all vows made and not yet fulfilled had been misinterpreted for generations by the enemies of the Jews. He likewise disdained all liturgical references to the Jews as the chosen people, a concept he believed jarred with American ideas of equality. He often sparred with congregants over how far such changes in language could go. But despite these differences, Kaplan began disseminating his ideas by publishing the nationally circulated *SAJ Review,* an intellectual forum for discussing the nature of Judaism and the need to reconstruct it in ways that were compatible with American and democratic ideals. During his first year at the SAJ he called on his daughter Judith to read from the Torah to mark her bat mitzvah, in the process setting in motion what amounted to a revolution in Judaism.[23]

None of these national developments, shaped by rabbis and leaders, would have taken place had not ferment bubbled up from the local and congregational levels. In 1824 fifty members of Charleston's venerable K. K. Beth Elohim petitioned the synagogue's board for the right to listen to a weekly "discourse" in English. They also requested that the board allow some prayers to be recited in English and that it take steps to ensure greater decorum during prayers. They wanted to tone down the boisterous fund-raising—the selling of honors—that punctuated religious services. The board refused to consider these requests, and the dissidents seceded and organized the Reformed Society of Israelites. Led by Isaac Harby, a journalist, drama critic, and educator, the members of the Reformed Society conducted services to suit their tastes until 1833.[24]

The society could not, however, survive the death of Isaac Harby, and in 1833 the seceders rejoined Beth Elohim, still the only synagogue in South Carolina. But the reforming of Jewish worship could not be stopped. By the end of the 1830s, as Beth Elohim moved into its grand Greek Revival edifice, differences over religious ritual once again split the congregation. One member, Abraham Moise, had been a follower of Harby and had edited his memoirs. He continued to push for reform even after his mentor's death. He persuaded the *hazzan,* Gustav Poznanski, a Polish-born lover of America, who had dubbed his new country "our Zion," to install an organ in the new building. This move agitated the traditionalists in Charleston. After a protracted legal battle between the two factions over who had custody of the building, those who opposed the innovations seceded and founded a congregation of their own, appropriately named Shearith Israel, "the remnant of Israel." Yet another fissure divided Beth Elohim in 1851 when a new group opposed to change left and founded B'rith Sholom. This congregation served Charleston's Orthodox Jews and listed itself as one of the first congregations to join the newly created Union of Orthodox Jewish Congregations of America in 1898.[25]

MORE CONGREGATIONS ARE BORN

Congregations continued to spawn yet more congregations according to the will of groups of members. A family tree of all the congregations would show many branches sprouting from a single institution. The Baltimore Hebrew Congregation provides a case in point. While a minyan might have existed in Baltimore before 1830, in that year the Maryland legislature passed a bill incorporating Nidche Israel, known more commonly as the Baltimore Hebrew Congregation, or in the next decade as the "stadt shul," the city synagogue, to distinguish it from the Fells Point Hebrew Friendship Congregation near the docks. (Later the Baltimore Hebrew Congregation would be known as the Lloyd Street Synagogue.) The Baltimore Hebrew Congregation functioned in a manner appropriate to a European institution and assumed that it could regulate the behavior of its members. Members could be—and were—fined for gathering on the sidewalk outside the synagogue, for chewing tobacco on the Sabbath, for removing their prayer shawls before the end of services, for not asking the permission of an officer to leave the synagogue, or even for singing louder than the cantor.

The Baltimore Hebrew Congregation can claim to have imported the first ordained rabbi to America. In 1840 Rabbi Abraham Rice came to Baltimore from Bavaria. He found everything in his congregation and in the lives of Baltimore's Jews abhorrent. "I live in complete darkness," he wrote to a teacher in Bavaria. "The religious life in this land," he continued, "is on the lowest level, most people eat foul food and desecrate the Sabbath in public. . . . Thousands marry non-Jewish women. . . . I wonder whether it is even permissible for a Jew to live in this land."[26]

Rice demanded that the board censure members who desecrated the Sabbath. It refused, less on ideological grounds and more because it believed that it alone should wield that kind of power. Rice's profound rupture with the congregation—and theirs with him—came in 1842. A member who, like increasing numbers of American Jewish men, belonged to the Masons, died. Rice refused to allow the deceased's Masonic brethren, many of them members of the congregation, to perform any Masonic rituals at the cemetery. A handful of members quit in disgust and founded America's first explicitly and continuous Reform congregation, Har Sinai. Har Sinai achieved fame not only for being the first congregation in America to be founded as a Reform institution, and to survive, unlike the earlier Charleston experiment, but also because its first rabbi, David Einhorn, whom it engaged in 1851, became a powerful force in the creation of an American Reform movement. The Hungarian-born Einhorn emerged in the 1850s and 1860s as the leader of the most extreme faction in the developing movement.

Rice continued to face dissension in the congregation among those who had not bolted in the 1842 schism. The remaining members of the Baltimore Hebrew Congregation imposed a series of innovations on the worship. Rice agreed to go along with some, such as giving up a few of the liturgical poems, *piyutim,* from the service, which many considered too long. But the majority found Rice unsatisfactory, and he, them. In 1845 Rice left and founded his own congregation, Shearith Israel.

The question of how far changes could be taken continued to plague the Baltimore Hebrew Congregation. In 1868 another rabbi, Abraham Hoffman, a moderate reformer, assumed the pulpit. Some of his members insisted on further innovations, including a shorter service, the exclusion of prayers calling for future animal sacrifice in a rebuilt Temple in Jerusalem, and the like. Hoffman agreed to these changes, since they engendered little controversy. But in 1870 the issue that again ripped the congregation apart was the introduction of a mixed chorus. An enraged minority went to court to try to block the change. The court refused to hear the case, so the dissidents formed Congregation Chizuk Amuno, "those who hold fast to their faith." Almost immediately the new congregation began reeling from its own internal divisions. In 1892 it joined the Jewish Theological Seminary Association, and in 1913 it signed on to the United Synagogue of America, thereby casting its lot with the newly founded Conservative movement.[27]

Similar stories could be told about congregations in almost every American city. Very small towns, where the Jewish population remained negligible, had difficulty supporting more than one congregation, and differences over institutional practices had to be ignored. But in all but the smallest of communities, this was a period of congregational disruption and diversification. Some of these break-offs and reformations grew out of deeply felt beliefs. One faction believed that certain practices had to remain in place, while another considered it equally crucial for particular changes to be made. Often such disputes surfaced when a congregation decided to buy a building and moved out of its rented space. Often they bought church buildings. These structures had no women's balcony or any discrete section where women could sit sequestered from the men. Some had an organ and a choir loft. The decision over how to proceed involved more than mere architecture, and congregations split over whether the physical spaces stayed the same or whether they were changed to conform to Jewish practice. Some groups could, and did, take offense.

National origins also played a role in the formation of institutions. In the early stages of any community's development, the small number of Jews did not warrant geographically specific congregations. But the broadening of the geographic base of the emigration made itself felt in the increasing number of congregations that represented the countries, regions, and towns of Europe. Lithuanians, Poles, Bohemians, Russians, Hungarians, and Greeks, when their numbers made it possible, all wanted to have their own congregations. Longing to hear the melodies of home, considering the practices of childhood homes authentic and authoritative, they created synagogues reflecting the towns, regions, and countries they had left. The growing class divide among American Jews, the creation of a solid middle class of prosperous entrepreneurs, and the increased number of industrial laborers and entrepreneurial proletarians led to congregations becoming divided along class lines. Well-off Jews built grand edifices, while the poorer among them worshiped in small spaces, sometimes storefronts or lofts.

Mixing and Matching Jewish Practice

The intense diversification of this period notwithstanding, ultimately the reality of how most Jews actually lived mattered more than the schisms in congregations over public ritual, the precise wording of the liturgy, or the specifics of doctrinal concerns. Most Jews in this century never belonged to any congregation. The larger the city, the smaller the number of Jewish men who actually participated in synagogue life. Among the eastern European immigrants in New York, Chicago, Philadelphia, and the other giant enclaves, synagogue members were a rarity. Few paid dues or followed the debates among the rabbis about matters of public worship. Most, however, did feel obliged to attend services during the high holy days of Rosh Hashanah and Yom Kippur. Those "days of awe" tapped into their deeply held beliefs about the Jewish calendar and Jewish duty. In large cities "mushroom congregations" started to sprout. Makeshift services took place in rental halls that overflowed with those who felt called to participate in this annual ritual. Likewise, home-based rituals, such as cooking a rich Sabbath meal, lighting candles at Hanukkah, and observing Passover united Jews, whether they belonged to congregations or, like the majority, did not.

Labels did not mean much. Members of Orthodox congregations violated the Sabbath and consumed unkosher food outside their kosher homes. At the same time, through the 1870s, Reform congregations affiliated with the Union of American Hebrew Congregations supported ritual baths and paid the services of a *shochet* to provide kosher meat. Most Jews, however, maintained and indeed insisted on retaining certain practices, including lighting Sabbath candles, having their sons circumcised, and supporting the institutions of the Jewish community as a form of obligatory charity. Throughout this century, some Jews did refrain from working on the Sabbath, upheld the laws of ritual purity, ensured that a *mikveh* existed so that the married women could immerse themselves in the pool of water after completing their menstrual cycles, and went to tremendous efforts to observe the dietary laws. Eastern European rabbis may have railed against America as a place where traditional practice could not be observed, but groups of Jews in cities across the country, particularly in New York, did build their lives around the observance of the commandments.

Always in the minority, though, most American Jews picked and chose among those obligations. Much of what they did reflected the circumstances in which they found themselves and not deep ideological speculation. Sabbath observance serves as a good example of this phenomenon. Throughout the nineteenth century and into the twentieth, vast numbers of American Jews made a living in small businesses. Most Americans shopped on Saturdays, and most states maintained laws restricting buying and selling on Sundays. This put the Jewish Sabbath in direct conflict with the very reason for the Jews' migration to America: making a living. But even if they kept their stores open, they still marked the Sabbath. Typically families gathered in their homes on Friday nights for a festive meal welcoming the Sabbath. They ate foods redolent with the aromas of the places they had left in Europe, such as chicken soup with noodles, gefilte fish, roast chicken, and kugel. Mothers lit candles. Fathers intoned the blessings over the wine.

Yet the next morning, these men opened their stores. This was true in small Midwestern towns in the 1860s and in early-twentieth-century large Jewish neighborhoods in the big cities, among Jews from Germany and those who had emigrated from Russia. A 1913 study of life in New York's eastern European community on the Lower East Side found that almost 60 percent of the stores in the neighborhood did a brisk business on Saturdays.[28] Memoirists have told of men who went to synagogue in the morning but in the afternoon donned their shopkeeper's apron. The same person who, under economic duress, sold goods across the counter of his store during the day on Saturday went home in the evening and made *havdallah,* the ceremony marking the end of the Sabbath. By strict standards of Jewish law, these men had violated the Sabbath, but they thought of themselves as good Jews who observed what and how they could.

Women, however, more often took the Sabbath off, working in the stores on weekdays. From the middle of the nineteenth century, American synagogues filled up on Saturday mornings with women worshipers, a profound change from European practice in which men flocked to synagogues and women rarely showed up. Although rabbis lamented the feminization of the synagogues, over the course of this century, they adjusted to the reality of women's dominant presence.[29]

Work alone did not lure Jews away from observing the Sabbath. American cities throbbed with venues for popular entertainment, and Jews, like others, rushed to consume the pleasures of urban life. In a community studded with Orthodox synagogues and small storefront *shtieblach,* or prayer houses, the Yiddish theaters on the Lower East Side often sold out on Friday nights and at Saturday matinees. One non-Jewish observer of life in the New York's Jewish quarter described the scene:

> The Orthodox Jews who go to the theater on Friday, the beginning of the Sabbath, are commonly somewhat ashamed of themselves and try to quiet their consciences by a vociferous condemnation of the actors on the stage. The actor, who through the exigencies of his role, is compelled to appear on Friday night with a cigar in his mouth, is frequently greeted with hisses and strenuous cries of "Shame, shame, smoke on the Sabbath!" from the . . . hypocrites in the gallery.[30]

To be sure, many Jews would not even think of attending a show on the Sabbath. But they found themselves in the minority within the population as a whole and within any specific community. Essentially, those Jews who felt that laws such as Sabbath observance could not be negotiated eschewed emigration to America, while those who believed that their Jewishness would not be compromised if they opened their shop doors on Saturdays, sometimes ate unkosher food, and failed to uphold family purity laws swelled the ranks of the immigrants. At holidays and key moments in their lives—marriage, the birth of sons, death—they insisted on ritual forms that they understood to be a part of traditional and never-changing Judaism, similar in tone and texture to what they had known in Bavaria, Bohemia, Posen, or the Pale of Settlement. All in all they picked and chose from familiar practices remembered from childhood, cobbled together inconsistently with American innovations and adapted to their need to make a living.

Forging a Strong Identity

At the core of this picking and choosing, however, lay their firm belief in themselves as Jews. This identity was beyond contestation, and however tenuously they adhered to traditional Judaism, they vigorously resisted outside efforts to win them over to Christianity. At the most a few hundred Jews a year fell under the influence of an evangelical movement that after the 1880s emerged with greater sophistication and organization, targeting eastern European immigrant Jews. These small numbers, drawn from the highly biased narratives of the evangelicals, stood in stark contrast to the zeal of the missionaries.[31] The fact that the Protestant missionaries did so poorly confirmed the strong sense of identity among the majority of American Jews. They may not have belonged to synagogues, and their relative disinterest in the activities and declarations of rabbis and rabbinical bodies may have reflected their nonideological engagement with Judaism. Yet most remained steadfast in their sense of themselves as Jews. The firmness of their self-image as Jews, independent of the religious establishment, essentially challenged the ability of rabbis to mold Jewish life.

After the 1820s the synagogues faced another challenge that perhaps proved more formidable than the schisms over theology and the inconsistency of practice. A variety of institutions providing Jewish services—charitable, social, cultural, educational, and even religious—developed, which destroyed the monopoly that the early synagogues had enjoyed. By the second decade of the nineteenth century, American Jews could live a full Jewish life and not belong—or even enter—a synagogue. In the prenational period, for example, the *shochtim* served as the paid employees of the congregations. To get kosher meat required synagogue membership and conformity to its rules. Starting in the 1820s, with the proliferation of the synagogues and the increase in migration, as well as the opening up of commercial opportunities in the growing cities, kosher butchers no longer served the congregations. Anyone could buy kosher meat. In an era that celebrated laissez-faire economics, anyone could open a butcher shop and hang whatever sign would attract shoppers.[32]

Likewise, in the earlier era, Jewish charity centered on the synagogue, and all assistance to Jews in need flowed from its offices. But this changed in the 1820s as well. In 1822 some recent Ashkenazic Jewish immigrants who belonged to Shearith Israel created the Hebrew Benevolent Society, or Meshibat Nefesh, in New York. The members wrote a constitution making clear that, although the Society was loosely linked to the synagogue, it existed as an independent body.[33] The unlinking of synagogues and Jewish charity and communal relief, not just in New York, but all over the United States, proved to be momentous.

THE IMPORTANCE OF COMMUNAL SERVICE

From 1822 on, American Jews, from the wealthiest to those of relatively modest means, launched a mammoth enterprise of social service, which included caring for the sick, the elderly, orphans, the unemployed, prison inmates, the hungry, and the destitute. By the 1920s this sizeable service network came to be one of the hallmarks of American Jewry and one of the characteristics of the Jews most admired by non-Jews. William Burder, who authored a massive encyclopedia of American religions in 1872, declared that the Jews "will never suffer the destitute to be an incubus upon society at large. Rarely is any of their faith an inmate of the almshouse, and more rarely is he arrested as a vagrant or an outlaw. Charitable associations supplying food, garments, fuel, and house rent . . . encourage the industrious: hospitals, orphan asylums; foster houses, and homes for the invalid and decrepit, are supported wherever a Jewish community exists."[34]

Communal service came to be the common denominator of American Jewry. Though Jews could not always—or indeed ever—agree on matters religious, they could, in literally thousands of community organizations, agree on their common obligation to provide assistance to Jews in need. Whether or not they were schooled in Judaic religious texts, they knew that they were obliged to help other Jews, whether in the form of providing an interest-free loan to help someone get a business started *(gemillat hesed)*, assembling a dowry for a poor bride *(hachnassat kallah)*, or providing a night's lodging for itinerant Jews *(hachnassat orchim)*. These practices had been long-standing Jewish communal obligations, derived from canonical texts. Unlike the Christian notion of charity, given out of the goodness of one's heart when one feels so inspired, these practices fell into the category of *tzedakah*, profound responsibilities.

The Jews' concern with helping the needy also contained an element of defense. Until the twentieth century almost all American charity derived from sectarian sources, with little assistance to the poor and those in distress coming from the state. Jews considered relying either on overtly Christian institutions or on those that mixed assistance with a subtler Christian message to be simply out of the question. Those institutions made no provisions for Jewish practices such as observing dietary laws or maintaining the Sabbath. More significant still, these charitable enterprises were wrapped up in the evangelical fervor of American Protestantism. A Jewish child entering an American orphanage would most likely emerge a Christian. Therefore, Jewish orphanages, a high communal priority, functioned both to assist parentless children and to keep them away from the missionaries.[35]

Among American Jews the creation of social-welfare services made clear the meaning of class and helped develop a desire to acquire American goods and styles of consumption. Those with resources, the backers of charitable projects, exposed the poor and the immigrants to the idea of the middle-class standard of living. Though the immigrants may have harbored resentment toward their patrons, through these charitable projects they came to develop a keen sense of how they would live if they could. Immigrant Jewish women, for example, flocked to cooking classes set up by middle-class American Jews in settlement houses. Their exposure to American tastes and styles in turn shaped the immigrant women's sense of entitlement to America's bounty.[36]

This charitable network also put a good deal of communal power and influence into the hands of the few wealthy women and men. Particularly as immigration from eastern Europe grew from a trickle to a flood, the actions of individual philanthropists left their mark on the community. Individuals like Jacob Schiff, Julius Rosenwald, and Minnie Low, to name a few, could, by the size of their contributions and the tenacity with which they monitored their projects, change the structure of Jewish community life.

One group of wealthy New York Jews—Isidor Straus, Samuel Greenbaum, Myer Isaacs, Jacob Schiff, and Isaac Seligman—believed that the new immigrants massing on New York's Lower East Side needed a transformative educational institution to help them negotiate the demands and challenges of America. They consolidated other smaller institutions, which they also had funded, including the Hebrew Free School Association, the Aguilar Free Library Society, and the Young Men's Hebrew Association, and merged them into the Educational Alliance, which opened its doors in 1893. A multifaceted enterprise dedicated to "Americanizing, educational, social and humanizing" activities, the Educational Alliance provided services and classes, involving nearly every aspect of their lives, to tens of thousands of immigrant Jews of every age.[37] Lectures, civics lessons, religious services, and classes and a library for adults that reached about a thousand people a day, all augmented by clubs, made the Educational Alliance a vital nexus of community life. A number of bureaus, such as the Legal Aid Bureau and the Desertion Bureau, attempted to mediate between the immigrants and the American legal system and between these relatively poor newcomers and the large Jewish charitable associations like the United Hebrew Charities. In 1901 the Educational Alliance founded a summer camp for boys at Cold Spring on-the-Hudson and a few years later one for girls at the New Jersey shore. While part of the Educational Alliance's vision involved top-down charity, the women, men, and children who used its facilities actively molded its programs. After all, they chose to attend and to seek its services.[38]

Although the Judaic system did not consider charity a matter of largesse and choice, in American Jewish communities it came to function that way. As early as the 1830s Philadelphia's Isaac Leeser called on Jewish charitable bodies to research carefully requests for assistance to "raise the character of the recipient of charity through a proper discrimination, by aiding those who are most deserving."[39] Into the early twentieth century, he, along with a string of community leaders, decried the amount of fund-raising going on for Jewish charities and the fact that American Jews found themselves subjected to multiple campaigns for their charitable dollars.

Locally, and eventually nationally, institutions competed to raise money, staging picnics, banquets, concerts, plays, and other kinds of recreational activities to entertain and to collect contributions. They sold raffle tickets and gave away prizes. Nineteenth-century American Jewish communities typically hosted annual Purim balls, gala affairs to enhance Jewish sociability and add to the coffers of favorite projects. In the early twentieth century, in New York in particular, charitable societies bought blocks of seats in the Yiddish theaters. Art and charity became dependent on each other. By offering popular plays, the charity earned money to add to its funds. By making the theater available to these benefits, the producers, directors, and actors of the Yiddish theater helped sustain a vibrant charitable infrastructure.

But Jewish communal leaders worried about the disorganized nature of the philanthropic project. By the end of the nineteenth century, as the immigration issue loomed so large and as the problems of the newcomers seemed so overwhelming, Jewish charities started federating, very much in the spirit of the age of reform. Beginning in Boston in 1895 and in Cincinnati in 1896, and followed by Chicago, Philadelphia, Cleveland, St. Louis, Kansas City, and a string of other cities, Jewish charities launched campaigns for all the federated agencies. By the early 1920s, when Congress froze immigration and when eastern European Jewry faced the crisis of postwar reconstruction, local federations also started raising money for international Jewish needs in a single community-wide drive.

While the basic institutions functioned on the local level, as early as the 1870s national Jewish bodies developed to lend coherence to Jewish charity. That year those involved in the United Hebrew Relief Association of St. Louis suggested that a National Association of Jewish Charities be formed. It took until 1899, when the National Conference of Jewish Charities was formed, for this to happen. It, as well as other national and international bodies, like the Baron de Hirsch Fund, the Jewish Agricultural Society, the Industrial Removal Office, the Hebrew Sheltering and Immigrant Aid Society (HIAS), and the National Desertion Bureau, linked American Jews, regardless of where they lived and of whether they were the donors or the recipients of charity.

During much of the great century of migration, a somewhat unclear boundary separated these two shareholders in the philanthropic effort. While each community had major donors whose funds made possible the most ambitious projects and whose names came to be chiseled on the marble tablets hanging in the entranceways of lofty buildings, in the many immigrant enclaves and in small towns, Jews provided assistance to each other informally. Through their own networks they gave each other jobs and fed and sheltered each other during hard times. Somewhat more formally, family circles, or clubs, provided interest-free loans to kinspeople down on their luck. Women's burial societies, known in America as Hebrew Female Benevolent Associations, fulfilled the religious obligations associated with death and burial, and they also extended loans to women in need, prepared dowries for poor brides, helped orphans, and generally looked after the welfare of Jewish women and children.[40]

Landsmanschaftn

Free-loan societies made no distinction between members, and most members at some point availed themselves of the benefit of an interest-free loan, just as they also contributed.[41] On a much larger scale *landsmanschaftn*, hometown associations that thrived in every large Jewish community, functioned as benevolent societies. Joined by common Old World origins, members of *landsmanschaftn* provided each other with an array of benefits that helped cushion the blows of industrial capitalism. While many *landsmanschaftn* also functioned as quasi-synagogues, they mainly served as agencies where immigrant men turned to their fellows for health insurance, for loans to make ends meet, for the services of a doctor, and for burial benefits.

Immigrants from the Polish city of Bialystok founded America's first *landsmanschaft* in 1868. During the next few decades forty separate Bialystoker societies formed in New York, with active lodges in Newark, Milwaukee, Chicago, Detroit, and Philadelphia. The larger the European community and the larger the American city, the more specialized *landsmanschaft* life became. The Bialystoker in New York, for example, divided into the Bialystoker Bricklayers Benevolent Associations, the Bialystoker Young Mens Association, the Bialystoker Ladies Aid Society of Harlem and the Bronx, and several dozen more organizations. Other towns and regions supported their own societies, all of them easily mixing sociability, mutual assistance, and concern for family and friends in Europe. Thousands of these societies existed in New York alone, and indeed, by the 1920s, many more American Jews belonged to *landsmanschaftn* than to synagogues. Even decades after migrating, it was here that immigrants turned when they needed assistance and when they yearned to hear familiar accents. Although most *landsmanschaftn* functioned as male-only groups, in some cases wives of members created auxiliaries, and in a few rare instances, men and women joined as equals.[42]

Immigrants not only created networks of support for themselves, utterly independent of the wealthy donors, but they also founded large-scale institutions to meet their own needs as they defined them. In 1909 a group of immigrant Jewish women in Boston's South End, mothers who met regularly at Hyman Danzig's Three and Nine Cent store, recognized the lack of adequate medical care in the poor neighborhood. These women formed a committee and came up with a scheme by which to raise money for a clinic—they constructed miniature bricks and sold them for fifty cents apiece. By 1911 they had made enough progress that they transformed themselves into the Beth Israel Hospital Association, and having enlisted several of the neighborhood *bikkur holim* societies—associations for visiting the sick—they incorporated and started to approach some of the city's major Jewish philanthropists and doctors to join in the effort. By the end of the year these immigrant Jewish women could claim the credit for a forty-five-bed hospital, Beth Israel, which later expanded and became Harvard University Medical School's teaching facility.[43]

Likewise, in 1914 the Bessarabian Verband Association, a *landsmanschaft* formed by a group of immigrants from Bessarabia living on New York's Lower East Side, confronted the crisis of a group of Jews in need. As one participant recalled, "four pitiful little brothers, parentless and neglected . . . were brought in by a very sick grandmother." At first the women of the association "took turns looking after the children.

Each day one would bring in the meals prepared in her own kitchen. Another stayed with the children during the day, until another relieved her in the evening." Out of these efforts was born the Hebrew National Orphan Home. The existence of their own orphanage most likely gave the members of the Bessarabian *landsmanschaft* a degree of comfort. Should tragedy befall them, their children would also be cared for by a friendly institution, one that they themselves had shaped.[44]

Starting in the 1820s, each communal enterprise, large or small, operating from the top down or flowing laterally within the ranks of the relatively poor, provided American Jews with a way to express their Jewishness outside the synagogue apparatus. Each enterprise allowed them to feel that they were fulfilling a basic Jewish commandment, that of *tzedakah,* the responsibility to give to those in need. At the same time each project reflected the overall American tendency to form and support voluntary associations.

The B'nai B'rith Is Born

Perhaps no organization represented more dramatically the complex fusion of the charitable and the social, and the challenge to synagogues, than the B'nai B'rith, the oldest of America's permanent Jewish organizations. In 1843 twelve young Jewish men, all immigrants from central Europe living in New York's *Kleindeutschland* neighborhood, were rejected as members at a local Masonic lodge. They met at Sinsheimer's Tavern on Essex Street on October 13 and pledged their support to each other, forming the Bundes Bruder, "band of brothers." Shortly thereafter they opted for a Hebrew name, B'nai B'rith, "the sons of the covenant."

They borrowed liberally from the Masons, the Odd Fellows, and other fraternal orders so immensely popular among nineteenth-century American men. They greeted each other with secret rituals and secret handshakes. Just like the Masons who had rejected them, they donned special regalia for meetings, but all with a Jewish flavor. The secret handshake, for example, went along with the words *shalom aleichem*—peace unto you—and the costume included the *arba kanfot,* the men's four-cornered fringed prayer undergarments. Lodges took on Hebrew names: Emes, B'er Chayim, Ramah, Ebn Ezra, Gal-Ed, and the like. Like other American lodges, the B'nai B'rith responded to the demands of the mercurial American economy by offering benefits to its members, particularly those addressing sickness and death. Because of the high rate of mobility among members, the B'nai B'rith allowed them to carry their package of benefits from lodge to lodge as they moved across America in search of new homes and more lucrative work. The B'nai B'rith, which started its first chapter outside New York in 1850, functioned as the first national American Jewish institution. In that same year it adopted English as its official language.

The Jewishness of B'nai B'rith, the first powerful secular male alternative to the synagogue, manifested itself in the organization's activities. In Albany, New York, the Shiloh Lodge briefly supported a Jewish all-day school, while the Champaign, Illinois, Grand Prairie Lodge provided Jewish children with instruction on Sunday mornings. At times B'nai B'rith lodges sponsored religious services, and they often provided a venue for lectures given by visiting rabbis and other learned men. In Philadelphia, New York, and Cincinnati, the B'nai B'rith established Jewish libraries, making Jewish books and magazines available to the public. These activities took place across the country, and although the main focus of the B'nai B'rith was the insurance benefits it provided to members, their families and the full and active social life it provided shaped the way the men spent their leisure time.[45]

Other Orders

American Jewish men created other lodges as well. In 1860 a group of men from eastern Europe, Poland in particular, founded Kesher shel Barzel. Unlike the B'nai B'rith, which, although it changed its language to English in 1850, tended to attract Germans, except in smaller communities where it alone functioned as the Jewish lodge, the Order of B'rith Abraham had a primarily Hungarian constituency. Regardless of what lodge they belonged to, by affiliating these men contributed to an American definition of Jewish manhood. By belonging to a lodge, a Jewish man could fulfill his responsibility to his family, protecting his wife and children from the accidental calamities and the vagaries of the marketplace. He could also feel surrounded by Jewish social and cultural activities, even though those activities existed outside the synagogue, disconnected from any concern with the details of Jewish law.

The lodges deeply embraced America. Their writings, programs, and meeting halls abounded with the symbols of their American identity, meshed with Jewish idioms, symbols, and ideas. The B'nai B'rith, for example, commissioned the sculptor Moses Ezekiel to create a statue for the 1876 exposition held in Philadelphia to mark the century since the American Revolution. Although the statue unveiled in Fairmont Park made little explicit reference to Jews or Judaism, the words "Religious Liberty" engraved in the stone extolled the American system, its constitution in particular, which defended all from the snake of "Intolerance."[46]

JEWISH EDUCATION DEVELOPS

Belonging to a lodge, to a Jewish literary society, or to a Young Men's Hebrew Association, a product of the 1870s, became in and of itself a Jewish act, no less sacred in the eyes of members than the fulfilling of mitzvoth, the commandments derived from canonical texts but determined by individual preferences.[47] How they transmitted formal Jewish learning to their children reflected their class status, how long they had been in America, what they considered fundamental to Jewish life, and the size of their community. Both American and Jewish impulses shaped Jewish education.

Much of the impetus for the development of Jewish education came from the state of general education in America. As the former changed, so did the latter. At first Jews created a number of day schools, where Jewish children could receive a secular education as well as study Jewish subjects. These schools achieved their popularity among immigrant parents partly because of the focus on transmitting Jewish knowledge. But these schools derived much of their rationale from the virtual absence of any public schools teaching general subjects acceptable to Jewish parents. Most government-supported schools had a decidedly Protestant agenda. Until well into the 1850s, public school children read from the King James version of the Bible, sang Christian hymns, intoned decidedly Protestant prayers, and studied from textbooks that posited Christianity as the highest achievement of civilization.[48]

Day Schools

Jewish day schools proliferated, offering, to those who could afford them, general education as well as Judaic instruction. Before the 1820s education had been a function of the individual congregation, providing one more way in which Shearith Israel, Mikveh Israel, and other original congregations exerted influence on their members. This dynamic did not come to a complete end with the immigration of the 1820s. Indeed, the central European immigrants who created new synagogues began, by the 1840s, to build day schools attached to the synagogues. New York's B'nai Jeshurun founded one in 1842, Ansche Chesed in 1845, and Rodeph Shalom and Shaarey Hashamayim in the mid-1840s. In the 1850s similar schools developed in Philadelphia and Cincinnati.

Alongside these synagogue day schools, some Jews created similar all-day schools that were not connected to any particular congregation. In the 1820s a series of Jewish schools, starting with the Polonies Talmud Torah of 1821 in New York, broke out of the congregational orbit. School and synagogue had become disengaged, and enrolling a child in a school like Polonies did not require membership in a congregation. Enough Jewish day schools existed in New York in the 1840s to inspire Rabbi Max Lilienthal to attempt to coordinate them. In 1845 he attempted, unsuccessfully, to bring the day schools of Ansche Chesed, Rodeph Shalom, and Shaaray Hashamayim together under the aegis of a single "Union School" to avoid duplication of boards, teachers, and fund-raising efforts. However, each congregation wanted to retain control of its school and balked at the idea of joining forces.

Both the synagogue-based day schools and those that functioned independent of congregations depended on student fees to pay the teachers' salaries. They tended to serve better-off immigrants and to cluster in large cities. Few existed in smaller towns, where parents sent their children to the public schools, using makeshift methods for imparting Jewish teachings.

The Jewish press repeatedly published advertisements from small-town congregations looking for teachers, and when possible parents hired private tutors to teach Jewish subjects to their children at home. In the big cities where Jewish schools existed, the poor had little chance of taking advantage of them; the combined need of their children's labor and the high fees kept them out. Rebecca Gratz's creation of the Jewish Sunday school as a form of communal charity reflected the fact that many Jewish parents could not afford to pay the day school tuition. It also demonstrated the degree to which Jews feared Christian evangelical activities among the children of the Jewish poor in particular.[49]

Those Jews who could afford to pay for their children to attend the day schools participated in a unique experiment. These schools represented a notable fusion of Jewish concerns—the teaching of Hebrew, Jewish texts, and Judaic rituals—and American child-oriented styles and issues specific to the newly forming immigrant communities. These coeducational academies were an American innovation. Jewish girls, who at that time received virtually no Jewish education in Europe, made up about one-third of the students at American schools. The schools came into being at a time when middle-class Americans considered the education of girls essential. In the early Republic, public discourse focused on women as key to the transmission of republican virtues and national identity. Americans emphasized the importance of teaching girls so that they would grow up to be educated mothers who would raise their sons in a manner appropriate to the needs and values of the growing nation.[50] Likewise, the influx of millions of immigrants from Ireland and Germany, as well as the westward expansion of the nation, made the public education of girls a matter of concern. Girls acquired an education so that they—at a lower cost than men—could teach the children of newcomers about America and bring civilization to the frontier.[51]

The girls educated at the Jewish schools benefited from an American ethos that invested great importance in women's intellectual development. These Jewish women saw themselves, and were seen by male community leaders, as the future mothers of Israel in America, a cultural idea akin to that of "Republican motherhood" that took root in the early decades of the nineteenth century among their Protestant neighbors. Educated Jewish women could be primed to teach the children of the newly arriving Jewish immigrants about both Jewishness and America.

The Female Role in Education

Jewish women made up the cadre of teachers who provided instruction in the Sunday schools. When the Hebrew Free School No. 1 was opened up in 1865 in New York's immigrant Jewish neighborhood, just a year after a Protestant mission school opened its doors nearby, it employed Jewish women to provide the educational antidote to the evangelicals. During the nineteenth century and into the early twentieth, Jewish women who taught in the various schools came to play a crucial role in the formation of Jewish communal life. They, more than the rabbis, came in contact with Jewish families and learned how American Jews articulated their Jewishness. They showed leadership and helped shape Jewish institutions.

Ray Frank was one of these women. Born in the middle of the 1860s in San Francisco, she taught in the Sabbath school of Oakland's First Hebrew Congregation at the same time that she gave private lessons in literature and elocution and wrote for various West Coast newspapers. By the 1890s Frank traveled extensively around the West and other parts of the country, giving lectures and sermons on a variety of Jewish topics in synagogues and other Jewish venues. She called on Jews to renew their commitment to Judaism and invoked in particular the power of women to give meaning to Jewish ritual. A group of Jews in Chicago actually approached her in 1893 to serve as rabbi for their congregation, despite the fact that no woman had ever been a rabbi and that the issue had never been broached in public debate. [52]

Over time the supplementary schools, like the one at which Frank taught, whether in session on Sundays or in the middle of the week, came to be the dominant American Jewish educational form. The all-day Jewish schools survived while Jewish parents expressed discomfort with the public schools, and as such they thrived only into the late 1850s. In large measure Jewish day schools declined because of the political pressure exerted by the Catholic Church on city and state governments. Catholics, who were rapidly becoming New York's majority population, forced officials to unlink general learning from the propagation of Protestant religion. As the schools in New York and elsewhere became increasingly neutral, Jewish parents had less need for the parochial academies and moved en masse to the public schools. Many, although not all, Jewish leaders hailed the change of climate in the public schools. Isaac Mayer Wise in Cincinnati, for one, pressed for the new kind of public school shorn of religion and urged Jewish parents to send their children to these schools once the Christian content had been removed.

Public Schools

Immigrants arriving later in the nineteenth century had a different set of options than those who came earlier. In many states, New York in particular, newly passed legislation raised the mandatory age through which children had to stay in school. Whereas the earlier era had emphasized work and experience rather than formal learning as the mechanisms of achievement, increasingly Americans linked extended education with the idea of economic mobility. The newly arriving immigrants attended public schools that operated in a less Christian context. These schools represented the best chance for children to receive an education, at least as long as the children did not have to seek employment.

While many Jews, even into the early twentieth century, needed their children's income to survive, by and large most children went to school. For most immigrant parents, coming to America offered them the chance to give their children a better education than what they could have had in Europe. They almost universally sought that education in the public schools, not Jewish ones. Jewish learning had to be sandwiched in between two decidedly larger concerns. For some, it had to be set aside so that the children could work. For others Jewish education had to make room for the dream of upward mobility that many believed could only be realized by attending public school. The statistics bear out both the salience of American education and the decidedly lower status of Jewish education. In 1917 nearly all Jewish children in New York attended public school, although fewer than a quarter of them received a Jewish education.[53]

Jewish communal leaders trumpeted the public schools as the best hope for the new immigrants' upward move into the middle class. In 1884 Julia Richman, the daughter of immigrants, became the first Jewish principal in the New York public schools. Her school served an almost exclusively eastern European Jewish immigrant clientele, and she waxed eloquent in articles she wrote for education publications and Jewish magazines about the importance of public education for Jewish children, but always in the context of the supplementary Jewish school system. She claimed to be on a crucial mission in the public schools, rescuing the entire immigrant "family from traditions which enslave the mind . . . and present stubborn obstacle to . . . Americanization of the alien." The Sunday schools, attended by Jewish children who went to public school during the week could, if properly administered, inspire in children a loyalty to Judaism. The two systems, she maintained, needed each other.[54]

This kind of rhetoric could be heard all over the country as American Jews pinned their hopes on the public schools. Rabbi Abram Simon of Washington, D.C., echoed these thoughts in 1911, claiming that "there is no greater friend of the American public school system than the Jew."[55] Samson Benderly, who played a key role in professionalizing Jewish education, considered the public school system no less crucial. He wrote in 1908: "What we want in this country is not Jews who can successfully keep up their Jewishness in a few large ghettos, but men and women who have grown up in freedom and can assert themselves wherever they are. A parochial system of education among the Jews would be fatal to such hopes."[56] Some American Jews disagreed with this outlook and remained committed to providing their children with an extensive Jewish education, despite the overwhelming tendency of the community in the opposite direction. They put the acquisition of a solid and traditional Jewish education on a higher rung than that of learning American skills. In 1857 Rabbi Pesach Rosenthal opened a Talmud Torah in New York at which teachers taught in Yiddish, with texts that deviated little from what was being taught at that time in his native Poland. In 1883 Rosenthal's school evolved into a more substantial institution, Machazikai Talmud Torah. In 1886 it was joined by the Etz Chaim Yeshiva to provide a small number of eastern European Jewish youngsters in New York with a decidedly non-American education. This kind of learning represented a small, atypical experience.[57]

Other Venues for Immigrants

Synagogues functioned as the key sites for Jewish education. Congregations mostly followed the Sunday school model, offering one day a week of instruction. Congregational schools enrolled both boys and girls, and most held up as their crowning achievement the confirmation ceremony, an American innovation, although one with roots in German reforms of the same era.[58] Typically taking place during the teenage years, and purposely later than the bar mitzvah age of thirteen, confirmation highlighted religious services during the late spring harvest festival of Shavuot, which celebrates the giving of the Torah at Sinai. Congregations led exercises at which young people, dressed in white, demonstrated what they had learned and took part in leading the service.

But in a community increasingly made up of immigrants and their children, synagogue membership lay well beyond the means of most, and very few actually belonged. Immigrant families relied on other sources of learning to prepare their sons for Jewish learning. Immigrant girls typically received less attention than American-born middle-class Jewish girls. A large number of Jewish children, boys and girls, simply received no Jewish education whatsoever. Boys might study privately for a brief time to learn to recite the blessings over the Torah at their bar mitzvah. Others spent some time in an after-school Jewish setting, perhaps during good economic times when their families had less need of the extra income from a son's part-time job. When boys attended a Jewish afternoon school, whether in New York, Chicago, Philadelphia, Baltimore, Newark, or Boston, they did so in one of the many hederim, single-room supplementary schools, which met in basements and storefronts. *Melamdim,* teachers, usually newly arrived from Europe, set up these classrooms and taught Jewish boys the basics of Hebrew letters, prayers, some Bible, and some Talmud. No agency regulated these Jewish one-room schoolhouses.

Some Jewish children learned the basics of Judaica in larger, more professional institutions formed in part out of charity. The Hebrew Free School in New York educated thousands of youngsters until it closed in 1899, as did the Down-town Sabbath School founded by women from Temple Emanu-El, particularly Minnie Louis, which mixed Jewish subjects with American ones.[59] Along with Hebrew, Bible stories, songs, prayers, and blessings, teachers imparted lessons about American citizenship, cleanliness, and physical education. The founders and teachers wanted to provide children of immigrant parents with models of *American* Judaism. They felt that Jewishness need not be the province of bearded, Yiddish-speaking rabbis who seemed far out of step with the American culture these children were rapidly absorbing.

Similar charitable schools run for immigrant children developed in the other large cities. In every place where they cropped up they reflected the same complex mix of impulses: genuine concern for the health and well-being of the immigrants' children, a desire to Americanize them but in a warm and loving Jewish environment, and a concern that without this kind of environment, these children would drift away from Jewish life. The schools that middle-class American Jews established for the immigrants out of philanthropic impulses tended to define girls' education as crucial, while more autonomous schools, products of the immigrant community, reflected the eastern European idea that only boys needed to acquire a formal Jewish education.

By the 1910s Jewish education moved in a decidedly different direction. As ideological splinterings within the Jewish communities became more pronounced, partisans of particular ideologies founded schools to teach the basics of Judaica, along with the particular belief system of the sponsoring organization. In 1892 eastern European Jewish Socialist immigrants created the Arbeiter Ring, or Workmen's Circle, for social, benevolent, and political purposes. One of the fundamental institutions of eastern European Jewish life in America, the Arbeiter Ring fused fraternalism with left-wing ideology. Since part of its ideology focused on the power of Yiddish as the tongue of the masses to transmit political ideas, from its inception it maintained an educational orientation. Likewise, it emphasized the need for unions, the rights of workers, and the dignity of the ordinary Jewish immigrant—as opposed to the rabbis and the intellectual elite—to create and sustain Jewish culture in America. Functioning alongside the Yiddish press and the Yiddish theater, the Workmen's Circle helped the immigrants become American at the same time that it mounted a critique of capitalism.

By 1900 the Arbeiter Ring went national. In doing so it sought strategies to broaden its appeal and to bring increasing numbers of immigrant Jews into its circles. Some leaders of the Workmen's Circle considered it crucial to reach out to less ideologically committed immigrants through Yiddish-language cultural programs. Others disagreed and saw the immigrants' ultimate linguistic assimilation into the American working class as the desired goal. From about 1912 onward an intense debate between those supporting these two approaches raged within the organization. By 1918 the former faction triumphed, and the Arbeiter Ring launched a network of Yiddish schools for children. The schools it founded in New York, Chicago, Philadelphia, Milwaukee, Newark, Baltimore, Rochester, Denver, and elsewhere first enrolled children of its own members, but over time children whose parents did not belong to the organization or share the organization's political perspective attended as well. By 1919 ten such schools existed. A year later, the number had climbed to thirty and to forty-seven in 1922. The children in the Arbeiter Ring schools grew up in Yiddish-speaking homes, and the schools provided systematic instruction in a language the children picked up in everyday life. The schools exposed them to Yiddish literature, Jewish folk music, Jewish history, and the history of the working class.[60]

Though the Labor Zionist movement had a different agenda, its educational story followed the same script. In 1905 the Poale Zion came into being. Five years later an ancillary group, the Farband, or the Jewish National Workers Alliance, joined it to make up American Labor Zionism. As a movement Labor Zionism stood between the two great revolutions in the Jewish polity of the modern age, Socialism and Zionism.[61] To its fellow Zionists, it stressed the importance of labor as a liberating force for the Jewish communities developing in Palestine and the need to advance the Socialist agenda in the diaspora as well. Jews, the Poale Zion argued, would never be free as long as class inequities remained. It admonished the other Zionists that the plight of the Jews could not be disassociated from the plight of other oppressed workers. Yet it rejected the politics of the other Jewish Socialists, like those in the Bund, who saw Zionism as narrow, chauvinistic nationalism. They offered a counterargument to those Socialists, who though Jewish, went out of their way to de-emphasize Jewish culture, heritage, and aspirations. Poale Zion sought to create in America, as well as in Europe, a renaissance of Jewish culture through the Hebrew language.

Like the Arbeiter Ring, the Poale Zion turned to the education of its members' children as a way to propagate the ideology. In 1908 it adopted as key to its mission "the education of the Jewish youth in the Jewish national spirit." To that end it created a network of *folkshulen,* "schools for the people," around the country. True to their ideology, Labor Zionist schools, as well as the summer camps it founded, emphasized Hebrew and Yiddish as living languages, Jewish history, Socialism, and those aspects of Judaism that could be translated into nationalist and

Socialist idioms. American Jewish children, descendants of eastern European immigrants, who attended the Poale Zion schools imbibed the music and dance coming out of the collective settlements, the kibbutzim, being formed in Palestine. From afar they were taught to think of themselves as helping in the building of that land.[62]

The Kehillah Gives Direction

These ideologically driven schools, as well as the Americanizing schools and Sunday schools that grew out of the philanthropic impulse, tended to teach loyalty to a particular vision of Jewish life rather than to the Jewish people as a whole. By the 1920s, Jewish education had no communal body to oversee it. It lacked direction, coordination, or a sense of operating as a unified entity. Schools existed independent of each other, and parents interested in securing a Jewish education for their children had no guide. In 1908 this high level of disorganization prompted New York Jewish leaders of both the "downtown" immigrant world and of the "uptown" American world to create the Kehillah, an overarching body of communal self-governance. In one of its first acts, the Kehillah formed a Bureau of Jewish Education in 1910 to impose order on the vast welter of schools that constituted Jewish education in New York. Kehillah leaders invited Samson Benderly, a trained physician who had dedicated himself to Jewish education, to come to New York from Baltimore to head the Bureau.

Benderly behaved like a prototypical progressive. He believed in order as a positive good and that by achieving order, New York's Jews could obtain a better Jewish education.[63] He considered the ideal Jewish education as one reflecting the values of American education and believed that it would succeed only if talented professionals could be enlisted in the cause. In a letter to Rabbi Judah Magnes, president of the Kehillah, Benderly wrote, "As the great public school system is the rock bottom upon which this country is rearing its institutions, so we Jews must evolve here a system of Jewish education that shall be complementary to and harmonious with the public system."[64] Benderly joined up with Rabbi Mordecai Kaplan, then head of the Teachers Institute at the Jewish Theological Seminary and an admirer of the progressive educational philosophy of John Dewey.

Like the progressives among whom they counted themselves, Benderly and Kaplan believed in rational planning, bureaucratic structures, and the need to amass accurate information on the nature of the problem. First they elected to conduct a thorough survey of Jewish education in New York to ascertain a statistically accurate picture of the nature of Jewish schooling. They learned how few children received any Jewish ed-

ucation and uncovered a disparate and unregulated educational world
for those who did. They found that very few teachers had received any
systematic pedagogical training, and that Jewish education seemed not
to be guided by any clear vision or purpose. They worried that so few immigrant children were receiving any Jewish education and that those
who did endured poor facilities and even worse instruction. That education, according to Benderly and Kaplan, could hardly be considered
worthy of the body of Jewish knowledge—the language, liturgy, scriptures, and codes—that had been the Jews' estate and had made them "the
people of the Book." These children could hardly be expected, in years
to come, to be leaders of American Jews.

Benderly and Kaplan shared a vision. Both believed that to retain the
loyalty of young people, Judaism could not deviate dramatically from the
basic contours of American culture. Jewish children needed to find something in Judaism that pertained to them as new Americans, something
they could proudly use to enhance their self-esteem. A dingy basement
classroom, taught by a *melamed* who knew no English, Benderly and
Kaplan believed, would do little to nurture Jewish pride in an American
setting. Furthermore, as more and more children came from homes that
were less and less racked by poverty, "uplift" education had lost its purpose.

To create an American Jewish educational system that taught children
to be Jewish in America, and American in the Jewish world, Benderly
brought together a group of young women and men named the "Benderly boys," whom he and Kaplan trained and then sent out to Jewish
communities across the United States. While New York's Kehillah did
not survive the strains of World War I, the young people taught and influenced by Benderly and Kaplan ventured far out of New York to create schools in numerous cities. By the middle of the 1920s they played
an instrumental role in forming bureaus of Jewish education in Pittsburgh, Minneapolis, Detroit, Baltimore, Boston, and Cleveland, as well
as a number of other cities. These bureaus did in fact create unified pay
scales for teachers, offering resources and programs citywide.

The development of integrated and more centralized Jewish educational systems on the local level led to the formation of Hebrew teachers' colleges and institutes in Chicago, Cleveland, Baltimore, and Boston,
all of which became centers for fostering Jewish learning. Some of the
Kaplan-Benderly disciples, like Albert Schoolman, developed Hebrew-
language Jewish summer camps where Jewish children could live for a
few weeks a year in an all-Jewish environment. The camps, like many

other progressive Jewish educational projects, owed a large debt to Zionism, emphasizing the creativity of the *yishuv*, the burgeoning Jewish community in Palestine, which had revived Hebrew, created new artistic forms, and which had taken its Jewish destiny into its own hands.[65]

The new schools, the camps, and the other youth-oriented activities operated according to a kind of marketplace model. Educators wanted to mold children who would grow up to be committed Jewish adults. The children and their parents had to be sold on the idea of expending time and money on Jewish education. If the schools helped make the youngsters proud of being Jewish, educators hoped, the families would be likely to buy into the system. In contrast, young people who grew up with few positive reasons to commit to Jewish life would be unlikely to keep the schools, camps, synagogues, and other institutions alive.

YIDDISH THEATER

The ability of ordinary women and men to choose became the dominant characteristic of American Jewry, one that set it apart from the many other diaspora communities. By the 1920s a seemingly boundless number of places—limited only by the number of Jews in the community—made it possible for American Jews to construct the kind of Jewish life they wanted. Providing venues for interacting with other Jews and for thinking about Jewish themes involved leisure as well as the serious business of religion and education. The emergence in the 1880s of the Yiddish theater in New York added another option to an already complicated mélange of congregations, lodges, and charitable societies, all of which offered ways of being part of a Jewish public. The theater articulated some of the deepest emotions of the newcomers and explored themes close to their hearts: the loss of European authenticity, the trials of the immigration experience, family conflict, the erosion of faith, temptation both material and sexual, and the burden imposed on families by the lure of America. They also offered dramatic and biblical themes, Jewish history, and scenes of Jews suffering outside America.

Some of the most popular dramas, like *Die Yiddishe King Lear* (1892) and *Mirele Efros* (1898), both directed and acted by Jacob Gordin, as well as Boruch Thomashefsky's *Dos Pintele Yid* (1907), probably the biggest hit of the era, mixed high emotionalism with serious issues familiar to the immigrants. In *Die Yiddishe King Lear*, the tragedy that befell Shakespeare's monarch happened instead to an old-style eastern European rabbi who faced the cold-hearted abuse and rebellion of his

American daughters. In Peretz Hirschbein's 1915 *Farvofen Vinkel*—an isolated corner—star-crossed lovers in a traditional village overcome the odds and find happiness. Biblical melodramas like Abraham Goldfaden's *Shulamith* (1880) and *Bar Kochba* (1887) wove together music and theatricality with Jewish history. Yiddish theater functioned as a highly interactive medium. Not only did the audience cheer and hiss, yell at the villains and encourage the heroes, but the Yiddish press also played a powerful role in shaping the life of the stage.

If the synagogues were noted for the paucity of members and the struggles of rabbis to fill the sanctuaries on Sabbath mornings, the theaters proved to be wildly popular. By the turn of the century the four main Yiddish theaters, Thalia, Windsor, Grand, and People's, presented eleven hundred performances a year for an audience of about 2 million. Charitable societies and lodges bought up vast blocks of tickets for benefit performances, and families came, brought food, and with their neighbors and *landslayt*—friends from back home—wept and laughed, shouting at the actors on the stage and offering advice to the characters in distress.[66]

By 1924 the Yiddish theater in New York, as well as secondary stages in Philadelphia, Chicago, and a few other large cities, was at its apex. Philadelphia-born singer-comedienne Molly Picon made her debut in front of theater audiences just the year before. In that decade the last two of the major Jewish theaters, Maurice Schwartz's Yiddish Art theater and the Public Theater, both elegant structures on Second Avenue (dubbed "Yiddish Broadway" or the "Yiddish Rialto"), raised their curtains. In that same decade a small Yiddish filmmaking industry and Yiddish radio joined the Yiddish theater as artistic media bringing America's Jews, the immigrants and their children, in touch with the sentiments of communal identity.

The theater, like other institutions of Jewish life, responded directly to the tastes and sensibilities of the Jewish masses. Institutions rose or fell, preserved tradition or changed, depending on the will of the community. Indeed, the ability of ordinary Jews to create, sustain, or put an end to institutions—and ritual practices—represented the essence of community building in the century of migration.

When the century of Jewish migration to America began in the 1820s, it shook up the status quo of a small, relatively inconspicuous string of communities that lacked much of an institutional infrastructure, a sense of itself as distinctive from its European counterparts, or the ability to produce its own culture. The explosion in numbers, the ethnic diversity within American Jewry, and the tensions associated with trying to negotiate two worlds provided American Jews with the impetus to define themselves. The breakdown of the cultural and political hegemony of the white Protestant elite enabled Jews to create and celebrate their communal distinctiveness in a society made up of immigrants hailing from Ireland and Italy, Germany and Greece, Scandinavia and the Balkans—nearly everywhere in Europe.

Indeed, by the time Congress closed the doors to further immigration in 1924, American Jewry boasted a broad and elaborate set of organizations and an expansive set of practices reflecting the many variants of Jewishness. Despite the array of values and the chaotic complexity of its institutions, American Jewry articulated an abiding sense of commitment to both a Jewish past and future. The Jewish women and men in America recognized that their future in America lay entwined with where they had come from and where they now found themselves.

The institutions of Jewish life in the century of migration took their shape in large measure from the existence of poverty and the newcomer status of large numbers of the Jews in America. As long as immigration continued, American Jewry would have in its midst a sizable number of poor individuals. That poverty was a quintessential characteristic of an immigrant population, since by and large those with ample means did not migrate. Therefore, many Jewish institutions in America took on, to one degree or another, the assistance of the newcomers, relieving their economic distress as best they could and attempting to hasten their achievement of security and comfort.

American Jews associated economic advancement with Americanization. Both the newcomers and those whose parents or grandparents had migrated in previous decades assumed that to succeed they needed to learn the language and mores of their new home. Regardless of their political and religious ideologies, immigrants and their friends and relatives already in America used community institutions to negotiate the process of becoming American. With few exceptions they embraced the idea of America as a place of economic possibility and religious freedom. They expected to gain political rights through their own volition and not as a matter of descent or birth.

Others in America did not always agree with their inclusive American vision, and the Jews realized that they had to be prepared to defend themselves in their American home. As citizens of a democratic nation, they also felt an obligation to speak out on behalf of Jews in distress elsewhere. That dual imperative of defense forced them to create a Jewish political project in the momentous century from 1820 through 1924.

5

A CENTURY OF JEWISH POLITICS

1820–1920

"With politics," Isaac Leeser declared in 1855 in his journal, *Occident and American Jewish Advocate*, "Jews have little concern, except to vote for those whom they individually may deem most fitting to administer the offices created for the public good."[1] Politically, during this formative century, Jews functioned as voters, officeholders, or as petitioners to government officials, and many, like Leeser, claimed that they did so as Americans—or Ohioans, Georgians, Californians, and New Yorkers—in the interest of the community as a whole. Yet the simplicity of Leeser's statement, articulated repeatedly by American Jews, belied a more complicated world of American Jewish politics. For during this era Jews in America founded a range of organizations to argue on their behalf and on behalf of Jewish people around the globe. These defense agencies reflected both the ways in which immigration shaped Jewish life and the lack of a clear boundary between American Jews and their sisters and brothers living elsewhere.

Leeser did offer a correct assessment in that American Jews in the century from the 1820s through the 1920s neither voted as a deliberate bloc nor took a unified stand on major political issues. Nothing demonstrated this fact better than the Civil War and the issue of slavery. Southern Jews regarded the matter no differently than did their neighbors. Three thousand Jewish men fought in gray uniforms, and Jewish women aided the cause with volunteer work. Northern Jews took a more complicated stance. Some ardently opposed the "peculiar institution" of slavery, and a handful of Jews who were part of militantly abolitionist groups, like

August Bondi, joined and fought with John Brown to make sure that Kansas would enter the Union as a free state. Rabbi David Einhorn fled Baltimore when a mob, incensed at his outspoken condemnation of slavery, came after him and destroyed the printing presses on which he produced his publications, *Sinai* and *Der Wecker*. Rabbi Samuel Adler of New York's Emanu-El regularly preached against the evils of slavery.

Other northern Jews, particularly those allied with the Democratic party, while not proslavery per se, opposed the abolitionists. For his harsh words against slavery, Adler met with stiff opposition among his congregants, who informed him that politics had no place in the pulpit. Isaac Mayer Wise, a staunch Democrat in Ohio, even as the nation was heading for war, claimed that he would tolerate slavery as a way to preserve the Union. But once the hostilities began, Jewish men in the North flocked to the Union, with about ten thousand of them serving in blue. Although by the end of the war most voting Jewish men supported the Republican party, neither the legacy of Lincoln nor the role of the party in reconstructing the nation shaped a Jewish political consensus.[2]

Not only did they refrain from taking a unique position on American political issues, but they never formed a political party representing their own interests. Until the third decade of the twentieth century American Jews did not vote in overwhelming numbers for any one party, and as such they did not emerge as an identifiable bloc. This had more to do with the nature of American politics than it did with the status or sensibilities of the Jews. In America the two-party system emerged as the norm early on. At times small interest-group parties interrupted the tug-of-war between the two big parties, be it between the Democrats and the Federalists, the Democrats and the Whigs, or the Democrats and the Republicans. But although the Know-Nothings, the Free Soilers, the Populists, the Progressives, and the Socialists all tried to break the two-party monopoly, none ever seriously disrupted the status quo.[3]

The Jews' disinterest in entering into electoral politics through a Jewish party was the consequence both of the two-party system and of the obvious smallness of their numbers. Likewise, the practice of politics in America disinclined them from forming a visible caucus or subgroup within any of the parties. Throughout much of this century the two parties found themselves relatively balanced in terms of voter preference, and control of the White House and Congress seesawed back and forth between them. The separation of powers between the presidency and Congress further weakened the possibility of one party dominating the political scene. Therefore, by and large the parties avoided ideology and instead emphasized compromise. Among the various constituency groups, defined by region, occupation, class, religion, and ethnicity, parties tried to appeal to as many different groups as possible, hoping to avoid giving offense and trading practical favors for votes.[4]

FUNCTIONING WITHIN A TWO-PARTY SYSTEM

Two crucial political realities emerged from this system for a minority group like the Jews. First, no political party in the United States in this century tried to gain political capital by engaging in anti-Jewish rhetoric, although individual politicians, on the state or local level, did at various times make negative references to Jews. In 1855 an irate speaker of the California House of Representatives, William Stowe, attacked Jews as unworthy and undesirable residents "who only came here to make money and leave as soon as they effected their object." He proposed a special head tax on Jews. His proposal, however, remained just that. It did not become policy.[5] In 1859 an unsuccessful candidate for the Oregon territorial legislature blamed the Jews for his defeat, claiming in fact that "the Jews of Oregon . . . have leagued together . . . to control the ballot box."[6] In the 1890s Populist leaders, most notably Georgia's Tom Watson and Minnesota's Ignatius Donnelly, found ample opportunity to blame the Jews, whom they called parasites and money-loving creditors, for the plight of the farmers of the South and Midwest.[7]

These malicious accusations notwithstanding, by the end of the nineteenth and the early twentieth centuries, the relative openness of American parties to Jews stood in stark contrast to the rise of virulent anti-Semitic parties in much of Europe. At no time did the Jews become the focus of political strife in the United States. America had no equivalent of France's 1894 Dreyfus affair, in which the parties lined up for or against the Jewish officer who had been falsely accused of treason. For several years the Dreyfus case functioned as the key dividing point in French politics. Not only did different parties argue about his guilt or innocence, but the halls of the assembly resounded with statements about the Jews, about their worthiness and loyalty to France or the lack thereof.

That no formally anti-Semitic political parties arose in America during this century does not mean that Jews had no political enemies or that their increasing numbers did not become fodder for political controversy. The movement to restrict immigration, for example, included individuals who expressed fear and loathing of the Jews. The American press abounded with articles and editorials about the immigration issue highlighting the widespread opinion that, according to *Harper's Weekly* in 1902, "these immigrants make very undesirable additions to our heterogeneous population."[8] Public officials, journalists, and commentators offered numerous statements about Jews as criminals, prostitutes, radicals, and subversives. Such rhetoric played a formative role in shaping the Jews' political behavior, which reflected a high level of insecurity over going public with their concerns and their specifically Jewish agenda.

These episodic bursts of political anti-Semitism never went beyond the local scene and therefore did not constitute a sustained and successful anti-Jewish political tradition. The most overtly anti-immigrant political party in the history of the United States, the Know-Nothings, had nothing to say about Jews. Rather, they focused on Catholics, the Irish in particular, as the nation's enemy bent on destroying American freedom. Some Jews actually belonged to the Know-Nothings, and even as a relatively successful third party, it launched no challenge to the Jews' comfort level in America.

Because no one party stood for or against the Jews, American Jews evinced no pronounced loyalty or aversion to any particular party. Both major parties attempted to present themselves to Jewish voters as friends, and in turn Jews responded positively to being wooed. In the early twentieth century both Democrats and Republicans took strong stands condemning, for example, the pogroms breaking out in czarist Russia. They made sure that Jewish voters in the large cities, New York in particular, knew that they and their party abhorred the Russian brutality.[9]

Democratic and Republican presidents also found opportunities to make visible appointments of Jews to prestigious posts. Republican Theodore Roosevelt, for example, eager to show the world the increasing diplomatic panache of the United States, reported mischievously that by appointing Oscar Straus as the American representative to the arbitration court at The Hague he wanted "to show Russia what we think of the Jews in this country."[10] Likewise, Democrat Woodrow Wilson took a serious political risk by naming Louis Brandeis to the Supreme Court, both because he was a Jew and because of his unpopular views. In 1916 the *American Hebrew* reported that as a result of his unswerving support for Brandeis, Wilson captured the majority of the supposedly nonexistent "Jewish vote."[11]

Only in the 1920s did Jewish voters—now including women—come to be clearly identified with the Democratic party, particularly with its urban, labor-oriented, liberal wing. But even then, while a majority voted for Democratic candidates, of the eleven Jews elected to the U.S. Congress, ten came from the Republican Party. The only non-Republican was Meyer London, who affiliated with the Socialist party. Only in 1922 did any Democrats begin to show up in the Jewish congressional delegation.

Second, Jews in America were politically protected by the reality that both parties had to court a diverse electorate, divided by religion, national origins, region, and class. The complex nature of the white male population forced politicians seeking office to court a mixed clientele and, as much as possible, to avoid overtly offending any potential group of voters. Particularly in places where specific immigrant groups clustered, those holding and seeking office expressed solidarity with homeland causes, visited ethnic neighborhoods, and met with community leaders. Political patronage also tended to bring immigrant men and their sons into the arms of one party or another, and both presented themselves as the friend of whatever group of voters they needed to woo. This dynamic tended to mute ideological distinctions and to transform the political machinery into a kind of ethnic brokerage system. Jews took their place under the broad umbrella of American politics and benefited from the fact that the parties and their operatives faced an ethnic mélange in which Jews did not so dramatically differ from the German, Polish, Irish, Italian, Hungarian, and other ethnic constituencies whose votes counted.

Jews Hold Office

But no such delegation ever formed. Whether they were Republicans, Democrats, or Socialists, Jews in public office did not organize themselves into any kind of ethnic association for the purpose of articulating a common platform. They did not meet as a caucus determined to speak with a single Jewish voice. Yet the fact that Jews did hold political office, both elected and appointed, wherever they settled indicated much about their place in the world of politics. In cities of every size and in small towns serving as the mercantile hubs of agricultural areas, Jewish men took advantage of political opportunities. Particularly in small communities at their early stages of economic development, Jewish men, most of whom made a living as merchants, stepped forward to help govern their communities.

In every region Jews served on county boards, city councils, school boards, and in state legislatures. Some became mayors, governors, and members of Congress. In 1851 Samuel Hirshl successfully ran for town council in Davenport, Iowa, as a member of the newly formed Republican party. The local newspaper commented dryly, "Mr. H. is a well known citizen and property holder and no doubt will make an excellent officer." Morris Goodman sat on Los Angeles's first city council, while by 1880 Portland, Oregon, had already elected two Jewish mayors, Bernard Goldsmith and Philip Wasserman.[12] In 1900 both the Republican and Democratic parties ran Jewish mayoral candidates. The candidate who lost in that election ran for governor in 1911. As early as 1910, just two decades after the first Jews had settled in Stamford, Connecticut, voters elected one of them to the state legislature and two others as justices of the peace. Two years later a Jew from Stamford ran for statewide office and became the secretary of state.[13]

From 1820 through 1920 Jews also showed up as loyal party operatives, as men devoted to the business of politics. Emanuel B. Hart played a crucial role in New York City's Tammany Hall, the heart of Gotham's Democratic party machinery, and in 1832 he had been a major campaigner in Andrew Jackson's presidential bid. A number of Chicago Jewish men organized monster public rallies for the fledgling Republican party in the late 1850s, and as a result of their ardent support for the party, one benefited handsomely from the patronage system and secured a very comfortable political position. He was Abraham Kohn, an immigrant from Bavaria, who had opened a clothing store in Chicago in 1843 and had become so deeply woven into the fabric of local business and Republican politics that by 1860, Mayor John Wentworth named him city clerk. One Illinois politician making his way to Washington in early 1861 stopped by Kohn's store to thank him for his political work and to pay homage to him. Kohn presented the newly elected president, Abraham Lincoln, with a flag that he himself had embroidered with the phrase, in Hebrew and English, "be strong and of great courage."[14]

The Role of Socialism

The fact that both the Democrats and, after the mid-1850s, the Republicans courted the Jews meant that even the small number of votes coming from Jewish men mattered. Additionally, after the beginning of the twentieth century, the emergence of a Socialist presence among immigrant Jews, particularly in New York, made the large Jewish vote there even more contested. While Socialism did not truly challenge the political status quo on the national or state level, in New York City elections its powerful appeal to immigrant Jewish voters meant that the other two parties had to try even harder than usual to win over neighborhoods like the Lower East Side. In 1914 the nine Jews who served in the state assembly included seven Republicans, no Democrats, and two Socialists. To make inroads in the city's Jewish enclaves, Tammany Hall, the Democratic machine, had to play to Jewish sensibilities and adopt some Socialist rhetoric. Tammany politicians like Charles Murphy and Al Smith realized that to keep Jews from voting Socialist required not only patronage but also some serious grappling with the moral issues raised by the Socialists. The Democrats, to woo the Jews, had to address some of the key issues concerning Jewish voters. After the horrific 1911 Triangle Shirt Waist Fire, for example, New York City Democrats began to respond to workers' calls for factory inspection. Essentially, the Democrats wanted to convince the city's Jewish voters that they had something to offer.[15]

The powerful role of Socialism in Jewish immigrant communities made Jewish politics more than just a mirror of American politics. That Jewish voters in New York elected Meyer London to Congress three times—in 1914, 1916, and 1920—testified to the diversity of political sensibilities in the immigrant community. In the 1910s and 1920s Jewish districts in New York City elected ten state assemblymen, a municipal judge, and seven alderman. Nationally, New York City provided Socialist candidates with almost half their votes, and most of those votes came from Jews. Additionally, Jewish labor organizations like the International Ladies Garment Workers Union, the Amalgamated Clothing Workers, the Cap and Hat Workers, as well as the umbrella United Hebrew Trades, with a membership of over two hundred and fifty thousand in 1917, took their tone from the Socialist affiliation of their rank-and-file members and leaders.[16]

Partly because of the Socialist ethos, Jewish politics in America transcended the horse-trading associated with the nation's practical, nonideological politics. But Jewish politics went even beyond the vision of the Socialists who waged political campaigns for economic justice. Rather, for a group of people who saw themselves as a distinct minority in their new home, as bearers of a religious tradition that sometimes posed problems for the Christian majority, and as those who had taken on themselves the obligation to help their coreligionists around the world, their politics reflected their consciousness as Jews. They developed a distinctive American Jewish political strategy by which they sought to ensure their place at home and to fulfill their responsibilities to the Jewish people abroad, even as they claimed, like Leeser, that they had no particular Jewish political agenda.[17]

AMERICAN POLITICS, JEWISH POLITICS

The election of 1868, which fell just about halfway through the great century of Jewish migration to America, offers a case in point. It demonstrated how American Jews sought to negotiate and use politics, despite their public rhetoric. It also showed how political participation became a vehicle for fulfilling Jewish goals.

Ulysses S. Grant, the Republican candidate in 1868, had a Jewish problem. In 1862, as a general in the Civil War, he had issued Order Number 11, an edict that classified all Jews in the "department of the Tennessee" as profiteers and ordered their expulsion within twenty-four hours. But for Abraham Lincoln's intercession, the result both of the visit of a delegation of Kentucky Jews led by Cesar Kaskel and of Jewish protest around the country, the Jews would have been forcibly evicted from the region. Chillingly reminiscent of their centuries-long history of victimization, of being collectively accused of some misdeed, and of enduring banishment at the whim of an official, Jews reacted with fear and determination to counter Grant's edict.[18]

Memory of that incident lingered, and in 1868 Jewish men divided over the appropriate electoral response to Grant's candidacy. Some publicly echoed Leeser's words. One letter appeared in the *Illinois Staatszeitung,* reprinted in the *Missouri Democrat,* commented on how Jews should best use their vote: "I am a Jew, when Saturday, the seventh day, comes; I am one on my holidays; in the selection and treatment of my food; it was always written on the doorposts. But when I . . . take a ballot in order to exercise my rights as a citizen. Then I am not a Jew, but I feel and vote as a citizen of the republic, I do not ask what pleases the Israelites."[19]

Others, however, expressed disgust at the prospect of Jews voting for Grant, stating that doing so would be akin to the behavior of those "who lick the feet that kick them about and like dogs, run after him who has whipped them." Isaac Mayer Wise, an Ohioan Democrat, noted that "none in this nineteenth century in civilized countries has abused and outraged the Jew" worse than Grant. Many, like Wise, believed that Jews had an obligation to stand up for themselves and help defeat the evildoer.[20]

Still others, like Simon Wolf, an official of the B'nai B'rith and the Union of American Hebrew Congregations, a lobbyist for Jewish rights at home and abroad and a lifelong friend of Grant's from Ohio, actively supported the Republican candidate. The election proved to be very close, and the former general understood that every vote had counted. For his support, and in line with the widespread cronyism typical of this era, Wolf received a fine political plum, the position of recorder of deeds for the District of Columbia. In fact, Grant went out of his way during his administration to demonstrate his friendship to the Jews. Despite their small number, Grant tried to cultivate, through Wolf, a better relationship with those who still remembered Order Number 11. In 1876 Grant attended the consecration of Washington D.C.'s traditional synagogue, the Adas Israel Congregation, the last year of his second term. His presence, duly reported by the local press, demonstrated the respectability achieved by the Jews as an American religious community and their growing presence in the American polity. Grant may have been remembered as the author of Order Number 11. But he can also be cited as the first president to enter a synagogue and witness the rituals and rites of Judaism.

He did so at a time when Christian evangelicals had begun to mount a massive campaign to "rechristianize America." Among the evangelicals a movement was afoot to change the wording of the preamble of the Constitution to read "We, the people of the United States, humbly acknowledging Almighty God as the source of all authority and power in civil government, the Lord Jesus Christ as the Rule among the nations, his revealed will as the supreme law of the land, in order to constitute a Christian government." On a number of other cultural and political fronts, including the issues of school prayer and the reading of the King James version of the Bible, as well as mandatory Sunday closings of businesses, militant Protestantism made religion a hot political issue.[21] By sitting in the pews of a traditional synagogue and standing with the congregation in the presence of Torah scrolls, Grant had made a statement about Judaism as an acceptable part of the American religious mosaic.

Grant's interest in wooing the Jews, however, went further than this ceremonial moment. As Grant's go-between to the Jews, Wolf played a crucial role in bringing to the president's attention the plight of the Jews of Romania. The dire circumstances of these Jews, who were suffering nearly as much as their sisters and brothers in czarist lands, became the focus of the world's concerns about the Jews. Nudged by Wolf, Grant made an unprecedented diplomatic move. He named a leader of the B'nai B'rith, Benjamin Franklin Peixotto, as the U.S. consul to Bucharest. The letter, fixed with the president's signature, that Peixotto carried with him could not have been clearer about the political fruits of American Jews' political engagement. Dated December 8, 1870, it read: "The bearer of this letter, Mr. Benjamin Peixotto . . . has accepted the important, though unremunerative position of U.S. Consul to Roumania. . . . Mr. Peixotto has undertaken the duties of his present office . . . as a missionary work for the benefit of the people he represents—a work in which all citizens will wish him the greatest success."[22]

Being appointed by the president to speak for the United States in international matters made Peixotto primarily a representative of the American people. Yet Wolf's intercession, as a result of the troubling reports of Jewish suffering in Romania, made it equally evident that Peixotto also represented the Jewish people. At the same time, then, Peixotto served a universal, American public and a specific, Jewish one. Reflecting much of American Jewish politics from 1820 through 1924, his mission straddled the American and the Jewish. Jewish politics, in fact, involved constructing a strategy by which the Jews could serve the latter in the name of the former. In advocating for their coreligionists, they simultaneously acted locally and globally—serving both the cause of Jews at home and of those around the world.

The Advantages of Being White

In this era American Jewish engagement in politics was influenced by a number of factors. First, Jews were white. While during this century Judaism would at times be regarded as alien to the Christian core of American culture, and Jewish people would be stigmatized for what many considered essential racial traits—greed, depravity, crudeness, and clannishness—their right, as white men, to be part of the polity never came into serious question. Although some raised questions about whether Jews really could be classified as white, at no point did any political movement seek to take from Jews their entitlement to citizenship and the other benefits enjoyed by white men such as voting, holding office, and serving on juries. They could expect and demand the protection of the state in matters involving their personal safety, their legal status, and their ability to move about freely and transact their business affairs.

After the 1880s as a racialized view of Jews among some Americans was on the rise, certain rights became compromised. Jews lost their access to certain posh resorts and hotels. They could not occupy teaching posts at some elite colleges and could not be employed in prestigious law firms and certain hospitals. Yet notably in this era (and until the late 1940s) these kinds of restrictions stood outside the law. Government—federal, state, or local—maintained a hands-off policy on these matters and allowed private employers and institutions to determine whatever policies they wanted. As such these discriminatory practices functioned beyond the scope of politics. Furthermore, the spread of this social anti-Semitism stopped at the gates of government.

Despite the discomfort caused by these practices, the Jews' political rights remained untrammeled, and their political influence only grew. It is interesting to note that as a more popularly disseminated rhetoric of racialized anti-Semitism spread, increasing numbers of Jews entered politics as candidates, office holders, and party leaders.[23]

This experience stands in stark contrast to the political history of African Americans, who began this century as slaves with no rights, let alone the full privileges of political participation, and ended it as a largely disenfranchised group, living under the shadow of lynching. Jewish politics in America continued to be predicated on the fact that Jews could exercise their constitutional rights at all times and could expect to be protected. Jews did not have to "become" white.[24] The experience of the Jews, as white immigrants, also ran a far different course from that of the Chinese, who in 1882 were explicitly forbidden to enter the United States. This exclusion offers a glaring example of how the American political system dealt with nonwhite ethnic groups. In contrast to the experience of the Chinese and other ethnic groups, Jews endured small acts and limited episodes of political marginalization.

In further contrast, the minor disabilities endured by a small number of Jews stemmed from their religion and not their perceived racial difference. In the decades after the 1820s and ending with the passage of the Fourteenth Amendment, a few states, holdovers from the earlier era, continued to use religion as a test for officeholding. Yet since few Jews lived in either New Hampshire or North Carolina, where these disabilities persisted the longest, these restrictions affected very few people and faded by the 1870s. A profession of Christianity, an oath taken on a Christian version of the Bible, automatically wiped away these disabilities in these isolated places. While few Jews chose this route, the existence of this option demonstrated the profoundly religious origins of their limitations. And as penalties for Jewishness these disabilities appeared particularly weak when compared to the limitations suffered by Jews outside the United States.

DEFENDING JUDAISM

Additionally, the religious qualification for officeholding that limited Jewish participation did not exist in the context of any other abuse—

legal, social, religious, or physical—of the Jews. In politics, Jews found themselves essentially forced to negotiate for Judaism as a religious system. At its core, public policy privileged Christianity and made Christian practice and institutions the norm to which other religions—Judaism—had to accommodate. Particularly through the 1880s, Jews sought to ensure that the government extended to Judaism the same benefits that it did to the majority faith. For example, the small Jewish community that formed in the nation's capital in the early 1850s had to contend with an act of Congress allowing for the conveyance of property to the trustees of churches.

The Jews found this act offensive. They had no way of knowing whether Congress had intended to slight Judaism when it legislated in 1844 or whether the fact that no Jewish congregation existed in the District of Columbia had shaped the congressional language. The Jews who did gather in the early 1850s to form the Washington Hebrew Congregation turned to Jonas P. Levy, a naval officer, Mexican War hero, and a visible political player in national politics, to intercede on their behalf. Levy obliged, and in 1856, with little debate or fanfare, Congress passed an "Act for the benefit of the Hebrew Congregation of the City of Washington." Despite the fact that the Jews in the District of Columbia had needed a well-placed intermediary to appeal to Congress, this incident demonstrated the degree to which a small religious community needed to learn to navigate the nation's political waters to defend their system.[25]

Across the country, synagogues, cemeteries, charitable societies, orphanages, nursing homes, schools, and other building-block institutions of communal life had to become incorporated. Not only did this process require that Jews know the political system and befriend key players, but it also made Jewish political participation, particularly on the local level, essential to sustaining Jewish life. While nearly all the funding for these institutions came from the pockets of the Jews themselves, public money also often sustained them. In newly formed western towns, legislatures and town councils at times made outright grants of land to synagogues and cemeteries, and in New York and other big cities, Jewish charitable projects were supported by public monies. The Hebrew Benevolent Society of New York financed its building, in part, with city and state funds. Additionally, courts remanded children in distress to Jewish orphanages and provided funds for their upkeep. Since American Jews defined *gemilat hesed*—acts of loving-kindness—as a core religious ritual of no less gravity than attending synagogue services (indeed, many would have said that it exceeded public worship in importance), then the degree to which the government helped make such projects possible entwined Jews in the web of politics.[26]

At times the political defense of Jewish practice became more overt. Jews sometimes found themselves in an uncomfortable position when an arm of the state limited their ability to practice Judaism. They faced such situations by marshaling their political capital to undo the religious discrimination. Few events demonstrated this dynamic more clearly than the issue of Civil War chaplaincy and the role of religion in the armed forces.

In July 1861 Congress passed an act that provided for "regularly ordained ministers" of "some Christian denomination" to serve as chaplains to the troops. The Young Men's Christian Association administered the chaplaincy, and YMCA workers visited the various army camps to ensure the proper conduct of the soldiers' religious affairs. Jewish soldiers in the Union army tended to cluster in particular regiments, and some expressed a preference for a Jewish religious presence on or near the bloody battlegrounds.

In 1862 the men of the Sixty-fifth Regiment of the Fifth Pennsylvania Cavalry, commanded by one Colonel Max Friedman, voted for Sergeant Michael Allen as their chaplain. Allen, a Hebrew teacher, had two strikes against him. He could not have been considered "regularly ordained," although he had briefly studied for the rabbinate. (No rabbinical seminaries existed yet in America, and few men could spend a lengthy period of time in Europe preparing for ordination.) But an even greater liability encumbered him. Allen clearly did not represent any Christian denomination. When the YMCA field-worker discovered the violation, Allen faced a dishonorable discharge.

The regiment persisted. On a second try, it voted on Arnold Fischel from New York's Shearith Israel, who could claim to have been ordained. Fischel dutifully applied to the War Department, which quickly rejected him. Rabbis and members of the Jewish press reacted to this rebuff. They saw it as an affront to Judaism and to the Jews, claiming that Jewish men wearing the uniform of the United States "have the same right, according to the constitution of the U.S., which they endeavor to preserve and defend with all their might."[27] It took nearly a year of protest, but in September 1862 Jacob Frankel became the first Jew to serve as a commissioned chaplain in the United States Army.

American Jews waged a constant battle as they asserted the rights of a minority religious community in a society that on the one hand separated church and state and on the other increasingly prided itself on its fundamentally Christian character. Matters such as mandatory Sunday business closings, Christian ritual in public schools, as well as the threat of adding a religious amendment to the U.S. Constitution, dominated the American Jewish political agenda of the last part of the nineteenth century. Out of their engagement with these issues, American Jews crafted a political position that demanded a strict interpretation of the constitutional principle of separation of church and state. Jews understood that any official reference to "religion" as a positive and elevating force in the life of the nation actually meant "Christianity," and that even small and seemingly innocuous religious ceremonies in public life posed a threat to their religious freedom.

Ironically, then, a good deal of American Jews' political vision emerged in their increasingly vocal calls for the greater secularization of America. Rabbinic bodies like the Central Conference of American Rabbis, despite their deep commitment to the salience of religion in organizing and conceptualizing Jewish life, boldly stated that America must evolve into a secular and religiously neutral society. In 1906 the CCAR published a pamphlet entitled *Why the Bible Should Not Be Read in the Public Schools* and distributed it wherever Jews found themselves locked in political battles over public school Bible reading.[28] Reform rabbis hardly opposed the Bible, but they believed it was a matter of private religious preference and had no place in the curricula of public schools.

At times the Jewish community as an organized body used politics to defend Judaism, petitioning legislatures and Congress when they saw their practice infringed on. They lectured and wrote, expressing their opinions both in Jewish and general venues. At times they went to court and made their political position quite public. In 1905 in a Brooklyn public school composed predominantly of Jewish children, the principal announced at a Christmas celebration, "I want you all to have the feeling of Christ within you." Angry parents demanded that the administration remove him, and the Union of Orthodox Rabbis hired a lawyer to represent the irate families. Although it took a lengthy Jewish boycott to bring about the principal's ouster, the Jews of this Brooklyn neighborhood learned that politics paid off for a community with an agenda.[29]

The defense of Judaism served as a basic common denominator in American Jewish politics. The fact that religion enjoyed the protection of the Constitution and that national or ethnic groups enjoyed neither constitutional recognition nor entitlement to protection explains in part the tendency of most American Jews to describe themselves as members of a religious group. Nevertheless, Jews were divided about how volubly they ought to engage in that defense. Over time the nature of their political behavior changed. Generally, until the latter part of the nineteenth century, almost all Jews who weighed in on these matters agreed that they should push for strict separation between church and state.

But subsequently some began to believe that increasing anti-Semitism, particularly after the late 1870s, required that they do as little as possible to draw angry public attention to them. On any number of religious issues, they had been doing battle for decades, and their actions had yielded few results, Sunday closing laws being the most dramatic case in point.

By the beginning of the twentieth century the Union of American Hebrew Congregations, which had previously spearheaded protests against any manifestation of Christianity in the public sphere, dropped its battle against blue laws, which forced businesses to close out of respect for the Christians' day of rest. Louis Marshall, a constitutional lawyer, a committed Reform Jew, and one of the key players in American Jewish politics, proposed in New York state that the law stand but that exemptions be made on a case-by-case basis for Sabbath-observing Jews.[30]

DEFENDING THE JEWS

By the end of the nineteenth century, the thrust of American Jewish politics shifted from the defense of Judaism to the defense of the Jews. That change took place partly because Judaism, despite Sunday closings and Christian evangelicals, had in fact come to be ensconced in America as an acceptable, if unusual, religion. Similarly, American public culture increasingly secularized and made room for people and practices removed from the scope of religion. Movies, public entertainment like vaudeville, advertising, organized sports—baseball in particular—and mass-market magazines represented neutral spheres where Jews could participate independent of their religion. But the change also took place because, by that time, in America as in England, France, and the rest of Europe, the Jews as a group had come to be imagined as a defective people whose moral and mental capacities reflected their essential natures.[31]

The discourse on Jews in the American popular press, while never articulated in a single voice, was taking a decidedly racist turn. A steady stream of articles in some of the most respected and most widely circulated publications asked such questions as, "Will the Jews Ever Lose their Racial Identity?" and, "Are the Jews an Inferior Race?" The answer to the first was decidedly no, while the second was answered in the affirmative.[32] The newly emerging social sciences pondered similar issues.

One of the founders of sociology, the University of Wisconsin's E. A. Ross, asserted that all Jews had a fixed temperament or character. Ross and other social scientists of the late nineteenth and early twentieth century envisioned humankind as divided into a number of fixed racial typologies. They thought of "Italians," "Slavs," "Irish" (or "Celts"), "Teutons," "Asiatics," and high-status "Anglo-Saxons" as coherent social and, more important, biological groups. Jews, sometimes called "Hebrews" or "Semites," took their—lowly—place in the racial cosmos. Even when praising their great intellect, race thinkers attributed it to their essential Jewish nature.[33]

Beginning in the late 1870s, the sources of this anti-Semitic language, and the deeds that accompanied such speech, emanated from a number of seemingly contradictory sources. Some anti-Semitism resulted from the fact that American ideas and attitudes functioned within a transnational intellectual context; American writers, thinkers, and shapers of public opinion read many of the same journals and books that circulated in Europe, the seed bed of this kind of thinking. Many American social scientists had received their training in Germany and England and functioned as part of an academic culture, attending conferences, for example, at which they could hear papers on the fixed nature of racial typologies and the inherent depravity of the Jews.

But domestic forces came into play as well. Some of the racialized rhetoric about Jews came from American elites, the native-born white Protestants who fretted over the incursion of Jews into their communities. The 1877 decision of the Grand Union Hotel in Saratoga Springs, New York, to refuse accommodations to Joseph Seligman, a Jewish millionaire, exemplified one type of anti-Semitism in evidence.

Yet the elites were not the only source of anti-Jewish talk. Poor farmers in the South and Midwest who faced first the devastation unleashed in the aftermath of the Panic of 1873 and then the even worse Panic of 1893, short but devastating depressions, found comfort in blaming the Jews for their travails. Some Populists believed that Jews made up a class of international financiers whose policies had ruined small family farms. Jews, they asserted, owned the banks and promoted the gold standard, the chief sources of their impoverishment. Agrarian radicalism posited the city as antithetical to American values, asserting that Jews were the essence of urban corruption.[34]

In the 1890s marauding bands viciously beat a number of Jewish storekeepers in the rural South. At least one Mississippian justified the attacks by saying, "the accursed Jews and others own two thirds of our land."[35] The legacy of rural anti-Semitism, born out of Populist protests, laid the groundwork for the notorious Leo Frank case. In 1913, Frank, a young northern Jewish businessman who managed a pencil factory in Atlanta, was arrested on the charges of raping and murdering a young girl who worked in his factory. Despite the flimsiness of the evidence, the jury found Frank guilty and sentenced him to death. The governor of Georgia, troubled by numerous evidentiary and procedural problems with the state's case, commuted the sentence to life in prison. This 1915 decision did not, however, find favor in the eyes of an inflamed band of white Christian Georgians, who dragged Leo Frank out of jail and hanged him. At the site of his hanging, the Ku Klux Klan, which would play a key role in American politics in the 1920s, came into being.[36] Yet despite the rumblings of anti-Jewish rhetoric among some Populists, the official party they created, the People's Party, never appealed to voters with an anti-Semitic plank in its platform.

Some anti-Jewish rhetoric flowed from the pens of the muckrakers, the Progressive Era journalists who sought to expose the evils of industrial capitalism and the horrors of America's urban poverty. They too fixed on the Jews and their racial traits as the source of corruption. Probably no piece of progressive anti-Jewish rhetoric made as much a stir as George Kibbe Turner's "Daughters of the Poor" in the popular muckraking magazine *McClure's* in 1909. In this article Turner declared that eastern European Jews in New York City, and around the world, controlled the apparatus of prostitution. According to Turner, not only did Jewish women swell the ranks of New York's prostitutes, but Jewish men worldwide were running the "white slave" trade as pimps and procurers. Turner's exposé proved so persuasive that in 1910 Congress passed the Mann Act prohibiting the transport of women for immoral purposes across state lines.[37]

In 1908 New York City's police commissioner, Theodore Bingham, added to the public discourse about the defects of the Jews and their deleterious impact on urban life. He reported that immigrant Jews, although only one-quarter of the city's population, made up half of its criminals. "Of that race," noted Bingham, in an article in the *North American Review,* "the men [are] not physically fit for hard labor. . . . they are burglars, firebugs, pickpockets and highway robbers . . . though all crime is their province."[38]

The more white Americans represented them as a race, the more skittish Jews became about how best to project themselves publicly. In the United States race mattered terribly in that it determined one's access to

basic civil rights and access to education, housing, and political influence. It determined the degree to which people could expect to receive
basic protection of their persons. In 1903 and 1907 the government
added "Hebrew" to the national and racial classification system used to
track immigrants arriving in the United States. This put American Jews
in a quandary. They knew that being Jewish meant much more than participating in a set of religious rituals. The Jews understood that according to their own texts they constituted a people with links to others in
their group, both past and present. But they worried that emphasis on
peoplehood compromised their American options. They did not want to
be viewed, certainly in matters of public policy, as a distinct race.[39]

The political project of American Jews in the latter half of the century
of migration took its basic form from their awareness of the spread of
anti-Jewish rhetoric and the increasing tendency for the discourse to be
acted on. They sought ways to make their case but remained ever conscious of the smallness of their numbers, sensing that just below the surface of American society lay a dangerously large reservoir of antipathy.
One Springfield, Illinois, Jew, Samuel Rosenwald, wrote to relatives in
Germany in 1881 in response to their query about the status of Jews in
America: "I quite forgot," he noted, "that you wanted to be exactly informed about the Jewish question, although there is not much *Rischus*
[literally evil, but in this context, hatred of the Jews] here, yet we are not
on the same level with the Christians. . . . In business one hardly ever
hears anything like that, but the children often hear about it, and that is
unpleasant enough."[40]

Although the Jews embraced America as a place with "not much
Rischus," they knew that it did exist and that they needed to marshal
some measure of vigilance. Americans, even those who seemed to accept
them, were still Christians who had been nurtured in a tradition that fostered animosity toward Jews. How loudly and in which venues the Jews
spoke out about their treatment always involved a complex alchemy of
fear of "rocking the boat" and the belief that to achieve a desired political end they had to cultivate relationships with those holding power and
influence. They weighed and measured anti-Semitic incidents and debated their pervasiveness, seriousness, and threat. They compared their
lot with that of Jews in Europe and of other Americans who fared much
worse. American Jews realized that although they needed to couch their
arguments in terms that would win over American sympathy, at the
same time they considered the necessity of standing up for their basic
rights.

Some responded to their anxiety by attempting to prove to Americans that Jews did not constitute an alien force. They sought to document the length of Jewish roots in America and the degree to which America had benefited from the Jews' presence. To that end, in 1892 such Jewish community notables as Oscar Straus and Cyrus Adler helped to organize the American Jewish Historical Society. Dedicated to using history as a weapon in the defense of the Jews, the Society and its publications included such articles as Simon Wolf's "The American Jew as Soldier and Patriots." Jews, the articles claimed, had been in America since its earliest days and had contributed both to the growth of its economy and to its democracy. One observer who attended the founding meeting of the Society, which had been held at the Jewish Theological Seminary, predicted—or expressed hope, anyway—that the activities of these amateur historians would "eliminate whatever prejudice lingers against the Jews."[41]

PHILANTHROPY AS POLITICAL RESPONSE

Many others hoped that the prejudice would evaporate if the Jews transformed themselves. In the many programs that Jewish women and men created to help newly arriving Jewish immigrants, the culture of anxiety became manifest. Many Jews reasoned that the more quickly newcomers could be made respectable, the less ammunition the critics of the Jews could use against them. They created a vast social service effort that blended core ideals of Jewish communal obligation with the very contemporary politically charged need to present a positive portrait of Jews.

Americanization of the immigrants ranked high on the American Jewish political agenda. The massive effort by Jewish charitable societies and schools to usher the new immigrants into American ways represented a political response to anti-Jewish sentiment in America. Many believed that the more Jews, immigrants in particular, acted in a manner that seemed to conform to popular racial stereotypes—that Jews are emotional, disputatious, greedy, clannish, dirty—the more all Jews would suffer. The progress the community had made and the respectability it had acquired could be easily lost. Latent hostility could easily be activated.

Running the gamut from teaching English to Yiddish speakers to teaching immigrants a useful trade, from cajoling Jewish employers and Jewish employees in the garment trade to come to terms with each other to helping immigrant Jews without work move out of New York and into small towns and farming communities, all attempts at group transformation had behind them the urgency of political anxiety. Each endeavor combined a sense of Jewish concern for those among them in need and panic over the rise of anti-Semitism, both actual and potential.

Where Jewish service left off and fears about the "alienness" of the immigrants began became blurred in this myriad of philanthropic activities. In the 1890s, for example, the Atlanta Hebrew Ladies' Benevolent Society, an offshoot of the city's Reform congregation, provided food, coal, clothing, and temporary housing to new immigrants. It offered them direct cash when needed as well as cooking and English lessons to hasten their integration. Women at New York's Shearith Israel congregation created an Oriental Committee, which set up a settlement house at 86 Orchard Street, deep in the heart of the city's Jewish immigrant enclave. Here they offered classes and services, including English lessons, to the new Jewish immigrants coming from the Ottoman Empire. In both the Atlanta project and the "Oriental" one in New York, the ties of Jewish kinship became bound with the deepening concern that poor foreign Jews would overwhelm America and in the process arouse greater anti-Jewish sentiment.

Formal institutions, well funded and employing professional staffs to assist in Americanizing immigrants, emerged as clear political projects of the 1890s. Although for decades assisting new immigrants and the poor in general had been a central element of American Jewish communal life, in the last decade of the nineteenth century these endeavors became better organized, more highly financed, and more extensive. Not coincidentally, during this time Congress passed the first piece of restrictive immigration legislation. This decade of worldwide depression had impoverished many Americans, making them less charitable to the flood of newcomers. It had also witnessed the emergence of anti-Jewish populism and the founding of the Immigration Restriction League.

Created in Boston in 1894, the League represented the efforts of an old New England elite that believed the nation could not cope with free, open, and relatively unregulated immigration. The Immigration Restriction League espoused a simple solution: "keep America for the Americans."[42] For Jews the simplicity of the message and the prestige of the founders, all graduates of Harvard and descendants of long-standing New England families, complicated their lives and jeopardized the transfer of the Jews from the perils of Europe to the opportunities of America. The American Jewish reaction to domestic threats therefore tended to be low-key and often involved self-improvement rather than an attempt to change Americans.

Reaching Out to Other Jewish Communities

At the same time that they sought to remake themselves, American Jews had another political project: succoring the Jews of other diaspora communities. Just as their domestic agenda became more complicated in the last quarter of the nineteenth century, so too did their foreign-policy strategies. Until then American Jews, along with the Jews of England and France, the other emancipated communities, had lobbied for the protection of Jews in distress. The objects of their concern—the Jews of Italy and of Damascus—lived and suffered in places where American Jews had no family members or personal connections. In some ways this kind of lobbying took place on an altruistic level. But starting in the 1870s the source of their anxiety shifted to precisely the places where they had kin, where many of them had left, and whose Jews sought to leave for the United States. Thus a blurry line at best separated the defense of Jewish rights abroad and the issue of immigration.

Since the 1840s American Jews had seen themselves as a community enjoying the fruits of a democratic society, a fact that made them feel responsible for Jews who suffered elsewhere, especially in places where Jews had few rights. In 1840 American Jews participated in a transatlantic Jewish effort to rescue a group of Jews in Damascus, Syria, who had been accused by Ottoman officials of kidnapping a Catholic priest and his servant. The rumor, which circulated throughout the city, went even further. Word had it that the Jews had killed the two Christians and used their blood to bake Passover matzo, the centuries-old blood libel.

In response, the Syrian government rounded up some Jewish notables and children. After being subjected to torture, they "confessed" to the truth of the accusation. This inspired officials to round up even more Jews, and seventy-two of them faced death sentences. In addition, the government claimed that up to thirty thousand Jews had been complicitous in the heinous crime. Although Jews in western Europe had organized two months before Jews in America did, when the Jews of the United States joined in the protest, they mounted a vigorous and highly public effort. They staged rallies in nearly every American city with a Jewish presence and called on Christian clergymen and politicians to speak out in condemnation of what they saw as a barbarous relic of medieval ignorance. They called on President Martin Van Buren to "use every possible effort to induce the Pasha of Egypt to manifest more liberal treatment towards his Jewish subjects." Jews couched their protest in the distinctively Jewish trope of citizenship. Leeser, for example, noted:

> As citizens, we belong to the country we live in; but as believers in one God . . . as the inheritors of the Law . . . we hail the Israelite as a brother, no matter if his home be the torrid zone or where the poles encircle the earth . . . oceans may intervene between our dispersed remnants . . . mountains may divide us, but the Israelite is ever alive to the welfare of his distant brother, and sorrows with his sorrows, and rejoices in his joy.

They then claimed as U.S. citizens the right to address their government and to expect a hearing, but they did so in the name of their "dispersed remnants."

Newly inaugurated President William Henry Harrison already had sent a stern rebuke to Ottoman officials, but he did take note of the Jewish protest. Secretary of State David Porter wrote to the American minister in Turkey, telling him again "to do everything in your power with . . . the Sultan . . . to prevent and mitigate these horrors . . . the 'persecution and spoliation' of Jews in 'Mahomedan dominions.' "[43]

That the United States meddled in the internal affairs of the Ottomans represented one element of a larger mission, namely, to make it clear to the European powers that America should be considered a player on the world stage. Diplomatic action on behalf of the Jews of Damascus allowed the United States to indicate its level of progressive civilization as a nation, which made "no distinction between the Mahomedan, the Jew, and the Christian," according to the secretary of state.

For the Jews, the Damascus affair launched modern Jewish politics on an international scale, and for American Jews it represented their first effort at creating a distinctive political agenda. Just as the United States had used this affair to proclaim its presence on the global stage, so too did American Jews, in their newspapers and at mass meetings, announce to their coreligionists in France and England that they too ought to be thought of as players in global Jewish diplomacy.[44]

During the next eighty years, culminating in the massive American Jewish relief effort on behalf of the Jews of central and eastern Europe after World War I, American Jewry followed the pattern set by the Damascus affair. They rallied as Jews and went out of their way to include sympathetic non-Jews in their efforts. They met and petitioned government officials, sending delegations to presidents, senators, and officials in the State Department, crafting an argument that by acting on behalf of Jews abroad, they were behaving like good Americans. While they did not always succeed in getting the ear of government officials and did not always achieve the desired results, their strategies rarely changed.

Sometimes, despite their numbers, their protests fell flat. In 1858 American Jews again gathered in protest when they heard of a Jewish child in Bologna, Italy, named Edgardo Mortara who had been secretly baptized by his Catholic governess. Because the church and state considered the six-year-old a Christian, Vatican police took him from his home, decreeing that he should not be raised by Jewish parents. In New York City alone two thousand Jews attended a rally. They begged President Buchanan to behave as his predecessor had and to pressure Pope Pius IX to release the boy and to revoke his baptism. Buchanan, a Democrat who relied heavily on the votes of Irish Catholic immigrants, refused.[45]

This issue resonated deeply with American Jews. Aside from their firm belief that Jews bore a responsibility to each other, they feared the aggressive actions of Christian missionaries at home. Many proselytizers prowled hospitals and tried to talk the sick and dying into making deathbed confessions. In the same year as the Mortara case, a Jewish patient in a St. Louis Catholic hospital received an unwanted baptism.[46] Undeterred by their lack of success in the Mortara affair, the Jews aproached the State Department in 1863 on behalf of Jews in North Africa. Secretary of State William Seward met with them and complied with the request of a delegation of Jews who had come to him asking that the offices of the United States be enlisted to help the Jews of Morocco, who had been enduring a seemingly endless cycle of physical attacks, expulsions, and other repressive measures.[47]

The Jews who constructed this foreign-policy strategy worked on the assumption that as their numbers grew no party would take their votes for granted. Both parties hoped to appeal to Jewish voters, and as such Jews could reasonably expect some satisfaction from the government when they pled their fellow Jews' case. They believed that if they met with the right officials, showed their deep patriotism as Americans, and behaved respectably, they could prevail. As they saw it, no real boundaries separated Jews, no matter where they lived, other than the degree to which they enjoyed the protection of the state. As they saw it, Jews in America had as much responsibility for Jews in Russia or Romania as they did for Jews in their home communities.

They made no clear distinction between domestic and foreign Jewish matters. Indeed, one of the first political encounters between American Jews, the U.S. government, and czarist Russia took place in the early 1880s and involved the right of American Jews traveling in Russia to be treated as Americans. Secretary of State James G. Blaine, as a result of complaints from American Jews journeying in Russia for business, protested vigorously to the Russian government. He threatened to abrogate a favorable trade treaty with Russia, which dated back to 1832, unless Jews with United States citizenship received appropriate treatment instead of being lumped together with Russian Jews.[48]

This protest notwithstanding, most of American Jews' political efforts on behalf of Jews in distress abroad did not involve the handful of Jewish businessmen who met discrimination in czarist lands. Rather, from the late 1870s on, most American Jews, as measured by the political capital they expended, focused on the increasingly difficult situation of Jews in eastern Europe. Jewish communal leaders and the Jewish press monitored closely the fluctuating condition of eastern European Jewry, noting periods when violence and discrimination peaked and subsided. They consistently maintained a clear agenda: asking the United States government to do what it could to protest abuses and to keep the doors to America open to Jews.

Jewish American leaders like Wolf, Marshall, Oscar Straus, and, most notably, financier Jacob Schiff succeeded in arousing sympathy and getting American governmental officials to attend massive public gatherings highlighting the suffering of the Jews by decrying the barbarity of Russia.[49] During the Russo-Japanese war of 1904–1905 Schiff, hoping to topple the czarist government, floated a loan to Japan of $200,000,000. Schiff not only refused to provide loans to Russia, which had also appealed to his firm, Kuhn, Loeb & Co. but also used his significant influence in the financial world to keep other banking houses from doing so. In their defense of Jews abroad, American Jews like Schiff took a stance marking them as distinctively Jewish and often quite out of step with American public opinion. In 1904, in response to the same war, American Jewry—at least as measured by press coverage—cheered Japan's victory against the Jews' foe. The *American Hebrew* stated:

> It is but the veriest human nature that causes us to exult at the initial victory of Japan over Russia. Aside of the fact that Japan seems to have justice on her side in the conflict that she has precipitated, that Russia, who has defied all the decencies of civilization in her own land, should seek to assume to control territory in the Orient in the name of civilization leads us to hope that she will be brought abjectly to her knees in the present war. Mean-

while, the Jew may hope for some peace in Russia. The revolutionary and socialistic elements there will undoubtedly assert themselves and keep the local authorities busy so that the Jews will be left to breathe freely for the time being.[50]

With this kind of rhetoric, a distinctive Jewish identity asserted itself in America. Most white Americans viewed the Japanese victory over Russia as chilling evidence of the growing "yellow peril." That a European nation could be defeated by an Asian one fed into American hysteria over the tilting balance of power on the Pacific Rim and exacerbated an American sense of the danger it faced in Japan. To American Jews, though, Japan's victory became a cause for celebration, an omen that perhaps Russia might be pushed to change.[51]

Jewish leaders, including financiers like Schiff and lawyers like Marshall, as well as rabbis, publishers, and leaders of organizations, communicated with each other and with Jewish leaders in Europe through a steady stream of cables and letters. Delegations of American Jews made their way to the White House, the halls of Congress, and the offices of the State Department whenever they believed that Jews were in great peril. Sometimes, as in 1904 while Theodore Roosevelt hammered out a treaty between Russia and Japan in Portsmouth, New Hampshire, American Jewish leaders had the opportunity—through the president—to meet directly with the Russian officials.[52] Later, at the end of World War I, when world leaders met in Versailles to contemplate a new map of the world, a delegation of American Jewish notables, held together by Louis Marshall, received the privilege of expressing their views about the needs of the Jewish people. The victory they brought home involved a clause in the peace treaty according civil rights to Jews and other minority groups in Poland, Czechoslovakia, Yugoslavia, Hungary, Romania, and Austria.[53]

Helping World War I Victims

Each crisis, from the Romanian ones of the late 1860s onward, loomed large in the minds of American Jews. But none did more to bring them together than the calamity brought about by World War I. Many issues that had been significant to them—birthplace in Europe, length of time in America, and religious ideology—faded in comparison to the enormity of Jewish suffering.

Jews suffered physically, economically, and politically not just when they got caught in the cross fire between the Axis and the Allies, but particularly in Russia and the eastern parts of the now-dissolving Austro-Hungarian Empire, when they became the targets of widespread murders, rapes, arrests, and expulsions.[54] Intact Jewish communities suddenly received hundreds of thousands of refugees needing immediate food, shelter, and medical care. In May 1915, for example, one hundred thousand Jewish refugees showed up in Warsaw alone, with the elderly, children, and women predominant.[55] The Jewish crisis did not come to an abrupt end with the armistice of November 1918. The civil war brought on by the Russian Revolution and the war between the new Soviet Union and Poland dragged on into the 1920s, and throughout this period, the Jews endured atrocities, seeing their homes, businesses, and lives destroyed.

American Jews responded with open wallets. Philanthropist Julius Rosenwald, owner of Sears Roebuck (the son of the Springfield Jew who noted the *Rischus* among his Illinois neighbors), alone contributed $3.5 million. The various *landsmanschaftn* collected what they could as well, and as soon as the war ended, they sent delegations to hometowns and to various regions to assess the damage in order to help Jews there rebuild.[56] By 1918 American Jews had contributed nearly $20 million for the relief of European Jews. Additionally, in the aftermath of the war, which for the Jews meant a continuation rather than a cessation of wartime carnage, Jewish leaders secured from the U.S. government and other relief agencies another $27 million for eastern European Jewish relief. Individual American Jews representing the relief effort traveled to eastern Europe, including the Soviet Union, to investigate the physical need of the Jews. In 1920, two of these men, Rabbi Bernard Canto and Professor Israel Friedlander of the Jewish Theological Seminary, met their deaths at the hands of an anti-Jewish gang in an ambush in the Ukraine.

The millions of dollars collected by American Jews proved to be crucial and represented a deeply felt sense of responsibility. The money provided by the U.S. government came from humanitarian sources and might have come to the Jews regardless of what had happened in the past. But decades of cultivating American public opinion and pleading the case of the oppressed Jews of Europe paid off tangibly, as measured in the soup kitchens, medical clinics, milk stations, homeless shelters, and reconstruction projects that revived Jewish life in eastern Europe.[57]

Caring for the Jews of Palestine

In their political calculations American Jews focused on another part of the world as well, Palestine, their ancient home, which Jews referred to in prayer as "our land." Before the end of the nineteenth century American Jews, regardless of class, European birthplace, place of residence in the United States, or ideology, offered charitable support to the messengers or representatives of the impoverished Jewish enclave in Jerusalem, who regularly traveled around the United States seeking alms.[58] In the 1880s just as the first groups of Jewish pioneers, the *Biluim,* left Russia to try their hand at agriculture in Palestine, so too a small handful of Jews in New York formed a Hoveve Zion, or "lovers of Zion," society. Chapters of this idealistic group sprang up in a number of other American cities, and although few joined, these societies contributed articles to American Jewish publications about the need for American Jews to support, financially and physically, the colonies in Palestine.

But what had been a minor force in America and elsewhere changed after Theodore Herzl called together the First Zionist Congress in Basel, Switzerland, in 1897. The following year some of the Hoveve Zion, along with Gustav Gottheil, a few of his fellow Reform rabbis, and others, formed the Federation of American Zionists. In the closing year of the nineteenth century FAZ claimed 125 societies, with a total of ten thousand members.

Zionism, as an organized political faction in the community, never appealed to a large number of American Jews, who found themselves torn by the movement's ideas. The most religiously observant opposed it because it clashed with their belief that in a future messianic age God would restore the Jewish people to their home. Many in the Reform movement asserted that the Jews of America had already found their promised land and that calls for a homeland halfway around the world would jeopardize their claims to American citizenship. Socialists in the eastern European immigrant community, the Bund in particular, mustered little enthusiasm as well. Zionism, they believed, represented just another petty nationalist ideology, and like all the others, it distracted workers from focusing on their class position. The fact that the Zionist camp itself suffered internal divisions did not help to boost its popularity. After 1914 personality and political squabbles beset the movement, further diminishing its appeal to the majority of American Jews. But despite the paucity of dues-paying members, the bickering within the Zionist movement, and the vigorous criticism hurled at it from various quarters of American Jewry, most American Jews in fact looked favorably on the small Jewish settlements developing in Palestine and continued to feel responsible for the poor religious Jews there who had long depended on Western Jewish charity.

World War I proved to be quite influential in the American Jewish relationship to Palestine and in Palestine's place in the American Jewish political agenda. The Jews of Palestine, regardless of whether they were yeshiva students in Jerusalem, *halutzim* (pioneers) in the Jordan River valley, or dwellers in the new Jewish cities of Tel Aviv and Haifa, like the Jews of central and eastern Europe, stood trapped among the great powers fighting for control of land, waterways, and resources of the crucial region. The direct clash between the British forces and those of the Ottoman Empire under whom the Jews of Palestine lived often put them in harm's way. As they had done before, and would do again, American Jews came to the rescue. Schiff, Marshall, and Nathan Straus played an instrumental role in sending money to the Jews of Palestine. They persuaded the U.S. government to allow a messenger carrying the money to travel aboard a U.S. battleship, the *U.S.S. North Carolina.*[59]

Likewise, when in 1917 Britain wrested control of the sliver of land along the Mediterranean from the Ottomans, it issued a pivotal document, the Balfour Declaration, in which it announced that it looked favorably on the Jewish resettlement of its historic land. Many American Jews hailed this development, and fifteen thousand of them gathered at Carnegie Hall on December 23 to celebrate. Twenty-five thousand marched down the main streets of Newark, New Jersey. While anti-Zionist Jews did not share in the celebration, most American Jews did, and they played a key role in trying to convince President Woodrow Wilson to support the Declaration.

AMERICAN JEWS PRESS FOR IMMIGRATION

Each crisis in Europe, Palestine, or elsewhere, brought forth the same reaction from American Jews. From the 1890s through the bloody years of the early 1920s when the newly created nations of eastern Europe, Poland in particular, subjected Jews to violence and discrimination, American Jews sought redress from the American government. They used personal contacts and worked quietly through back channels if they had to. They considered public meetings with notable non-Jews an important element in the campaign to win over American public opinion, but they eschewed noisy, hostile, and aggressive public demonstrations. The handful of the very wealthy who had an impact on international finance and banking used their resources and influence to help Jews and punish their enemies. Because they had been relatively successful in getting public officials at least to utter sympathetic words, they persisted in

this strategy. While they never succeeded in getting the government to intervene militarily in Russia to protect the Jews, for example, American
Jews could balance most of their political failures with small victories.
They felt that the government sided with them and that they had devised
a reasonable strategy to meet most crises.

Moreover, they pinned many of their hopes on allowing continued
immigration to the United States as the most effective way of saving European Jewry. As long as America remained open, they reasoned, the suffering of Jews elsewhere could be mitigated. Along with the massive assistance provided to newly arriving immigrants, American Jews sought
to prevent the passage of all proposed pieces of immigration legislation
restricting access to the United States. In the 1880s although some of the
notables, like Schiff, expressed some reservation about the eastern European immigration, within a decade they offered wholehearted support.
In 1891, for example, when Congress excluded certain classes of what it
defined as mentally and physically handicapped and of "paupers or persons likely to become a public charge," American Jews protested vigorously in print and before congressional hearings. Simon Wolf wrote to
Charles Foster, the secretary of the treasury, that "a very large number
of Russian Hebrews sought this land of liberty as a haven of rest. They
have been assimilated in the mass of citizenship."[60] Foster accepted
Wolf's request for a lenient interpretation of the newly passed law with
regard to admitting Jews but suggested that American Jewry do what it
could to prevent the immigrants from concentrating in New York and
other industrial cities.[61]

Likewise, each time that Congress debated legislation mandating a lit-
eracy test as a way of excluding some immigrants, as it did in 1896,
1898, 1902, 1906, 1913, and 1915, Jews registered their opposition.
They pleaded with friendly officials, testified before congressional hearings, and launched a barrage of press reports detailing what fine Americans the new immigrants were becoming and claiming that the United
States had nothing to fear by allowing the free flow of more Jews to a
country where they could prosper. When some Americans asserted that
Jews represented a radical threat to the American social order, Jewish
leaders sought to prove the opposite. The immigrants, they argued,
quickly integrated, learned English, and embraced the American way of
life. Indeed, in 1895, one year after the Immigration Restriction League
was founded, Simon Wolf published the first book detailing the service
of Jews in the American military. His chronicle of Jewish service to the
United States, he hoped, would counter the mounting accusations of the

Jews' inability to assimilate, claims that he believed could jeopardize the flow of Jewish immigrants into the United States.[62]

The bargain struck between Wolf and the secretary of the treasury involved a three-pronged dynamic that continued to manifest itself until 1924. First, Jews flowed out of eastern Europe, and their desire to leave not just Russia but also Romania and parts of the Austro-Hungarian Empire, particularly Galicia, seemed boundless. While they left for complicated reasons, American Jews, the shapers of communal opinion and those with access to public officials, emphasized repeatedly how their emigration represented a flight from death, not just an ordinary migration. The Kishinev pogrom of 1903, the bloody wave of pogroms that stretched until 1906, the blood libel against Mendel Beiliss, a Jew in Kiev, that stretched from 1911 to 1913, and the devastation during and after World War I all created an American Jewish communal rhetoric that sold the American public on the urgency of the immigration and on its uniqueness as a response to the pogroms. The Jews, they argued, should not be considered typical immigrants, migrating in search of bread; eastern European Jews should be seen as fleeing persecution. Allowing them to come to America amounted to a supreme act of humanitarianism.

Despite this urgency, American Jewish leaders often disagreed about which strategies to use and how best to approach particular officials. Yet they agreed, although not explicitly, on the basic tenet, that eastern European Jews should be able to keep immigrating. Notable American Jews such as Wolf, Schiff, Marshall, and their allies may have had little or no personal warmth for the immigrants, and the well-established elite and the newcomers shared very little common ground. But all shared a belief in immigration and a sense that it had emerged as *the* political issue among American Jews. On this issue, they staked their political fortunes. Third, American Jews understood that to make their case for keeping immigration flowing, they had, in essence, to vouch for the behavior of the new immigrants. Thus, if Americans feared a massive influx of poor "aliens," then it became the political responsibility of the leadership to ensure the immigrants' economic mobility and their social and cultural adaptation to America.

The goal of the leaders, which they imposed on themselves at the same time that others imposed it on them, became to facilitate the immigration without making the new Jews conspicuous in their foreignness and poverty. But the care and monitoring of immigrant Jews by Jewish agencies in and of itself complicated the project. Non-Jews, not particularly favorable to Jews and Jewish immigration, had ample access to the mountain of writing and commentary by Jews about the condition of the immigrants. Robert Hunter, who wrote a widely read exposé of poverty in America, could point to the data amassed by the Jews themselves proving the high degree of economic distress among the immigrants. Calling the Jews the "most oppressed peasantry of Asiatic countries," Hunter declared that among the Jews,

> who have been admitted in great numbers to this country, and who have settled almost entirely in the largest cities, distress and poverty are widespread. Not to speak from observation, but to quote only from published reports, there is more than enough to be said. The annual report of the United Hebrew Charities for 1901 says: "A condition of chronic poverty is developing in the Jewish community of New York that is appalling in its immensity."[63]

Numerous American Jewish projects stemmed from this political concern. In 1907, for example, Jacob Schiff, in collaboration with Oscar Straus, then secretary of commerce and labor, and with the encouragement of President Theodore Roosevelt, unveiled the Galveston Plan. The idea behind it was to divert newly arriving Jewish immigrants from the urban East Coast, steering them instead toward the American interior through the port of Galveston, Texas. Schiff believed firmly that if the Jewish wave crested on the shore at Texas, not New York, more Jews could in fact make their way to the United States. In the remote West few would see or comment on them. The immigrants could settle in more dispersed communities away from the glare of public attention.

Schiff expressed great faith in the immigrants from eastern Europe. In 1910 he wrote to Jacob Billikopf, another Jewish community activist, that he found the typical immigrant to be "of splendid stock." Schiff continued in his praise, speculating that "he not only makes it possible through his work that we maintain and extend our commercial supremacy, but he also brings his ideals and a religious background of which, with our materialistic tendencies, we stand in good need." He wanted very much to keep immigration flowing. Indeed, at one point he expressed a hope that he might somehow make it possible to "take every one of our persecuted people out of Russia and bring them to the United States." Schiff, however, believed that the more the immigrants concentrated in one city in particular, the harsher the reaction to them would be and the more likely that the restrictionists would win over public opinion. Thinning out the New York ranks by diverting the ship traffic to other, smaller points seemed an attractive solution.

In 1901, after several years of discussion, Jewish communal workers created the Industrial Removal Office in an effort to realize Schiff's vision and that of others who worried about overcrowding in New York. The IRO served as a kind of employment office. In New York immigrant Jewish men without work applied to get their fare paid to some smaller community, where a local Jewish community would help them with jobs and housing. If successful, they would send for their families to join them, be it in another large city, like Detroit, or a small community, like La Crosse, Wisconsin. A network of agents employed by the IRO scouted out likely places where immigrant men could find jobs and fit in with some degree of comfort, while the New York office assessed the character of the applicants, trying to ascertain who could function well in the hinterlands.[64]

American Jews saw immigration as a positive good, and indeed as the only feasible alternative to life in eastern Europe. The Zionists' weakness rendered them unable to offer a counterargument proposing Palestine as the solution to the escalation of anti-Jewish violence in Europe, and few, even by the 1910s and 1920s, considered the weak and tiny *yishuv*—the Jewish population in Palestine—a viable option for housing millions of European Jews. The fact that immigration to the United States became the only concrete option increased the pressure placed on American Jews to accept what they could get from the U.S. government, and to do so with gratitude. They had to depend on friendly officials and on a sympathetic American public to keep their one safety net in place and had little choice but to adopt a defensive posture that eschewed confrontation. The fact that the leaders of American Jewry witnessed with dread how the country inched its way to extreme restrictionism as embodied in the passage of the temporary 1921 legislation and then finally the 1924 law, shook their confidence but offered them no new strategy to pursue in years to come.[65]

A "Nation of Immigrants"

By making immigration key to their political agenda, American Jews deviated quite dramatically from Jews in England, France, and Germany. In those countries Jews could also count among their number a cadre of well-connected, affluent individuals who called on heads of state, legislators, and bureaucrats and pleaded for themselves and for Jews elsewhere in distress. Eastern European Jews created communities in London, Paris, and Berlin that in some ways resembled the communities forming in New York, Chicago, and Philadelphia.[66] But in those countries where national identity remained closely tied to ancestry and to an ideology of belonging to a nation through descent, further Jewish immigration did not become a policy or goal actively encouraged by the native-born Jewish elite. German Jews, for example, did not pin their hopes for their people on a constant and growing immigration from the east. On the contrary, they intended Germany to serve as a humane way station ensuring that eastern European Jews would not linger there too long. Likewise, Jews in France and England did not fashion a political agenda predicated on a larger, future influx of Jewish newcomers.

That Americans generally prided themselves on being a "nation of immigrants" gave Jews the chance to behave politically unlike Jews in other western democratic societies. American Jews could develop a rhetorical strategy to call for open doors, citing the American political tradition as a way of fulfilling their obligations to other Jews. By the beginning of the twentieth century, they understood that other Americans had embraced a more racialized definition of citizenship, one assuming that some immigrants, Jews among them, would never be transformed into "real" Americans.

In their defense, American Jews pointed to their success in raising the throngs of impoverished immigrants as evidence that an older American ideology, based on Enlightenment thinking and associated with republican ideology, could still work. They invoked the idea of America as a "fine and liberty-loving country, that has always opened its gates to the down-trodden and unjustly persecuted" and argued their case by praising the essence of America. They asserted that "to close the avenues" into America "would be against the underlying genius and theory of our glorious and beloved constitution."[67] The American Jewish discourse on nation, identity, immigration, and citizenship involved high political stakes. Much rode on the persuasiveness of their argument.

Politically, American Jews made little distinction between their domestic concerns and their global perspective. When thinking about how to deal with the matters specific to American Jewry, they calculated how their actions would affect Jews in other places, eastern Europe in particular. In essence the immigration issue served as a bridge between their two political agendas, domestic and foreign-policy strategies.

Journalism as a Political Vehicle

The newspapers and magazines that American Jews published and read expressed deep concern over both agendas and pointed to the connectedness of all Jewish people. From the first American journalistic venture,

The Jew (1823–1825), until 1924, when Congress passed, and the president signed, restrictive immigration legislation, hundreds of publications, both local and national, informed American Jews of the affairs of the Jewish world. Some of these publications served as journalistic vehicles for rabbis with particular religious and political agendas. Leeser's *Occident and American Jewish Advocate* circulated from 1843 until 1860, and as a journal it did exactly what its masthead claimed: it advocated for the Jews at the same time that it championed Leeser's particular brand of traditionalism.[68] In 1854 Isaac Mayer Wise launched *The Israelite,* which functioned in a similar manner, but from a different ideological standpoint. Although one publication came from Philadelphia and the other from Cincinnati, they both commanded a national readership, and both commented extensively on the achievements and crises of Jews around the world.

During the century of migration, Jewish publications could be found in many languages, including German, Hebrew, Yiddish, and Ladino, each targeting specific segments of the population. These publications focused mainly on the particular part of the world from which its readers came and where they still had family and friends. Along with the English-language local Jewish newspapers, which were usually weeklies—like Philadelphia's *Jewish Exponent* (1887) or Minneapolis-St. Paul's *Northwestern Jewish Advocate* (1894)—the nationally circulating Jewish periodicals made politics a key part of their mission. They chronicled in detail the words and deeds of American politicians and officials, identifying the Jews' friends and enemies. They highlighted malicious acts perpetrated on the Jews at home and abroad, and they urged Jews to speak out on matters of concern to them. Local Jewish newspapers took stands on the constant turmoil in America and in world politics.

Politics never strayed far from the press's attention. The Hebrew press existed in large measure as a vehicle for Zionism. The coverage of developments in the *yishuv* as well as the distress of European Jewry gave the movement and such papers as *ha-Leumi* (New York and Newark, 1888–1889) and *Hapisgah* (New York, 1888–1990) their raison d'être. The longest lasting of the Hebrew publications, *Hadoar* (1921), never shied away from making political commentary.[69]

Politics also deeply informed the Yiddish press, and many publishers actively engaged in local party politics. Kasriel Sarasohn, the pioneer of Yiddish journalism in America and the publisher of the first daily, the *Yiddishes Tageblatt* (1885–1928), labored ardently for New York City's Republicans.[70] He used his paper to lambaste the two other political parties eager to capture the loyalty and votes of the immigrant community, namely Tammany Hall and the Democrats on the one side and the Socialists on the other. The latter group won a good deal of support among the immigrant Jews in New York after 1897 through *Forverts,* the newspaper edited by Abraham Cahan.[71] Both newspapers, despite the vast differences in their politics, advocated for Jewish rights at home and around the world, commented with passion on the evils of racism in America, and argued fervently for immigrant rights, expressing the position that immigration should be kept open to eastern Europe's Jews.

Given the highly political nature, sometimes subtle, often blatant, of the American Jewish press, the mere act of reading a newspaper or magazine could be construed as a political act. That a reader chose one paper over another, or subscribed to a particular magazine, could not be disconnected from his or her ideology and political preferences. But regardless of ideology, all American Jewish journalism covered the worldwide connections between Jews and the centrality of immigration to the United States as the best possible option for the largest number of Jews.

COMMUNAL AND DEFENSE ORGANIZATIONS

It is within the context of this double agenda that the development of American Jewish communal and defense organizations may best be understood. From 1859, when representatives of twenty-four congregations gathered in New York to create the Board of Delegates of American Israelites, through 1922, when an American Jewish Congress, a product of World War I, came into being, a relatively small elite of leaders sought to direct the American Jewish political agenda and to bring about unity in their otherwise scattered efforts to defend Jewish rights.

As with the issue of immigration, the organizational profile of American Jewry differed substantially from that of other modern Jewish communities. The fact that the U.S. government recognized no one as representing or speaking for the Jews—or for any other religious or ethnic group—meant that in political matters different individuals, factions, and organizations could claim to be the voice of the Jews. In England, just as the chief rabbi regularized religious matters with the blessings of the crown, so too did the actions of the Board of Deputies of British Jews carry official sanction. Founded in 1760, the Board of Deputies had been officially recognized by Parliament in 1835 as the single representative body speaking for the Jews.

The Board of Delegates

The rabbis of the growing number of congregations in and out of New York clearly had the British model in mind when in 1858 they assembled at Cooper Hall after being called together by Rabbi Samuel M. Isaacs of Congregation Shaarey Tefilla. The Mortara affair precipitated the meeting at which the religious leaders of twenty-five congregations assembled. The rabbis hoped to find a way in which American Jews could be represented so that they could protect their interests and influence the government. Initially the Board of Delegates structured itself as a union of congregations, although the majority of the country's congregations did not join. As it became increasingly clear that American Jews conducted much of their Jewish lives outside the synagogue, in 1869 the Board of Delegates decided to include delegates from the secular Jewish organizations that increasingly commanded the loyalty of American Jews.

The Board of Delegates developed an agenda that could be described as both limited and elastic. It took on the task of monitoring developments in the Jewish world, collecting data on American Jewry, and strengthening Jewish education. Over its lifetime, the Board of Delegates attempted to fulfill all three missions. It raised money for the relief of Jewish suffering during wars in Tunisia, Morocco, Romania, and Russia. It lobbied with the U.S. government to remove anti-Jewish language from trade agreements between the United States and Switzerland, Russia, and Romania, and it championed the cause of Jewish chaplains in the U.S. army during the Civil War. Furthermore, the Board waged a battle to erase the religious requirements for officeholding in the last few states maintaining them. When Cesar Kaskel came to Washington to bring to Lincoln's attention the looming crisis of Order Number 11, he consulted first with Adolphus Solomons, a Washington Jew who sat on the executive committee of the Board of Delegates. Despite its prodigious efforts, however, the Board faded from the American Jewish political scene at the end of the 1870s.[72]

Its death knell tolled in 1876 when it merged into the Union of American Hebrew Congregations, the synagogal body of the Reform movement. While the UAHC continued some of the lobbying and defense-oriented tasks that previously had been associated with the Board of Delegates, its sectarianism made it quite different from its predecessor. Traditionalists could not accept the leadership of a body connected to Reform. The Board of Delegates, even before its merger with the Reform Union, never came close to attaining either the clout or the consensus that characterized British Jewry. Its weakness demonstrated the complexity of American Jewish life and the difficulty of American Jews, given both their diversity and the voluntary nature of their community, to take a single stand.

The Political Projects of B'nai B'rith

Even before the Board of Delegates had been called together, the B'nai B'rith had adopted a range of political projects in the name of all American Jews. Despite the fact that B'nai B'rith essentially began as a social and mutual-aid association for men, it spoke out for Jewish rights early in its history and used its national chain of lodges as a way to exercise political influence on behalf of world Jewry. In 1851, for example, petitions circulated around the country, from lodge to lodge, urging Secretary of State Daniel Webster to demand that Switzerland, which banned Jews from living in certain cantons, change its discriminatory policy. The impetus for the B'nai B'rith petition drive stemmed from the fact that the United States had begun renegotiating a trade treaty with Switzerland. To B'nai B'rith members, this seemed a propitious moment to ameliorate the status of Jews.

Into the 1920s the B'nai B'rith continued its political work by joining in the delegations and lobbying efforts through which American Jews sought to influence public policy. Like much of American Jewry, it believed that by assisting the newly arriving eastern European newcomers it was fulfilling a Jewish mission and enhancing the status of all Jews in America. For its part, the B'nai B'rith published widely used manuals for immigrants, in Yiddish and English, on how to apply for naturalization and how to acquire citizenship. In 1901 its lodges became the conduit through which the Industrial Removal Office tried to find jobs for poor Jewish immigrants outside New York.[73] It also played a crucial role in transnational Jewish politics. When President Grant sent Benjamin Peixotto to Romania to investigate the conditions of the Jews, he dispatched an official of the B'nai B'rith. The spread of the organization around the world, first to Germany in 1882 and then to Palestine, Romania, Poland, Czechoslovakia, Austria, France, England, and elsewhere, made it a nerve center of intra-Jewish communication and mutual endeavor.

The Anti-Defamation League

On the domestic level the political work of the B'nai B'rith became most manifest in the United States in 1913, when fifteen members of the

Chicago lodge, called together by an attorney, Sigmund Livingston, created the Anti-Defamation League. In light of the arrest of Leo Frank in Atlanta that year and the proliferation of offensive images of Jews on the stage and in the press, the ADL's work focused on disseminating the "correct aspects of Jewish culture and heritage."[74] Although initially it favored the idea of calling on state and city governments to censor defamatory language, it quickly took another tack, instead focusing on educating the public about the dangers of racism. In the early 1920s it worked with other groups to counter the rhetoric of the Ku Klux Klan.[75]

That the sponsoring body of the ADL, the B'nai B'rith, saw little distinction between its everyday activities, its fraternal and benevolent functions, and its defense work at home and abroad provides a good way of understanding American Jewish political life. Local and national, domestic and global, social and defensive, cultural and political blended together as the nineteenth century brought Jews around the world both the possibility of emancipation and the specter of destruction.

The National Council of Jewish Women

Similarly, the activities of the National Council of Jewish Women blurred conventional distinctions and demonstrated the highly political nature of American Jewry. Founded in 1893 by a group of middle-class women in Chicago and led by Hannah Greenbaum Solomon, the NCJW devoted itself to the self-education of Jewish women in an effort to help them better defend Judaism and make a place for themselves in American Jewish life. Solomon placed the Council, both its national organization and its many chapters around the country—which by 1905 enrolled over ten thousand members—squarely in the progressive camp. It took stands on nearly every political issue, including birth control, women's suffrage, disarmament, civil liberties, racial justice, labor legislation, and the responsibility of government—state and federal—to provide for the welfare and social improvement of the lives of citizens. It mattered little to the Council leaders that some rabbis and editors of Jewish newspapers criticized its intensely prosuffrage stance. It understood that as long as women were excluded from the political equation, American politics would not represent the majority and as such would be tyrannical.[76]

The Council's outspoken political actions often put it in conflict with the many organizations that remained male run until the 1912 founding of Hadassah. The NCJW's work on the issue of prostitution provides a revealing case in point. The Council consistently supported unrestricted immigration, and like other organizations, lobbied against proposed legislation that would have imposed limits on the number of immigrants allowed into the country. Like most American Jews and Jewish organizations it considered the protection of the immigrants a crucial part of the Jewish political project and a way to deflect criticism of immigrants and of all American Jews. The NCJW concerned itself in particular with the dangers faced by immigrant women, realizing that the public discourse about Jewish women as prostitutes harmed all Jews. Turner's sensational article "Daughters of the Poor" had proven that many Americans associated Jews with vice.

The Council launched a series of initiatives to address the problem. It lobbied Congress for the protection of immigrant women. It hired agents and stationed them at Ellis Island and at the port in Philadelphia to offer protection to unaccompanied Jewish women, whom they considered vulnerable to pimps. In 1908 alone NCJW agents met and greeted over ten thousand Jewish women. If those newcomers had no place to go, it provided them with shelter in Council houses. The agents handed out brochures in Yiddish marked with the words "Beware of those who give you addresses, offer you easy, well-paid work, or even marriage. There are many evil men who have in this way led girls to destruction. Always inquire in regard to these persons of the COUNCIL OF JEWISH WOMEN, which will find out the truth, and advise you."

Regardless of how much Turner and others overstated these claims, the NCJW reacted to the fact that Americans consumed a steady diet of reports about Jews as pimps, procurers, and prostitutes. The NCJW's role in the antiprostitution movement also connected it to the activities of Jewish women in Germany and England who were also taking up the cause. The plight of young Jewish women, lured into prostitution by Jewish men, became an international Jewish women's concern. To the NCJW and their sisters in Berlin and London, prostitution constituted a Jewish political problem requiring a political solution.

In this project, one of many taken on by the NCJW, it combined ministering to the needy and addressing a Jewish concern with how they were projecting their image. Many male communal leaders, rabbis in particular, considered the NCJW's public discussion of prostitution unwise. By warning Jewish women away from "white slavers" and procurers, they argued, the Council was drawing too much public attention to the issue and to the negative depictions of Jews. Furthermore, the Hebrew Sheltering and Immigrant Aid Society wanted to supplant the Council. It asked the Baron de Hirsch Fund, which provided money to both it and the NCJW, to give it the authority to replace the female "volunteers" with male professionals. The Council won the battle and, on a grassroots level, was able to continue its work.[77]

Local sections of the Council also did political work, taking on the stereotyping of Jews in the press a half decade before the Anti-Defamation League came into being. In 1907 leaders of the Portland, Oregon, chapter met with the publisher of the *Oregonian,* the most widely circulating newspaper in the state. They informed him that affixing the word "Jew" to the names of individuals arrested for crimes was "uncalled for . . . unless newspapers all adopt the same system against all others and designate them as Presbyterian, Episcopalian, Catholic, Unitarian or otherwise as the case may be."[78] In their hometowns throughout the United States, Jews, through the National Council of Jewish Women, B'nai B'rith, or any of the broad panoply of local organizations, made defense a large part of their political endeavor. They responded quickly when words slandering the Jews appeared in print or when public officials disparaged them.

The Kehillah and the American Jewish Committee

In 1908 in New York, Police Commissioner Bingham's statement about excessive rates of Jewish criminality led to the founding of the Kehillah, a classic body of Jewish self-government but one designed to fit America's democratic mold. Well-off Jews representing the Americanized "up-towners" and the new immigrants, most of whom dwelled "downtown," organized the Kehillah in large part because of the frighteningly high level of anti-Jewish rhetoric. Bingham's statements led the city's Jewish press, both English and Yiddish, to speculate on the gravity of the situation. Most of the press coverage of Bingham's remarks focused on the inaccuracy of his figures and the possibility that his words would aid both restrictionists in America and anti-Semites in Russia. New York Jewish leaders and commentators agreed that a crisis loomed.

But despite that unanimity of views on the gravity of the problem, New York Jews responded in many different ways to it. Each group weighed in, and each publication had its own words to add to the tempest. But after a meeting on September 5 at Clinton Hall on the Lower East Side, a consensus began to emerge: New York Jews needed to be able to respond to defamatory rhetoric in a coordinated and calculated manner. By March 1909 the Kehillah had been born. During the ten years that it existed, it attempted, with modest success, to centralize Jewish charity and education in the city. The Kehillah would be a clearinghouse for disputes in the kosher meat industry, a constant and vexing problem, and it would collect statistics of various kinds. Members designed a Bureau of Social Morals to investigate illegal activities among the immigrant population, and its Bureau of Industry, its advocates hoped, would help mediate labor disputes between Jewish employers and Jewish laborers.

The Kehillah fused purely Jewish issues with external ones involving Jewish interaction with the non-Jewish world. They two could not, in fact, according to the Kehillah, be disentangled. As long as Jews did nothing about crime in their communities, for example, they fed Jew-baiters like Bingham with ammunition. But even if Jewish organizations could do little to root out criminality, the fact that they were trying assiduously absolved the community of charges of inaction. If Jewish criminals existed—and they did—their criminality could not then be seen as stemming from the fact of their Jewishness. Criminality would not, they hoped, be viewed by others as an essentially Jewish trait.[79]

The American Jewish Committee, an organization that had been founded just three years earlier, represented the "uptown" Jews in the Kehillah experiment. The AJC did indeed function, as its name declared, as a committee. Because of the prestige, status, and connections of its handful of members—Cyrus Adler, Jacob Schiff, Oscar Straus, Louis Marshall, and Mayer Sulzberger—it carried great weight in communal politics, and it had no desire to be an organization based on mass. The Committee developed as a result of the Kishinev pogrom. The men who founded it sought to involve the U.S. government in the internal matters of czarist Russia to protect the Jews there at the same time that it considered increased and unchecked Jewish immigration to the United States the only way to solve the crisis of Russian Jewry.

Through the decades after its founding, the AJC consistently opposed every piece of immigration restriction and pressed, sometimes privately, a succession of presidents, congressional representatives, and diplomats to intervene on behalf of Russia's Jews. Gaining access to those in power emerged early on as the Committee's mode of operation, and it positively rejected the idea of including more members who articulated diverse perspectives. Like most other American Jewish bodies, including those with mass membership, it believed that one—though not the only—way to combat anti-Semitism involved prevention. Accordingly, the AJC looked favorably on and participated in the Galveston Plan, a tactic it hoped would take away from the restrictionists one of their most effective pieces of propaganda, the massing of thousands of new immigrant Jews in a single neighborhood in a highly visible city.[80]

Because it consisted of a small coterie of like-minded men sharing a single political perspective, the Committee could respond quickly to crises. And since the members had ample resources at their command, they had no need to raise funds from the masses or to derive income from dues. The Committee, therefore, expected to dominate in its endeavors, and it cooperated nominally with other very different groups. This dynamic indeed contributed to the Kehillah's eventual failure, given that the other groups representing the immigrants had no desire to defer to the Committee's hegemony.

The American Jewish Joint Distribution Committee

Despite its inability to work well with other Jewish organizations, the American Jewish Committee did play a significant role in organizing massive relief for European Jews during and after World War I. Its contribution of money and resources played a crucial role in the founding, in October 1914, of the American Jewish Joint Distribution Committee. The relief effort had been initiated earlier by the Union of Orthodox Jewish Congregations, which had formed a Central Committee for the Relief of Jews.[81] Louis Marshall of the AJC decided that the problem had gotten too big to be handled by the Orthodox group or indeed by any one organization. Therefore, he insisted that AJC become the pivotal body in a joint venture. Men associated directly or indirectly with the AJC would direct the American Jewish Joint Distribution Committee. Felix Warburg served as chairman, and Nathan Straus spearheaded the fund-raising drive.[82]

Through Warburg the Joint interceded on behalf of the Jews with the larger American Relief Administration headed by Herbert Hoover. Hoover believed that all European war victims ought to be treated the same. But Warburg, the Joint, and the American Jewish Committee knew that Jews occupied a place in society that made them very different from other people. They had particular needs, such as kosher food, and they faced unique problems, such as anti-Semitism, that would complicate the relief effort. As a result of this kind of input, ARA earmarked funds especially for Jewish relief.[83]

Like the American Jewish Committee, the Joint found itself criticized by many American Jews for its neutrality on Zionism. In the aftermath of World War I and in the face of escalating anti-Jewish violence in eastern Europe, activists representing other Jewish organizations considered rebuilding European Jewish communities futile and suggested that the money and energy instead go into the building up of Jewish Palestine.

They believed that the Jews had no future in eastern Europe and that the *yishuv* in Palestine would be able, with American Jewish money, to accommodate the immigrants. By the 1920s more American Jews had moved toward a warm embrace of Zionism, even if few American Jews paid dues to Zionist organizations or contemplated moving to Palestine. A benevolent, philanthropic form of Zionism rapidly gained hold among American Jews, particularly among the masses of eastern European immigrants and their children favorably disposed toward the romance of the Jewish people re-creating themselves as a nation in the ancestral land.

The American Jewish Congress

Two other organizations constituting the political infrastructure of American Jewry owed their origins and popularity to the spread of Zionist sentiment and to the idea of communal democracy. The American Jewish Congress may be seen as the political reaction of the immigrants, who objected to the American Jewish Committee's rejection of both Zionism and communal democracy. Since the first decade of the twentieth century, when the Committee was founded, some American Jews started to agitate for a different kind of organization, a representative, democratically elected central body that would speak for all, not just for a few dozen wealthy individuals.

World War I provided the opportunity for such a congress to be considered, even by the Committee. After a series of negotiations between a newly formed Jewish Congress Organization Committee and the American Jewish Committee, delegates met toward the end of the war to form an American Jewish Congress. The Congress staged elections all over the United States in June 1917, and over three hundred and fifty thousand Jewish women and men cast their ballots. A month after the armistice, on December 15, 1918, the Congress convened. Originally the delegates had intended to operate only temporarily, expecting to disband as soon as the Congress completed its work monitoring the global fate of the Jewish people, in the aftermath of the immediate war.

At the peace talks being held in Paris, the American Jewish Congress defined its mission as representing American Jewry. It sent representatives to Versailles to demand that the rights of Jews and other minorities be added to the treaty, in which the signatories would draw a new map of Europe, and that the world leaders "recognize the aspirations and historic claims of the Jewish people" to Palestine, in line with the Balfour Declaration.[84] After they had accomplished this, members of the Congress began dissolving the body. But some of those involved, particularly

Reform Rabbi Stephen Wise, believed that the Congress had much work left to do. The Romanians and the Poles had accepted only bitterly the minority-rights clauses of the treaty, and violence and economic discrimination engulfed the Jews in those countries, despite the professed commitment of the new governments to protect their minorities. The outbreak of Arab violence against the Jews of Palestine made the lofty words of the Balfour Declaration seem insubstantial.

Wise and others suggested that the Congress continue. Accordingly, in 1922 a new American Jewish Congress came into being, although without the participation of the American Jewish Committee from the one side or the National Workmen's Circle Committee from the other. Through the 1920s the organization struggled with a shaky treasury, a blurred mission, and a minuscule membership. Though its goals were supporting Zionism and defending Jewish rights, it had no firm idea how to accomplish either or how to enlist American Jews in its projects.[85]

The American Jewish Congress differed from the Committee in large part because of the status of those who had been elected to the initial body and who remained active into the early 1920s. First, unlike the Committee, women participated in the Congress, and while they did not enjoy equal representation, their presence in the organization helped to broaden the definition of who could conduct Jewish politics. Class differences also distinguished the Congress from the older, more established bodies. While the elected members did not come from the ranks of the industrial workers and the new immigrants, they did represent a new class of American Jewish communal activists. Often the children of immigrants, they had received American educations, they held professional credentials, and they wanted to work for and within the Jewish world. Many had participated in local Jewish communal organizations and had direct knowledge of the conditions of immigrant life and the problems associated with adjusting to America.

Elizabeth Blume of Newark, New Jersey, one of the more interesting, and not very well-known, Congress members, represented that new kind of leader. The daughter of immigrants, Blume was born in 1892 and graduated from New Jersey Law School of Newark at age nineteen. Too young to be admitted to the state bar, she had to wait until 1913 until she could practice, eventually practicing criminal law. Throughout her early adulthood she participated in Jewish communal activities in Newark. She belonged to the Zionist Organization of America, the Malbish Arumim Society (a benevolent association that provided clothing to the needy), Hadassah, and numerous other organizations. In 1917 Blume won election to the first American Jewish Congress. Accomplished and educated, she brought to Jewish politics a set of ideas emphasizing participation and mutuality. To Blume Jewish politics represented the collective understanding of Jews in their communities, not simply the actions of a handful of the prominent, wealthy, and well-connected.[86]

Hadassah

The other American Jewish organization founded in this era, Hadassah, never called itself political. From the start Hadassah developed a highly effective strategy to secure its finances by effectively growing its membership and by exerting its influence, both among American Jews and within the circles of world Zionism. Hadassah put its energies into practical action rather than fiery rhetoric. It began small. In 1907 Judah Magnes, the leader of the Kehillah and rabbi of New York's Temple Emanu-El, collaborated with Henrietta Szold, a writer, the editor of the Jewish Publication Society of America, and a Zionist leader, to organize a study group for seven young women. B'noth Zion, which became a model for the later, national organization, combined self-education and friendship with a focus on Zionist ideas and projects. In 1909 Szold traveled to Palestine, where not only was she shocked by the health conditions but she also saw how the failure of the Zionist parties in Europe and America to engage in practical, rather than rhetorical, work had produced little of substance.

Szold, along with a group of thirty other women, many of them the wives of notable Zionist men, met in New York in February 1912 to contemplate forming an organization, the purpose of which would be "the promotion of Jewish institutions and enterprises in Palestine, and the fostering of Jewish ideals" in America.[87] Szold understood that by enlisting women around a specific concern in Palestine, Hadassah could become the only national Zionist mass organization in America. It went out of its way to recruit women regardless of their religious orientation or birthplace. It functioned as a body for all American Jewish women. Likewise, it made a point of recruiting women who had no particular affinity to Zionism but who wanted the companionship of other Jewish women within the context of doing good. Szold's plan was, in essence, to win them over to Zionism by doing rather than by being lectured to. Szold emphasized that to be effective the group needed a "definite project" as a way to garner members and command their loyalties.

That "definite project" was medical care. In 1913 the newly formed organization dispatched two nurses to Jerusalem to set up a clinic whose first projects were a maternity facility and an eye-care facility. Within a few years it opened the first emergency hospital in Jerusalem, and as early as 1915, just three years after its founding, it had opened the Henrietta Szold-Hadassah School of Nursing. In America Hadassah organized chapters around the country that quite quickly accommodated single and married women, American born and immigrants, the young and old. It avoided one of the main obstacles to the progress of the other Zionist societies: splintering and bickering over different agendas and points of ideology. Hadassah emphasized what all members had in common: their interest as Jewish women in improving the lives of the people in Palestine.

Hadassah consistently fought to control its own work, funds, and organizations. In 1917, for example, it decided to create its own youth group, Junior Hadassah, although the larger, male-dominated Federation of American Zionists insisted that Hadassah support its youth group, Young Judea. Likewise, in 1918 the Zionist Organization of America demanded that all independent Zionist publications be suspended so that a single voice of American Zionism could be heard. Hadassah complied for less than two years and then boldly launched its *Hadassah Newsletter* as an assertion of its political independence and confidence. In 1921 Hadassah defied the Keren HaYesod, an international Zionist funding agency, by insisting on controlling its own funds.

Hadassah succeeded in providing its members with a social life, a sense of purpose, and an avenue toward self-education. In 1914 Szold organized the Hadassah School of Zionism to give "intellectual substance" to the members' lives. Since Hadassah focused both on promoting projects in Palestine and on fostering Jewish ideals, it could gain the loyalty of thousands of members around the country by emphasizing service and sociability. It could be political without claiming a partisan agenda. Reflecting American Jewish politics as a whole, Hadassah made little distinction between the promotion of Jewish interests abroad and the solid American identity of its members. Like most American Jews, Hadassah leaders believed that they belonged to a collective, a worldwide people whose fate they considered their responsibility.[88] Regardless of the articulated purposes of their organizations—political or benevolent, social or defensive—American Jews never strayed far from their belief that as Jews they bore responsibility to each other. How they fulfilled that responsibility revealed much about them as Americans.

In the century shaped by immigration from Europe, American Jews consistently considered integration into America a positive ideal. Those who abhorred America and its culture rarely made the journey to the United States, and when they did, their inconsequential number rendered them irrelevant to the development of a political and communal agenda. Throughout this century few American Jews believed that integration and Jewish concerns had to be mutually exclusive. Rather, the majority believed that the two went hand-in-hand, and judging by most details of Jewish life in America, they took satisfaction in the kinds of Jewish communities they had built. They successfully integrated Judaism into the American religious and political landscape.

Their understanding that America offered the most viable source of protection to the Jewish people, including those who already lived there, those who wanted to live there, and those who made their homes elsewhere, deeply influenced American Jewish politics. American Jews recognized that they could exert some influence on the political process most effectively when they did not call attention to the parochialism of their concerns. They could take pride in the fact that politicians and political parties courted them, and although they claimed that no "Jewish vote" existed, the eagerness of Republicans and Democrats alike to win them over at the ballot box convinced them that they had chosen a wise path.

Politically they adopted a strategy that they believed fit the needs of a small group living in a complex society. Most defined themselves in ways that they hoped would resonate positively with the majority. They celebrated America—even the Socialists among them embraced American symbols—as the best solution to the problems of the Jews yet behind the scenes fretted over the precariousness of their condition. The Zionists held up the ideal of another home, Palestine. But most American Zionists thought of it as the place of refuge for Europe's, not America's, oppressed Jews. As Americans they did not see themselves as living in an exile from which they needed to be delivered. But beneath the surface lay a reservoir of foreboding, a feeling of deep insecurity about the potential for anti-Semitism. In essence, those involved in discussions about the political life of American Jewry always looked over their shoulders. They looked over one shoulder to try to gauge American—that is, Christian—reaction, and they looked over the other to determine the condition of their sisters and brothers worldwide.

The National Origins Act of 1924 proved to be a major moment in the history of the Jewish people. For European Jewry, which in a decade would be swept up in the maelstrom of Nazism and in the decade after that in World War II, America could no longer be a place of refuge. The National Origins Act did not count Jews as Jews but indirectly imposed on them restrictive quotas as nationals from Poland, the Soviet Union, Romania, Hungary, and elsewhere in eastern Europe. Despite their mighty effort, the inability of American Jews to block the legislation seemed a chilling omen of the limitations of minority politics. The year 1924 marked American Jewry's greatest political failure, although no evidence suggests that a different political strategy would have secured a different outcome. And no one could have foreseen the even greater failure that would confront American Jews in the not-too-distant future.

This *ketubah*, the traditional Jewish marriage contract, attested to the union of Haym Salomon and Rachel Franks. Salomon, known as the "financier of the Revolution," raised substantial amounts of capital for the Revolutionary War. Rachel Franks came from a notable eighteenth-century Jewish family. Courtesy of the American Jewish Historical Society; Waltham, Mass.; New York, N.Y.; #1344.

Haym Salomon served his country, alongside Robert Morris and George Washington, by seeking loans and financing for the nascent American government. Salomon later served in the department of finance of the new government. A wealthy man during the revolution, Salomon died penniless in 1785. American Jews built a monument to Salomon, pictured here, in Chicago (1941). Courtesy of the American Jewish Historical Society; #1344/8.

Maryland's proposed "Jew Bill," passed in 1826, paved the way for Jews to hold elected office. Courtesy of the American Jewish Historical Society; #601.

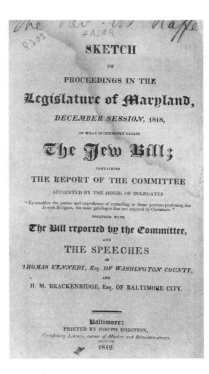

The cover page from the first prayer book printed in America, 1761. No rabbis arrived in the United States until the 1840s, and American Jews designed and published their own liturgies. Courtesy of the American Jewish Historical Society; #70.

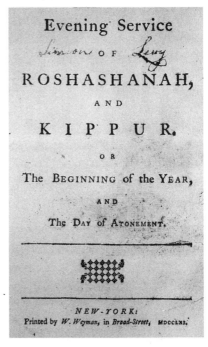

At a time when many Americans lived on farms or in small communities, Jewish peddlers provided people with their everyday necessities. Like J. Meyer, shown here with Native Americans, they roved America's hinterlands selling items like buttons, stoves, glass, needles, old clothes, and plates. Courtesy of the American Jewish Historical Society; #1047I.

לאור   מחושך

Happy New Year   לר שובה תכתבו

A New Year's postcard heralded the immigration to America as a journey "from darkness to light." Courtesy of the American Jewish Historical Society; #1151.

Esther Katzov studied at and even graduated from a gymnasium in Mirgorod, Russia. She came to America and went to work as a milliner in Chicago and Los Angeles. Courtesy of the Museum of Jewish Heritage, a Living Memorial to the Holocaust.

Detail of Esther Katzov's diploma. Courtesy of the Museum of Jewish Heritage, a Living Memorial to the Holocaust.

Esther Katzov's mother also made the journey to the United States. She lived on Chicago's West Side not unlike how she had in Europe, retaining the head covering considered appropriate for an observant married woman. Courtesy of the author.

Esther Katsov, whose entire family changed their name to Kite, frolicked in the surf in Venice, California. Courtesy of the author.

Esther Kite married in her late thirties in California, far from her family in Chicago. She married a Hebrew teacher, Moshe Schwartzman, himself an immigrant from Russia's Vholin province. They shared a belief in Zionism, and both belonged to the Labor Zionist wing of the movement. Courtesy of the author.

Newly arrived Jewish immigrants from Russia adopted American clothing styles, at least when posing for the camera. This photograph traveled back to family members still in Russia as evidence of the successful search for work and a more acceptable standard of living. Courtesy of the author.

The young people of Rypin, a town in the Budgoszcz province of Poland, formed a branch of Hechalutz, a Zionist youth movement. In the 1920s, Jews made up about 35 percent of Rypin. Courtesy of the author.

Helen Fenster, a member of Hechalutz, left for America in the mid-1920s with her father and sister. Her stepmother and younger siblings waited until the American contingent had earned enough to pay their fare and set up a household for them. Fenster made her living in a garment factory sewing blouses. Courtesy of the author.

Camp Nitgedeiget— "Do not worry"—provided year-round activities for members of the Jewish left in New York. A young worker, Helen Fenster, found time to enjoy wintertime leisure in a comfortable Jewish setting. Courtesy of the author.

William Fenster, born in Poland, graduated from New York's City College in the spring of 1936. He expected to find a job in his field, engineering, but the combination of anti-Semitism and the Depression closed that door to him. He went to work as a token seller in a subway station, working his way up to become the system's chief financial officer. Courtesy of the author.

M. KRAMER

NEW AND SECOND HAND

CLOTHING

MOHAIR LONG COATS & SUITS
READY AND MADE TO ORDER

607 Maxwell St., Chicago

Clothing provided much of the basis for the Jewish economy. M. Kramer represented merely one of millions of Jews in America who played a role in the garment industry. Courtesy of the author.

Leslie's Weekly showed Jews buying fish from a peddler's pushcart in the food market on the Lower East Side. Courtesy of the American Jewish Historical Society; #1108.

On April 23, 1903, *Leslie's Weekly* depicted a bustling shopping thoroughfare on the Lower East Side. In 1910 540,000 Jews lived in this one-and-a-half-square-mile area of New York. Courtesy of the American Jewish Historical Society; #1107.

To eradicate crowding in the Jewish neighborhood, the Baron de Hirsch Fund encouraged immigrants to take up farming. Although agricultural settlements in Louisiana, South Dakota, and Oregon survived only a few years, farmers like these prospered in New Jersey. Courtesy of the American Jewish Historical Society; #901.

Founded in 1826, B'nai Jesurun, or the Elm Street Synagogue, was the first Ashkenazic synagogue in New York City. Courtesy of the American Jewish Historical Society; #651.

JEWS' SYNAGOGUE, ELM STREET.

In August 1877 *Frank Leslie's Popular Monthly* showed Jews purchasing matzah, unleavened bread for Passover, by the pound. Courtesy of the American Jewish Historical Society; #36/3.

Many Jewish left-wing organizations, like the Workmen's Circle, established schools, or folk *schuln,* to teach Jewish children to participate in Jewish life through Yiddish culture, mutual aid, and the pursuit of social and economic justice. Courtesy of the American Jewish Historical Society; #709 B-16.

The Yiddish theater provided an essential medium for Jews to embrace Jewish culture outside the synagogue. This handbill from Boston advertised a production of *Shulamith,* among the most famous plays of Abraham Goldfaden, one of the first great Yiddish playwrights. Courtesy of the American Jewish Historical Society; #1195.

Manual training schools like this one in Chicago taught Jewish immigrants skilled professions. These young women from the "science department" learned needle trades. Courtesy of the American Jewish Historical Society; #634.

Lizzie Black Kander created the Abraham Lincoln Settlement House, and its cookbook, in Milwaukee under the auspices of the National Council of Jewish Women. Courtesy of the American Jewish Historical Society in Waltham; #87.

A sign-painting class at the Baron de Hirsch Training School, which funded many immigrant assistance programs and provided grants and trained immigrants in agriculture and the trades. Courtesy of the American Jewish Historical Society; #1294.

Originally published in the *New York Herald* on May 28, 1893, this drawing depicted scenes from the Baron de Hirsch Training School. Courtesy of the American Jewish Historical Society; #650.

Mothers lined up to enter their children in the "Better Baby Contest," sponsored by a settlement house in 1924. Jewish settlement houses not only served Jewish clients, but they also reached out to all residents of the neighborhood. Courtesy of the American Jewish Historical Society; #709B-5.

A settlement house worker at the Irene Kaufman Settlement House in Pittsburgh helped an applicant for citizenship fill out his papers. Courtesy of the American Jewish Historical Society; #709 A-27.

Michael M. Allen, the first Jewish chaplain in the U.S. Army. Allen's election as chaplain for his unit caused a widespread controversy in the Union Army, which stipulated that all chaplains must hold official ordination and represent a Christian denomination. Courtesy of the American Jewish Historical Society; #1120.

Jews began participating in the civic life of the nation almost immediately after their arrival in the United States. In a parade honoring the reception of President Lincoln's remains, the Hebrew Benevolent Association marched alongside the German Workmen's Society in the fourth division of the parade. Courtesy of the American Jewish Historical Society; #1032.

A Boston election poster in Yiddish called on voters to vote for William Berwin for alderman in an election to be held on December 13, 1898. Courtesy of the American Jewish Historical Society; #1482

Jonah J. Goldstein's election poster reflected New York City's culture of ethnic politics during the first decades of the twentieth century. Goldstein's poster plays on numerous themes important to his potential Jewish constituents. Courtesy of the American Jewish Historical Society; #635/2.

THE JUDGE.

4

THE RUSSIAN JEWS AND THE STRIKE.

Observant Policeman.—"May be as how these fellers ain't no good for this work, but in a few years they'll own all the railroads."

Anti-Semitic cartoons accused Jewish men of being effeminate and unable to perform manual labor but possessing extraordinary economic prowess. Courtesy of the American Jewish Historical Society; #1747.

The Judge published this anti-Semitic cartoon on July 22, 1882, depicting America as overrun by Jewish immigrants. Note the street sign, which reads "Levi St., formerly Canal." Courtesy of the American Jewish Historical Society; #179.

MENAUHANT HOTEL

❉❉❉❉❉❉❉❉❉❉❉❉❉❉ MENAUHANT. MASS. ❉❉❉❉❉❉❉❉❉❉❉❉❉❉

Date of
Opening

THIS House, is situated in Falmouth Township, on the South Shore of Cape Cod, at the confluence of Nantucket and Vineyard Sounds, it is directly on the beach, and is nearly surrounded by water; it is owned and managed by Mr. Floyd Travis, and will be open for the season of 1906, on June 16th.

MENAUHANT WHARF.

A great many conditions combine to make Menauhant the most delightful summer resort on Cape Cod.

We have no HEBREW patronage.

It became common practice for hotels and vacation resorts to refuse Jewish guests. Courtesy of the American Jewish Historical Society; #1285.

During World War I, organizations like the American Jewish Relief Committee sent money and supplies to European Jews caught in the cross fire of the warring nations. Courtesy of the American Jewish Historical Society; #1719.

BREAD AT LAST

LODZ — Bread made from flour bought by the Joint Distribution Committee is the only daily sustenance for nearly 500,000 Jews in Poland.

The American Jewish Joint Distribution Committee provided financial and material support to Jewish communities throughout Europe during World War I. Here Jews in Lodz receive bread, the only daily sustenance for almost five hundred thousand Jews in Poland. Courtesy of the American Jewish Historical Society in Waltham; #578II.

The Jewish South.

DEVOTED TO THE INTERESTS OF JUDAISM.

VOL. I.   RICHMOND, VA., FRIDAY, AUGUST 25, 1893.   No. 1.

Plate IV
Vol. I No. 1, The Jewish South

Jewish newspapers sprang up wherever Jews settled. Southern Jews relied on regional papers rather than local ones, since they lived in small and scattered locales. The press became one of the primary means for communities to discuss politics, communicate, and receive news from other parts of the country and the world. Courtesy of the American Jewish Historical Society; #18078.

During the 1930s, Jews throughout the United States participated in the anti-Nazi movement. Jewish organizations mounted rallies like this one, held on March 27, 1933, in New York's Madison Square Garden, to protest Nazi anti-Jewish policies. Courtesy of the American Jewish Historical Society in Waltham.

American Jews gather on March 23, 1933, to protest the rise of the Nazi party in Germany. Courtesy of the American Jewish Historical Society; I-7 roll 17.

HELP RESCUE THROUGH EMIGRATION HELP

שפּען מיט גערעטעוועטע דורך האיאס
קומען צו אונזערע ברעננען!

העלפט זיי קומען

ווייזט אייער דערבארמונג היינט

העלפּט **האַיאַס** העלפּט

אין דער הייליגער רעטונגס ארבעט

שנדר'ט פאר האיאס

 ## CONTRIBUTE TO HIAS

HEBREW SHELTERING and IMMIGRANT AID SOCIETY
10 TREMONT STREET, BOSTON, MASS.

The Boston chapter of the Hebrew Immigrant Aid Society implored American Jews in Yiddish to contribute to assist postwar Jewish refugees to immigrate to America. Courtesy of the American Jewish Historical Society; #623.

This poster, from World War II, advertises a "grand artistic performance" about the Warsaw Ghetto revolt. The production demonstrated the concern American Jews had for their coreligionists' suffering in Nazi-dominated Europe. Courtesy of the American Jewish Historical Society; #526/92.

A Hanukkah service held at Harvard-Radcliffe on December 7, 1945. At that time, Harvard still enforced a quota on admitting Jewish students. Courtesy of the American Jewish Historical Society; #1619.

April 17, 1947

Miss ████████████████████
████████████████████
Elkins Park, Pennsylvania

My dear Miss ████████:

    It is with regret that we are obliged to
return your application but our Jewish quota
has been filled for some time.

    Trusting that you will find another college
to your liking, we are,

                Sincerely yours,

                W.H. Moore, III
                President

WHM:B

Eng. 2

During the first half of the twentieth century, many institutions of higher learning imposed quotas on Jews. Often institutions overtly acknowledged their exclusionary policies, as did this one to an unsuccessful applicant to the Maryland College for Women. Courtesy of the American Jewish Historical Society; #1286.

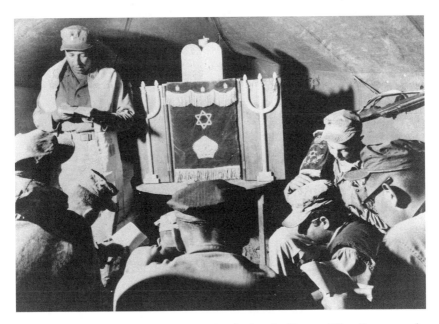

Jewish GIs participate in a prayer service during the Korean War. Courtesy of the American Jewish Historical Society; #560.

Rabbi Abraham Joshua Heschel, one of the most important twentieth-century Jewish theologians, marched alongside Martin Luther King Jr. on the historic march from Selma to Montgomery in March 1965. Courtesy of the Jacob Rader Marcus Center of the American Jewish Archives; #2232.

Andrew Goodman and Michael Henry Schwerner traveled to the South during the Freedom Summer of 1964. Shown in this FBI poster, the two students were murdered, along with James Earl Chaney, while investigating the bombing of African American churches in Mississippi. Courtesy of the Jacob Rader Marcus Center of the American Jewish Archives; #2220.

In the 1980s members of the Jewish-Black Dialogue, organized by the Washington branch of the American Jewish Committee, picketed the South African embassy in protest of that nation's apartheid policy. Courtesy of the author.

The late 1960s made it possible for Lubavitcher Hasidism to begin large-scale outreach activities. The group endeavored to persuade as many Jews as possible to practice Judaism according to Jewish law, including observing Succot, the fall harvest festival that involves eating a festive meal in a "booth." Courtesy of the American Jewish Historical Society; #P-358.

The 1970s witnessed the rise of Jewish student organizations on America's college campuses. Here students participate in Israeli dancing, which has become popular in America since Israel gained its independence in 1948. Courtesy of the American Jewish Historical Society; #P-358.

During the 1970s the Soviet government's persecution of its Jewish citizens galvanized Jews throughout the world to stage protests calling for the liberation of Soviet Jewry. Courtesy of the American Jewish Historical Society; #P-358.

PART THREE

TWENTIETH-CENTURY JOURNEYS

6

AT HOME AND BEYOND

1924–1948

The quarter century between 1924 and 1948 proved to be one of the most momentous periods in Jewish history. It raised wrenching questions about the future of the Jews and severely tested the proposition that real emancipation would be possible and that modernity would mean true integration for the Jews. In this relatively short period European Jews experienced an unprecedented escalation of anti-Semitism in the countries that had been cut out of the patchwork quilt of the Austro-Hungarian Empire, including Poland, Hungary, and Czechoslovakia. They endured the rise of National Socialism in Germany in 1933 and later the devastating loss of 6 million Jews at the hands of the Nazis and their allies.

This period also witnessed another transformation. The Jews, who had been stateless since the beginning of the Common Era, established a home of their own with the creation of the state of Israel on May 14, 1948. The emergence of an independent Jewish homeland shifted worldwide Jewish geography; most survivors of Nazi persecutions moved as soon as they could from Europe to Israel. The Jewish communities of North Africa and the Middle East—Morocco, Libya, Tunisia, Egypt, Algeria, Syria, Yemen, Iraq, and Iran—converged on the newly formed state and in the process redrew the Jewish map. From that date forward American Jewry would place Israel and its security high on their political agenda.

These momentous developments, involving loss and gain, tragedy and redemption, took place far from the United States. This transformative quarter century demonstrated emphatically how differently American Jews experienced history from their sisters and brothers living most other places. During these two cataclysmic events—the Holocaust and the struggle for an independent, sovereign Jewish state—American Jews stood on the sidelines. This does not imply that they were unconcerned with the fate of their coreligionists. On the contrary, they actively worked to rescue Jews from the rising calamity in Europe, watching in horror as "the Jews of Europe were marked for, and came close to extermination at the hands of the Nazi hordes."[1] They also rallied enthusiastically around the idea of a Jewish state. Indeed, these events, particularly the rising threat in Germany and the spread of the destruction into eastern Europe, their "old home," shaped the consciousness of the Jews in the United States.

The "main event" in the lives of American Jews actually involved the lengthy and complicated process of middle-class Americanization. Jews were taking steps toward reconciling the realities of their mobility with the society's mixed signals about their place in the life of the nation. The Jews simultaneously experienced welcome and rejection, embrace and disdain, opportunity and restriction, dramatic success and discrimination. Indeed, this time period began with the passage of the National Origins Act, which, while not specifically aimed at reducing Jewish immigration, did accomplish just that. Many of the bill's proponents articulated negative opinions of Jews, particularly of the potential emigrants from eastern Europe who would have continued to pour into the United States, had they been permitted.

This era of uncertainty culminated in the 1945 passage of the Ives-Quinn antidiscrimination bill in New York, the first of its kind in the country. Jews benefited early and profoundly from this act, which prohibited discrimination in employment on the basis of race, creed, or color. Other states with large Jewish populations, such as New Jersey and Massachusetts, followed shortly thereafter with their own legislation.[2] In 1948 the *American Jewish Yearbook* heralded the report of President Truman's Committee on Civil Rights. That report, and the civil rights efforts on the state and local levels, worked to the advantage of America's Jews and demonstrated the important role that Jewish organizations played in spearheading the "fight against discrimination."[3] In that same year, with the landmark case *Shelley v. Kramer,* the U.S. Supreme Court invalidated restrictive covenants that had barred Jews from buying houses in neighborhoods whose residents had, since the 1920s, wanted to exclude them. Finally, in 1948 New York, home to more Jews than any other state, passed the Fair Education Practices Act, making discrimination in college and university admissions illegal.

These pieces of legislation and judicial decisions brought this quarter century to a close in a way that met with the approval of the Jews. At the beginning of this period colleges and universities had begun to enforce quotas on Jewish students. Likewise, certain large employers, like the telephone companies in Boston and New York, went to great lengths to pass over Jewish applicants. Yet despite these discriminatory practices, the conditions of the lives of Jews in the United States highlighted the vast differences between them and their fellow Jews across the Atlantic. Rather than being utterly marginalized, they moved closer to the comforts available to other white middle-class Americans, even amid the realities of anti-Semitism. As Jews in Germany, central Europe, and eastern Europe began to lose their citizenship, legitimacy, and their lives, American Jews were increasingly moving away from the poverty and immigrant status of the past to relatively unfettered participation in American life.

Some of them achieved wide recognition as articulators of American culture. They made movies, composed music, and wrote plays accepted by the public as exemplars of American popular culture. Many Jews taught in public schools. They increasingly participated in civic affairs, owing to the expansion of the federal government under the aegis of the New Deal, crafting legislation that would affect the lives of all Americans. The limitations on their access to some white-collar jobs and to elite colleges and universities actually reflected the ascendant position of the Jews, who gradually navigated from outsider to insider status in America.

Yet the fact that some achieved renown and moved closer to the center of American society did not spell the end of a distinctive Jewish culture. The path taken by Jewish institutions—such as synagogues, schools, and community centers—reflected the twin aims of American Jews: to live as Jews and to be accepted as Americans. In basic matters such as jobs, place of residence, and family structure, though the Jews could take advantage of expanding opportunities in America, they did so in idiosyncratically Jewish ways. In essence, they lived through the prosperity of the 1920s, the ravages of the Depression, and the intensity of World War II differently from how other Americans did.

AMERICAN ANTI-SEMITISM

Moving incrementally away from the margins did not spell the end of anti-Jewish behavior and rhetoric in this period from the 1920s through the 1940s. To the contrary, this era saw the peak years of American anti-Semitism during both the "tribal twenties" and the Depression years. Not until the United States entered the war did anti-Semitism begin to abate, and in the years right after the war ended, only those on society's fringes dared to express anti-Jewish sentiment. The upsurge in anti-Semitism in America in the 1920s owed its existence to a number of factors. America functioned in the context of a Western cultural system, linking it, despite the widespread isolationism in the aftermath of World War I, to intellectual and cultural trends in Europe. Although American anti-Semitism was much milder than its European counterpart, it reflected the same ideas attributing to different "races" radically different moral and mental abilities.[4]

Further, for some Americans, like small-town white Protestant fundamentalists, the visibility of Jews in the movies as music producers and in other areas of popular entertainment proved that urban Jews were bent on destroying the essential qualities of America's Christian civilization. They believed the culture to be slipping away from them, the white Christian majority, and loathed the idea that the Jews had seized it.[5] Jews did indeed play a prominent role in popular entertainment. Most of the moguls of the movie industry—Louis B. Mayer, Adolph Zukor, the Warner Bros., Harry Cohn—were Jewish. Jews like Al Jolson, Irving Berlin, Sophie Tucker, Fanny Brice, George Arlen, George Gershwin, Benny Goodman, Ziggy Elman, Yip Harburg, Eddie Cantor, Lorenz Hart, Jerome Kern, Oscar Hammerstein II, and Mezz Mezrow, many of them immigrants themselves or the children of immigrants, helped to create an American musical vernacular.

They borrowed heavily from styles associated with African American culture and by doing so raised the specter of racial mixing, a dreadful taboo to the overwhelming majority of Americans. Jewish musicians not only incorporated African American styles into their tunes, but they also publicly crossed the color line. In 1938 jazz clarinetist Artie Shaw featured Billie Holiday, an African American singer, in his signature piece "Begin the Beguine."[6] In the process, he began an assault on American definitions of cultural purity. Likewise, Chicago-born clarinetist Benny Goodman ignored a performance taboo in 1936 when he brought Lionel Hampton into his quartet.[7] In his 1930 movie *Whoopee!* Eddie Cantor helped a white woman defy her father and reunite with her Indian lover, thereby both condoning interracial romance and confirming the American idea that "love conquers all," even race. The wildly popular corpus of creative work created by American Jews seemed to challenge the idea that white Christians still guarded American culture.[8]

Many Americans began to believe their civilization to be in great peril. A resurgent Ku Klux Klan with a national constituency played on the idea that Jews, as Bolsheviks, had led the Russian Revolution, and that they were poised to lead another revolution in America.[9] With equal conviction, some, particularly in America's agricultural belt who did not benefit from the prosperity of the 1920s, believed that the Jews, whom they assumed were controlling Wall Street, along with those making the transgressive movies in Hollywood, conspired to destroy American rural life, which should have remained Christian to the core. For seven years, beginning in 1922, Henry Ford waged a vigorous campaign against the Jews in the name of decent, hard-working small-town America. In 1919 Ford had purchased a nearly defunct newspaper, *The Dearborn Independent,* and started to write editorials attacking Jews. While his assault began with scattered anti-Semitic remarks, it quickly became a more formidable threat when in 1920 he published, in a series called "The International Jew: the World's Foremost Problem," the notorious forgery *The Protocols of the Elders of Zion* imported from Russia. The readership of the newspaper extended beyond those who already subscribed to anti-Jewish thinking. Ford insisted that his dealerships stock copies of the paper, making his ideas about the "international Jewish conspiracy" available to anyone who came to buy an automobile.[10]

American anti-Semitism did not just reside in those with visions of a return to a homogenous, Protestant "old-time" rural America. It emanated from elite circles as well. From the early 1920s through the mid-1940s, most American colleges and universities, particularly those on the East Coast, imposed quotas on Jewish students. Schools like Harvard worried that if academic merit alone became the standard in the admissions process, they would become "too Jewish." State universities in the South and Midwest as well as law, medical, and dental schools also devised strategies to limit their Jewish students. Some public universities in the North, in states with large Jewish populations, found ways to restrict the number of Jews. Rutgers College in New Jersey, for example, admitted in 1931 that it would put a cap on the Jewish students "to equalize the proportion" of Jews in the student body and to prevent Rutgers from becoming "denominational." Its sister institution, New Jersey College for Women (later Douglas College), accepted 61 percent of all applicants in 1930, but only 31 percent of the Jews, although the commit-

tee on admission admitted that "their scholastic standing is usually better than that of the other students."[11]

In the realm of high culture, Jewish artists, with their modernistic edge
and their willingness to experiment with racial hybridism and mixed
genres, provoked a negative reaction among the custodians of the arts.
Virgil Thompson, on hearing George Gershwin's 1935 opera *Porgy and
Bess,* declared that Gershwin "does not even seem to know what an
opera is." He could, continued Thompson, "never compete with *us* for
intellectual prestige."[12] In nearly every locus of elite life in America, Jews
found the doors shutting in their faces. In the 1920s many affluent communities started using restrictive covenants to prevent Jews from buying
homes. Social clubs and resorts that had excluded Jews since the turn of
the century continued to do so. The number of such places spread. A
hotel in Michigan emblazoned its front with a sign saying "A hotel exclusively for gentiles," while another declared "No Hebrew or tubercu-
lar guests received."

In many professions, particularly those to which American Jews aspired, various degrees of restriction barred their entry. Some hospitals refused to give privileges of treating patients to Jewish doctors. The most
prestigious law firms would not consider hiring Jewish attorneys. Banks
and many public utilities refused to employ Jews, regardless of their
skills. Through the early 1930s no more than one hundred Jews held
professorial positions in American universities, while many of the daughters of Jewish immigrants, eager to enter white-collar occupations, encountered advertisements for secretarial positions specifying "Gentile"
as a qualification.[13]

Jews Blamed during the Depression

If the 1920s saw the building up of a substantial edifice of anti-Jewish
rhetoric and behavior, much of it considered acceptable, the 1930s represented anti-Semitism's apex. Americans facing unemployment and the
loss of economic status blamed the Jews for their problems. As many
Christians saw it, Jews seemed to be suffering less than other Americans
from the Depression. Jews, American Gentile writers noted, benefited
from their economic power, which protected them from the economic
pain felt by the majority. Increasingly, Gentiles in America voiced the
opinion that Jews took care of their own, and in the process everyone
else suffered, reflecting the common belief in Jewish clannishness and
self-centeredness. The Jew, according to the liberal *Christian Century* in
1936, "will never command the respect of the non-Jewish culture in

which he lives so long as he huddles by himself, nursing his own 'uniqueness,' cherishing his tradition as something which is precious to *him* but in the nature of things cannot be conveyed to others, nor participated in by others."[14]

At times this kind of talk developed into political action against Jews. In a number of Polish American communities residents noisily protested in the streets the presence of Jewish merchants. They argued that Jewish shopkeepers robbed Polish businessmen of their livelihood, and picketers encouraged the women and men of *polonia* to buy from their own.[15] In some urban African American neighborhoods, anti-Semitic rhetoric could be heard from street corner speakers who blamed the Jews for the devastating economic woes of the black community. Many Jewish merchants in Harlem, who had been there since the days when the neighborhood was heavily Jewish, became the target of resentment that spilled over into a stream of anti-Jewish venom.

Highly visible campaigns in Harlem and Chicago to boycott merchants who did not hire African American employees thrived. Speakers admonished African American consumers with such slogans as "Don't Shop Where You Can't Work." These efforts targeted many small Jewish mom-and-pop stores that had long relied on the labor of family members. Particularly during the Depression, those who held on to such stores tried to help out unemployed relatives first. But in the eyes of Sufi El Hamid, the organizer of the campaign in Harlem, this made the Jews evil exploiters of black people, and he went so far as to state that he could easily sympathize with Hitler. In 1935 a riot in Harlem saw the destruction of Jewish shops and stores at the hands of an African American mob that regarded the Jews as interlopers. Ironically, the Yiddish newspapers described Sufi El Hamid as the "Black Hitler" and drew for their readers a parallel between his deeds and the stripping of Jewish economic rights in Germany.[16]

Anti-Semitic rhetoric was heard not only on street corners but also on the airwaves. Father Charles Coughlin of Detroit ranted to an estimated 30 million radio listeners about the Jewish domination of America. His newspaper, *Social Justice,* carried the same message.[17] Coughlin did not represent a lone example of this kind of talk. Rather, from the middle of the 1930s through the end of World War II, a stream of anti-Semitic organizations, publications, and speakers competed in viciously vilifying the Jews. The Silver Shirts, the Friends of Democracy, and the National Union for Social Justice, all short-lived anti-Semitic organizations, each with its own leader, members, and publications, also vied with one another in their denunciation of the Jews, all acknowledging the potency of the example of Hitler and the Nazis.

Average Americans with anti-Jewish proclivities also expressed their dislike of the Jews. In opinion polls, an innovation of the 1930s, they admitted to their belief that Jews benefited from the suffering of Christians. In 1938 almost 50 percent of Americans answered affirmatively when asked if they had a low opinion of Jews. Polls continued to reflect the fact that many believed Jews to be less trustworthy and honest than other Americans. As late as 1946, 64 percent of those asked claimed that they had heard negative talk about Jews.[18]

Surveying the American scene in 1947, near the end of this time period, the Anti-Defamation League noted both the contradictions of the era and the direction in which American sentiments were headed. The ADL noted in its summary that it had discerned "broadly speaking and with certain significant geographic exceptions . . . a very real increase in" what it labeled "unorganized anti-Semitism." In this category it included "acts of anti-Semitism not directed by professional hate-mongers. This includes individual acts of hostility against Jews, and economic, social, and educational discrimination." Yet two years after World War II had come to an end, the report, put together by Arnold Forster, the national director of this organization wrote, "With respect to organized anti-Semitism, the picture is somewhat different: There appears to be less organized anti-Semitic activity than at any time since 1933."[19]

The ADL did not randomly choose 1933 as its benchmark year. In that year, the lowest point of the Depression and the beginning of the New Deal—and the year that the Nazis came to power in Germany—many non-Jewish Americans seized on the idea not only that the Jews had caused their affliction but also that they controlled the government. Many Americans who disliked President Roosevelt and his policies believed that he had surrounded himself with Jews who made policy from a Jewish perspective for their own benefit. Some serving in the administration recognized the pervasiveness of this belief and felt the need to respond to the public discourse about what some derisively termed the "Jew Deal." Adlai Stevenson, for example, noted that among the attorneys working alongside him on the staff of Jerome Frank, general counsel to the short-lived Agricultural Adjustment Administration, "there is a little feeling that the Jews are getting too prominent." Whatever Stevenson himself thought about Jews and their role in the administration, he obviously felt that this New Deal agency needed to win public support, particularly from the farmers. If the AAA's constituents believed that the agency had become dominated by Jews, then the administration's efforts to woo the farmers might be put in jeopardy.[20]

Stevenson no doubt knew how widely Roosevelt's critics questioned what they saw as the undue power of the Jews on Franklin Roosevelt and his activist wife, Eleanor, whom they frequently reviled as a "Jew lover." Some went so far as to claim that Roosevelt himself was really a Jew named "Rosenfeld." One popular verse depicted a conversation between Eleanor and Franklin:

> You kiss the niggers,
> I'll kiss the Jews,
> We'll stay in the White House
> As long as we choose?[21]

Others close to Roosevelt also expressed overtly anti-Jewish attitudes and believed that Jews manipulated his policies. Roosevelt named Joseph P. Kennedy to become ambassador to England in 1938. While there, Kennedy met with German officials and complained to them that Roosevelt had fallen into the clutches of the Jews. Kennedy had amassed part of his fortune in the movie industry, which he believed also represented Jewish interests. He considered the press to be controlled by them as well. Kennedy, who maintained a friendship with Father Coughlin, urged the United States to tread lightly in its dealings with Hitler. After all, he noted, Hitler opposed Communism and might prove helpful to the United States.[22]

Issues involving the rescue of European Jews also played themselves out in the context of this heightened atmosphere of anti-Semitism and the discourse about Roosevelt and "the Jews." Most Jewish organizations recognized that power politics in Washington and the general mood in America did not favor easing immigration restrictions, pushing them toward adopting a quiet, behind-the-scenes approach. They staged few noisy rallies, called out few provocative slogans. They believed that drawing attention to their agenda would only exacerbate the anti-Semitism from which they already suffered.

A Faint Echo of Europe

American anti-Semites in the 1930s had a powerful model to follow. After all, in this same decade Hitler assumed power in Germany, eliminated Jewish citizenship, barred them from the professions and schools, put into effect the Nuremburg Laws of 1935 to protect German racial purity, launched the pogrom of November 1938—*Kristallnacht*—and took Germany and the rest of Europe down the inexorable road toward the Final Solution. In 1930s New York Fritz Kuhn's German-American Bund enrolled a small but highly vocal membership that spouted rhetoric from Berlin and, joining up with other anti-Semitic groups like the Christian Front, desecrated synagogues, sporadically picketed Jewish retail establishments, and in New York and Boston engaged in random acts of street violence against Jews. The Bund held Nazi meetings in the *Turnverein*—an institution used by Jewish men for recreation in the middle of the nineteenth century. It held mass rallies in Madison Square Garden, and its members proudly displayed their swastikas in the city's Yorkville neighborhood, a heavily German enclave. In many other American neighborhoods as well Jews had good reason to fear for their safety.[23]

From the 1920s through the middle of the 1940s anti-Semitism in America paralleled the swelling tide of anti-Jewish sentiment in Europe. It relied on European-inspired race theory, which understood the Jews as a separate race whose distinctive phenotype they associated with certain inherent depravities. American anti-Jewish rhetoric echoed the economic arguments of its European counterpart, which simultaneously blasted Jews as capitalist exploiters and as Bolshevik revolutionaries. In America as in Europe, anti-Semitism operated within a deeply Christian culture and relied on age-old religious metaphors.

Yet America's relatively muted anti-Jewish behavior posed little threat, particularly in comparison to the situation in Europe, including England and France. Although it caused personal pain and communal discomfort, most American Jews remained safe as individuals and as members of a community, undeterred in their desire to live as they wanted. That fact, however, did not mean that they did not take anti-Semitism into account when making basic decisions about work, residence, education, and leisure. Although anti-Semitism in these years may have seemed tame when set against the cataclysm engulfing Europe, it continued to mold Jewish political consciousness. On a personal level it caused Jews discomfort and even anguish as they negotiated their path into the middle class.

Jews reacted in a variety of ways to the anti-Semitism of these years. Agencies like the American Jewish Committee, the American Jewish Congress, and the Anti-Defamation League defended Jewish rights as much as they could. They lobbied and testified in Congress against immigration restriction, which they saw as only slightly disguised anti-Semitism.[24] They issued propaganda to counter anti-Jewish stereotyping on the stage and in the press and joined with other organizations of goodwill to eliminate racism in American society, by supporting, for example, anti-lynching legislation and exposing the nefarious goals of the Ku Klux Klan. They argued that racism ran counter to American ideals and violated the essentially liberal and egalitarian spirit of the American creed.[25] They worked behind the scenes to have anti-Semitic publications withdrawn. Louis Marshall of the American Jewish Committee labored successfully to have Henry Ford's newspaper withdrawn, threatening a lawsuit if the automobile manufacturer did not comply.[26]

By and large, Jewish organizations shied away from airing their fears publicly, loathe to express their anger or to point out the "Jewish" angle of their political vision. Noisy demonstrations and impassioned public proclamations drawing attention to Jewish concerns did not suit their desire to be viewed as sober, respectable citizens. As they dealt with anti-Semitism in their communities, leaders of the American Jewish organizations sought to disprove the images purveyed by their enemies. They calculated that this strategy would have only minimal negative implications for Americans Jews. In the final analysis, only a handful of Jewish stores had been vandalized, a limited number of synagogues had been defaced, and very few individual Jews had been roughed up on the streets. And although many Jewish students may have been barred from certain colleges and universities, in New York, at least, they could flock in large numbers to Hunter College or City College. For those rejected from medical school or who felt too discouraged to apply, other careers, in pharmacy, for example, provided alternatives.

RESCUING EUROPE'S JEWS

This political posture of limited assaults on anti-Semitism had deep repercussions on the kind of leverage the Jews had hoped to have with regards to the crisis in Europe. With the Nazi accession to power, the German occupation of Austria and Czechoslovakia, and the outbreak of the war in 1939, Americans—non-Jews—strongly desired to stay isolated from Europe's problems. Some believed that Jewish efforts to enlist the U.S. government in the rescue of their sisters and brothers in peril compromised America's neutrality and amounted to a Jewish campaign for Jewish interests, to be waged on the backs of young American soldiers.

Southerners, many of whom represented areas steeped in Christian fundamentalist thinking, dominated Congress. Chairmen of key congressional committees came from districts where few Jews lived and where many considered them a powerful threat to American values.

Roosevelt depended on these congressmen and their constituents for his programs. He did not want to appear overly solicitous to Jewish groups at the same time that most Americans did not take seriously the trickle of news documenting the plight of the Jews in Europe.[27] What small steps the government did take, like issuing an invitation to the leaders of thirty-two nations to meet in Evian, France, to discuss the refugee situation, had to be carefully orchestrated by Roosevelt and the Jewish communal leaders who applauded such action. In his invitation to join the conference and at the meeting in Evian, Roosevelt made clear that no country's immigration laws would be jeopardized. Jewish leaders expressed great joy at the outcome of this meeting, but in the final analysis because of the constraints within which Roosevelt operated, his actions made almost no difference to European—or American—Jews.

Organization leaders and rabbis, molders of American Jewish public opinion, understood that Roosevelt did not have a totally free hand in his dealing with the State Department, which controlled the visa process. The department had long been a bastion of anti-Semitism. Individuals with the power to decide who got visas and who did not and who showed little overt friendliness to the Jews staffed the U.S consular offices in Europe. Roosevelt, whom many believe wanted to do more, walked a fine line between a public that was not terribly fond of Jews, was wary of Jewish power, and sure that Roosevelt did the bidding of the Jews and the Jewish organizational leaders who were encouraging him to do more.[28]

This set of realities shaped the behavior of American Jews as they faced the emerging crisis in Europe. Their efforts starting in 1933 flowed organically from the activities they had engaged in during the 1920s. Through *landsmanschaftn* and other organizations, and particularly through the actions of philanthropists and communal leaders, they participated in the rebuilding projects made necessary by World War I. Starting in the middle of the 1920s American Jewish agencies scrambled to create programs in central and eastern Europe designed to rebuild Jewish life in the aftermath of the Great War, with its widespread Jewish dislocations. Committees formed to support the autonomous Jewish region of Birbidjian in the Soviet Union in the middle of the 1930s, providing Jews with a project combining their Jewish and pro-Soviet loyalties.[29] They also sought to publicize to the U.S. government the rising crisis of anti-Semitism in Poland, Romania, and elsewhere in eastern Europe.

By 1933 the situation had grown graver. From that date on, culminating with the war's end in 1945, prominent American Jews, either on their own or through organizations, appealed to President Roosevelt, to the American public, and to Congress to act. They beseeched those with power to help rescue the Jews, especially those trapped in Europe facing horrible persecutions. Even before it became clear that the Germans intended to annihilate the Jews of Europe, American Jews met with government officials and sent a barrage of telegrams and letters, begging for assistance. In 1944 the American Jewish Conference, founded the previous year at the suggestion of B'nai B'rith president Henry Monsky to promote unity in the face of the grave threat, proposed to Roosevelt that the United States negotiate with the Germans directly. They should empty out the death camps, and the Allies would return to them all German prisoners captured in battle.[30] Both as individuals and as leaders of organizations American Jews tried to awaken their non-Jewish colleagues to the enormity of the problem. They constantly strategized to find ways to advance the cause of their fellow Jews caught in the lethal clutches of the Germans.

Organized Efforts

Nearly all sectors of American Jewry responded. Each approached the crisis in its own way, reflecting its particular style and constituency. As early as May 1933, shortly after Hitler's ascension to power, the American Jewish Congress sponsored a number of mass demonstrations and public rallies in New York and other cities. Its national leader, Rabbi Stephen Wise, urged a nationwide boycott of German goods. He had been preceded in this by the Jewish War Veterans, who had also suggested that an economic boycott would harm the infant Nazi economy. As a result, the JWV hoped, the Germans would vote Hitler out of power. Supporters of the boycott picketed stores that continued to carry German-made products. Wise's boycott eventually took on a global dimension, as Jews in other countries joined the effort, and as a result, the World Jewish Congress came into being in 1936 under the leadership of Nahum Goldman.

In 1934 Jews from the trade union movement responded by creating the Jewish Labor Committee. It sought to inform American organized labor about the evils of totalitarianism and provided direct aid to Jewish trade unionists fleeing Germany. As early as 1934, Baruch Charney Vladek of the Committee addressed the annual meeting of the American Federation of Labor, the largest and most powerful labor organization in the United States, about Germany's persecution of the Jews. The B'nai B'rith, in part because of its past history ferreting out anti-Semitism in the United States, mobilized its resources to expose organizations in America that maintained links to the Hitler regime, although it opposed the idea of the boycott. The American Jewish Committee, long uncomfortable with Zionism, went so far as to criticize the British government for its refusal to allow large numbers of Jewish refugees into Palestine, although, like the B'nai B'rith, it believed that boycotts and noisy street demonstrations would be counterproductive.

Hadassah, which since its inception had stressed direct service to those in need, adopted the Youth Aliyah project in 1935. Youth Aliyah had been founded the previous year in Germany by Recha Frier to resettle German Jewish children in Palestine. Henrietta Szold saw this kind of undertaking as conforming to her organization's vision. Hadassah became the agent for Youth Aliyah in the United States, raising money and the consciousness of American Jews about the plight of German Jewry. Likewise, the National Council of Jewish Women took on the cause both of German Jewish children and of the resettlement of Jewish refugees in the United States. In 1939 Orthodox rabbis founded the Vaad-ha-Hatzala, "the rescue committee." Initially the Vaad looked out for rabbis and yeshiva students attempting to flee Lithuania and Poland. During the war it expanded its efforts, participating in more general rescue efforts. In 1943 it organized a march on Washington, hoping to focus public attention on the catastrophe taking place on the other side of the Atlantic.[31]

On July 21, 1942, when news of the wholesale slaughter of Jews in eastern Europe reached America, twenty thousand people massed at New York's Madison Square Garden for a rally called by the American Jewish Congress, the B'nai B'rith, the Jewish Labor Committee, and the American Jewish Committee. Thousands more stood outside, overflowing the arena. Notable Americans—public officials, labor leaders, representatives of the Christian clergy—participated, while President Roosevelt sent a telegram declaring that all Americans "hold the perpetrators of these crimes to strict accountability." Following this giant rally, the Synagogue Council of America declared on July 23, Tisha B'av (the day of mourning recalling the destruction of the Temple in Jerusalem), to be a special day in memory of the victims of Nazis, while Jews in Chicago, Milwaukee, Hartford, and elsewhere lent their voices to the chorus of lament.[32]

Some American Jews thought that words of compassion meant little in light of the grave threat, and they rallied to the call of Peter Bergson (originally Hillel Kook). He thought all these resolutions to be mere exercises in futility, and he shook up the ranks of American Zionists who sought to link the rescue of Europe's Jews with the creation of a Jewish homeland. Bergson called on Jews to form an army to directly take on the Third Reich. His splashy advertisements in American newspapers claimed "We Shall Never Die." Bergson won the support of journalist Ben Hecht, who staged a pageant invoking the same idea. "We Will Never Die" enlisted prominent Hollywood personalities—Paul Muni, Edward G. Robinson, Paul Henreid—who went to a number of American cities with the message that Jews had to take their destiny in their own hands. The words may have been bold, but ultimately they revealed merely a high level of wishful thinking.[33] Other Zionists representing the mainstream of the movement gathered at New York's Biltmore Hotel for a meeting of the Zionist conference in May 1942. They too expressed deep concern about the plight of Europe's Jews, and they rose in thunderous applause to the suggestion made by Rabbi Abba Hillel Silver that the time had come to declare a Jewish state. Only with sovereignty would rescue be possible.[34]

Could More Have Been Done?

American Jews' concern for the Jews of Europe and their awareness of the unfolding crisis evolved gradually. The *American Jewish Yearbook*, published by the American Jewish Committee, had sounded the alarm as early as the late 1920s as the Nazi party began to gather strength in Germany. From that point onward, throughout the 1930s and 1940s it annually provided meticulous details about the decrees of the German government and the spreading desperate plight of European Jewry, both their increasing impoverishment and the physical peril they were increasingly facing. From 1938 to 1939 it succinctly described the Hitler regime policies toward the Jews as "all-embracing and diabolically ingenious," bent on making "living in Germany impossible for all Jews."[35] By the waning years of the 1930s it warned its readers that it felt "no doubt . . . that the Nazi Government was bent upon annihilating the last vestiges of the German Jewish community."[36]

Jewish newspapers abounded with ominous reports from Europe. American Jews, far removed from the European crisis, did what they believed they could. They approached their Christian colleagues in the press, the pulpit, and the other professions to join in their protests. The growing catastrophe began to change the structure of many Jewish organizations. In 1938 the Joint Distribution Committee, the National Coordinating Committee, which provided assistance to refugees, and the

United Palestine Appeal merged to create the United Jewish Appeal, which in its first year raised $16 million intended to relieve distress.[37] In late 1944, when some of Europe's Jews had already experienced the thrill of liberation while others still faced the death camps, American Jews, through the United Jewish Appeal, raised $27 million for overseas needs. At the same time the Joint Distribution Committee expended nearly $24 million.[38] HIAS opened offices around the world, showing up literally as soon as a territory had been liberated by Allied armies.

When opportunities to help came their way, Jewish activists seized them. Ruth Gruber, for example, a journalist and confidant of Secretary of the Interior Harold Ickes, enthusiastically accepted an assignment from him in 1944. President Roosevelt, who over the years had offered almost nothing to American Jews who had asked him to provide refuge for Europe's Jews, decided to allow a thousand into the country. He proposed that they be housed in an abandoned military installation in Oswego, New York. Ickes approached Gruber to take a secret flight to Europe and bring the refugees back to the safety of the United States. He gave her the rank of general for her own protection. If, he warned, "you're shot down and the Nazis capture you as a civilian, they can kill you as a spy. But as a general, according to the Geneva Convention, they have to give you food and shelter and keep you alive." Gruber took the assignment and brought the thousand refugees safely to upstate New York.[39]

Gruber's story stood out because of its successful, albeit limited, resolution. Most American Jews talked and wrote about the crisis but had little to show for their anxiety. Historians have cited the high level of bickering and conflict that frayed American Jewish politics and pointed to what they saw as disastrous blunders. Stephen Wise, for example, has been condemned for his decision not to provide American Jews with information he had in August 1942 about the Final Solution.[40] Abba Hillel Silver has been blamed for putting too much emphasis on Zionist projects and not enough on rescue. With so much squabbling over methods and jealousies over organizational prestige, historians have argued, American Jews could accomplish precious little, effectively sitting by while 6 million perished.[41]

Although these historians correctly point out the high degree of rancor and turf protecting that went on within the ranks of organized American Jews, little evidence suggests that a unified community could have budged Roosevelt, the State Department, with its encrusted anti-Jewish bureaucracy, Congress, and the American public. The administration mainly focused on the lingering effects of the Depression, and it continued to adhere to a profound isolationism, shaped in part by the country's negative experiences of World War I. The forces at work in American society to block assertive action on behalf of European Jewry far outweighed what even a unified and more strident American Jewish community could have accomplished.[42] Additionally, American Jews worked according to the inherited wisdom of the past. They knew what had succeeded at other times when they sought to alleviate the suffering of their coreligionists, and they relied on those strategies to steer a course in this crisis. By the time it became clear that the crisis of the 1930s far surpassed anything they could have imagined, no real alternatives existed.[43]

However much American Jews were hobbled by their in-fighting, and however exaggerated their fears that any militant behavior would have profoundly negative repercussions, they did all share the hope that something could—and would—be accomplished. As a group American Jews felt frustrated by their inability to make so little difference. In 1938 the *American Jewish Yearbook* informed its readers that it considered the year that had just passed "the most somber and disheartening twelve-months for Jews since the close of the World War."[44] Particularly after September 1939 when Hitler's troops invaded Poland—the heartland of European Jewry—they had little they could even contemplate doing, other than read the news reports and face an uncertain future.[45]

For many American Jews, enthusiastic support of the war after December 7, 1941, blended Jewish sensibilities with American patriotism and gave them a sense that they now could somehow change the course of their people's history. Abba Hillel Silver, the Reform rabbi who dominated American Zionism in those years, encouraged America's Jews to "fling themselves resolutely into the fight with Amalek," the biblical foe of the Israelites and a symbol of Hitler and Nazism.[46] Many American Jewish men served in the U.S. military, and while they fought as Americans, part of their commitment to the war effort grew out of their recognition that they found themselves battling the Jewish people's greatest enemy of modern times. Jewish men made up 8 percent of those in uniform, about twice their proportion to the population as a whole. A substantial number of Jewish women volunteered for military service. Three hundred and forty thousand of them served as nurses and in a variety of other capacities. Twelve graduated in the first class of officers commissioned as the Women's Auxiliary Army Corps. One of them, Frances Slanger from Boston's Roxbury neighborhood, landed on the beach in Normandy in advance of the massive invasion that marked the beginning of the end of Nazi domination of Europe. She was also buried there, a casualty of the war.[47]

Supporting a Jewish State

The degree to which American Jews wished they could have done more was also reflected in the amount of time and energy that their organizations devoted to planning for the postwar world. Even as the war raged they sought to influence the postwar fate of the Jewish people. In the early spring of 1943, Henry Monsky, president of the B'nai B'rith, called together the leaders of thirty-four Jewish organizations to plan for the radically changed Jewish world that would exist at the end of the war. The American Jewish Conference that emerged from that meeting assumed that Palestine would play a key role in that future. The war and the destruction of European Jewry played a crucial role in rallying American Jews around the Zionist cause. Although only a minority joined any Zionist society or participated in Zionist politics, even when it became clear that European Jews faced extinction, most American Jews did see a Jewish homeland as the only logical and morally correct outcome of the catastrophe in Europe.

The war and the European crisis caused those who did belong to Zionist groups to sharpen their message and to enhance their organizational structure. In 1945 American Zionists across the ideological spectrum formed the Zionist Emergency Council to direct their propaganda efforts with the American public, the Jewish public, and most important, their lobbying efforts with the U.S. government. A few of the most committed young Jews, through Zionist youth groups like Habonim and Hashomer Hatzair, smuggled arms to the embattled *yishuv,* the Jewish community in Palestine. A handful went there to fight against the British and against the Arab armies in the War for Independence. Most American Jews cheered the announcement from Tel Aviv on May 14, 1948, that Israel had been born as an independent country. There were a few exceptions to the nearly universal support of American Jews for Israeli independence. Members of the American Council for Judaism, founded by anti-Zionists in 1942, for example, did not join in the cheering. But it had no more than twenty thousand members and did not reflect most American Jews, who regarded the independent state of Israel with pride and warmth.[48]

NEGOTIATING JEWISHNESS AT HOME

All the organizational activities of American Jews reflected their knowledge that they did not have numbers on their side, that the American public did not give great weight to their concerns, that many Americans thought Jews too powerful and pushy, and that despite its friendliness, the Roosevelt administration had to juggle numerous interests against theirs. How much these organizations and factions differed depended on how they assessed American attitudes toward them. Their strategies reflected their assessments of the non-Jewish majority.

On a more personal level, from the 1920s through the end of World War II, American Jews sought different ways to cope with the all-too-real limitations they faced. They developed various strategies to circumvent restrictions. A great many found the discomforts too great and the emotional benefits of being Jewish too limited, and they moved away from Jewish life, leaving few traces behind. Some even converted to Christianity.[49] Others drifted into the American mainstream, maintaining no affiliations with Jewish institutions, including the informal networks of neighborhood life, and denying their Jewish antecedents. Intermarriage provided some Jews with a way out. To them Jewishness offered too little when set against the opportunities that total integration would provide.

Some who chose not to sever their connection to Jewishness felt compelled to move cautiously when entering areas in which intolerance of Jews predominated. They knew going in that being Jewish would pose a problem. Lionel Trilling, a major literary critic and professor in Columbia University's English department, recalled that "When I decided to go into academic life, my friends thought me naive to the point of absurdity, nor were they wholly wrong—my appointment to an instructorship in Columbia College was pretty openly regarded as an experiment, and for some time my career in the College was complicated by my being Jewish."[50]

Some Jews found that changing their name offered a reasonable way to "pass" publicly as a non-Jew. Julius Garfinkle, for example, became Jules Garfield and eventually John Garfield. Betty Persky evolved into Lauren Bacall, Marion Levy into Paulette Goddard, and Emanuel Goldenberg into Edward G. Robinson. Leo Jacobi came to be known to American moviegoers as Lee J. Cobb, while Muni Weisenfreund, a star of the Yiddish stage, shone in American movies as Paul Muni. Melvyn Douglas began his life as Melvyn Hesselberg. In the realm of American letters, critics acclaimed the 1939 Day of the Locust by Nathanael West. As Nathan Weinstein, though, the author suffered the humiliation of being a Jewish student at Brown University. In academia, another zone in which a Jewish name limited one's options, a young man born with the last name Shkolnik became the sociologist Robert K. Merton.[51] Writers on the left felt equally compelled to cloak overtly Jewish names in more "American"-sounding ones.[52] Thus Irving Horenstein emerged as Irving Howe, and Ivan Greenberg, as Philip Rahv. Emanuel Garrett had once been Emanuel Geltman, and Albert Gates began his life as Albert Glotzer.[53]

For others, women in particular, cosmetic surgery offered a chance to pass as non-Jewish. Or at least changing their faces provided them with a way to mitigate what they considered the conspicuousness of their Jewishness. For centuries anti-Jewish caricatures had fixated on the "Jewish nose" as a distinctive and comic feature. Jewish women and men in America recognized the prevalence of the stereotype, and some found the surgical procedure a small price to pay for easing the anguish of appearing "too Jewish" and therefore being denied the chance to integrate as well as access to jobs and schools. An English-language article in *Der Tog,* a Yiddish newspaper, spoke directly to Jewish women about this issue: "Many Jewish girls are of the oriental type of physique. This may be very beautiful in its proper setting, but in an Occidental Gentile country a really graceful curved nose is regarded as a 'hooked nose,' the vivid coloring: black eyes, full mouth . . . appear 'common' and 'loud,' the full well-developed figure is 'blowsy' or 'fat.' " The best thing a girl might do for herself would be to "offset these intimations of vulgarity" by whatever means possible. If even friendly Jewish publications dispensed this kind of advice, then Jewish women must have felt a great deal of pressure to fix their defects. No wonder Jewish women began to turn, when they could afford it, to cosmetic surgery to make themselves more "beautiful," more Western, and thereby less "vulgar" and Jewish.[54]

The need to change names and faces went along with a kind of self-censorship in the realm of popular culture. As screenwriters, actors, producers, directors, movie studio owners, songwriters on Tin Pan Alley, and movie theater operators, Jews strove to present themselves as thoroughly American. Most of the movies they made depicted up-beat stories about life in America, a relatively happy place where obstacles could be overcome and where every drama had a happy ending. In contrast to the era of the silent films that came to an end in the middle of the 1920s, most Jewish filmmakers of the 1930s and 1940s assiduously avoided Jewish themes. Sometimes Jewish themes functioned as a kind of hidden message in a movie ostensibly devoid of Jewish content. Eddie Cantor's *Whoopee!* provides a case in point. In the movie the protagonist, Henry Wilson, is ostensibly a Gentile. But at moments Henry lets it be known that he once spoke Yiddish, attended Hebrew school, and had another "real" name, Izzie Horowitz. But these references fly by in rapid-fire dialogue, and audiences could easily miss them. For all intents and purposes *Whoopee!* and its protagonist would not be recognized as Jewish.

Only occasionally did Jewish topics show up in the movies. And in these few films the idea of America as the promised land loomed large. *The Jazz Singer* of 1927 provides an interesting exception to the general tendency to steer clear of Jewish subjects, but it did confirm the industry's trope of happy endings. Inspired by the 1922 short story "The Day of Atonement," the first talking motion picture told the story of a young man—played by Al Jolson—who decides to abandon the Jewish tradition represented by his father, a cantor, for a life of show business. The film depicts traditional Judaism as rigid, unyielding, and without compassion, forcing Jake Rabinowitz to make painful choices. "Show business," as the embodiment of America, welcomes him, allowing him, his mother, and his (presumably) non-Jewish girlfriend to live "happily ever after." The Judaism of his father, whose death the plot dictated, left no room for happiness, compromise, and personal choice.

A whole range of works created by Jewish artists emphasized the essential Americanness both of products and creators. In the late 1930s and early 1940s, a Jew, Irving Berlin (once Israel Baline), wrote "God Bless America," "White Christmas," and "The Easter Parade." In 1943, another Jew, Oscar Hammerstein II, offered to the American public *Oklahoma*, a rousing musical about the power of the American frontier to reconcile personal differences. The show opened with the rousing song "Oh, What a Beautiful Morning." Its title song ended with a rousing chorus, "the land we belong to is grand." A third, Aaron Copland, adopted American musical themes in his 1943 "Fanfare for the Common Man" and "Appalachian Spring" of 1944, for which he won the Pulitzer Prize the following year. Copland, highly identified with left-wing causes, associated himself, through his music, with the richness and inclusive nature of American themes and idioms. Regardless of the criticism hurled at the Jewish producers of American culture, the artists could be confident that what they presented to the public ultimately celebrated the beneficence of American values.

Jewish Enclaves Offer Escape

Most Jews confronted the realities of anti-Semitism in more quotidian matters. For Jewish college students, Hillel, founded in 1923 on the campus of the University of Illinois, offered young people a chance to spend leisure time with their Jewish peers, away from the hostility that pervaded so many college campuses. It allowed Jews who did not feel particularly at home in America to partake of American experiences but with the protection of a comfortable and familiar environment. In classes they sat side by side with non-Jews, but when it came to social life, their comfort came from being apart from them.[55] At the University of Wisconsin, Hillel kept a list of Madison landlords who would rent to Jewish students. Students looking for a place to live could spare themselves the embarrassment of being turned down as soon as the landlord heard their names or saw their faces. Hillel essentially served as a buffer against the hostile world that Jewish students inhabited.[56]

Most Jews, though, lived in primarily Jewish neighborhoods. No doubt part of their decision to live among fellow Jews grew out of their awareness of residential and social exclusion and their fear of encountering hostility in more mixed neighborhoods. It also reflected their understanding of the physical community as an essential component of Jewish life. Little evidence suggests that in those years large numbers of Jews wanted to live in predominantly non-Jewish sections but could not do so. In New York, Chicago, Philadelphia, Boston, Baltimore, and the other cities with large Jewish enclaves, Jews clustered in particular places. The streets, the public schools, the shops, and the parks resounded with Yiddish words. Delicatessens selling corned beef, salami, and pastrami; appetizing shops offering herring, smoked fish, and pickles; and bakeries that turned out aromatic loaves of rye bread marked Jewish space. Newsstands sold Jewish publications, and the basic tempo of life followed the cycle of the Jewish calendar, even when large numbers of residents had drifted away from observing Jewish law. Most Jews, a majority of whom had immigrated to the United States, found this a pleasant way to live, and as such discrimination in the housing field seems to have touched them very little.

Exclusion also may have pushed the Jews to create their own recreational culture. But again, many Jews most likely preferred to spend their social time with other Jews, restrictions or not. In these years, New York Jews created an elaborate culture of leisure in the Catskill Mountains. Staying in simple bungalow colonies, known as *kochaleins*—"cooking by yourself"—or elaborate resorts like Grossinger's and the Concord, they found pleasure in the country, mixing with other Jews, eating Jewish foods, and enjoying the entertainment that made this "borscht belt" famous. The fact that Jews, including those still considered working class, considered themselves entitled to this kind of vacation is perhaps a more notable historical phenomenon than their exclusion from Gentile places of leisure.[57]

American-Brand Zionism

No single measure can be used to determine how at ease American Jews in the 1920s through the 1940s felt. Certainly the vast outpouring of literature, journalism, and film points to a cautiously positive assessment of both America and their place in it. That so few embraced Zionism may demonstrate how little anti-Semitism pervaded their consciousness, or at least how much faith they placed in the basic values and structure of American society. They did not feel the need to seek another home. Zionists recognized this lack of enthusiasm, stressing primarily the need to rescue persecuted Jews and to provide them with a safe, Jewish homeland. Additionally, many Zionist groups, particularly those working with the young, emphasized the fostering of positive Jewish identity rather than the need for American Jews to search for another homeland.

Likewise, the political machinations of American Zionist leaders and the multiple factions splintering the movement did not resonate with American Jews, who concerned themselves more with making a comfortable place for themselves in America than with arguing points of Zionist ideology. Factionalism tore apart American Zionism with particular ferocity in the 1920s and 1930s. Louis Brandeis and Louis Lipsky each represented a different faction within the movement, but neither had much of a popular constituency.[58] In 1941 about forty-six thousand belonged to the Zionist Organization of America and fifty-five thousand to the many smaller Zionist parties like the Labor Zionists or the Mizrachi (religious) Zionists. Membership in Zionist organizations did climb as the plight of European Jewry worsened during and immediately after World War II. The majority of American Jews saw the creation of an independent Jewish homeland as the only way to resolve the trauma of the diaspora created by the Holocaust, but that did not translate into formal affiliation with the movement.[59] But notably, American Jews did not include themselves among those living in exile. Hadassah, the women's Zionist organization, offered a powerful exception as a mass organization that enlisted the time, energy, and loyalty of tens of thousands of members around the country. Through the talented leadership of Henrietta Szold and its work, Hadassah had by the 1920s actually become the largest Jewish organization in America. In 1941 it had eighty thousand members, and its branches, with their weekly meetings and activities, provided a focus for Jewish women's communal lives. It played a significant role in giving shape to American Jewish identity on the community level, and because of its grassroots power, it played an independent political role in the Zionist movement. The secret of Hadassah's success, when other Zionist groups remained fairly weak, grew out of its understanding that Jewish life in America needed to be nurtured and developed, since the vast majority of American Jews planned to stay there.[60] While it focused on succoring other Jews, for example, through its role in Youth Aliyah, Hadassah recognized the need to provide a Jewish context for female social life. In that spirit, in 1934 it launched the School for the Jewish Woman in New York, which offered afternoon and evening classes. In 1940 it created the American Zionist Youth Commission, sending speakers to chapters around the country to lecture on contemporary affairs, Jewish history, and Jewish tradition.

In all these endeavors it sought to provide its members, and by extension other American Jews, with a positive focal point for Jewish life in those uncomfortable decades. Hadassah leaders perceived a vacuum in the lives of American Jews. They understood that increasing numbers of them sought entry into mainstream American institutions and found their paths blocked. To Hadassah activists and to numerous others who systematically observed and commented on the American Jewish scene, this bode ill for the future of Jewish life in America. If young American Jews considered themselves hampered from ascending to professional positions and obtaining the comfort they craved in America, they would no doubt blame their Jewishness rather than American bigotry.

SURVIVING THE DEPRESSION

In the 1920s through the 1940s, some analysts believed that the reality of exclusion, and the widespread Jewish awareness of it, caused deep psychological and cultural distress, particularly as experienced by the young, American-born who represented the emerging majority. In 1922 Harry Wolfson, a Jewish philosopher at Harvard, issued a pamphlet entitled *Escaping Judaism* in which he opined that anti-Semitism should be recognized as a permanent condition that American Jews would have to learn to endure. "Some are born blind," he wrote, "some deaf, some lame, and some are born Jews." Because of that disability, Jews "must be prepared to give up some of the world's goods."[61] Other voices joined the chorus of lament. Louis Wirth, writing in the late 1920s, believed anti-Semitism to be widespread, endemic, and insolvable. Like Wolfson, he knew for certain that as long as Jews existed, they would be dogged by anti-Semitism. While Wirth did not advocate Jewish assimilation and intermarriage, he did predict that only those forces would bring an end to anti-Semitism.

Kurt Lewin, a social psychologist who came to the United States in 1932 from Germany, had witnessed the swelling popularity of the Nazi party. He agreed with Wirth's proposition, asserting that anti-Semitism caused irreparable damage to Jewish children. Unlike Wirth, he believed that a solution other than assimilation existed. The empirical research he conducted for the American Jewish Congress's Commission on Community Interrelations in the mid-1940s led him to advise Jewish parents and institutions to work assiduously on instilling group pride and loyalty in children: "[A]n early buildup of a clear and positive feeling of belongingness to the Jewish group is one of the few effective things that Jewish parents can do for the later happiness of their children. In this way parents can minimize the ambiguity and the tension inherent in the situation of the Jewish minority group, and thus counteract various forms of maladjustment resulting therefrom."[62]

Lewin made an important point. Anti-Semitism poisoned the atmosphere, made Jews uncomfortable, and forced them to find ways to hide or compromise their identities. Certainly on an individual level, Jewishness had an impact on career choices, place of residence, and recreation. But little evidence suggests in fact that anti-Semitism, from 1924 through the end of the 1940s, significantly hampered Jewish economic and educational mobility. It may have altered the paths taken by Jews to achieve these, but it did not stall the process in any measurable way, nor did it bar, for an appreciable number, their entry into the middle class. In essence, despite the fact that anti-Semitism had become more pervasive and virulent, Jews continued to find ways to move out of the working class.

In the 1920s, when immigration came to an end, most Jews still made a living as industrial workers and petty shopkeepers. By the end of World War II, the number of Jewish factory workers had dwindled significantly. Those in retail business now operated more formidable establishments, while the majority of American Jews fell into the category of white-collar workers, including managers, by the middle of the 1940s. Like many Americans, Jews had experienced the 1920s as a flush time. Their experience, however, differed from that of other Americans. They had long shunned heavy industry and farming, and Jewish factory workers tended to be skilled laborers in the needle trades. Even those who still labored in factories did so under the protection of effective unions. In the

1920s Jews had enough excess income to fuel a building boom in synagogues, community centers, schools, resorts, summer camps, and philanthropic ventures for others less fortunate than they. Their coffers bulged enough to allow them to send millions of dollars overseas to relieve Jews in distress in eastern Europe and Palestine.

In fact, by the end of this period, American Jews made up the richest and most powerful Jewish community in the world, and they ranked among the most affluent ethnic groups in America. With regard to education, earning power, and the elaborateness of their communal infrastructure, they far outpaced the children and grandchildren of their co-immigrants from Italy, Greece, Poland, Hungary, and the rest of Europe. Despite the Depression, and the discrimination that remained in place even after the passage of civil rights legislation in the northern and western states, Jews experienced a steady move out of industrial employment into proprietorship, white-collar occupations, and the professions. Owing to the success of Jewish trade unions, the general prosperity of the 1920s, and continuing Jewish investment in the education of their children, by the end of World War II, as school teachers, social workers, civil servants, doctors, lawyers, dentists, accountants, and business owners, Jews occupied a decidedly middle-class position in the nation's economy.[63]

American Jews achieved this solidly middle-class profile by the end of World War II by virtue of having been in the right place at the right time. As white urban dwellers massing in American cities in the heady years of the 1920s, they had taken advantage of the prosperity. They had almost no stake in the agricultural sector, the sick spot in the American economy even in the boom years of the 1920s and the place to suffer the first blows of the Depression. They possessed the right combination of skills and ethnic networks, particularly in commerce, to allow them to take advantage of the good times and to cushion them against the bad. Their concentration in the garment industry, an enterprise needing relatively little start-up capital, gave some of them a chance to become employers. When the Depression set in, few Jews made a living in heavy industry, the worst-hit sector of manufacturing.

As people with white skin, no small credential in a segregated society, they could take advantage of whatever educational and economic opportunities society offered. Exclusion from some colleges and universities still left many institutions of higher learning open. Factory workers assumed—rightly—that their children, those who came of age in the 1920s, 1930s, and 1940s, would not follow them into the garment shops, except perhaps as employers. By the end of the 1930s Jews constituted about 40 percent of the workers in America's garment factories, a dramatic drop from earlier decades.[64] The large numbers of Jewish women and men who had received an education, qualifying them for civil service jobs, teaching in particular, cushioned Jewish families and communities against the worst of the economic downturns and positioned them to segue into the ranks of the American middle class when wartime expansion fueled real recovery. Figures from one relatively typical small Jewish community, Stamford, Connecticut, demonstrate the Jewish insulation from the harshest of conditions. In 1938, well before prosperity had returned, of 960 Jewish households, only twenty-one had no family member bringing in an income. In one-quarter of the households, two individuals drew a paycheck and contributed to the family's welfare. Stamford Jews experienced this Depression year with relatively high employment.[65]

By the end of World War II, all the Jews' economic differences that had splintered the immigrant generation had disappeared. One economist has concluded that there were "no systematic differences among Jews by parent's country of birth" when it came to partaking in the affluence of the late 1940s. This too constituted a significant shift in this era, which had begun at a time when birthplace mattered tremendously.[66]

But in the middle of this era lay the difficult years of the 1930s. Like all Americans, Jews were affected by the Depression. Jewish businesses, like others, failed. Jews owned a large number of New York's fur and jewelry stores, and between 1929 and 1933 over 1,400 of the 2,855 fur stores closed, and half their jewelry stores vanished. In New York's furniture business, both wholesale and retail, Jewish businesses failed at an alarming rate, dashing the hopes of the proprietors for a comfortable existence and tempering their expectations for their children's upward mobility.[67] A fixture of the Lower East Side since 1913, the Bank of the United States—despite its lofty name, a small immigrant-era establishment—failed, and its depositors watched their savings vanish.[68] Many Jews struggled with unemployment or underemployment. Fifty thousand Chicago Jews found themselves without work for some period in 1931, an increase of over 200 percent from earlier years. Jewish social service and charitable agencies reported increases in the number of requests for assistance.[69] Those same agencies were incapable of dealing with the gravity of the problem, and for the first time Jews found themselves on public relief rolls.

Jewish social workers noted with alarm the ways in which Jews seemed to revert to earlier patterns of coping. Among the unemployed, practices from the era of immigration came back. Families doubled up, sharing space. They returned to the diet of their early years in America, filling up on soup and potatoes and eating less meat. Since the turn of the century American Jews had reveled in shedding the practices of poverty. Their eating habits, especially meat consumption, represented the fulfillment of the aspirations of the immigration.[70] Yet the Depression seemed to be compromising the progress made during the 1920s, a time when immigrant dreams started to come true.

American Jews, however, did not entirely lose their sense of entitlement in the face of Depression scarcities. Even when faced with the exigencies of unemployment they tried to adhere to an American standard of consumption. In New York and other cities with large Jewish communities, housewives protested noisily in the streets against high food prices. They argued that even though they might be poor, they still deserved the right to eat meat and other rich and nourishing foods at a reasonable price. In the 1930s Clara Lemlich Shavelson, who as a young woman had been a union organizer at the turn of the century, organized consumer protests among the Jewish housewives with whom she lived in Brooklyn. She led them to demand, despite their straitened circumstances, the benefits of middle-class status, including good food and adequate housing.[71]

American Jews could not but express fear of the future, disillusionment with earlier dreams of American success, and uncertainty about whether conditions would ever improve. Irving Howe, who in later decades would emerge as a powerful voice of American Jewish literary culture and author of the epic chronicle of east European immigration, *World of Our Fathers*, remembered those years: "We were never hungry but almost always anxious."[72] In 1930 Mike Gold, a pseudonym for Itzok Granich, published his grim *Jews without Money*, a hopeless novel, scathing in its indictment of America, a country that forced millions of immigrants to "eat the bread of sorrow and shame."[73]

Jewish Charities Step In

Jewish charities geared up to ease the burden of the Depression. Jewish communities contained social-service agencies staffed by trained social workers, ready to spring into action. During the Depression agencies that had existed for decades or more began to make their operations more sophisticated and rational. They consolidated procedures for studying Jewish social problems and devised more efficient means to provide services. It took the Depression to bring together local bodies under a national umbrella. The National Council of Jewish Federations and Welfare Funds came into being in 1931.[74] Similarly, in 1938 concerned individuals convened a national conference on the problems faced by Jews professionally. The Conference on Vocational Adjustment Policies and Problems in turn led to the founding of the Jewish Occupational Council the following year. The activities of communal leaders, lay and professional, in these areas reflected not just the gravity of the problem, although they knew the situation to be grave enough, but also the sense that the Jewish community bore an obligation to its members to see them through the hard times.

Social workers and other Jewish community activists, both in large cities and in smaller communities, created programs to give direct aid in money, food, and clothing and to help find jobs for the jobless. Typical of the sophisticated agency response, New York's Federation of Jewish Philanthropies created an employment bureau in 1934. This Federated Employment Service brought together a professional staff trained in vocational services and psychology, committed to efficiency in the delivery of services, and knowledgeable about economic trends.[75] In neighborhoods aid came from within and functioned without bureaucracy and planning. One man who grew up in Rochester during these trying years recalled his grandmother:

> [S]he was a saintly lady. A true old time Jewish woman with a great heart and a concern for her fellow beings. And she made it a project during the Depression years to make baskets in her home, *erev shabbes* [Sabbath eve]. She would call Alfred Hart [a local wealthy Jewish businessman] and ask him for all his seconds on Thursday. . . . She made these packages for all the people. She made it a personal project to find out where all the people were who had no food.[76]

From the most organized agencies that serviced the Jewish communities to the individual efforts of the "old time" possessors of "great hearts," the 1930s taxed communal resources. More children lived in New York's Hebrew Orphan Asylum in the 1930s than at any time in its history since the 1860s.[77] Baltimore's Jewish charities marked a 75 percent increase in requests for assistance. In 1930 the thirty-nine largest Jewish family service agencies in the country carried a caseload of twenty-five thousand families. In 1931 the number had gone up to twenty-nine thousand, and in 1931 and 1932, thirty-one thousand Jewish families received services from these agencies.[78] Social workers, rabbis, and others surveying the Jewish scene worried that hard economic times would bring back crime, marital desertion, and other social ills of the immigration era.

While the 1930s did witness the flamboyant career of gangster Meyer Lansky and the development of Murder, Inc. in Brooklyn, Jewish delinquency did not return despite the bad times. In 1931 a court official in New York observed that "there has been a drop in delinquency and criminality among the Jews almost beyond belief. The number of Jewish prisoners is sinking to practically a negligible quantity."[79] The worry expressed by Jewish communal leaders, partially shaped by rising levels of anti-Semitism, inspired Jewish welfare agencies to pioneer in psychiatric social work and to seek out the newest methods for dealing with social problems. Social workers felt that Jews in America had too much at stake not to avail themselves of the best methods and most sophisticated practices emerging from the top social-work schools in the country.

But this pioneering work took place in an environment in which Jewish charities, always dependent on donations, had diminishing resources from which to draw. The once wealthy lost fortunes. Those who held on to some part of their assets had less to give. Those who in the past had made small contributions had little room in their strained budgets to fulfill the obligations of *tzedakah*. In 1930 the Philadelphia Jewish Federation found itself over $300,000 in deficit.[80] Newark's Beth Israel hospital could not collect on promised pledges.[81]

Jewish charities had a few options as they confronted the steep decrease in funding, which had previously come from philanthropic donations. One solution involved combining their fund-raising efforts. Since the end of the nineteenth century American Jewish charities had been moving toward federated structures, and the Depression accelerated a process long in the making. By 1936, 145 such federations served local Jewish communities. Of those, forty-eight had been established since 1931.[82] Jewish communal workers recognized that even after individual charities became federated, the problem still exceeded available resources. For the first time, Jewish agencies began to accept money from nonsectarian funds like the Community Chest or the United Way. In 1935 Jewish agencies in sixty-three cities, with operating budgets of over $7,000,000, received 43 percent, or about $4,000,000, from community chests or similar citywide bodies.[83]

Perhaps even more dramatically, Jewish agencies began to advocate that relief efforts for the unemployed be put under the auspices of the federal government and that Jews avail themselves of those programs.

Maurice Karpf, surveying the very bleak landscape of Jewish communal services in 1938, predicted that the future of Jewish agencies "will depend entirely upon the programs of the Federal and State governments." In his own statistics, compiled for the *American Jewish Yearbook,* he demonstrated that Jewish reliance on the federal government had already made a difference. In 1934, when the first of the New Deal relief programs went into effect, the number of Jewish families receiving aid from Jewish agencies dropped down from thirty-one thousand to twenty-three thousand, and the amount of money that went in and out of the treasuries of these agencies dropped from $4,000,000 a year in 1932 and 1933 to $1,716,000 in 1935.[84]

All three solutions had disadvantages. In their attempts to manage the organizational chaos, the federations compromised the essential democracy of American Jewish life. They centralized authority in the hands of professional staffs and big donors, depriving Jews of control over communal funds. A political climate in which anti-Semitism hovered over all Jewish-Christian encounters influenced the operation of community chests. At worst this meant that Jewish agencies would be less likely to receive the kind of funding they felt they deserved. Most leaders of community chest agencies were non-Jews. Even if they harbored no antagonism toward Jews, they knew little about them and could not make decisions based on any knowledge of Jewish culture. Finally, the growing reliance of Jews on the government for relief reversed a long-cherished fundamental of Jewish life in the diaspora: that Jews should take care of their own. In America Jews believed passionately in the separation of church and state. They feared the political and cultural costs associated with a new paradigm in which sectarian agencies would come to the government for money.

In the 1930s the situation of American Jewry seemed grim indeed. Isaac Rubinow, a noted economist and Jewish communal activist, lamented the extent of Jewish unemployment. He predicted with authority that "American Jewry is likely to develop a growing class of educated workers who will drift unhappily from one temporary occupation to another, most of them maladjusted." Furthermore, there would be "a small minority in the field of big business, an increasing number employed in the hectic field of salesmanship, an unwilling drift to factory work, and a growing intellectual proletariat without permanent occupational status."[85]

Rubinow assessed correctly that American Jews, young people in particular, hoped to continue their educations so that they could enter the professions, despite the grim realities around them. The Federated Employment Service reported that most of the applicants to its vocational services aspired to professional employment. But Rubinow erred in stating that in the short term they were finding no outlets for their aspirations. In 1936 a New York survey found that while Jewish youth made up one-third of the city's working population, they made up 56 percent of the managers and proprietors, 43 percent of sales and clerical personnel, and 37 percent of the professionals. In Buffalo, New York, though Jewish men may have had less access to the professions to which they had once aspired, they turned to another profession, high school teaching. It may have offered them lower salaries than medicine or law, but it hardly turned these men into an "intellectual proletariat."[86]

Rubinow's concern for Jewish youth facing the limitations of the Depression exceeded actual conditions. He fretted that frustrated, overly educated Jewish young people would become bitter and in their bitterness turn to radical politics. Here too he made an incorrect prediction by overstating young Jews' embrace of the far left. The attraction of Jews during the Depression to the left, the Communist Party in particular but also left-leaning unions and fraternal orders, grew out of complex roots. Many joined left-wing organizations out of anger at the political system and out of the belief that political action could produce change. Studies conducted during the 1930s found that Jews, unlike most other Americans, did not blame themselves for their lack of good jobs, or indeed of any jobs. If they had aspired to being engineers but ended up selling subway tokens, they did not see the fault in themselves. While most other Americans tended to internalize responsibility, considering their narrowed straits evidence of their own deficiencies, Jews, when questioned by relief workers, blamed anti-Semitism, the economy, and the American capitalist system in which resources had been unequally distributed. They may have fallen on hard times, but they believed that they were entitled to better.[87]

Some Jews, many of whose parents had come to America already influenced by Socialist ideals, turned to left-wing politics as a solution to their own and to the nation's ills. A small number of Jews made up the majority of the Communist Party's members. Jews also comprised the bulk of those who joined other left-wing organizations. They believed that the Depression represented the logical result of the economic system. They also believed that it would be the final crisis of capitalism and that the United States as well as Europe stood on the brink of revolution. Their involvement with the Young Peoples' Socialist League, the International Workers Order, and the Young Communist League reflected their critique of the economic order and their unwillingness to blame themselves. Communists attempted to wrest control of the Jewish-dominated unions, the Arbeiter Ring, and even the American Jewish Congress. Even Jewish communal service agencies contended with the radicalization of Jewish social workers.[88]

The New Deal

Yet if Rubinow correctly assessed the leftward leanings of some American Jews, he over-represented the scope of this tendency. Although Jews made up an inordinate percentage of the members and leaders of left-wing groups in the United States in the Depression years, the vast majority in fact voted with the Democratic party. They supported the established unions, which offered them a modicum of protection. After the Hitler-Stalin pact of 1939, among many Jews Communism lost its luster as a solution to the ills of industrial capitalism.

Rubinow expressed his exaggerated fear of a widespread Jewish embrace of the Marxist left at a moment when, for the first time, Jews started to play a prominent role in the national government. Most Jews, even if they declared themselves Socialists, enthusiastically embraced Franklin D. Roosevelt and his New Deal. They saw in Roosevelt someone who understood them. More Jews served in the Roosevelt administration than in any previous administration. Roosevelt seemed to surround himself with Jewish advisers: Sidney Hillman, Joseph Proskauer, Henry Morgenthau Jr., Felix Frankfurter, Benjamin Cohen, and Samuel Rosenman considered themselves among his closest advisers and confidantes.[89] Rose Schneiderman began her career in the 1910s organizing garment workers and creating an alliance between feminists and working women. In 1933 Roosevelt named her to the Labor Advisory Board of the National Recovery Act. Anna Rosenberg sat on the board of the National Recovery Administration and on the War Manpower Commission in the department of defense during the war. Secretary of Labor Frances Perkins named Dorothy Jacobs Bellanca to chair the Maternal and Child Welfare Committee, while in 1936 Pauline Newman brought a delegation of garment and textile women workers to spend a week at the White House, at the invitation of her friend Eleanor Roosevelt.[90] On the second tier of what anti-Semites called the Jew Deal, Jerome Frank, Nathan Margolin, Abe Fortas, David Lilienthal, Saul Padover, Albert Arent, Felix Cohen, and dozens of other newcomers to government gave the administration a decidedly Jewish cast.

At the lower echelons of government hundreds of young Jewish women and men flocked to Washington, D.C., to work in the new government programs and regulatory agencies, which they believed would recover prosperity, relieve suffering, reform the economy, and give them a chance to carve out meaningful careers in public service. In a period of no Jewish population growth in the United States, the number of Jews in the nation's capital went from sixteen thousand in 1930 to over thirty thousand in 1947, a testimony to the growth of public-sector employment and the attraction of Jews to such jobs.[91]

The New Deal did not escape criticism by some Jews. Social activists like Abraham Epstein believed that it did not go far enough in revamping the social inequities of the American economy. Epstein, an economist who had come to the United States from Russia at age eighteen in 1910, had been an advocate of old-age pensions throughout the 1920s. In 1927 he founded the Association for Old Age Security, an organization that as its first act called on Congress to adopt the same old-age insurance laws that existed in Europe. Epstein emerged as a critic of the 1935 Social Security Act because it linked benefits to a percentage of prior earnings. He argued that the program as enacted would deny benefits to those in greatest need, African Americans in particular.[92]

On a specifically Jewish issue, community leaders expressed frustration, privately, with what they saw as Roosevelt's weak reaction to the mounting plight of European Jews. Yet that disappointment was not expressed at the ballot box or in party politics. Alone among Jewish leaders Abba Hillel Silver declared himself a Republican because of his annoyance with Roosevelt's small and ineffective rescue efforts and out of a sense that Jews lost political influence by being so thoroughly associated with one party precisely when they needed maximum clout.[93]

Yet to most American Jews Roosevelt's New Deal represented their, and America's, best chance. The New Deal saw a dramatic shift in Jewish voting, which through the 1920s had been almost evenly divided between the Republican and Democratic parties. Despite many relentless discussions in the Jewish press about the need to rescue European Jewry and the clear evidence that the Roosevelt administration had done little, the presidential election of 1944 saw the highest percentage of Jewish Democratic voting. Over 90 percent of American Jewish voters cast their ballot for Roosevelt. In some heavily Jewish precincts in Chicago the Democratic tally exceeded 95 percent.[94] Roosevelt and his New Deal, in fact, transformed American Jews into the party's staunchest white ethnic constituency for decades to come. One New York rabbi declared

F.D.R. "the Messiah of America's tomorrow," while Stephen Wise, rabbi and Zionist leader, expressed a wish for his "immortality."[95] In the architect of the New Deal they saw the possibility of the United States government acting toward its citizens as the *kehillot*, Jewish communities, had historically related to the Jews: providing a level of aid below which none could fall and working on the principle that assistance to those in need constituted a communal obligation. Their view of Roosevelt paralleled their views of America as a whole. They articulated in words and deeds a profound faith that he represented the best choice possible. He—like the country he led—needed to be prodded to do better. But he—like the United States—could not be matched by any available alternative.[96]

MOVING INTO THE MIDDLE CLASS

Perhaps Rubinow's greatest error in his assessment of the Depression's impact on America's Jews, however, lay in his gloomy prediction. While the economic crisis of the 1930s inflicted a great blow on the Jews it did so in the short term, in what amounted to a brief delay in a nearly unilinear trajectory. It left few marks on the Jewish economy, on Jewish attitudes toward America, or on the movement of Jews toward the professions and the middle class.[97] The Depression did little to stem the steady migration of Jews out of older urban slums into more comfortable neighborhoods of second and third settlement. In Chicago, for example, the development of a massive Jewish enclave in the Lawndale neighborhood, as well as substantial residential pockets on the northwest side, heralded to some in the 1920s the "vanishing ghetto," meaning the death of the old Maxwell Street market as *the* Jewish neighborhood. Steadily Jews moved to other, newer Chicago sections. Author Louis Wirth observed: "mobility seems to be cumulative, gaining momentum . . . as they leave the ghetto, and move to the area of second settlement. The movement becomes more frequent and covers a wider range as the confines of the ghetto are left behind."[98] In New York in the 1920s Jews had already begun abandoning Brownsville, Williamsburg, and Harlem, which two decades earlier had been considered desirable neighborhoods by upwardly mobile Jews who thought them finer than the old East Side.[99] In Buffalo, New York, the movement launched in the 1920s went from the East Side's William Street area to the city's North Side, leapfrogging first to the Elmwood and Humboldt sections. By the end of the 1940s the entire community found itself on the very border of the city, in North Park.[100]

While some Jews remained in the original neighborhood of first settlement, spaces such as the Lower East Side thinned out, and the Jews left behind tended to be older, poorer, and most in need of social services.[101] But most moved away, and with each shift Jews moved further away from the old neighborhoods and found larger, airier apartments or even single-family houses with lawns, homes that afforded privacy and a feeling of self-sufficiency. Each time Jews moved to new enclaves they ended up living in neighborhoods that were more thoroughly Jewish than where they had lived before. In 1920, 54 percent of New York's Jews lived in areas where they made up at least 40 percent of the population. By 1930, in the scattered enclaves around New York, 72 percent of them lived in such densely Jewish spaces. In these new neighborhoods, however, old loyalties, such as those based on European places of origin, diminished in importance.[102]

The shifting Jewish geography of the years from the 1920s through the end of the 1940s differed from previous patterns of mobility. Until the 1920s whenever Jews moved out of a neighborhood, new Jewish immigrants arrived and took their places. Once Jewish immigration halted, however, other newcomers to American cities replaced them, rather than immigrant Jews. In many cities African Americans from the South, participants in the northward migration, opted for the neighborhoods that Jews left. In fact, from the 1920s through the 1940s, Jews and blacks occupied the same spaces. Yet the members of the two communities understood those spaces very differently. While Jews expected to abandon these streets, for African Americans these neighborhoods represented their first steps outside the rigid boundaries of older "black belts." In the 1930s through the mid-1940s Jews and blacks coexisted in North Lawndale, Chicago, and in parts of Boston's Roxbury neighborhood. With the war's end, Jews rapidly left these places, while blacks stayed put.[103]

For Jews the movement to better housing, the process by which one Jewish family after another became homeowners, trading in bad housing for adequate, and adequate housing for even better residences, revealed their sense of themselves as worthy of the bounties of American life. They would not just "make do." In the years spanning the two world wars, this physical mobility of Jewish women and men in America reflected a profound transformation. At the beginning of this era immigrants made up the majority. By the end, those born in America outnumbered those of foreign birth. This change represented more than just a simple matter of demographics. For a hundred years American Jews had been notable for their foreignness, for their need to learn American ways, for the differences between them and other Americans, for the internal fissures in their communities based on European place of origin and length of time spent in America.

But their children did not stand out in these ways. They could list the United States as their birthplace on forms and applications, they spoke English with ease, they knew how to negotiate American institutions, and they considered themselves entitled to the full benefits of citizenship. Their sense of American identity was reflected in shifting patterns of loyalty to and identification with the various places in Europe that their parents had left. Through the early decades of the twentieth century, *landsmanschaftn,* benevolent societies linked to towns and cities in eastern Europe, enjoyed a mass membership and were one of the most popular venues for Jewish gathering and membership in America.

In the late 1930s a study conducted by the Federal Writers' Project concluded that one out of every four New York Jews belonged to a *landsmanschaft.* Though this number sounded impressive, of those *landslayt* who affiliated, only 15 percent had been born in the United States. The American-born joined markedly different organizations, casting their lot with the growing number of family clubs, groups of kin who met for social purposes, sometimes incorporating and providing interest-free loans. Over half the members of New York's Jewish family clubs had, in fact, been born in the United States. Old World towns meant relatively little to them. They had no memories of those places to draw on for the construction of identity, while they *could* draw on loyalty to family and identification with other Jews in building a sense of self. Particularly with the advent of the war, loyalty to European towns came to be associated with loss and pain. After all, many of those places no longer existed or had any Jews living in them.[104]

Shifting Demographics

That a majority of the country's Jews were born and brought up in America directly influenced some of the institutions created by the immigrant generations. The Yiddish press, which had peaked in 1917, reaching about six hundred thousand daily readers, began to diminish in the 1920s. By 1923, when immigration still flowed, circulation had dropped to 383,638. Those newspapers that survived began to include English pages to retain the loyalty of their readers, who now demanded news and feature stories in their new language. With each decade the number of Yiddish papers sold declined.

By 1948 all the Yiddish daily newspapers that had been published outside New York had closed. In 1924 two different local Yiddish newspapers hit the streets every day in Chicago, one in Cleveland, and one in Philadelphia. But during the next two and a half decades, those papers ceased publication.[105] Of the five Yiddish daily newspapers that survived into the post–World War II period, only the Communist *Frieheit* could claim relatively recent vintage, having begun publication in 1922. The dearth of new Yiddish daily newspapers revealed the emergence of an Anglophone Jewish population.[106] The Yiddish weekly, monthly, and quarterly magazines being published in the late 1940s served the needs of the organizations that published them. None were new, and many now devoted up to half their issues to material in English.

Though the Yiddish theater, like the Yiddish press, enjoyed continued popularity throughout this period, it too was headed in an unmistakable direction. The size of its audience dwindled, the number of theaters shrunk, and aspiring actors turned to English-language theater in their search for a larger stage on which to display their talents. The year 1916 represented the high point of Yiddish theater, as it did for journalism, but from then on, the numbers spiraled downward. In New York, the center of Yiddish theater, twenty theaters put on tragedies, farces, comedies, musicals, and domestic dramas. Yiddish theaters existed in Newark, Detroit, Philadelphia, Chicago, and elsewhere. By 1927 the number of Yiddish theaters across the United States had dropped to twenty-four. New York audiences supported eleven Yiddish theaters; Chicago, four; Philadelphia, three; while Newark, St. Louis, Boston, Cleveland, Detroit, Los Angeles, and Baltimore each had one.

The decline began outside New York first. Yiddish-speaking communities ceased to support local professional companies with their own theaters. During the 1930s and 1940s these communities enjoyed Yiddish theater only when visiting companies from New York came to town. A few cities, like Milwaukee, brought Yiddish theater to the Jewish masses with amateur groups. The Perhift Company, named for the playwright Peretz Hirschbein, put on both new and classic plays in Yiddish, but the actors all pursued other occupations to make their living. The production of Yiddish culture had to be left for leisure hours, since there and throughout the country, audiences continued to shrink.[107]

The Yiddish theater might have experienced an even more precipitous decline had not the Depression and the flourishing of Jewish radicalism in the 1930s rescued it temporarily. The Federal Theater Project of the New Deal and the left-wing political ferment of the 1930s provided an antidote to the diminution of the theater's audiences. The infusion of money from the federal government made it possible to fill the seats in the Yiddish theaters, which had been constructed on the "Jewish Rialto" along New York's Second Avenue in the 1910s and 1920s. In 1928 Artef, a Communist-affiliated ensemble theater founded as an amateur company, grew with the left-wing activity of the 1930s. It became professionalized, bought a building of its own, and stayed afloat until the end of the decade. But when the radical tide receded and the federal funds dried up, the Yiddish theater's decline began in earnest.[108] The year 1945 might be considered the symbolic end of large-scale Yiddish theater in America. For decades New York's Yiddish theatrical world centered on the Cafe Royale on Second Avenue and Twelfth Street, next door to the Yiddish Art Theater. Cafe Royale had served as a hiring hall as well as a meeting place for actors, directors, managers, costumers, dressers, scene painters, agents, journalists, and loyal fans eager to see their favorite stars. But in 1945 it served its last cup of tea.

The creeping decline of the Yiddish press and theater dovetailed with the cessation of immigration of Yiddish-speaking immigrants. After 1924 few Jewish immigrants came to America, and of those who did, most came from Germany, not from eastern Europe. The gathering clouds in Europe did bring some Yiddish cultural institutions to the United States and in the process helped to revive, albeit in a different form, Yiddish culture in America. In 1940 the Yiddish Scientific Institute, or YIVO, brought what books and manuscripts it could to the United States for safekeeping. YIVO's library, activists, and activities invigorated the study and preservation of Yiddish. It did not, however, spawn the flowering of a Yiddish-speaking community in America.

After Hitler came to power in Germany, about one hundred and fifty thousand Jewish refugees made their way to the United States. Some left on their own, while others received the support of American Jewish and professional organizations. New York's New School for Social Research created a "university in exile" for some of the leading Jewish intellectuals and academicians forced out of their positions in Germany. A number of the psychology, sociology, and political science professors who fled Germany took teaching positions in southern black colleges.[109] In 1940 the Reform movement's Hebrew Union College brought the theologian Abraham Joshua Heschel, an exponent of neo-Hasidism, to the

United States. HUC's president, Julian Morgenstern, brought a number of others, who formed a Jewish College in Exile in Cincinnati.

Jewish institutions also facilitated the flight of rabbis and scholars out of Germany. Rabbi Hugo Hahn, whose synagogue in Essen had been destroyed on *Kristallnacht* by German mobs, took advantage of the rabbi of New York's Central Synagogue's invitation to come to America and serve as his assistant rabbi. Once safely in America, Hahn felt a call greater than rescuing himself and his own family. In 1939 he and other German newcomers in New York banded together to found the appropriately named Congregation Habonim, "the builders."

The founders of the Habonim envisioned their congregation, which occupied space in the Central Synagogue, as a central synagogue for New York's German Jews and as a re-creation in exile of German Jewish life. Unlike American Reform congregations, which used the Union Prayerbook and adhered to standard Reform liturgical and ritual practices, Habonim defined itself as liberal but in its early years used a traditional prayer book on the weekdays and Sabbath, and at holidays worshiped from a Conservative one. Habonim initiated an adult education project modeled after the Frankfurter Lehrhaus and conducted classes for children in German. In 1941 Habonim created a summer camp for its youngsters in the Catskills. By 1945 Habonim outgrew the Central Synagogue and moved into its own rented building.[110]

The evolution of Congregation Habonim mirrored the relationship between American Jews and the Jews fleeing Nazism who managed to come to the United States. The former considered the fate of German (and other European) Jewry their responsibility, even though they had few options for fulfilling that self-imposed mission. Yet ultimately the institutions that sustained the previous waves of immigrants did not speak to the needs or sensibilities of these newcomers. Most immigrants from Germany of the 1930s possessed higher levels of education than most American Jews at that time, and they had enjoyed a higher standard of living in pre-Nazi Germany than that of their fellow Jews in the United States. Those who stayed in New York, about 60 percent of the refugees, and those who went to other cities, to small towns, and to rural areas, experienced a decline in their material conditions.

The arrival of Jewish refugees from Germany caused American Jewish organizations to improve on their ability to deliver service to those in need. The immediate needs of the immigrants, housing and jobs in particular, became the concern of existing American Jewish organizations. The National Council of Jewish Women, both on the national and the local levels, HIAS, and individual synagogues and federations all attempted to help. The NCJW in particular provided direct service. Its members greeted refugees at the train stations and at the seaports, helping them find housing, jobs, clothing, and other essential services. They taught women how to shop in American stores. In Washington, D.C., Jews involved in various philanthropic and social-service agencies considered the problems of the refugees to be beyond the ability of any one organization to solve. The arrival of refugee families provided them with a crisis, which they attempted to address by changing the structure of the community. Because of the enormity of the problem, they decided to create a federation of all local Jewish philanthropies and a Jewish Community Council, an umbrella body to represent all local Jewish organizations.[111]

Most refugees, while availing themselves of the resources offered to them, founded an array of their own institutions that spoke to their needs and reflected their sense of apartness. They founded about thirty synagogues, spanning the religious spectrum from the highly reformed Hebrew Tabernacle to the Orthodox Breuer community centered in Washington Heights, in upper Manhattan. Where their numbers could not sustain a synagogue, they created their own burial societies. They banded together for lectures and other kinds of social and cultural activities. In 1934 about two thousand German Jews in New York founded the New World Club, which in turn launched the publication of *Aufbau*. The German-language newspaper, with a circulation of fifty thousand, linked the scattered refugees to each other and introduced them to the process of Americanization in their own language.[112]

The Jewish refugees made their way to the United States in the 1930s in numbers too small to make an impact on American Jewish social and cultural patterns. They could not transform the existing organizations or the cultural landscape of American Jewry. Within a generation their children received thoroughly American educations and married non-German American Jews, leaving the refugee community.[113] Further, the one hundred thousand survivors of the Holocaust who arrived in the late 1940s hardly made a dent on the demographic profile of American Jewry, a population whose number had been frozen in the middle of the 1920s. Indeed, after that decade, the number of Jews in the United States never grew again.[114]

Their numbers remained fixed not only because no sizable contingent of new immigrants had arrived, but also because American Jews, eager to achieve middle-class status, opted for small families, much smaller than those of most other Americans in the working class. Jewish women and men chose to have just two, or at the most three, children. By 1938 half of all Jewish families in America limited themselves to two children.[115] One specialist on American population trends writing in 1939 commented with amazement on how "urban American Jews constitute the most ardent birth-controlling group in the population. Regardless of economic or educational status the Jews seem overwhelmingly to be of the opinion that contraception is the thing."[116] With smaller families, these Jews believed they could invest in their children's education and ensure a higher level of material comfort for their families.

The Depression intensified the American Jewish commitment to small families, but it did not cause it. From the 1920s through the 1940s, Jewish doctors played a crucial role in the birth control movement. Hannah Stone, Lena Levine, Bessie Moses, Rachelle Yaross, Sarah Marcus, and Nadine Kavinosvky all ran clinics and dispensed medical information on contraception. Dr. Stone, along with her husband, Abraham Stone, wrote an important and accessible book on contraception, *A Marriage Manual*. She worked closely with Margaret Sanger, the pioneer of the American birth control movement, and in 1936, with Sanger, successfully appealed to the federal courts to allow physicians to import contraceptive devices and transport them through the mail.[117] Similarly, Caroline Klein Simon, a lawyer in New York City, edited *Birth Control Review* in 1939 and 1940.[118] These professionals' Jewishness did not necessarily influence Jewish wives and husbands in their decisions about family planning, but their public visibility did conform to prevailing American Jewish sensibilities.

MIDDLE-CLASS AMERICAN JEWISH LIFE

Nor did pro–birth control statements by the Union of American Hebrew Congregations and the United Synagogue of America influence the intimate decisions made by Jewish women and men. Rather, American Jews' emerging profile as efficient controllers of their own fertility reflected their overwhelming desire to experience mobility into the middle class. This quest for middle-class stability transcended place of origin in Europe. Indeed, an emerging American Jewish identity, unaffected by differences in birthplace, also influenced how Jews conducted their religious lives. The intricate splinterings of the immigrant era among the congregations representing the towns, regions, and countries of Europe fell by the wayside. In their place emerged middle-class synagogues catering to new needs. Most of these came into existence in the 1920s, either as brand-new congregations, starting from scratch in the new communities, or as new incarnations of older congregations transplanted to the second and third areas of settlement.

All these synagogues, regardless of denomination or the birthplace of their founders, functioned in an environment in which only about one-third of American Jews belonged to a congregation. Even those Jews who paid dues to a synagogue generally attended only during the high holidays, at the anniversary of the death of a beloved family member to recite kaddish, or to life-cycle events of family and friends, particularly *b'nai mitzvah*. Most Jews, members of synagogues included, did not observe the Sabbath. Rabbis knew full well that Sabbath services competed with their members' need to make a living and their desire to enjoy their free time in various forms of recreation.

Indeed, competition provided the framework for Jewish religious life in the early twentieth century. All the synagogues had to compete with other venues for the loyalty and membership of a fixed population of American Jews. Jewish community centers had evolved in the 1920s out of the Young Men's Hebrew Associations of the 1880s and 1890s, coordinated on a national level by the Jewish Welfare Board. They also had to compete with B'nai B'rith lodges, Hadassah chapters, Zionist organizations, and a wide panoply of social organizations that allowed Jews to interact comfortably with each other.[119]

Each type of Jewish institution offered activities to children and adults, men and women, members and potential members. Each developed programs simultaneously to provide a Jewish content to American life and a way to promote their particular visions of Jewishness. Each worked to win over new members and foster loyalty among those already affiliated. The incremental increase in the Jews' level of material comfort and their growing acceptance as Americans allowed for an outburst in Jewish cultural creativity in the 1920s. That concern with Jewish culture stemmed in large measure from the diversity of American society and the place of Jews as one of many ethnic groups in the nation's mosaic. One example can stand in for the many stories played out around the country, on the local level in particular. Fanny Goldstein had immigrated to the United States, to Boston's North End, at the beginning of the century as a five-year-old. She became a librarian in 1913 and worked in the North End Branch of the Boston Public Library for a few years. In 1922 she moved over to the West End branch, and in this mixed-immigrant neighborhood she began to run special "book weeks" for the various groups who used the library. She not only organized

Negro History Week, Catholic Book Week, and Brotherhood Week, but she also marked off special time in the library for Jewish Music Month and Jewish Book Week, which she started in 1925. This local endeavor, an effort to highlight to the library's patrons what kind of Jewish books sat on the shelves, grew into the National Jewish Book Week and eventually lead to the founding of the Jewish Book Council of America.[120]

In 1927 American Hebraists—those women and men devoted to the promotion of the Hebrew language—established a summer camp, Camp Achvah, or "brotherhood." Founded by Samson Benderly, this camp, as well as Camp Massad, which began enrolling youngsters in 1941, tried to create a kind of mythical all-Hebrew-speaking world in rural New York. During the summer months, children swam, played ball, hiked, danced, and spoke nothing but Hebrew. These camps emphasizing Hebrew and Jewish culture functioned within a national organization, Histadrut Hanoar Haivri—the "organization of Hebrew youth"—organized in the 1930s.

Histadrut Hanoar Haivri had to compete with programs set up by other Jewish organizations that also emphasized Hebrew. At almost the same time that Histadrut Hanoar Haivri began its efforts to win over American Jewish young people, Labor Zionists created both a youth movement—Youth Poale Zion, which in 1935 became Habonim—and a network of camps, starting with New York's Camp Kvutzah. Habonim in turn competed with such other left-wing Zionist youth groups as Hashomer Hatzair, Gordonia, Avukah, and Massada.[121] At the same time all these Jewish institutions had to compete with the dazzling array of cultural attractions, particularly ones that beckoned on the Sabbath. Theaters, movies, shops, and sports all provided ways to spend leisure time, and synagogues had to vie with these enjoyable activities. The fact that places of entertainment like the Yiddish theater operated on the Sabbath only compounded the difficulty.

Perhaps the competition among the religious denominations represented the most telling form of rivalry of the era. Until the 1920s a kind of rough division marked the institutional life of Judaism in America. Most of the descendants of the nineteenth century, immigrants from central Europe, made up the constituency of Reform Judaism. Until the end of the nineteenth century not only did immigration continue from Germany, but relatively high fertility rates made for a steady stream of new congregants filling the pews of Reform temples. Traditional congregations, those labeled Orthodox, served the needs of those eastern European Jews who had not been converted to Socialism. Regardless of their level of observance most, if they attended a synagogue, attended one that fell at the traditional end of the American Jewish religious spectrum. Conservative Judaism, a product of the early twentieth century, remained too small a movement to have any natural constituency. This small sector of American Judaism, centered on the Jewish Theological Seminary in New York, did not in fact emerge as a movement until the end of the 1910s.

Reform Judaism Responds

But all of this changed by the 1920s. The majority of American Jews, whether they were inclined toward Reform, Conservative, or Orthodox Judaism, were the children and grandchildren of immigrants from eastern Europe who had come to America starting in the 1870s. Leaders of Reform Judaism understood that their movement, which had been the bastion of the central Europeans, had to attract the descendants of the eastern European immigrants or it would die out. The simple demographics of immigration made that proposition inevitable. By 1930 the number of Reform congregations had begun to decline. It stood then at 285 congregations with a total of sixty thousand members. In 1931 a survey found that the proportion of members of "German parentage and of East European parentage" were equal.[122]

Changes within Reform also came about as the Reform rabbinate began to change. Sons and grandsons of immigrants from Poland, Russia, and Lithuania started attending Hebrew Union College, even in the second decade of the twentieth century. The best-known Reform rabbi of this era, Abba Hillel Silver, had been born in Lithuania, had grown up on the Lower East Side, but found Reform attractive. He received his ordination at Hebrew Union College in 1915. Other students at the Reform seminary in Cincinnati had made this particular journey as well, and they collectively pushed Reform to accommodate a changed American Jewry.

Reform Judaism also began to change because of American Jewish marriage patterns. The boundary between "German" and "eastern European," however much it may have manifested itself at the turn of the century in neighborhood life, by the 1920s did not carry over to the wedding canopy. Denominational lines began to blur. As a case in point, the wife of Reform rabbi William Ackerman, Paula Herskovitz, had been born in 1893 into a family of immigrants from Romania. Her observant father enrolled Paula in a Reform Sunday school in Pensacola, Florida, but he hired an Orthodox rabbi to supplement her education with private lessons. Upon her marriage to William, not only did this daughter of eastern European Jewish immigrants involve herself with several Reform congregations as the rabbi's wife, but as an educator and choir leader she also played an important role in the life of Reform Judaism in Natchez and then in Meridian, Mississippi.[123]

Individuals like Silver, Ackerman, and others helped Reform Judaism to recognize the need to woo those Jews whom they previously had not considered their constituency. They pushed the movement, both overtly and more subtly, to adopt change. Thus congregations that had once acknowledged the importance of class hierarchies abolished family pews. Open seating fit a democratically oriented American Jewry that did not pay homage to an elite merely because of its wealth or the length of its membership in the congregation. Reform rabbis turned to new technology, particularly the radio, to address Jewish issues and to project to potential members the image of an active rabbinic presence. In 1924, for example, Rabbi Harry Levi of Boston's old prestigious Temple Israel began broadcasting his sermons throughout New England, as did the rabbis of Beth El in Detroit and Mt. Zion in St. Paul the following year.[124]

Many Jews who had grown up with the rites of traditional Judaism became uncomfortable with the choreography of the classical Reform service, and in the 1920s and 1930s the bar mitzvah ceremony, once rejected by Reform, came back. In addition, prayers that had been excised reappeared, and more Hebrew could be heard in the liturgy. For most of the children and grandchildren of the eastern European immigrants who saw Judaism as a dense social experience, the Reform temple as a grand palace of religion did not feel comfortable. As a result, Reform congregations tinkered with ways to enhance synagogue sociability. Many congregations created youth groups in these years, and by 1939 so many Reform congregations had added on organized clubs for young people that the National Federation of Temple Youth was founded.

These innovations in Reform that put it in touch with the sensibilities of the descendants of the eastern European immigrants coincided with the growing crisis in Europe. In the 1930s Reform shed much of its disdain for Zionism as a political movement. The path toward change had been paved by the many Reform rabbis and laypeople who had been long sympathetic to the Zionist idea. Reform rabbis like Silver and Stephen Wise, as well Judah Magnes and James Heller, played key leadership roles in American Zionism. Further, Reform-affiliated laypeople like Chicagoan Julian Mack helped to direct Zionist politics. They tried to bring their two Jewish affiliations into harmony and throughout the 1920s pressed Reform to express greater sympathy for Zionist ideas. As a small but telling example, in 1930 they succeeded in getting the Zionist anthem, "Hatikvah," added to the movement's official hymnal. In 1935 an outspoken Zionist, Felix Levy, won election to the presidency of the Central Conference of American Rabbis. All these early steps made possible the sharp break with Reform's past. In 1937 the annual meeting of the CCAR, held in Columbus, Ohio, issued a statement of principles that rewrote the 1885 Pittsburgh Platform and that expressed support for the idea of a Jewish homeland.[125]

The Conservative Movement Competes

The Conservative movement's project grew from other roots, although it adopted programs and strategies not all that different from those adopted by Reform. Its history in these years can also be understood in the context of denominational competition. From the 1920s through the end of World War II the movement assumed its basic identity, although it inherited an organizational structure from earlier decades, namely the Jewish Theological Seminary founded in the 1880s, the United Synagogue of America founded in 1913, and the Rabbinical Assembly, originally an association of Seminary graduates created shortly after that. Additionally, in 1915 Mathilde Schechter, wife of Solomon Schechter, president of the seminary, had founded the Women's League for the United Synagogue of America. Although she demanded that the organization be autonomous and not controlled by United Synagogue, it served as its arm and provided support for the seminary and its students.

Numbers can in part help us to trace the movement's odyssey. In 1919 a mere twenty-two congregations affiliated with Conservative Judaism. Ten years later that number reached 229, almost equal to the number of those affiliated with the more established Reform movement. By the time America entered the war, Conservatism could claim to be the single largest American Jewish denomination. The growth in numbers made it imperative for it to distinguish itself from its competitor to the left—namely Reform—and from that on the right, Orthodoxy. Conservativism sought its constituency among those immigrants from eastern Europe who had moved out of their original neighborhoods and had Americanized enough to be uncomfortable with Orthodox synagogues, particularly with the widely enforced segregation of women and men during services. Like their Reform counterparts, Conservative congregations stressed decorum and the aesthetic enhancement of Judaism and

blended American middle-class style with the ancillary activities that became its hallmark.

Yet the movement stressed how its restraint in prayer and the propri-
ety of those attending services, as well as mixed seating, did not constitute a break with tradition. Conservative rabbis at the Jewish Theological Seminary and in the pulpits believed themselves to be traditional in
their understanding of Jewish law. Halakah mattered to them. Between
1928 and 1948 they deliberated, through the Rabbinical Assembly's
Committee on Jewish Law, how much they could mold Jewish law to fit
American times without admitting that they viewed the law as contingent. Throughout these two decades the "conservative" Conservatives,
particularly Louis Ginsberg and Boaz Cohen, held the majority of the
committee, and the movement made few decisions that put it in conflict
with traditional practice and law. It also made few efforts to discuss publicly with its members—actual or potential—the exact nature of its principles. Notably it published a *Festival Prayer Book* in 1927, to be used
on Passover, Succoth, and Shavuot, times when many congregants did
not attend services. It did not, however, publish a high holiday prayer
book or a Sabbath prayer book until after World War II, in the process
remaining silent about major theological and liturgical matters for those
holy days likely to attract larger numbers of congregants.

The reluctance of the movement to tackle squarely matters of ideology and liturgy grew out of its desire to offend neither the traditionalists
nor the innovators among its potential and growing number of recruits.
The movement did not want to alienate the majority of American Jews
who, though they cherished their identities as Jews, had little interest in
theology and did not look to Jewish law in determining how they should
lead their daily lives. The women and men who affiliated with Conservative congregations did so because of the familiarity of the rite, so long
as that rite did not conflict with their idea of themselves as modern
Americans. They joined these congregations because the worship service
had not departed radically enough from what they had grown up with
to seem alien. Yet the setting and even the form of the services differed
just enough so that it felt American and middle class.

Adherents to Conservative Judaism hoped to anchor their children to
Jewish life without jeopardizing their trajectory into the middle class.
Conservative congregations specifically courted young families, women,
children, and teenagers as key constituent groups. Rabbis and officials
of the movement saw these groups as those most likely to respond to special services, clubs, lectures, and programs, all designed to fit their par-

ticular interests and schedules. Conservative congregations pursued, with particular zeal, the synagogue-center model.[126]

Much of the movement's attention was focused on women, both as actual and potential members. In many of the country's Conservative synagogues, the Women's League chapters devoted many hours to adult education. They stocked and staffed congregational libraries and gift shops and sponsored leisure activities, emphasizing music and crafts to enhance the practice of Judaism. The Conservative movement's effort to appeal to women might be best demonstrated by its 1927 publication *The Three Pillars: Thought, Worship and Practice* by Deborah Melamed and Betty D. Greenberg, and Althea O. Silverman's 1941 *Jewish Home Beautiful*.[127] These books and the other activities sponsored by Conservative congregations were motivated by a clear conviction: Judaism had to compete with the rich offerings of middle-class American culture. To do so it recognized that it must emphasize the beauty of the tradition and its compatibility with the bourgeois standards of American respectability.

In the most elaborate of the movement's synagogue-centers, religious functions coexisted with recreational and social functions. They boasted swimming pools, gymnasia, meeting halls, and social rooms, places where Jews could "show the world the ideal that you can be a Jew and enjoy life, and will express in everything you do that the same thing can be done in a Jewish way." This "Jewish way" involved Jews spending their leisure time with each other. Though not all the activities had a specific Jewish content, the fact that all the participants were Jewish transformed them into Jewish pursuits.[128]

The movement also aimed to win over the hearts of the youngest Jewish children and their parents. It attempted to do so, among other strategies, by providing a set of activities and accessible texts that could hold their own against other available options. As one example, in 1935 the Women's League issued an enduring children's book, *The Adventures of K'tonton,* a delightful set of stories about the "Jewish Tom Thumb." Through the antics of a very little boy, parents and children explored the world of Jewish holidays and rituals. By using the idioms of Western culture, Conservative movement activists hoped to help Judaism—and their movement—compete against the constantly expanding possibilities opening up for middle-class American Jews.

Kaplan and Reconstructionism

The idea of competition as the driving force in American Judaism in the period between the world wars emerged as the essential theme in the most important book to come out of the Conservative movement, indeed probably the key text in the history of American Judaism. Mordecai Kaplan's 1934 *Judaism as a Civilization* encapsulated the conflicts experienced by the Jewish system as it took root in the soil of American democracy.[129] Kaplan had been born in eastern Europe in 1881, in Lithuania. He came to America as a young child in 1890, and in 1902 graduated in one of the first classes of the Jewish Theological Seminary. He began his rabbinical career as an Orthodox rabbi but increasingly found himself unable to reconcile traditional Judaism with American ideals. In *Judaism as a Civilization,* in the synagogue he created, the Society for the Advancement of Judaism, and in his long career teaching at the Jewish Theological Seminary, he spoke of the crisis he had endured, which he believed reflected the dilemma of most educated American Jews.

Kaplan argued that American Jews lived in two competing civilizations, the Jewish and the American. These two worlds had to operate harmoniously with each other for Judaism to win and hold the loyalty of its American daughters and sons. Judaism would surely lose in that struggle unless it accommodated itself to America. Kaplan believed that American Jews had the right to massage tradition to fit American democratic values as long as it still served a Jewish purpose. He coined the aphorism "*halacha* should have a vote, but not a veto" as American Jews created new forms and texts for worship.[130]

The fundamental Judaic principle of chosenness bothered him deeply. This idea, Kaplan asserted, may have served deep emotional needs for Jews when they lived under the threat of persecution and sought divine meaning for their seemingly endless suffering. In America, where Jews could expect increasing inclusion, the idea seemed repugnant and jarred with American ideas of democracy and equality. Kaplan also argued that in the competition between American and Jewish loyalties, Judaism had to find ways to provide for the social and cultural needs of American Jews. If it did not, they would seek that meaning elsewhere. The idea of creating an "organic Jewish community" lay at the heart of his prescription for the future. Jewish communities should develop elaborate recreational, artistic, political, and educational activities, able to vie successfully with the richness of American society. Consistent with his overriding concern with creating and sustaining community, Kaplan saw great cultural power in the Zionist movement. In the growing settlements in the *yishuv,* Jews acted assertively by creating a new Jewish civilization. He believed, as did many American Zionists like Henrietta Szold and Kurt Lewin, that the example of Jews building a new, vibrant, and modern society in Palestine would give American Jews a positive model, which they could follow to enhance their own Jewish loyalties.

As a professor at the Jewish Theological Seminary, Kaplan influenced many of his students. Some joined with him to create a kind of movement within a movement, Reconstructionism. In 1935 they launched a magazine, *The Reconstructionist,* and in 1940 they came together to create the Jewish Reconstructionist Foundation. Shortly thereafter, in 1941, Kaplan and his followers issued a *New Haggadah* and published a Sabbath prayer book in 1945, which reflected Kaplan's rejection of chosenness. It also removed all references to the idea of the resurrection of the dead and the inevitable coming of the messiah. Both of these liturgical texts caused a storm of controversy, and a group of Orthodox rabbis held a public ceremony in 1945 at which they issued a *herem,* a ban of excommunication against Kaplan.

Orthodoxy and the American Jewish Competition

That a group of Orthodox rabbis gathered together one day in New York at the McAlpine Hotel to issue their harsh decree against Kaplan and his tampering with tradition reveals much about Orthodoxy in this period. These defenders of tradition did not represent a movement per se. Rather, they acted through a particular organization, the Union of Orthodox Rabbis. Their actions reflected their own views and not those of the many other rabbis and organizations that also called themselves Orthodox. Indeed, from the 1920s through the 1940s, Orthodox Judaism differed from the other two denominations in large measure because of its lack of an overarching structure. As compared to its more organized rivals, Orthodoxy's inner divisions fostered less consensus over how to relate to American conditions, and competition within Orthodoxy exacerbated, and was exacerbated by, its competition with the other denominations, particularly Conservatism.

Some Orthodox Jews found room for modernization and made it possible to include those who may not have conformed to halakah in their behavior. American-born, English-speaking, university-trained Orthodox rabbis, particularly the emerging graduates of Yeshiva University, founded in 1925 under the leadership of Bernard Revel, went into congregations that could just as easily have hired graduates of the Jewish Theological Seminary. Likewise, in this interwar period, graduates of the Hebrew Theological College in Chicago, founded in 1922 by

Rabbi Saul Silver, served synagogues that might join United Synagogue and move over to being Conservative. Most of the members of the National Council of Young Israel, founded in 1924, of the Rabbinical Council of America, organized in 1935, and of the Union of Orthodox Jewish Congregations (OU), which went back to the end of the nineteenth century, though they expressed tremendous frustration with the fact that they had to compete with the other branches, acknowledged the reality of the competition.[131]

Indeed, it may have been this lack of clear boundaries between American Orthodoxy and Conservatism that provided the impetus for the Union of Orthodox Rabbis (UOR) decision to declare Kaplan's prayer book and ideas anathema to Judaism in a highly public ceremony. In New York and its environs, Conservative and Orthodox congregations had become about evenly matched in numbers. In the 1930s, for example, eleven Conservative congregations functioned in Queens and on Long Island, as opposed to nineteen affiliated with the Orthodox Union. In the Bronx the eleven Conservative congregations stood, figuratively, alongside the same number of Orthodox-affiliated ones. Outside New York, particularly in smaller cities, Orthodox congregations became increasingly overshadowed by those belonging to Reform or Conservative, particularly in the neighborhoods to which Jews headed in search of better housing.

Orthodox synagogues in the areas of second and third settlement and in smaller cities can perhaps best be described as heterodox. Not all of them separated men and women during services. They allowed men known not to be observers of the mitzvoth to hold office and share in ritual honors. Members of Orthodox congregations sent their children to public schools. They even, at times, found ways, city by city, to cooperate with Reform and Conservative congregations. In 1935, for example, rabbis who belonged to the OU worked with those from the United Synagogue and the Central Conference of American Rabbis to sponsor a "Back to the Synagogue" campaign.[132]

The following year Rabbis Moses Margolies and Joshua Lookstein of New York's Kehillath Jeshurun founded a coeducational Orthodox day school, thus breaking out of the traditional pattern of sex-segregated Jewish education. Additionally, they added many of the same ancillary programs for young families, women, and children that the Conservative and Reform congregations were developing to enhance synagogue life and help them in the competitive world of American Judaism.[133] Under the spiritual leadership of Rabbi Joseph Soloveitchik, appointed to the

Talmud faculty of Yeshiva University in 1939, American Orthodoxy proclaimed, if reluctantly, its modern credentials.

But not all Orthodox institutions considered themselves engaged in competition with the liberal denominations. Rather, they believed that the real struggle was against the more compromising elements within Orthodoxy. This traditionalist critique of American modern Orthodoxy emanated first from a number of yeshivas that came into being primarily in the 1930s. The first challenge actually had been sounded in 1921 and came out of Brooklyn's Williamsburg neighborhood, through the activities of Rabbi Shraga Feivel Mendelowitz and the Mesifta Torah V'daath Yeshiva. In 1933 Rabbi Jacob I. Ruderman founded the Ner Israel Yeshiva in Baltimore, while in Manhattan Rabbi Moshe Feinstein founded Yeshiva Tifereth Jerusalem in 1937. Yeshivah Chaim Berlin in Brooklyn opened its doors in 1939. These institutions served as beachheads for a traditionalist, educationally oriented assault on Orthodox flirtations with the lures of secular American society.[134]

The transplanting of the Breuer community from Germany to Washington Heights in the 1930s also complicated the profile of American Orthodoxy. Members of this community built a full, largely self-sufficient Orthodox community, organized around the rabbinic leadership of the group known as Kahal Adas Jeshurun. Among Jewish refugees from Austria could be found a contingent of Hungarian Jews who set up schools and synagogues in New York. Led by Rabbi Samuel Eherenfeld and Rabbi Levi Grunewald, these new American Jews demanded higher levels of meat inspection and the provision of kosher milk.

In the years leading up to World War II, during the war, and in the immediate aftermath of the Holocaust, a stream of European Orthodox congregations and rabbis made their way to America. Rabbis, heads of yeshivas, Hasidic rebbes, and their followers, from Hungary in particular, but also from Lithuania, arrived in America. In 1941 Rabbi Aaron Kotler of Kletzk, Poland, reorganized his yeshiva and his community in Lakewood, New Jersey. Unlike the American Orthodox rabbis and laypeople who filled out the ranks of Young Israel or who joined the congregations affiliated with the OU or the Rabbinical Council of America, these "yeshiva-world" Orthodox defined themselves emphatically as self-segregating. They had, when immigration to the United States had been open and unlimited, affirmatively chosen not to come to America, having listened carefully to traditionalists in Europe who had warned about America as a godless land. When they came to the United States under duress, they sought specifically to re-create the world of European tradition as much as possible. In later decades the institutions these last arrivals founded would shake up the American, modern Orthodox consensus.

But from 1924 through 1948, the main trajectory of American Jewry did not involve refashioning a separate, "Torah-true" existence on American soil. Rather, American Jewish life took its basic shape from the period's liminality. This period stood between the century of migration and the "golden age" to follow, an era of an almost barrier-free access to American life. The constant influx of immigrants, which ended in the middle of the 1920s, had shaped Jewish institutional life and given American Jewry its basic character. It had caused a "constant expansion" and had "made room for enormous diversity within the community." Throughout that long century, Jews in America had been "challenged by the contrast" between native-born and newcomer. Throughout that period, second-generation Jews "always strained to reconcile the two forces," the European and the American. Where Jews had come from and when mattered a great deal.[135]

In contrast, by the end of the 1940s, parents' and grandparents' birthplaces in Europe had become little more than interesting matters of family history, revealing nothing about the education, income, residence, politics, or the nature of the Jewish participation of their American-born descendants. As the decade of the Holocaust drew to a close and the second half of the twentieth century began, the *American Jewish Yearbook* offered its readers an article entitled "A Century of Jewish Immigration to the United States," written by historians Oscar and Mary Handlin. "The events of the Second World War," they wrote, "left the United States the center of world Judaism."[136]

They might have added that Jews now stood just a few steps away from fully entering the central institutions of middle-class American life. How they would negotiate that journey away from the margins emerged as their main project in the decades ahead. Yet however much Jews became prime beneficiaries of the prosperity of the post–World War II era, the events of the 1920s, 1930s, and 1940s—the virulent anti-Semitism at home set against the powerful bonds linking them to their coreligionists around the world—would remain with them.

7

A GOLDEN AGE?

1948–1967

If any era in the history of American Jewry could be considered a "golden age," it would be the twenty years following World War II. In this relatively brief era American Jews pushed the troubled memories of the recent past—the uncertainties of the Depression, the anti-Semitism of the 1920s, 1930s, and 1940s, and the horrors of the Nazi era—to the margins of their concerns. Instead of feeling anxious about their status, they crafted a series of new communal practices that reflected the dominant themes of the postwar age: prosperity and affluence, suburbanization and acceptance, the triumph of political and cultural liberalism, and the expansiveness of unlimited possibilities.

This is not to say that because of this optimism they had become complacent or that this period offered no challenges to their place in American life. Rather, American Jews had ample reason to feel optimistic as they continued to negotiate between their minority status and the unfolding of new opportunities. In this era, the positive forces, as they saw them, outweighed the negative. The cold war certainly hung over them as they confronted challenges to their patriotism, and they could not ignore the loud chorus of vehement accusations that Jews did not subscribe to true American ideals. Yet in the face of these trials, or perhaps in spite of them, they joined forces with other Americans of goodwill who worked to change the status quo both for themselves and for America's larger minority population, the African Americans. To counter anti-Communist and anti-Semitic rhetoric, Jews, in their associations and organizations, emphasized that they supported America's

increasing commitment to end privilege based on race, religion, and national origin.

In this era dominated by a new kind of Jewish mobility—the move
from the cities to the suburbs—American Jews found ways to combine
middle-class comforts, social activism, and Jewish commitments. The
grassroots activities of Jewish women, largely played out in the new suburban communities ringing America's largest cities, helped to foster a
Jewish consensus. The newly independent state of Israel, while not the
primary influence on communal identity, inspired pride among American Jews. In this "golden age" religion functioned as a unifying force,
breaching the divisions not only among Jews but also between Jews and
Christians. In this era, which emphasized the benign and indeed benefi-
cent effect of worship and religious affiliation, Judaism joined Protestantism and Catholicism as a mainstream American faith, becoming a
third jewel in the crown of American civic religion.[1]

American Jews participated avidly in the rush to the nation's suburban communities, a phenomenon of profound significance ushered in by
postwar technology and facilitated by federal and local social policy that
defined the central city as a problem to be solved in part by enticing
white families to leave.[2] They took advantage of the G.I. Bill, the Ser-
vicemen's Readjustment Act of 1944, which provided free tuition and
living stipends to the demobilized soldiers returning to civilian life.[3]
While in their homes they observed fewer and fewer details of Jewish law
and ritual, in their high levels of synagogue affiliation and their intensely
Jewish social lives they continued to manifest an unswerving loyalty to
their inherited identity. More American Jews affiliated formally with
synagogues and Jewish community institutions than at any other time
since before mass migration began in the 1820s. Well over half joined
congregations.

Unlike eighteenth-century American Jews, however, who, because of
the paucity of Jewish resources were wedded to their synagogues,
post–World War II American Jewish women and men chose their synagogues as the places where they could express themselves as Jews. Similarly, at no time before or after this period did as many children receive
a structured Jewish education. In some communities the percentage
climbed to 80 percent.[4] While some critics bemoaned the quality of that
education and lamented what they saw as the shallowness of the religiosity of suburban synagogue culture, the very magnitude of these figures indicates that American Jews were unequivocally voicing their
choice to live as Jews and to bring their children into Jewish life. As a

group they celebrated the reality that being Jewish carried few liabilities in society.

For American Jews the era as a whole was defined by choice. In the schools they attended—and hoped to attend—as well as in the race for professional positions and the quest for improved dwelling places, Jews could compete without being burdened by their ancestry. Outside forces had little impact on what they did as Jews and how they constructed their identities. Stuart Rosenberg, a rabbi writing in 1964 about the mood of American Jewish life, got it right when he noted that in the minds of Jews "America [was] different." During this twenty-year span Jews also widely shared the expectation that they would be part of the effort to bring about what he called *"the America that is yet to be."* Rosenberg claimed that America's Jews would help to construct "the Judaism that *can yet be, in such an America.*"[5]

His words offer a window into the complexities of the era. In the culture of the 1950s and 1960s, Jews found America to be a hospitable place in which to enjoy their ascending status and to celebrate their heritage. They had a deep faith in the possibility that in "the America that is yet to be" the last barriers would crumble. They had ample reason to believe that a time would soon come when they could cease to feel anxious about themselves and their status as "others."

Yet that time lay in the future. Indeed, the phrase "the America that is yet to be" made amply clear that the America of the present still left much to be desired. Post–World War II Jews lived between expectation and the reality of their circumstances. Part of that reality lay in the fact that in those years they were also living under the shadow of the recent calamity that had befallen European Jewry in the 1930s and 1940s. Contrary to later historical accounts claiming that with the war's end American Jews refused to think, write, or talk about the tragedy, as individuals and as members of organized communities, they expressed their awareness that they had just witnessed one of the most horrendous eras in the history of their people.

REMEMBERING THE TRAGEDY

They did not turn to the pursuit of upward mobility, gaining acceptance, and avoiding memorializing the tragic events that had destroyed much of European Jewish life.[6] In 1953, less than a decade after the war's end, historian and writer Rufus Learsi composed a reading of remembrance, distributed nationally and locally through Jewish community councils and their constituent organizations, as well as in synagogues and the Jewish press. Printed on a simple sheet of paper, the reading, intended for home use at Passover seders, linked the almost universally observed family ritual with the uprising that had taken place in the Warsaw Ghetto on Passover eve in 1943. Dedicated to the memory of "our brothers" who were killed "at the hands of a tyrant more wicked than the Pharaoh who enslaved our forefathers in the land of Egypt," the reading described the Nazis as "the evil ones" whose brutal acts "defamed the image of God in which human beings were created."[7] The liturgical text claimed that the survivors of the concentration camps and ghettoes emerged from their trauma envisioning a day "when justice and brotherhood would reign among men." In 1948 the Reconstructionist movement published a *mahzor,* or high holiday prayer book, in which the "martyrology" liturgy for Yom Kippur, a lengthy and lachrymose prayer memorializing the ten rabbis killed by the Romans because they had taught Torah in defiance of an imperial decree, now included prayers memorializing the Jews of Europe, destroyed by "the demonic power of Nazism." Given the young movement's commitment to liturgical innovation it comfortably followed the traditional "Eleh Ezkerah" with a poem written by resistance fighter Hannah Senesh, who perished in the Holocaust, as well as a "Tribute to the martyrs of the Bialystok Ghetto."[8] And in May 1950 students and faculty at the Jewish Theological Seminary lit a memorial lamp in the library tower as a perpetually flickering reminder of the destroyed European Jewish communities.[9]

Seminary officials designated the observance of the Rabbi Akiva Memorial Month "dedicated to the study of Torah in memory of the six million Jews martyred during World War II," thereby connecting the recent horrors with examples of Jewish martyrdom from late antiquity. Similarly a 1950 Haggadah published in New York offered three illustrations to accompany the "Pour Out Your Wrath" section of the liturgy. One depicted Passover night among a group of hidden Jews in Spain, with the caption "The Inquisition interrupts a seder." The other two directed the wrath of seder participants to the evil deeds that only recently had engulfed the Jews. One photograph of the portal to Auschwitz, with its "Arbeit Macht Frei" sign, drew attention to "Oswiecim, where 4,000,000 Jews were slain." The other, a grainy photograph depicting smoke wafting around a stark and menacing chimney, bore the caption "Treblinka, death house of 731,000 Jews."[10]

This connection between contemporary Judaic practice and the events of the preceding decade manifested itself at the local level as well. One of the first congregations to be founded in Levittown, New York, the prototypical Jewish suburban community of the age, marked its opening with the dedication of "a Sefer Torah which was the first Sefer Torah to be returned to Germany after liberation by American troops." The history of this scroll, sacred in and of itself, made it a "very treasured one."[11] Throughout the 1950s, in fact, the Synagogue Council of America distributed religious objects salvaged from the destroyed European communities, offering them to the new ones cropping up all over America. The Synagogue Council made sure that newspapers covered the distribution of salvaged sacred objects and thereby kept in public view the horrors of the Holocaust. Through these Torah scrolls, filigree silver pointers, crowns bedecked with bells, and ornate bejeweled breastplates gracing their worship services, congregants could feel linked to the vanished past of European Jewry.[12]

Jewish communities across the country held Warsaw Ghetto memorial evenings every April, and Jewish summer camps used the midsummer fast day of Tisha B'Av, the commemoration of the destruction of the Temple, to remember the recent devastation. From the end of the 1940s and into the 1960s, literary, autobiographical, and historical texts in Yiddish, Hebrew, and English detailing the events of the war heightened Jewish discussion of the Nazi era. Publications for children, including pedagogic material, also began in the 1950s to draw American Jewish youngsters into the culture of memory. In May 1958, for example, *World Over,* a weekly "magazine for boys and girls," published by the Jewish Education Committee of New York but distributed nationally, offered its young readers a "Story with a Happy Ending." The vignette, with an accompanying photograph, told of "a tireless search by a father for his four-year-old daughter, snatched from him by the Nazis 14 years ago." The girl, Batya Galprin, "had been taken from her parents in a labor camp in Vilna in 1944." Her father "wandered in vain through the liberated camps, emigrated to Israel . . . and continued the search" for his missing child. As Barbara, she had been in the care of a Christian family in Poland who, believing that her parents had perished, arranged for her to go to Israel through Youth Aliyah. The *World Over* story made patently clear to American Jewish children how traumatic the destruction of the Holocaust had been and how it had affected those who had been caught up in it. It described the meeting between the girl and her long-lost family: "She began to ask, 'Are these my real parents?' [and] her mother started to sing a Yiddish lullaby which she had sung to her daughter as a child. As her memory stirred, Barbara started to sing the same song. She had found her parents."[13] While this story echoed the dominant American motif of the "happy ending," American Jewish rhetoric and performances of the Holocaust, including those aimed at the young, in the 1950s did not minimize the death, destruction, and pain.

By 1960 American politicians, both officeholders and aspiring politicians, began to attend Holocaust gatherings, voicing their solidarity with the Jewish people at these Jewish communal events. In April of that year, as three thousand five hundred people gathered in New York to commemorate the Warsaw Ghetto uprising, Democratic hopefuls John F. Kennedy, Hubert Humphrey, and Stuart Symington sent messages of solidarity to be read aloud to the assembled crowd.[14] The trial and subsequent execution of Adolf Eichmann in Jerusalem in the early 1960s further opened up the floodgate of American Jewish references to what in the late 1960s would universally come to be called "the Holocaust."[15]

From the beginning of the 1950s American Jews not only found time to think about the annihilation of the Jews of Europe, but they also increasingly used its imagery to describe contemporary events. In the early 1950s American Jewish communal concern about the fate of Jews in the Soviet Union and elsewhere behind the Iron Curtain mounted, as in Poland, Czechoslovakia, Romania, and other Communist countries, where Jews faced persecution and Judaism was increasingly suppressed. Anxieties began to be expressed in historic terms. When the *American Jewish Yearbook* commented on this situation it wrote, "With the memory of Nazi Germany's murder of 6,000,000 fresh in their minds, American Jews were in the main convinced that only a tremendous worldwide protest could stop the further development of the Communist anti-Semitic campaign."[16]

Similar language could be heard on a local level as well. When the Jewish community of Hamden, Connecticut, found itself in a heated debate over Christmas observance in the public schools, tempers flared. The New Haven Jewish Community Council had raised objections to the annual Christmas pageant, which in turn unleashed an angry reaction among the town's Christian majority. Some accused the Jewish minority of robbing the New England town of its holiday. A Jewish resident of Hamden, a member of Congregation Beth Sholom who participated in the controversy, described to the press an intense public meeting as vicious, "comparable to a mob in Munich under Hitler."[17]

While in the 1950s and 1960s American Jews did not place the events of World War II at the top of their public and communal agenda, they did make room for it in a communal discourse and political strategy. Although American Jews, until the late 1960s, had no single name by which to refer to the tragedy, they still found ways to weave it into their writings and other cultural expressions, both those aimed at Jews and those that the larger, non-Jewish world could partake in as well. Oscar and Mary Handlin, writing a history of the acquisition of Jewish civil rights in America, referred to "the barbarities that culminated in the extermination camps." In *Adventures in Freedom*, Oscar Handlin's history of American Jews written to mark the tercentenary of Jewish life in North America in 1954, he remarked somberly that "we cannot blot out from memory," even amid the celebrations marking the 1654 date, "the tragic decade that has just closed. Jews have not recovered from the shock of the six million victims of the European catastrophe." A 1951 synopsis in the *American Jewish Yearbook* of several memoirs described the books as "dealing with the European Jewish community that was the victim of the Nazi catastrophe."[18]

SUPPORTING CIVIL RIGHTS

That the Levittown Torah had been liberated from Nazi hands by American soldiers allowed the young families of the suburban synagogue to think about the connections between Jewish suffering and the expansive, tolerant vistas opening up to them as Americans. That the American Jewish Congress Passover reading depicted the survivors as envisioning a messianic future of brotherhood and justice made it possible for Jews to express feelings that echoed more general sentiments about the civil rights imperative. Jewish presentations of the Nazi era emphasized the suffering of the Jews juxtaposed against an admonition that Jews, and all other Americans, needed to work for a more just society. American Jewish thinking about the trauma of the recent past and the political climate of the postwar nation came together in the Jewish participation in and support of the civil rights struggle. Rabbi Joachim Prinz, who represented American Jewry among the speakers featured at the 1963 civil rights march on Washington, said it simply: "When I lived under the Hitler regime, I learned many things." His lesson consisted of recognizing that discrimination against some diminished all and that ending discrimination against a minority would benefit the polity as a whole.[19]

With this goal in mind, American Jews actively worked on the national, state, and local levels with other civil rights organizations, and sometimes on their own, to push through civil rights bills, in the process helping to change American life. While Jews had participated in the freedom struggle of African Americans since the beginning of the twentieth century, and American Jewish publications, both in Yiddish and English, had decried racism for five decades, only in the aftermath of World War II did the organized Jewish community—synagogues, synagogal bodies, defense organizations, and the like—become actively engaged in the movement. Notably, previous anxiety over their own status in America had prevented them as a community from risking the opprobrium of the non-Jewish majority.

A legion of examples of Jewish participation, large and small, in the civil rights struggle of the postwar era can be drawn from every Jewish community. Jewish support for the civil rights struggle encompassed the actions of thousands of individuals who felt obligated to act to create a more just America. As only one example, in 1950 Bella Abzug, a product of the Hashomer Hatzair youth movement and a graduate of Columbia Law School of the early 1940s, went to Mississippi to defend Willie McGee. McGee, an African American, had been accused falsely of raping a white woman, and Abzug hoped to save him from the electric chair. She argued in front of the U.S. Supreme Court, unsuccessfully, that McGee had never had a fair trial because Mississippi routinely disqualified black people from jury service. Abzug was pregnant at the time of her last futile journey to Mississippi to get McGee a stay of execution. Her actions fit into a tradition going back to the early part of the century of Jewish lawyers using their professional expertise to bring racism to an end.[20]

On the organizational level, the same sense of responsibility shaped Jewish behavior, and many of the institutions of communal life staked their reputations on their active support of a movement considered controversial by most Americans. In 1961 the County Council of Montgomery County, Maryland—a suburban destination of many Washington, D.C., Jews—discussed repealing its antidiscrimination legislation. The Jewish Community Council of Washington alerted all the rabbis, presidents of congregations, and leaders of Jewish organizations to voice their strong opposition to their elected officials. Similarly, the Jewish Community Council, which included a few organizations from the Virginia suburbs of Arlington, Alexandria, and Fairfax, organized a delegation to go to Richmond and lobby on behalf of school integration, sending " 'a good group from the Jewish congregations' . . . to let the legislators know that the Jewish community stood for integration."[21]

Some forms of participation took on a highly visible and political cast, contributing mightily to the judicial and legislative triumphs of the era, culminating in the 1964 and 1965 Civil Rights Acts. In 1950 the American Jewish Committee hired a black psychologist, Kenneth Clark, to study the psychological impact of school segregation on children. Clark's finding that segregation damaged self-esteem fed directly into the legal brief prepared by the National Association for the Advancement of Colored People, which in 1954 had triumphantly won *Brown v. Board of Education*.[22] Rabbi Leo Jung, spiritual leader of the New York Orthodox synagogue Kehillat Jeshurun, called that decision "a red-letter day in American history," and in a similar tone the Reform movement's Maurice Eisendrath—who shared little terrain with Jung on Jewish matters—described the court's mandate as "a veritable fulfillment of our own Jewish purpose and our American dream of destiny."[23] Jewish communal leaders like Isaac Frank in Washington, D.C., used the offices of the Jewish Community Council, of which he served as executive director, to facilitate the desegregation of the city's schools, playgrounds, and swimming pools.

Jews saw themselves as shareholders in the moral crusade of the 1950s and 1960s. They recognized that they also suffered from laws and social practices that prevented them from being considered as individuals rather than as members of a group. Discrimination against Jewish applicants to colleges and universities, for example, still lingered in numerous places. While some states, like New York, passed civil rights bills outlawing such practices as early as 1945, other states had not, and as such the discrimination remained firmly in place in most of the nation. By the mid-1950s Jews, like—and along with—African Americans, began to press for federal legislation, something that had not been possible since the days of Reconstruction. The kind of legislation that the civil rights coalition envisioned would check the free hand of private institutions to discriminate as they chose.

In this vision they did not distinguish between the actions of the government and those of the private sector. Jewish defense groups and religious organizations understood that the divide between public and private meant little in a place where the state gave employers, realtors, admissions offices, hotels, and others the right to do their business as they pleased. In a new kind of America, they believed, people would be able to put themselves forward as applicants for jobs, schools, housing, and places of recreation as individuals, and no one would be able to bar entry to them as Jews or blacks. In 1963 the Jewish Community Relations Council of Cincinnati summarized the confluence of Jewish interests and the African American freedom struggle when it declared that

"the society in which Jews are most secure, is itself secure, only to the extent that citizens of all races and creeds enjoy full equality."[24]

This sense of common purpose manifested itself in innumerable symbolic actions. Jewish leaders repeatedly intoned their support for ending
America's system of racial injustice. Rabbi Samuel Berliant used his 1952
inaugural address as president of the Orthodox body, the Rabbinical
Council of America, to advocate that synagogues play a role in creating
racial justice.[25] In 1955 the Central Conference of American Rabbis declared that each of its congregations should hold a "Race Relations Sabbath" during the month of February.[26] In March 1956 one hundred Hebrew Union College–Jewish Institute of Religion personnel were arrested
in Montgomery, Alabama, during the bus boycott. In the summer of
1961 Jews made up about two-thirds of the white freedom riders who
challenged racial discrimination in public accommodations. During the
1964 Mississippi Freedom Summer, the *American Jewish Yearbook* reported with pride that Jewish students made up from one-third to one-
half of the young white women and men who traveled to the South. It
lauded Jews as "well represented in the legal and medical corps in Mississippi," providing services to those who put their lives on the line in the
fight for freedom. While this quasi-official book, an annual compendium
of the "state of the Jews" of America, decried the savage beating of
Rabbi Arthur J. Lelyveld of the American Jewish Congress in Hattiesburg, where he had gone to work on voter registration, it also highlighted the fact that a prominent member of the Jewish community had
risked his health and safety in pursuit of black civil rights.[27]

Jewish organizations, including the Anti-Defamation League, the
American Jewish Committee, the National Council of Jewish Women,
Hadassah, the American Jewish Congress, and the National Community
Relations Advisory Committee (NCRAC), publicly honored civil rights
leaders, issued statements encouraging the civil rights effort, and counseled their members and local chapters to lobby on every political level
for civil rights. They sent letters to members of Congress, their state legislatures, and their city councils; they met with presidents, governors,
mayors, and senators, stating with utter clarity that the civil rights effort
ranked high on the American Jewish political agenda.

This urgency about civil rights made itself felt in ways large and
small. In 1961 the United Synagogue gave its annual Solomon Schechter
award to Ellen Steinberg, a native of New Orleans, who had offered the
city $500,000 to facilitate the integration of its schools. Although New
Orleans rejected the money, the United Synagogue felt the gesture

brought honor to the Jews, while giving good publicity to the cause and to Conservative Judaism. In 1963 over two hundred Reform, Conservative, and Orthodox rabbis participated in the historic March on Washington, and Jewish organizations heaped awards on Martin Luther King Jr., a featured speaker at numerous programs sponsored by Jewish organizations.[28]

Perhaps two moments best capture Jewish participation in the movement. In 1964 two young men, Andrew Goodman and Michael Schwerner, felt called to go to Mississippi as part of Freedom Summer. On June 20 they went with a coworker, James Chaney, to investigate one of the all-too-frequent bombings of black churches, a stratagem employed by local white opponents of civil rights. Chaney, Goodman, and Schwerner never returned, and two months later their bodies were found in a makeshift grave. While Schwerner and Goodman may not have articulated a connection between their actions and their Jewishness, American Jews saw them as their martyrs in a common moral crusade. The Jewish imperative felt by Rabbi Abraham Joshua Heschel as he participated in the struggle requires less speculation. In 1965 Heschel joined with Martin Luther King Jr. to make the historic march from Selma to Montgomery, Alabama. Heschel, considered one of the greatest Jewish theologians of the twentieth century, declared that civil rights grew out of the prophetic tradition. For Jews, he thundered, supporting civil rights should be considered a mitzvah, an obligation, not a choice. He wrote in his diary after returning from Selma that the walk across the bridge had afforded him "a sense of the Holy."[29] American Jews in those years took pride in the fact that so many of the white people who actively labored in the civil rights movement came from their community. Jewish sources expressed pride that so much liberalism persisted into the civil rights era, despite the Jews' overwhelmingly middle-class status. They continued to vote not only in support of liberal candidates but also in favor of referenda that chipped away at discrimination. In 1964, for example, in Kansas City Jews who lived overwhelmingly in wards eight and nine voted almost universally to uphold an ordinance for nondiscrimination in public accommodations. In the Jewish precincts in Detroit, Jews voted ten to one against an ordinance designed to protect white homeowners against possible racial integration.[30]

Yet many involved in the movement, including Jewish communal leaders, rabbis, and activists, saw the Jews' flight to the suburbs as a kind of middle-class complacency, a tacit acceptance of racial privilege, and did not mince words when castigating Jews whose behavior seemed to support the oppressive racial status quo. Rabbi Marvin Braiterman of Baltimore, speaking at the 1959 meeting of the Union of American Hebrew Congregations, declared his "scorn [for] those Jews who because of the invasion of white neighborhoods by non-whites, fled from the cities to the suburbs, carrying their temples with them." He labeled such actions a "moral disaster."[31]

Braiterman's words reflected a sense on the part of some Jewish leaders that beneath the bold words of the organizations, the decisive actions of the institutions, and the brave deeds of the activists, most Jews, like most other white people, feared the long-term implications of living in a truly integrated society. American Jews, Braiterman implied, did not realize how many of their rights and opportunities came to them by virtue of their skin color. Other rabbis and leaders directly lambasted the masses of American Jews for their complicity with American racism, a complicity that was not manifested in overt and violent behavior but in their silence and willingness to enjoy the benefits of a racially divided society. In 1964 Rabbi Arnold Jacob Wolf wrote an article in *Conservative Judaism* stating that Jews "approve of integration, but oppose every possible step toward it." The average American Jew, he wrote, "lives by his superiority to and distance from the American Negro and the American poor."[32] One Philadelphia rabbi went so far as to compare American Jews to ordinary Germans who had cared little about the fate of the Jews.[33]

The imperative to bring about desegregation as defined by national Jewish organizations and national Jewish publications reflected the settlement patterns of American Jews, most of whom lived in the North and in large cities. They experienced the late 1940s through the late 1960s as a period of geographic mobility into increasingly comfortable suburbs. They had no problem with integration in as much as the challenge being launched against the status quo did not disrupt their own, increasingly affluent lives and continued to broaden their range of options. It would not be until the latter part of the 1960s when the battle for equality began to focus on the vast disparity between city and suburb, particularly outside the South, that the Jewish place in the civil rights struggle became widely recognized as problematic.[34]

Southern Jews and the Quandary of a New Era

Until 1964 and 1965, with the passage of the two monumental pieces of civil rights legislation, the movement mainly looked to the South, the region that persisted in maintaining a rigidly divided legal system built on

the binary of black and white. The bulk of Jewish public opinion and political action called for a swift end to that division and demanded that
the federal government act decisively to bring about a change. But notably, few Jews lived in the South, and the kinds of changes the civil
rights effort called for, and to which Jews acceded, affected hardly any
of them. As of 1954, the year of the *Brown* decision, only about two
hundred and thirty thousand of America's Jews lived in the South, a region whose population numbered about 40 million. Southern Jewry constituted about 2 percent of the country's roughly 5.2 million Jews. They,
unlike most other southerners, resided in a handful of the region's largest
cities, New Orleans, Atlanta, Charleston, and Memphis in particular.
Mostly merchants, they depended for their livelihood on the goodwill of
non-Jews.

By every possible measure they had done well in the South. Jews
earned more than most of the whites in the same communities. One
study of income levels in New Orleans conducted in 1960 revealed that
although 43 percent of the city's Jews earned over $10,000 annually,
only 7 percent of the city's white population as a whole did so.[35] Southern Jews had higher levels of education than all other southerners and
claimed access to the best resources their communities offered. Yet as
non-Christians they stood out in the Bible Belt. Historically they had
struck a kind of compromise with regional mores and practices and subscribed to an ethos demanding that they draw no attention to themselves
as demanding, deviant, or different from their neighbors. Rabbi Charles
Martinband of Hattiesburg, Mississippi, who in the early 1960s emerged
as an anomaly, a supporter of the civil rights effort, characterized the
southern Jewish mentality in a short but pointed doggerel:

Come weal,
Come woe,
My status is quo.[36]

The outspoken support of national and northern Jewish organizations
for civil rights, and particularly for the imposition of those rights by the
federal government on a very reluctant South, put Jewish southerners in
a complicated and uncomfortable position. What Jewish leaders, organizations, and the press were calling for indeed involved dismantling the
status quo and upsetting the cherished equilibrium that had allowed
southern Jews to thrive. And thrive they did. Notably, anti-Semitism had
greatly decreased in the South ever since the Leo Frank case of the early
part of the twentieth century. The kind of anti-Jewish violence that flared

in ethnic neighborhoods in New York, Boston, and Chicago in the 1930s and 1940s had no southern equivalent. No one in southern communities complained about Jewish merchants. Rather, they valued these low-profile providers of goods.

But in the 1950s as southern whites confronted civil rights agitation and the possibility of change in their cherished racial system, Jews and Jewish institutions became targets of white violence. Starting in the late 1950s synagogue bombings in Nashville, Atlanta, Charlotte, Gastonia, Jacksonville, Miami, Alexandria, and elsewhere shook the Jews in the South, making them feel vulnerable. These bombings and the rising anti-Jewish rhetoric manifested in print and in speeches by advocates of militant segregationism made it painfully clear to southern Jews that they could no longer hide under the protective cloak of invisibility.[37] Yet many southern Jews strove to maintain that cover. A writer for the *Southern Israelite* noted that the "Jews who espouse and defend the cause of civil rights jeopardize the security of isolated Jewish communities in the South, threaten their social integration and economic position, and ultimately even their physical safety."[38] This statement accurately reflected southern Jewish opinion, both popular and rabbinic.

Yet some rabbis decided that they could no longer acquiesce to fear. Rabbi Perry Nussbaum of Jackson, Mississippi, recognized his congregants' preference for silence but decided that he bore a moral obligation to visit young northern Jews imprisoned for their participation in the Freedom Rides in 1961. He spent the next few years advocating tolerance and urging the South to retreat from its commitment to racism. On September 18, 1967, some in Mississippi decided that he had gone too far. A bomb ripped through Temple Beth Israel. On November 22 of that year, they bombed his home as well. Some of his congregants believed that Nussbaum's outspoken stance had jeopardized the congregation and the Jewish community.[39]

By the late 1950s most southern Jews realized that a conflagration beyond their control would soon engulf them. This put them at odds with their northern coreligionists. In 1958 at the annual meeting of the Rabbinical Assembly, southern Conservative rabbis met in a closed-door session to strategize. One of them, Rabbi William Malev of Houston, published an article in *Conservative Judaism* in which he demonstrated their discomfort with the evolving situation. After noting, "I am on the side of integration. Morally and religiously it can be the only way of solving the problem," he went on to detail the ways in which the national organizations, particularly the "so-called 'defense' organizations in Jewish life," complicated everything. Malev counseled that matters involving the Jews be left to local rabbis because only they could mediate between the very nervous Jewish community and the white southerners who did not understand the idea of Jews as a political and ethnic group. Despite the problems faced by southern Jews, the Conservative rabbis of the Rabbinical Assembly voted overwhelmingly not to meet at segregated hotels and to support integration through legislation.[40]

As Jews and their communal bodies outside the South became increasingly vocal and public in their support of the civil rights effort, southern Jewish discomfort rose. Jewish civil rights workers agitated local whites eager to preserve the racial order. Northern rabbis seemed to be coming in by the busload, and Jewish organizations felt no need to play behind-the-scenes roles in lobbying for civil rights legislation. All of this spelled trouble for southern Jews. Rabbi Eugene Lipman, executive secretary of the UAHC's Commission on Social Action, articulated, with some empathy, the southern Jewish plight best. Southern Jews, Lipman wrote in 1956, could not identify with the civil rights effort because "to do so, they feel, would call down upon them the furies of hatred which now buffet the Negro community, would open the Pandora's box of long dormant anti-Semitism." He felt for his southern colleagues who "are frustrated and torn by conflicting demands," buffeted by "their timid laymen and the nagging dictates of conscience."[41]

When the civil rights movement shifted into high gear, Jewish organizations sided with those eager to change the structure of American life. Historically, Jews feared social disorder, since they long had been the scapegoats of political turmoil. Those most concerned with the welfare of the Jewish community fretted the most, and with good reason, that upheavals led to persecution of the Jews. But in the postwar era, most Jewish organizations and rabbis made clear, in action and in word, that the time had come for America's Jews to risk their short-term security. They did so partly because of the legacy of the Holocaust and a communal belief that American Jews had been far too nervous about their own well-being to engage in disruptive behavior. They behaved as they did for moral and ethical reasons, as well. They believed that Judaism required them to pursue justice, however they could. They also did so because they understood that a society that did not mete out rewards and benefits on the basis of skin color would grant Jews the most options. They recognized that the civil rights legislation pending before Congress in the late 1950s and early 1960s, designed to outlaw discrimination in housing, employment, and education, would greatly improve their lives.

As individuals, as communal leaders, and as members of Jewish organizations, they decided, in essence, that the benefits of activism far outweighed the dangers of social discord.

Even the sputtering of anti-Semites who claimed that the "Jew-Led NAACP Wins School Segregation Case" or that "Jewish Marxists Threaten Negro Revolt in America" did not in the end deter Jewish activism and support.[42] Throughout the South, and around the country as well, anti-Jewish segregationist rhetoric asserted that African Americans took their orders from Jews who pushed them to overturn the long-comfortable arrangement of American race relations. Racist pamphlets and publications declared that blacks did not have the brains or the money to launch such a formidable assault on American values, that only the Jews, who had both, could have made this possible. Even outright threats did not dampen the energy of the organized Jewish communities. Although leaflets appeared on the street in Jacksonville, Florida, claiming that "Jews Must Be Driven Out of Florida," Jewish enthusiasm for the effort remained high.[43]

Rifts between Blacks and Jews

Toward the end of this "golden age" fissures began to appear in the political alliance between Jews and blacks. As the focus moved northward, social practices that worked well for Jews but that disadvantaged African Americans emerged as points of tension. In New York City controversies over racial inequities in public education immediately pitted Jewish interests against those of blacks. For most New York City Jews with children, the public schools worked well. The vast majority of children received what their parents considered an excellent education, and children graduating from these schools proceeded to college at a staggering rate.[44] Public schools also happened to employ a majority-Jewish teaching force, and the educational infrastructure, the teachers' union included, represented Jewish interests.

Some Jews strove to level the playing field in the North where de facto segregation reigned supreme. National Jewish organizations like the American Jewish Congress recognized the gravity of the problem for African Americans. In 1961 its officials, Will Maslow and Richard Cohen, asserted that little distinguished the North from the South in matters of education other than the fact that segregation "in the South is imposed by racial laws and in the North by school districts."[45] It sketched out a plan for a number of northern and western cities to experiment with new kinds of school boundaries to integrate schools, and in 1962 it filed a statement with the House Committee on Education and Labor that stated, "Negroes in our northern metropolises are herded together in black ghettos [and] attend school[s that are] segregated."

Yet when some black parents and organizations launched boycotts, marches, and lawsuits against the New York City schools, trying to force the city to confront the rampant inequities, blacks and Jews found themselves on opposite sides. Despite the recognition by the American Jewish Congress, a pillar of the Jewish organizational infrastructure, of the gravity of the problem, other Jewish organizations opposed changing the basic educational structure. The NCRAC, an umbrella body of all national Jewish organizations, expressed only tepid support for the American Jewish Congress's plan. Rather, it saw virtue in "the neighborhood school as having important educational values." In essence the NCRAC expressed the view that the public educational system, as it existed for most Jews in the 1960s, worked well and tampering with it would not necessarily bring about something better.[46]

This kind of intra-Jewish debate over urban public education, an area of public policy about which they cared tremendously, led to heightened tensions across group lines as well. In 1964 nearly all Jewish organizations opposed a boycott of the New York public schools, and the Jewish Education Committee of New York worried that if the city adopted mandatory busing, as demanded by the civil rights community, Jewish children would suffer. Nearly fifty thousand New York Jewish school children went to their local synagogue or neighborhood Hebrew school for Jewish education directly after school. A widespread system of busing, the group's statement claimed, would "infringe upon the limited time and energy that our children have available for study of the religious beliefs, ethical precepts, and cultural heritage of our people."[47]

In the explosion of unrest in northern black communities, set off by the "long hot summer" of 1965, Jews found themselves the victims of civil conflict and African American anger. In New York, Philadelphia, Los Angeles, Rochester, and numerous other cities, rioters, mostly young black men, expressed their frustration at the lack of real improvement in their lives by looting and damaging the stores of their neighborhood. Jews owned large numbers of those shops—grocery stores, appliance stores, clothing stores, and liquor stores. In Philadelphia Jews owned up to 80 percent of the damaged stores. In Los Angeles's Watts neighborhood Jews owned 80 percent of the furniture stores, 54 percent of the liquor stores, and 60 percent of the food shops.[48] Many of the stores dated back to the days when these neighborhoods had been predominantly Jewish, and the shopkeepers represented the last vestiges of what had once been a substantial Jewish presence. Local Jewish communal bodies, with long histories of working with African American and civil rights organizations, found themselves in a quandary. Although they represented the Jewish community, they did not want to overplay the Jewish aspect of the riots. The director of Rochester, New York's, Jewish Community Council counseled that "Jewish businessmen were not the prime targets because they were Jews" and that the riots should not "be interpreted as anti-Semitism."[49] At that point few Jews were seriously worried about the rise of anti-Semitism among African Americans, and from their point of view since the alliance between Jews and blacks had achieved worthy goals, for the benefit of both, that confluence of interest need not be questioned.

The more heated manifestations of black-Jewish tension over matters of policy and urban turf and a swift Jewish reaction to anti-Jewish rhetoric by African American orators lay in the near future. Indeed, the escalation of animosity between the two, at the end of the 1960s, heralded the end of this putative golden age. By that time, and in the decades beyond, many Jews and blacks began to question if there had ever been an alliance or if the history of American Jewish liberalism had ever been as grand as it loomed in Jewish collective memory. But the rhetoric of American Jewry and the thrust of local and national Jewish communal politics in the postwar era did highlight the convergence between Jewish interests and the civil rights effort, regardless of the tension when Jews and blacks confronted each other with different agendas. That convergence took on added significance in light of the fact that it happened during the tense years of the cold war.

JEWS AND THE COMMUNIST "MENACE"

Many white Americans, comfortable with the prevailing norm of racial segregation and inequity, considered calls for radical change, even by legal means, to be the work of "outside agitators," Communists in particular. The hostile and often violent reactions to any efforts to break down racial barriers cannot be disassociated from the hysteria that swept the country in the aftermath of World War II. That fear increased in intensity with the Communist victory in China in 1950, the Korean War, which ended in 1953, and the ongoing conflict between the United States and the Soviet Union. White Christian Americans easily made the connection between an enemy abroad and an enemy at home bent on over-turning American practices.

The flood tide of anti-Communism put Jews in an uncomfortable and compromised position. As political liberals, Jews articulated positions that many Americans considered suspect. Not only advocacy of civil rights and civil liberties, but support of the United Nations, federal aid to education, and efforts to take religion out of public schools—a key issue for American Jews—set them apart from many, possibly most, Americans. Jews responded differently to the political events of the period than did most other Americans. According to a 1952 Gallup Poll, for example, 56 percent of all Catholics and 45 percent of all Protestants considered the anti-Communist tactics of Senator Joseph McCarthy acceptable. In contrast, 98 percent of all Jews polled disapproved.[50] That Jews reacted so differently from others loomed as a potential problem in an era when the government sought ways to suppress free speech and when accusations about suspect political affiliations ruined careers and lives.

Jewish anxiety about the escalation of anti-Communist rhetoric and the spillover from words into deeds also reflected the fact that Jews had been over-represented among the supporters of left-wing causes in the United States throughout the twentieth century. Jews had played an inordinately large role in organizations and endeavors that to many Americans deviated from basic American values. Many Jews in America and elsewhere had, in fact, supported Socialist and Communist organizations.[51] In an era when the word *un-American* carried heavy political weight, the history of Jewish involvement with unions, the civil rights movement, liberalism, and civil liberties—as well as the Jews' own foreign antecedents—inspired fear in the hearts of the Jews.

Their sense of discomfort loomed large and emerged early in postwar America. In the summer of 1950 federal agents arrested a Jewish couple, Ethel and Julius Rosenberg, on charges of conspiracy to commit espionage, for passing atomic secrets to the Soviet Union. They arrested a friend of theirs, Morton Sobel, also Jewish. Ethel Rosenberg's brother, David Greenglass, and his wife, Ruth, likewise ended up in federal custody. The U.S. government indicted, tried, and found Ethel and Julius Rosenberg guilty, executing them in June 1953 on the electric chair at Sing-Sing Prison. Since they were a group of people who just decades before had been labeled inassimilable foreigners, the Rosenberg case specifically, and the anti-Communist crusade generally, made the Jews exceedingly nervous.

The arrest, trial, and execution of this Jewish couple, as well as the worldwide publicity generated by the event, could not have come at a worse time for American Jews, particularly for those most prone to worrying about their status. The fact that at the height of American anti-Communism, the two people executed by the United States government happened to be Jewish sent a shudder of fear through a community with a profound historical memory of being scapegoated. Various Jewish organizations debated internally how best to respond and how to ensure that the furor not turn on all American Jews. The American Jewish Committee, for example, commissioned sociological research to ascertain the links between intense anti-Communist sentiment and anti-Semitism. The research pointed to a strong and chilling connection between the two, propelling this defense organization and others to strategize. They had to balance the reality of the correlation and its obvious threat to American Jewish comfort and the broad—indeed nearly universal— American Jewish support for civil liberties.

Jewish Anti-Communism

One strategy Jewish organizations turned to involved proving to the public that Jews could not, in fact, be Communists. They produced material for the press highlighting the very real persecution of Jews under Stalin in the Soviet Union and elsewhere in Communist east Europe. Large public rallies held in many American Jewish communities in the early 1950s against Soviet anti-Semitism reflected genuine concern on the part of American Jews for the plight of their sisters and brothers in eastern Europe and followed a pattern set by earlier generations who had taken on the defense of diaspora communities in distress. They genuinely worried about the Jews of Czechoslovakia, for example. In 1952, the Communist government there arrested eleven Jews, all of whom had been active Communist party members. Accused of being "crypto-Zionists," nine went to the gallows. That same year a number of Soviet Jewish writers and intellectuals, branded disloyal counter-revolutionaries, met their deaths as well, amid a barrage of anti-Semitic rhetoric.

By the late 1960s, as anti-Communism had lost much of its virulence, American Jews, young people in particular, continued to agitate over the plight of Soviet Jewry, no longer yoking their protests to anti-Communism. But at the beginning of the decade, as Americans imagined a vast Communist threat at home and abroad, Jews staged demonstrations and held protests in a number of cities focusing on the desperate condition of Jews in Communist countries. This assertive behavior, they hoped, might convince Americans that they ought not to think of Jews as Communists, members of the party, sympathizers, or just "fellow travelers."[52]

Some Jewish organizations also cooperated with the various governmental bodies designed to ferret out the domestic Communist "menace." "Judaism and communism are utterly incompatible," a representative of the American Jewish Committee informed the powerful House Committee on Un-American Activities, and it, as well as other Jewish organizations, allowed HUAC to go through their files. Defense organizations took on the task of defending the Jews against a potent threat, the resurgence of anti-Semitism as a by-product of cold war hysteria, by cooperating with the state. In 1953, out of similar instincts, a staff member of AJC wrote a pamphlet, *The Rosenberg Case*, which validated the jury's finding of the couple's guilt and supported the death sentence imposed on them. *American Legion Magazine* reprinted the piece, written by S. A. Fineberg, as did *The Reader's Digest*. Historian Lucy Dawidowicz, writing in *Commentary*, a magazine founded by the American Jewish Committee in 1945, argued that the execution should go on. Calls for clemency would, she claimed, hurt the Jews. Other Jewish publications, some Yiddish papers included, accepted the Rosenberg's guilt but argued that the punishment did not fit the crime.[53]

When commenting on public policy, Jews found a variety of opportunities to defend themselves against charges questioning the depth of their loyalty to America. This dynamic led the Jewish Community Council of Washington, D.C., to expel the Jewish Peoples' Fraternal Order, a subsidiary of the International Workers Order, from the Delegate Assembly, the representative communal body. On a national level, nearly all organizations conducted internal purges of Communists. The American Jewish Committee, the American Jewish Congress, Hadassah, the National Council of Jewish Women, the Federation of Jewish Philanthropies of New York, and the Anti-Defamation League participated in this effort, although Hadassah went on record as opposing both the formation of HUAC and the McCarthy investigations, as did NCJW.[54]

Jewish anti-Communism developed differently from the type of anti-Communism taking hold in society at large. Jews articulated a connection between Communism as a repugnant ideology and all forms of totalitarianism, focusing most on Nazism. They also framed their abhorrence of Stalin and Communism around a passionate defense of civil liberties in the United States. Despite the purges of Communists that took place in the ranks of American Jewish organizations, the United Synagogue proclaimed in 1950:

> The only important fear which we need have of communists in this country today is that they will provoke us into suicide, by piece-meal destruction of our own free institutions. Police-state tactics will not destroy Communism. We must not forget that in Czarist Russia, the first nation in which Communism triumphed, these tactics turned out to be a boomerang. By refusing to adopt police-state tactics, America will strike the heaviest possible blow against communism, and preserve its own democracy.[55]

Despite the fact that Jewish organizations showed up cooperatively at hearings of the House on Un-American Activities, the Women's League for United Synagogue urged the abolition of HUAC and condemned the passage of the 1950 McCarran Act, the Internal Security Act requiring the registration of all "subversive" organizations.

Jewish tactics also involved linking anti-Communism to progressive causes, particularly to the growing American acceptance and tolerance of difference. Thus, when Rabbi Jung applauded the 1954 Supreme Court decision on *Brown v. Board of Education,* he hailed the event as a triumph against Communism.[56] The Jewish press found ways to affirm their anti-Communism while at times condemning the tactics of the anti-Communists. They hedged their language to protect themselves. The 1952 volume of the *American Jewish Yearbook* commented that international tensions in Korea and Europe "dramatized the threat of Communist imperialism. . . . This necessarily increased concern that proper safeguards be taken . . . against native Communist agents of Soviet Russia." Yet having indicated that it, as an authoritative voice in the community, agreed that Communism constituted a problem, the *Yearbook* went on to note that everyone concerned should ask if "unjustified attacks on civil liberties" have been taken as well.[57]

By all accounts American Jews walked a tightrope from the end of the 1940s through the 1960s. They remembered the anti-Semitism that had flourished through World War II. They had seen from a distance where hatred of Jews could lead. They knew that many individuals in the community had been involved with causes and organizations deemed questionable by large numbers of Americans. They perceived of anti-Semitism as sleeping but not dead.

Taking on Universalist Causes

Despite their fear of being labeled "pink" or "red," the majority of Jews in the 1950s and 1960s adamantly supported civil rights, civil liberties, the separation of church and state, federal aid to education, the United Nations, and a panoply of other causes defined by some Americans as out of step with national values. On the issue of separation of church and state in the realm of public education they deviated quite substantially from most Americans, Christians who did not see the issue through minority eyes. After World War II Jewish defense organizations stated unequivocally that public schools, which served as the common ground for all Americans, should not be the venue for religious rituals, readings, or exercises. In cases such as *McCollum v. Board of Education* (1947) and *Zorach v. Clausen* (1952) they appeared before the U.S. Supreme Court arguing for a religiously neutral state and for public schools shorn of religious ritual. Both cases involved programs in which students would be released from school for religious instruction.[58]

Jews stayed on the liberal side of American politics in large measure because they believed that certain positions would assist both Jews and America as a whole. Jews would benefit from enforced antidiscrimination legislation and strong public education. And they cared a great deal about Israel, the newly Jewish independent state. Given the realities of Middle East politics, they believed that Israel's security would be strengthened by a strong system of world governance embodied in the United Nations. Notably, their political rhetoric and style of political activity in the postwar era emphasized what America as a whole would gain. They employed a rhetoric of universalism, obscuring the distinctively Jewish interests at stake. While Jewish publications discussed anti-Semitism in minute detail, in the public sphere they attacked prejudice in general. Using film, television, radio, and print journalism, they issued a steady barrage of propaganda stating that prejudice stemmed from ignorance, that no intellectual or moral justification existed for racist thinking. While differences existed among Jewish organizations, most strayed very little from a communal consensus maintaining that Jews could secure themselves by making alliance with others of goodwill and fighting for general causes in the name of "intergroup relations" or "human relations."[59]

The American Jewish Committee played a particularly prominent role in leading the fight against intolerance through education. The defense body engaged social psychologists to research the phenomenon of prejudice. It launched the Studies in Prejudice series, which included Theodore Adorno's *The Authoritarian Personality,* Bruno Bettelheim and Morris Janowitz's *Dynamics of Prejudice,* and Nathan Ackerman and Marie Jahoda's *Anti-Semitism and Emotional Disorder.* The last specifically called attention to anti-Jewish prejudice in its title, but it, like the others, sought to teach Americans that the roots of prejudice lay in deep psychological pathology, not in rational assessments of the social order.[60]

In the work Jews did to combat or prevent anti-Semitism, they appealed to universal liberalism rather than to specific group interests. Even the most dramatic event of this era, the creation of a separate Jewish institution of higher learning as a response to discrimination, demonstrated the fusion of the particular and the universal as a communal strategy. The academy, as a place to provide students with university training and as an employer of scholars, had long excluded and restricted Jews. In 1948, inspired by Israel Goldstein, a Conservative New York rabbi, and a group of Boston Jewish businessmen, Brandeis University opened its doors to a small class of 107 students in Waltham, Massachusetts. It hired a heavily Jewish faculty and early on included Judaic studies in its curriculum. Brandeis, however, proclaimed itself to be a nonsectarian university that would serve all Americans as it advanced the common good.[61]

Subsequent historians have accurately emphasized how little anti-Semitism existed from 1948 through 1967, particularly after the early 1950s. They have shown how despite the political agitation over anti-Communism, Jews escaped much of the viciousness, other than that directed at them by fringe groups.[62] Despite their over-identification with civil rights, as perceived by other white Americans, Jews did not suffer in any meaningful way, with the bombing of southern synagogues by defiant white supremacists a regional anomaly. Although Jews took public positions on religion that many Americans considered a threat to Christianity, they in fact were experiencing increased mobility, broader acceptance, and expanded opportunities.

Yet Jewish organizations worried that their positions on public policy would in fact put them in harm's way. Therefore they carefully monitored anti-Jewish rhetoric and reported in exquisite detail on episodes large and small. They also tracked the fates of Jews who had applied to universities and professional schools, noting with some surprise how swiftly barriers had fallen.[63]

Those barriers did not just fall on their own. They did not crumble merely because American Christians of goodwill decided to abandon the quotas, housing restrictions, and employment practices that in the recent past had hampered Jewish aspirations. Rather, through organizations and communal bodies the Jews waged a vigorous campaign, in public education—broadly defined—and in the press, as well as in legislatures and courtrooms, to bring such practices to an end. Their participation with

African Americans in the civil rights struggle played a crucial role in making those practices obsolete, and as such they brought America with them in their quest for a more open and barrier-free society.

THE SUBURBANIZATION OF AMERICA'S JEWS

Jewish anxieties had not been completely unwarranted, as evidenced by the vast amount of work it took to gain acceptance. Yet editors and writers of Jewish publications, rabbis, communal leaders, professional staffs and grassroots members of many organizations also realized that worries about latent anti-Semitism, the Soviet oppression of its Jews, and the fate of Israel competed in intensity with the demographic, economic, educational, and religious developments of this period. And these developments all emanated from a single reality: the massive suburbanization of America's Jews.

Jewish suburbanization of the postwar era represented an acceleration of a process that had been in the works for many decades, by which an economically mobile group moved from an area of first settlement to second and even third neighborhoods. Each move represented a step up in amenities and status. With each relocation, though some element of the Jewish community and some institutions stayed put, the trajectory was outward, even if the new neighborhood existed within the jurisdictional boundaries of the city. Although new Jewish neighborhoods pivoted around the large cities, they could increasingly be found situated farther and farther away from the urban core. In the 1950s two-thirds of America's 5,500,000 Jews lived in or just outside of the country's ten largest cities. New York, Chicago, Philadelphia, Cleveland, Baltimore, and Boston remained major centers of Jewish life, although the majority of the population lived on these cities' suburban fringe.[64] For some post–World War II American Jews, the suburbs that beckoned could be found in new states and regions. Los Angeles and Miami, in particular, became magnets for Jewish migrations from the "old" Northeast. One hundred and thirty thousand Jews lived in Los Angeles before World War II, but by 1951 the number had grown to three hundred thousand. As of 1958 half the city's Jews had arrived in the previous thirteen years, making it a city of Jewish newcomers. In the 1960s Los Angeles ranked just below New York and Tel Aviv in its number of Jews.[65]

The attraction of the suburbs, whether in a new place or a familiar one, whether within the political borders of the city or nestled in a separate county, could be explained by recent history. The Great Depression and the war had dramatically reduced the already low Jewish fertility. Couples who married during the hard times of the previous decade had put off having children. Many had doubled up with parents and other family members to save money. With the war's end, and stimulated by the G.I. Bill and the opening up of these new communities, many of which, like Levittown, New York, and Levittown, Pennsylvania, had been developed by Jewish builders, families could now have homes of their own.

The move to the suburbs meant a slow but steady abandonment of the central city. Notably, Jewish removal to the suburbs did not take place in tandem with any Jewish influx into older neighborhoods. Since this period witnessed little new Jewish immigration to the United States, no new Jews took the place of those leaving the city neighborhoods. The law inherited from the 1920s made certain of that. In the years immediately after the war, some Holocaust survivors made their way to America. In the year that saw the largest wave of postwar migration, 1949, just under forty thousand new Jewish immigrants entered the United States, most of them from the Displaced Persons camps of Europe. Subsequently, small trickles of Jewish immigrants came to America in response to crises in other lands. In the late 1950s, about ten thousand refugee Hungarian Jews came to America; about one thousand, from Egypt in the early 1960s; and four thousand, from Cuba in the aftermath of the 1959 Revolution.[66] Throughout this period, several thousand Jewish immigrants arrived every year from Israel, a country that in fact annually filled its quota, as allotted by the McCarran-Walter Act, the law enacted in 1952 that imposed even stricter limits on immigration than the 1920s law.

These new immigrants also settled in the Jewish neighborhoods forming on the edges of America's large cities. Certainly some Jews remained in the urban neighborhoods. Older and poorer, they made up the dwindling membership of inner-city synagogues. They constituted the readership of the last of the Yiddish newspapers, the *Tog-Morgen Zhurnal*, the *Forverts,* and for those on the far left, the *Freiheit*. In some cases forces beyond their control compelled even these Jews to move. Urban renewal projects in most cities demolished poor neighborhoods, defined by policy makers as run-down slums. In places such as Washington, D.C., the last traces of the old Jewish enclave on Half Street met with the bulldozer. The leveling of Half Street and the adjoining area near South East sent the capital city's Jews, most of whom owned and operated small stores, out to the suburbs. Most of them headed for Montgomery County, although some settled within the District itself, but at the outer edges of North West. Their new neighborhoods, whether in the city or on its margins, lacked the street life of the "old neighborhood."

Whether like the majority who opted for the fresh new suburbs or like the minority who lost their homes through urban renewal, Jews could take advantage of new housing opportunities because of their skin color. The practices of suburban developers, strongly buttressed by government policy, opened up wide vistas for white people. Banks and other lending institutions played a role in hastening the segregation of northern cities by not giving loans to black applicants and "block-busting" older urban neighborhoods to hasten white flight. African Americans filled the neighborhoods being abandoned by those flowing to the suburbs.

The dwindling of the Jewish population in particular neighborhoods and the corresponding increase in the non-Jewish black population stimulated the outward movement of the stragglers. This process had tremendous implications for the institutions that served as the building blocks of Jewish communal life. Synagogues, schools, community centers, and entrepreneurial networks followed the movement of the Jews. As Jews and their institutions left, the few remaining Jews found themselves bereft of the services and social life that had made Jewish life possible. Kosher meat markets and bakeries, for example, had no reason to stay open when the majority of their customers left for other neighborhoods. The few Jews who remained, lacking the essential ingredients of Jewish life, found themselves joining their friends and family who had already made the suburban move. In essence, suburban migration begot further suburban migration.

Jewish economic affluence accelerated the process. Whatever reservations they may have had about leaving familiar places—South Shore in Chicago, Boston's Roxbury, vast parts of the Bronx and Brooklyn, and analogous Jewish enclaves in Philadelphia, Baltimore, Cleveland, and St. Louis—Jews could afford to do so more easily than many of the Italian and Irish Catholic residents of adjacent neighborhoods.[67] Surveys of Jewish communities in the mid-1950s found that from 75 to 96 percent of those identified as Jews made a living in nonmanual occupations, as opposed to 38 percent of all other Americans. As of 1953, one-sixth of American Jews over the age of eighteen had graduated from college, as opposed to one-twentieth of the general population.[68] As early as 1948, before the benefits of the G.I. Bill had had much of a chance to change the Jewish educational and economic profile, among Jews in Charleston, South Carolina—a Jewish community of two thousand—

eight doctors, seven dentists, eighteen lawyers, five pharmacists, nine teachers, eighteen engineers, seven social workers, and four accountants could be found. Ten years earlier, when the community stood at about the same size, only one Jewish doctor and one dentist, a few lawyers, two pharmacists, and three teachers had constituted the community's professional class. Postwar affluence and the benefits of social policy only enhanced the Jews' professional ascendancy.[69]

The intensity of the Jewish move out of old central city neighborhoods, so deeply associated with the immigration era, took place with little regret, at least on the part of those who rushed to suburbia. The exodus did, however, launch an era of literary retrospection. In the aftermath of World War II and in the face of the suburban trajectory, such memoirs as Alfred Kazin's *A Walker in the City* and Meyer Levin's *My Father's House* described with ironic fondness the sights, sounds, and smells of the old immigrant neighborhoods of Brooklyn and Chicago, respectively.[70] The 1951 publication of *All-of-a-Kind Family* by Sydney Taylor marked not only the first juvenile book on a Jewish subject to be embraced by the public at large but also the first mass-market veneration of the Lower East Side. The warm story of five little girls growing up in a loving family and an intense community on the East Side, *All-of-A-Kind Family* and its sequels valorized the old immigrant neighborhood—a place that Jews had left as soon as they could.[71]

A communal culture that particularly venerated New York's Lower East Side as the American Jewish equivalent of eastern Europe unfolded as Jews planted themselves in green and leafy suburbs, far removed from the gritty streets and grimy tenements that their mothers and fathers had once called home. Publishers reissued books set on the Lower East Side that had been written in earlier decades and then forgotten: Hutchins Hapgood's *The Spirit of the Ghetto* (1909), Abraham Cahan's *The Rise of David Levinsky* (1917), Henry Roth's *Call It Sleep* (1934), and Anzia Yezierska's *Bread Givers* (1925). These books found receptive audiences among American-born Jews whose parents or grandparents had been part of the great wave of immigration from eastern Europe. In 1966 the Jewish Museum staged a major exhibit on the Lower East Side entitled "Portal to America." Journalists noted with a degree of irony how crowds of suburbanites lined up to enter the august building on Fifth Avenue to see photographs of sweatshop workers, old sewing machines, and enlargements of pages from the Yiddish press.[72]

The wildly popular Broadway musical *Fiddler on the Roof* also echoed a sense of nostalgia for an era gone by. American Jews, like millions of other Americans, and indeed people around the world, became captivated by the drama and music of *Fiddler*. Yet the 1964 musical, based on short stories by Sholom Aleichem and set in a fictional Russian town, Anatevka, spoke to American Jews in a very particular way. Their immigrant origins lay so far in the past that they no longer had any reason to be embarrassed by them. They could embrace with warmth the world of Tevye and his daughters, their poverty, and their singing about "Tradition" precisely because such motifs carried no stigma. They enthusiastically incorporated the musical and its songs—particularly "Sunrise, Sunset"—and its evocation of a mythic shtetl into their communal culture. Now they felt safe to do so, since such places no longer had to be fled from, either physically or culturally.

Despite the warm feelings expressed for long-gone immigrant urban neighborhoods and the small towns of the Pale of Settlement, American Jews continued to race to the comfort and privacy of the suburbs. Jews very much resembled the other middle-class white American suburban migrants of their generation. Typically, young men who returned from military service married and moved to these communities first. In these places a young family just starting up could afford to buy a house. Suburbs, with their cheap and abundant land, offered roomier and greener accommodations than city spaces. Jewish suburb-seekers settled among others like themselves, young couples with new babies in tow. They created a lifestyle and a cultural milieu built around family life, recreation for couples, and the educational and social needs of their children. Few women held down jobs when they had young children. Husbands commuted to the city every day for work.

Yet while on the surface suburban Jews seemed like other white suburban Americans, they made their choices in very Jewish terms.[73] They did not settle randomly in the new communities ringing the central cities. Rather, they clustered in places with a substantial Jewish presence and that supported the Jewish institutions that they themselves had created. They maintained social lives built around Jewish networks. As they formed Jewish enclaves in Skokie, Illinois; Shaker Heights, Ohio; Newton, Massachusetts; and Silver Spring, Maryland, they drew other Jews to them, eager to partake in the good life these communities had to offer. Their decision to live among other Jews, however, was not in reaction to the reality or fear of anti-Semitism. Analysts commenting on Jewish suburbanization marveled at how little hostility Jews met in their new neighborhoods. Jews, women in particular, worked amiably with their non-Jewish peers in pursuit of common civic goals, like building good schools, maintaining fine playgrounds and parks, and supporting public libraries.

Synagogues Move to the Suburbs

The kinds of Jewish public spaces that developed in the suburbs reflected the selectivity of the migration. In the suburbs the Jews de-emphasized their ethnic distinctiveness, in contrast to the city neighborhoods where they had lived previously. Before the suburban move they had lived in places with an unmistakable Jewish flavor. Neighborhoods in the Bronx, for example, supported kosher butcher shops, bakeries, fish mongers, and delicatessens, other food shops that catered to Jewish tastes, Yiddish schools, Hebrew schools, Yiddish bookstores, and the storefront offices of Jewish organizations, all of which visibly marked the streets as Jewish. Newspaper stands sold Yiddish newspapers, and older residents, Yiddish-speakers, gave public spaces a bilingual tone. The atmosphere itself had made the city spaces Jewish.

But suburban life changed all this. Jews moved to new communities that had no pre-existing Jewish space. Since the older generation did not move to the suburbs in the same numbers as the young, the full range of Jewish institutions did not get transplanted beyond city limits. Suburban Jewish life tended to be built around the synagogue, which emerged as the central institution providing Jewish education and the social context for raising Jewish children. In fact, the period from the end of World War II through the early 1960s witnessed a massive explosion in synagogue construction. Between 1945 and 1950 alone, American Jews spent between $500,000,000 and $600,000,000 on new religious edifices.

In some cases established urban congregations did get transplanted to the suburbs. They often sold their old buildings, heralded just a few decades earlier with pride as magnificent Jewish structures, frequently to African American congregations. The markers of Jewishness—six-pointed stars, Hebrew letters, plaques engraved with the Ten Commandments—could be seen for decades peeking out from behind the crosses as historic reminders of old Jewish neighborhoods. But in most cases residents of the new communities founded new synagogues from the ground up. Members tended to come from the same age group and to be at the same point in the life cycle. In these congregations few, and often no, old people worshiped. The congregants, mostly American-born, had no memories of immigration to shape their attitudes. Poverty did not exist among them, and few—or none—made a living as manual laborers. A scant number made a living as proprietors of small retail

businesses. Rather, as professionals and owners of more substantial enterprises, they could all claim high levels of education measured both by
national standards and by the standards of their parents' generation. In
essence, the homogeneity of the community replicated itself in the homogeneity of the synagogues.

Sometimes Jewish developers fostered synagogue formation. As early
as 1946 Sam Eig, a key player in the development of Montgomery
County, Maryland, offered a free grant of land to the 550 Jewish families
already living in the Bethesda and Chevy Chase area. Eig stipulated that
the land had to be used to create an inclusive Jewish institution serving
all Jews who had moved beyond the District of Columbia line rather than
one serving a particular denomination. Out of this condition came the
Montgomery County Jewish Community, a synagogue-center. By 1958
over five hundred families belonged, and over twelve hundred young
people partook of its classes, clubs, dances, and other social activities.[74]

Those who joined suburban synagogues expected these religious institutions to provide for most of their Jewish needs. More than half of
all American Jews belonged to a synagogue through the middle of the
1960s. Their decision to join transformed the face of Jewish affiliation
in America. Rates of synagogue membership grew dramatically. In 1937,
527 Conservative and Reform congregations serviced 125,000 of America's Jewish families. Two decades later 1,200 congregations from these
liberal movements enrolled 455,000 families.[75] Many of the families who
joined synagogues when they arrived in their new suburban homes had
never belonged to one before. But moving away from the familiarity of
the urban neighborhood where Jewishness pervaded everyday life and
dominated the streetscape meant renegotiating the terms of Jewish affiliation. Jewish culture, however they defined it, would no longer be a
given that came just from living in a particular neighborhood and participating in the quotidian details of going to school, shopping, meeting
friends on the street, and the like. In these new communities they had to
determine exactly how to be Jewish and then act on their choices.

The Jewish Baby Boom

In this resettlement of America's Jews from city to suburb, concerns with
the needs of children loomed large. American Jews launched their own
"baby boom" in tandem with that same trend characterizing postwar
American demography. In the immediate postwar era few Jewish
teenagers showed up in community surveys or in suburban communities,
reflecting the suppression of childbearing during the 1930s through the

end of World War II. But small children abounded. While the Jewish
spike in population did not equal that of non-Jews, it did signal an important communal agenda.[76] The fact that in the late 1950s 60 percent
of all Jewish children in both Lynn, Massachusetts, and New Orleans fell
between the ages of five to twelve indicated much about who had moved
to the suburbs and what the communities looked like. The Jewish residents of America's suburbs expected synagogues to convey to their children a sense of Jewishness, to enculturate them into a Jewish life, and to
help them to mark Jewish life-cycle events.[77]

Parents sought a Jewish education for their children in those suburban synagogues, and community-wide Jewish schools that functioned independent of synagogues declined in number. Synagogue schools, usually meeting one or two weekday afternoons and Sunday mornings,
registered increases in enrollment each year from the late 1940s through
the mid-1960s. The congregational school prepared boys for bar mitzvah, an event that in this age of widespread Jewish affluence allowed parents to celebrate their material achievement and their family stability in
style. For the first time in these postwar suburban synagogues, girls appeared equal in number to boys as consumers of Jewish education. By the
late 1950s both Reform and Conservative congregations began to offer
girls a chance to demonstrate their learning and to mark their coming of
age with a bat mitzvah. If not initially as elaborate in ritual as the boys'
event, the bat mitzvah did at least offer girls a chance to ascend the
bimah—the raised platform—and stand before the Torah scrolls, a privilege previously enjoyed solely by males.

Children occupied a place at the top of the Jewish communal agenda.
Communal leaders and parents defined Jewish education as more important than they had in any previous era. As a field it made strides toward greater coordination and professionalization as communities
began to invest greater resources in teaching children the basics of Judaism. Before 1920 only four American cities—Boston, Detroit, Minneapolis, and Pittsburgh—coordinated Jewish education through some
kind of central communal body. By 1950 most communities, large and
small, "had discovered wide areas of social activity where they could
plan and work cooperatively for the attainment of common goals" in
fostering Jewish learning. Boards, sometimes referred to as bureaus, of
Jewish education hoped to bring higher standards to the enterprise of
learning by pooling resources, developing curricular materials, and enhancing the status of teachers.[78]

Jewish youth groups sought to inspire loyalty and organize the leisure time of youngsters, and their flowering in the postwar suburbs likewise demonstrates the emphasis on the young. In an era when educators and psychologists worried about teenagers and their seeming alienation from and rebelliousness against accepted social norms, Junior Hadassah, Young Judea, Habonim, Hashomer Hatzair, B'nai Akiva, B'nai B'rith Youth Organization, as well as the Conservative movement's United Synagogue Youth, Reform's National Federation of Temple Youth, and the Orthodox National Council of Synagogue Youth, together enrolled thousands of young Jews. They all sponsored overnight camps during the summer and activities in town during the school year, published magazines, and employed paid staffs to plan programming. The Conservative movement, for example, opened its first Camp Ramah in the summer of 1947, in Eagle River, Wisconsin.[79]

Additionally, congregations successfully introduced the institution of "junior congregations." On Sabbath mornings boys and girls gathered for their own services, under the gentle guidance of a teacher or assistant rabbi. They fulfilled all the ritual roles ordinarily the province of adult men. They chanted the service, delivered the sermons, and read from the Torah. The youth-oriented thrust of American Judaism created an environment in which youngsters became accustomed to functioning as Jews in age-segregated settings. Junior congregations—as a harbinger of future developments—tended to ignore gender difference to a degree unmatched in the adult service being held in the sanctuary. Here girls had the opportunity, unavailable to their mothers, to take part in the actual worship service.

Synagogues as the Focus of Jewish Life

Synagogues provided suburban Jews with a locus for being Jewish, a place to celebrate life-cycle events, and to socialize with other Jews. Classes and clubs met in the synagogues, which maintained men's clubs, sisterhoods, teen groups, theatrical troupes, Boy and Girl Scout troops, and nursery schools. They set aside space for gift shops where families could buy ritual objects, many of them made in Israel, a country whose struggles and achievements elicited their sympathy. The synagogue became *the* center of Jewish expression and behavior. In November 1963, Jews, like other Americans, reacted with profound grief to the assassination of President John F. Kennedy. Synagogues across America, suburban ones in particular, opened their doors to Jews to memorialize the fallen leader. In White Plains, New York, six thousand Jews, more than half the town's Jewish population, showed up for a memorial service.

Local rabbis estimated that more Jews went to the synagogues to mourn Kennedy than attended high holiday services that year.[80]

Synagogues may have loomed so large because the vast majority of suburban Jews had arrived only recently in these communities. Previously they had lived in other neighborhoods, and now they found themselves without extended family networks in the immediate vicinity. Likewise, many moved multiple times within their suburban communities. In 1953, for example, 18.5 percent of Jews recently arrived in the Los Angeles suburbs planned to move again within the year. Their synagogues provided a certain kind of stability as they constantly relocated in pursuit of bigger and better housing.[81]

The development of an American Jewish culture that pivoted around these suburban synagogues reflected the importance of social networks and continued identification with the Jewish people. Generally speaking, the social part of synagogue life inspired members much more than the religious part. American Jews did not evince high levels of religiosity. Most had moved away from traditional observance of kashrut and Sabbath restrictions. Few attended weekly services. Certainly, the sanctuaries overflowed during Rosh Hashanah and Yom Kippur, when Jews behaved differently from the people around them, staying away from their places of work and school to be with other Jews in the synagogue. But other than during the high holidays, most Jews did not regularly attend synagogue, despite their high rates of membership. Crowds piled into the sanctuaries usually only to celebrate the bar or bat mitzvah of a friend or family member. Often lavish and large, the *b'nai mitzvah* of this era emphasized the celebration of the birthday and the status of the family. Many commentators, rabbis in particular, worried that the events neglected the fact that "the important thing is Judaism and not [the boy's] immature self."[82]

But on the Sabbaths most Jews preferred to spend their leisure time in other pursuits. Writing at the end of this era, theologian Eugene Borowitz commented, "the paradox emerges. If the American Jew were truly religious, he would create a living American Jewish community, but though he organizes his community along religious lines, his life shows little religious belief and practice. . . . Secular Judaism, which could not dominate American Judaism under its own name, now may do so under the auspices of the synagogue."[83] The Jewish religious expression of the 1950s involved finding a place to teach their children what Jewishness meant and to mingle with friends in social activities. As such the suburban synagogue fulfilled more of an ethnic function than a religious one and used the cover of religion to express social instincts. Which congregations families opted to join probably had little to do with theological or halakic concerns.[84] In this peculiar type of secularism, American Jews differed from their Protestant and Catholic neighbors. Christians underwent a religious revival in the 1950s, and while theologians in the Protestant and Catholic seminaries questioned the depth of the sentiment behind that revival, they noted the overflow crowds who routinely came on Sunday mornings to churches of every denomination in communities around the country.

THE RELIGIOUS LANDSCAPE OF SUBURBAN JUDAISM

The social origins of American Jews in the 1950s helps to explain the particular denominational choices made by American Jews. While each of the "big three" of the Jewish denominations, Reform, Conservative, and Orthodox, found itself on the suburban frontier, these two decades represented the golden age of the Conservative movement. It thrived partly because of its history as a middle-of-the road denomination that emphasized the idea of *k'lal yisrael,* the unity of the Jewish people. It also became the majority denomination in these years as a result of the handicaps endured by the other denominations.

The mismatch between American suburbs and Orthodox Judaism had nothing to do with its institutional weakness. Indeed, despite the gloomy prognostications of sociologists like Nathan Glazer in *American Judaism,* who predicted the disappearance of Orthodox Judaism, the postwar era heralded a new burst of life for traditional congregations.[85] In the 1950s and 1960s, while it did not grow much in numbers, Orthodoxy intensified in the depth and breadth both of observance and learning among its adherents. Its institutional infrastructure became richer, despite the absence of substantial numerical growth, as measured in terms of members. Part of the intensification of Orthodoxy was due to the efforts of refugees coming immediately before, during, and after World War II, who found much in American observance, particularly in Orthodox congregations, wanting. The influx of Hungarian Hasidim after the end of the war had a particular impact on fostering intense piety and religious observance. In neighborhoods like Brooklyn's Williamsburg, Crown Heights, and Boro Park, as well as in Lakewood, New Jersey, and Monsey, situated in New York's Rockland County, they tried to do something that had never been done before in America: establish all-Jewish, Hasidic communities, made up of women and men who had no interest in "fitting in." They felt no anxiety about how to adapt to American expectations. Rather, these Jews wanted to remain separate from American culture and believed that conducting their lives based on traditional Judaism far surpassed in value the benefits of American success and acceptance.

These new Orthodox immigrants set a standard that gradually came to dominate Orthodox institutions, particularly those made up of the American-born, usually defined as modern Orthodox. Orthodox congregations, which for years had not placed a *mehitza,* a physical barrier between the men's and women's sections, felt called on to erect one. Others who before had considered a low *mehitza* perfectly acceptable agreed to raise the height of the divider to indicate a commitment to stricter standards of sex segregation. Orthodox rabbis and laymembers began to demand, in part inspired by the model set by the refugees, that higher standards of observance be met in their institutions. This pressure from the newcomers played a key role in the growth of intensive, all-day Jewish schools in the years after 1945. Throughout most of the century, and most of the country, observant parents, like nearly all other American Jews, sent their children to public schools in pursuit of an education that would help their children achieve professional success. But in 1944, for example, a group of Orthodox rabbis and laypeople founded the Torah Umesorah movement, known also as the National Society for Hebrew Day Schools. It launched a national effort to create schools that offered both quality American education and intensive learning of traditional Jewish texts. By 1957 such schools existed in 235 communities and educated over twenty-five hundred students.[86]

Orthodox groups, although still disunited and pursuing separate goals, found ways to bring their message to other Jews. The Rabbinical Council in 1953 organized "Torah Tours" for visiting Jews in their communities and college campuses to spread the word that the commandments of Jewish law should be followed. The Union of Orthodox Jewish Congregations set up regional offices in Philadelphia and Boston.[87] In 1954 Yeshiva University added a women's branch, Stern College, expanding opportunities for the observant by offering daughters of religious families an alternative to pursuing higher education in non-Jewish, gender-mixed settings.

American Orthodox bodies also asserted a new level of militancy as they began not only to criticize their members' level of observance and to chide them for their lukewarm commitment to traditional learning but also to challenge the other branches of Judaism with a zeal not manifested since the late nineteenth century. In 1954, for example, Rabbi Oscar Fasman of the Hebrew Theological College of Chicago declared that Orthodoxy as an organized entity should not recognize the legitimacy of Conservative and Reform Judaism.[88] That same year Rabbi Joseph Soloveitchik, leader of America's modern Orthodox, issued a ruling that forbade observant Jews from entering a non-Orthodox synagogue for any purpose.[89] In 1958 the Orthodox Rabbinical Alliance recommended that Orthodox Jews in America disassociate themselves from activities that brought them in contact with non-Orthodox Jews.

Orthodox rabbis and educational organizations sounded a discordant note in the Jewish consensus on issues involving the separation of church and state with regard to public aid for religious schools. In the postwar era American Jewry spent considerable time, money, and political energy disentangling the state from matters of religion, particularly in education. Leo Pfeffer of the American Jewish Congress emerged as the most powerful figure in the Jewish community in proclaiming that Jews had "an enormous stake" in the public schools. They, like all Americans, he declared, would suffer by the "opening of the public treasury to private and parochial schools."[90]

Orthodox groups disagreed vehemently. Siding with Catholics rather than other Jews, leaders of Torah Umesorah, and of the National Council of Young Israel and the Rabbinical Council of America, opposed the "hand-off" policy in relation to state support of parochial education, which served as the rallying cry of the Jewish organizations.[91] Except for Rabbi Moshe Feinstein of the Union of Orthodox Jewish Congregations, American Jewish groups applauded the U.S. Supreme Court's ruling in the *Engel v. Vitale* decision, which struck down school prayer.[92] Similarly, in 1963 when Brooklyn's Beth Jacob School asked permission to use an underutilized public school building, the American Jewish Congress objected, claiming that any mingling of religion and state in education posed a danger to America.[93] This kind of independence on the part of the Orthodox challenged communal bodies such as local boards of rabbis and community councils and, on a national level, the National Community Relations Advisory Council (NCRAC), which attempted to construct a Jewish consensus. It also questioned the depth of the American Jewish belief in integration.[94]

If local circumstances drove a wedge between the Orthodox and the other denominations, the newly created state of Israel surfaced as another source of tension. In Israel, unlike the United States, not just one but two chief rabbis—one Ashkenazic and the other Sephardic—acted as

state functionaries, empowered by the government to make crucial decisions about matters such as marriage, divorce, burial, and other concerns
of personal status. Orthodox groups in America opposed any efforts by
Reform and Conservative Judaism to establish themselves in Israel.
They jumped to the defense of the Israeli religious establishment whenever the liberal denominations questioned the power put in the hands of
the religious parties there. Yet ultra-Orthodox groups in New York
threw up pickets around the consulate of the State of Israel, objecting to
the policy of drafting women into the army or the carrying out of au-
topsies by medical examiners, both practices that they believed violated
Jewish law.

Although the vast majority of American Jews rallied to its support and
felt pride in its accomplishments, Israel could not unite them. In moments of political crisis, first in the initial months after the May 14, 1948,
declaration of independence, during the subsequent war, and during the
Suez Crisis of 1956, Jews in America expressed great support for Israel.
But in the realm of religion, the issue of Israel and matters relating to it
exacerbated internal divisions and helped make the Orthodox seem different from all other American Jews.

The Orthodox stood out from other American Jews most profoundly
for their commitment to an ideology that seemed impervious to calls for
compromise. In an era that stressed consensus and the pursuit of common objectives, the tone of American Orthodoxy sounded discordant.
Not just in the Jewish community, but in America as a whole, the years
after World War II represented an "end of ideology."[95] Scholars like
David Riesman, Nathan Glazer, and Daniel Bell noted, with a degree of
alarm, that conformity dominated public life. Under pressure from advertising and the mass media, Americans in pursuit of middle-class suburban comfort hesitated to stand out as markedly different from their
neighbors.[96] In the throes of the cold war, intense ideology seemed suspect, and unyielding adherence to a parochial creed seemed out of step
with the ethos of the time. Calls for separatism jarred with the era of civil
rights, which created a public culture that increasingly celebrated the
common identity of all Americans. Despite, or perhaps because of, its
passion, Orthodoxy did not fit the suburban Jewish ideal that supported
Jewishness so long as it did not prevent Jews from participating in civic
life.[97]

The geography of the American suburbs also slowed the spread of Orthodoxy to these new Jewish population centers. American suburbs
functioned as automobile enclaves. Middle-class Americans opted for

the suburbs because of the privacy they afforded, the substantial distance between homes boasting green lawns, and the rigid separation between residential and nonresidential areas enforced by zoning. For a group of people who could not drive on the Sabbath, the suburbs seemed inhospitable. Where no sidewalks had been built, Orthodox Jews had trouble getting to and from synagogue on Saturdays and holidays, when they could not operate cars. Much of American Orthodoxy remained bound to the cities, rooted in the older neighborhoods where they could live in harmony with the law.

At the other end of the spectrum of religious observance, Reform Judaism also lagged behind the Conservative movement in tapping into the sensibilities of suburbanizing Jews. In an era when many American Jews were deciding for the first time formally to join synagogues, Reform had to liberate itself from the burdens of its past before it could become the dominant denomination. Most of the new Jewish suburbanites and potential synagogue members were the children and grandchildren of eastern European immigrants, products of Jewish neighborhoods. Although few had grown up in synagogue-going families, they considered Orthodoxy the standard of religious life. They regarded it as "really" Jewish. Even if they observed few of the traditional mitzvoth, the obligations, they thought of them as the true reflection of Judaism. The idea of a service at which men sat in the presence of a Torah scroll with uncovered heads and without prayer shawls seemed wrong. A Rosh Hashanah service at which paid musicians marked the new year by sounding a trumpet instead of a shofar, a ram's horn, did not seem to them an appropriate fulfillment of the yearly ritual. That no bar mitzvah marked a boy's thirteenth birthday and that not a word of Hebrew could be heard jarred with their idea of authenticity and of Jewish synagogue practice.

Through the Central Conference of American Rabbis and the Union of American Hebrew Congregations, the Reform movement decided that the tide would turn against it if it remained committed to the ideological constructs developed during the century since the movement's founding. Under the leadership of Rabbi Maurice Eisendrath of the Union of American Hebrew Congregations and Rabbi Nelson Glueck, president of Hebrew Union College, Reform began to incorporate elements of ritual practice once discarded as relics of antiquity, inappropriate to modern America. *B'nai mitzvah,* optional head coverings, as opposed to obligatory bare heads, the chanting of the kiddush to welcome the Sabbath, Hebrew prayers, and a range of other traditional elements of the Jewish service increasingly began to appear in Reform congregations.

Temples in the suburbs added more days and hours to their religious school calendars. The movement clearly felt the need to change its position that Judaism constituted a religious entity and not an ethnic one. As evidenced by the summer camps, youth groups, social clubs, and recreational activities supported by the movement, Reform in postwar America emphatically affirmed the widespread idea that Jewishness constituted a social and cultural way of life in which formal religious worship played just one part.

The reintroduction of the bar mitzvah, a process begun earlier in some Reform congregations, became nearly universal after World War II. Between the 1930s and the 1940s the Reform movement launched a number of studies of the advisability of making the bar and bat mitzvah normative. The rabbis received a resoundingly affirmative answer that congregants, actual and potential, wanted the ritual. One Reform rabbi in Brooklyn noted that allowing *b'nai mitzvah* "has rescued the Saturday service from disappearing altogether."[98] The movement recognized that to attract the young families that had once known the dense Jewish neighborhoods of the cities, Reform had to shed its image as the exclusive domain of the elite and the rich.

The growth of Reform congregations testified to the increasing appeal of the movement and its successful renegotiation of ideology. In 1940 UAHC claimed 265 affiliated congregations with 59,000 members. In 1955, during the suburban religious boom, it claimed 520 congregations with 255,000 members. By 1964 the number of temples had climbed to 660. Part of Reform's success can be attributed not only to the re-Judaization of its ritual and the increasingly social aspects of its congregational life but also to its solid commitment to social action. Throughout the 1950s and 1960s Reform led organized American Judaism in its demonstrative advocacy of the liberal causes of the day, including civil rights, church-state separation, and by 1964, opposition to the U.S. war in Vietnam. In 1961 the movement opened its Social Action Center in Washington, D.C., from which it lobbied for causes that they believed linked Jewish traditions to the best interests of all Americans. More than the other denominations Reform invoked the idea that Judaism's prophetic legacy demanded that Jews play a role in bringing about a better world.[99]

In a 1962 book sponsored by the UAHC's Commission on Social Action, *A Tale of Ten Cities,* Rabbis Eugene Lipman and Albert Vorspan sent a message about the ideal balance in America between the particular and the universal: "America is, and will be, a pluralistic society in which, ideally, different races, creeds, national, ethnic and cultural groups try to persuade their adherents to retain their characteristic values generation after generation, even while all Americans try to live together and work together, combining competition and cooperation in a creative and healthy way." Such a vision of America allowed Reform to urge Jews to take pride in what set them apart, but only in the context of what united them with other Americans. This message could have been sounded by the movement only after it had reinvented itself and had gone about the process of retrieving distinctive Jewish practices and idioms.[100]

The Conservative movement, which emerged in the 1950s as the largest and fastest growing denomination, had a different project. It became the most popular denomination, at least as measured by the number of affiliated congregations and members, because it found a way to strike a balance between tradition and innovation, between commitment to Jewish law and the realities of postwar Jewish life. Conservatism succeeded in convincing a plurality of American Jews that it stood midway between Reform and Orthodoxy, and as such carried none of the liabilities of the others. The Conservative movement, its rabbis, congregations, lay leaders, and seminary projected itself as the most American and most Jewish of the movements.

Conservatism experienced a period of unprecedented growth in the postwar suburban era. At the end of World War II it included about 350 congregations. Between 1955 and 1957 the United Synagogue welcomed 131 new congregations to its ranks, and another 138 between 1957 and 1961. Although some suburban Conservative congregations had functioned earlier as urban congregations, most could claim purely suburban origins, the creations of the young Jewish families that had flocked to the suburbs. Clearly suburban Jews found much in Conservatism that appealed to them. The variety of clubs, classes, and activities appealed to them and their children. In 1961 so many young people had applied to the movement's Ramah camps that over three thousand had to be rejected because of lack of space.[101] By 1951 its national youth movement, United Synagogue Youth, founded in 1948 by a handful of teenagers in Minneapolis, held a national convention that drew over five hundred delegates to New York. By 1965 it could call together twelve hundred youngsters to meet in Washington, D.C., to discuss the meaning of "the Ethical Society."

Unlike Reform, Conservatism had always been associated with the descendants of the eastern European immigrants and had always emphasized the group or national aspects of Jewish life. Because support of the Zionist cause had always been part of its mission, an enthusiastic embrace of Israel fit its image. It had always valued the symbols of Judaism as key to shaping identity. Yet, at the same time, Conservative Judaism represented traditionalism in the suburbs without any of the burdens of Orthodox observance. Unlike in Orthodox services, in Conservative synagogues men and women sat together, rabbis gave English sermons on current events, and congregations paid a great deal of attention to decorum and aesthetics. The "Americanness" of Conservative rabbis could not be clearer. As of 1957 the Jewish Theological Seminary noted that more of its rabbinical students had graduated from Harvard than from Yeshiva University.[102] In essence, the suburban Conservative synagogue could compete with Reform on its own terms and could trump Orthodoxy in allowing its congregants to participate fully in suburban life.

Because Conservative movement changes in liturgy tended to be cosmetic, they did not offend those who retained a fondness for or a commitment to familiar symbols, tropes, tunes, and styles. Modifications in the liturgy that appeared in the *Sabbath and Daily Prayer Book,* issued in 1948 under the editorship of Hartford's Rabbi Morris Silverman, would have been noticeable only to those who actually knew Hebrew well and could detect the minor alterations. The Shema, the traditional morning prayer in which Jewish men thanked God for not having "made me a non-Jew" ("goy") appeared now as praise for "having made me in his image." Since most American Jews knew little Hebrew and did not have a deep knowledge of the original sources, the changes, if even recognized, meant little to them. Likewise, the English texts accompanying the Hebrew prayers stressed the compatibility of the Judaic outlook with American liberalism. The Silverman prayer book discussed the concept of the "chosen people" directly, indicating that this fundamental principle did not constitute a belief in racial superiority. Rather, it indicated that the gift of the mitzvoth —the commandments—had been granted by God to Jews alone. Chosenness, Silverman wrote in defense of the concept, should not be thought of as "petty and insular," nor should it be construed as a matter of "group vanity." Rather, it compelled Jews to facilitate "the progress of humanity." One prayer, the "Aleinu," which in Hebrew extols God for not having made Jews "like the nations of the land who has not situated us like the families of the earth," in Silverman's postwar ideology of liberalism, became "He hath not made us like the pagans of the world, nor placed us like the heathen tribes of the earth."[103]

The most significant changes made by Conservative Judaism in the postwar era reflected a tight connection between the movement and suburban life. In 1950 the Committee on Jewish Law and Standards of the Rabbinical Assembly ruled that Jews may drive to synagogue on the Sabbath. The ruling recognized the reality of suburban life. Rather than excoriate congregants for their behavior, it sanctioned an already common practice and garbed it in the language of halakah. The other powerful change made by the Conservative movement in the 1950s reflected another defining characteristic of the "golden age" of suburban Judaism. In 1954 the movement declared that women could be called to the Torah to recite the blessings over the sacred scrolls, a privilege previously enjoyed only by men. By amending a practice that had been in place for millennia, the Conservative movement, despite its commitment to halakah, realized that it had to respond to a revolution in American Jewish life, in which women played the most significant role.

Women's Role in the Congregations

Women emerged as the most powerful and sustaining force in the suburban synagogues, Reform or Conservative. They dominated congregational activities, and their efforts made almost all religious functions possible. Like other middle-class suburbanites, Jewish women tended to drop out of the labor market when they had young children. Their husbands earned comfortable incomes that allowed families to live well on a single paycheck. Few families operated small businesses, like their parents had, requiring wives to work behind the counter. Highly educated, many suburban Jewish women had worked as teachers, social workers, and librarians before the birth of their children, and many would return to these professions when their children started school. But while they chose not to be employed outside the home, women made much of suburban synagogue life possible. These women did volunteer work and ran the libraries and gift shops. They directed the education committees and many, as unpaid teachers, taught the children. They oversaw the social events that drew in new members, and they staffed the committees that sustained congregational life.

Women flocked in particular to the adult education programs, perhaps in an attempt to make up for the paucity of Jewish learning they had experienced as girls. Rabbi Albert Gordon, a Boston-area Conservative rabbi and trained anthropologist—and appropriately the author of the 1957 book *Jews in Suburbia*—lauded the commitment of women to acquiring a Jewish education: "Something quite remarkable is happening to the Jewish woman in the suburbs and, through her, to her husband. Never in all the years of my rabbinical career have I seen such concern for factual knowledge about Judaism and the Jews. . . . Whatever it is that impels them, I must pay my tribute to them. It is they, even more than their husbands, who are re-establishing today's Jews as 'the people of the Book.' " Gordon noted that other rabbis he spoke to told the same story. "In practically every suburban community," he noted, they "speak enthusiastically of the women's encouraging response to the call for Jewish education."[104]

Outside the synagogues, suburban Jewish women created a vast range of Jewish voluntary associations. They labored for the federations, the local Jewish fund-raising bodies that collected money for international, national, and local Jewish needs. National Council of Jewish Women, Hadassah, Organization for Rehabilitation through Training (ORT), the Brandeis Women's Clubs, and Pioneer Women represented some of the more popular Jewish women's organizations sustaining Jewish community life, along with the activities associated with the synagogues. While these organizations allowed a warm and informal social network for women, they also functioned as significant political bodies in the suburban communities, nationally and around the world. Jewish women in Hadassah and in the National Council chapters in Montgomery County, Maryland, for example, listened to speakers from the Committee for a Sane Nuclear Policy (SANE), advocating for nuclear disarmament, and to those from the local fair housing group at that time pressing for antidiscrimination legislation in the newly opened up suburban counties. In the 1950s American women's ORTs supported, through its fund-raising efforts, a network of vocational schools for Jewish youngsters in western Europe, North Africa, and Israel, as well as in Iran and India. These same women participated in civic organizations, particularly those bringing them into contact with like-minded middle-class suburban women. The League of Women Voters, the Red Cross, the local Parent-Teacher Association, and the board of the public library all attracted the attention of Jewish women whose years away from paid employment allowed them to help shape community life.

In the American suburbs of the postwar era Jewish women did not articulate a feminist agenda—that lay in the future. In those decades, in fact, they made few demands for greater equality in Jewish practice, either in the Conservative or the Reform movement. Rather, they seemed content, in public, at least, to acquire knowledge, sustain synagogues, and build communities—Jewish and general—as they took care of their families. At times they expressed a belief that Jewish women possessed a different history than men. In 1954, the year American Jews marked the three-hundredth anniversary of the Jewish presence in North America, for example, the National Federation of Temple Sisterhoods of the Reform movement prepared and distributed a filmstrip entitled *Through the Years: Jewish Women in American History.* On the surface, at least, they shared with their husbands in a communal consensus that allowed them to exercise indirect influence and participate in community work without garnering public recognition, behavior that did little to challenge the status quo. Few Conservative congregations actually took advantage of the ruling of the Rabbinical Assembly, and few women demanded the rights now granted to them.[105]

Beneath the surface, however, young women began to question that Jewish communal consensus. After all, they had received the same Jewish education as their brothers had. They had led junior congregations and at summer camp had served as "rabbis." Sally Priesand, for example, asked as a teenager in the 1960s if she might some day in fact become a member of the clergy.[106] Others like her started posing similar questions about the ways Jews worshiped, organized communities, and presented themselves to the larger society. The kinds of questions that the young increasingly asked about the nature of Jewish life in America became more challenging in the latter part of the 1960s, inspired both by the civil rights movement and the counterculture. As the decade drew to a close many American Jews interrogated the sincerity and content of American Jewish life, perceiving tarnish rather than gold in the condition of post–World War II American Jewry.

To some of those challengers of the late 1960s, the decades after World War II appeared in retrospect to have been shallow, compromising, and overly concerned with materialism and respectability. They could in fact draw on the words written in the 1950s and 1960s by some American Jews, theologians, novelists, essays, and journalists who also believed that suburban Jewish culture had little of substance to offer. Writers like Philip Roth, Saul Bellow, and Bernard Malamud entertained American readers with the foibles of the Jews who sought to make themselves into Americans on the suburban frontier and who in the process lost most of what had been distinctive and meaningful in their culture. Roth in particular, with his 1959 *Goodbye, Columbus,* which included such short stories as "The Conversion of the Jews," "Eli, the Fanatic," and "Defender of the Faith," satirized with a sharp and devastating eye what he believed to be a spiritual vacuum in the lives of suburban Jews.[107]

Even a relatively uncontroversial medium like television started to broadcast widely the anxieties of American Jews and with humor to expose their willingness to give in to the demands of superficial materialism. One of the most popular television shows of the era, *The Goldbergs,* devoted an episode to the anguish felt by Molly's teenage daughter about her overly Jewish face. In "Rosie's Nose," aired in 1955, Rosie hated her nose and yearned for "a plastic job" to change her appearance so she could measure up to contemporary standards of beauty. While in the end Molly used psychology to talk Rosie out of the operation, this episode fit into an internal Jewish discussion of the era, one that decried the cultural trends of the period and the ease with which Jews seemed to be willing to sacrifice depth and substance for conformity.[108]

Historian Herbert Strauss made the same point, but in more academic terms, when he commented: "Most observers agree that American Jewry's organisational and philanthropic excellence is not paralleled by its cultural achievements. The American Jewish middle class, like much of the rest of its peers in other religions, has not used its affluence and its ethical and political culture to create an aesthetically or intellectually satisfactory style of life, away from mass media, sports, small talk, or status-seeking consumerism."[109] By the late 1960s, an era that took its tone from the cultural and political militancy of the civil rights movement, many Jews found the behavior of the defense organizations in the postwar era to have been obsequious at best and at worst dishonest. By the late 1960s the communal cooperation that generally had prevailed during the postwar golden age lost much its luster. Indeed, just as the latter part of the 1960s announced the fraying of America's postwar age, to be replaced by social discord, cultural experimentation, and heightened group tension, so too American Jewry seemed to be "coming apart."

For the Jews of the United States, in fact, the late 1960s stood out as a watershed after which almost everything seemed less coherent. This period marked the challenge to all that the postwar era had stood for.

8

IN SEARCH OF CONTINUITY

1967–2000

The last three decades of the twentieth century constituted an era of bold contrasts in the lives of American Jews. In the thirty years ushered in by the Six-Day War in Israel and shaped by the upheavals in American culture that rocked the late 1960s, many Jews committed themselves more intensely to the Jewish component of their lives than they had in the past, while others maintained fewer involvements with things Jewish than ever before. This age of contradictions in the way American Jews lived—as Jews—and how they thought about their Jewishness caused many to worry about the future of the group in America.

About certain matters most American Jews agreed in principle and converged in behavior. The vast majority enjoyed a comfortable upper-middle-class economic status and benefited from more years of education than the population as a whole. By and large American Jews exhibited a low birth rate and as such were older than the general population. Nearly all understood that, as individuals, Jews actively participated in the production of American culture, and few—if any—points of access lay beyond their reach. In American intellectual, economic, political, and artistic endeavors, the names of American Jews surfaced as influential leaders in their field. The prominence of Jews in nearly every sector of American life became increasingly less notable and noted.

Yet American Jews were profoundly divided among themselves over the Jewish aspect of their lives. They could not agree over what constituted "Jewishness" and the degree to which being Jewish actually mattered. For some Jewishness intensely defined them and their daily lives, and they talked about Jewish life boldly in public, parading their identity in front of other Americans in unprecedented ways. Yet for an increasing number of others, Jewishness became a matter of minor significance, a mere fact of parentage, perhaps a curiosity, but devoid of personal meaning and making no difference in how they led their lives. Many did not involve themselves in the ongoing struggles over the nature of Jewish life, nor did they search for ways to express their identity. They did not participate in efforts to create new Jewish cultural forms or feel a responsibility to sustain community life. For many "being Jewish" ceased to determine with whom they socialized, whom they married, where they resided, or how they spent their leisure time.

THE PROBLEM OF INTERMARRIAGE

From the middle of the 1960s, American Jewish communal leaders noted escalating levels of intermarriage with alarm. Indeed, in 1964 a general-market magazine, *Look,* launched the public phase of the communal discussion, which had, in fact, begun earlier. The article in *Look,* entitled "The Vanishing American Jew," predicted that the Jews' integration would carry with it the seeds of their disintegration as a people, as had Jewish communal leaders like Rabbi Robert Gordis, who noted in 1966 that exogamy should be thought of as "part of the price that modern Jews must pay for freedom and equality." Yet they fretted over the fact that "our children may desire to marry persons of another faith."[1] Historically the Jewish family functioned as the locus for imparting identity and socializing children into the tropes of Jewishness, be they formal religion or a more amorphous, but still powerful, sense that being Jewish mattered. Whether absorbed in classrooms and organizations or through the tempo and atmosphere of family and neighborhood, Jewish families historically conveyed personal identity. Communal leaders and the committed rank and file worried that as more and more Jewish children were being raised in homes with a non-Jewish parent, with one set of non-Jewish grandparents, and a host of Gentile cousins, aunts and uncles, the glue binding together Jewish life would lose its hold.

A plethora of studies, both local and national, tried to fix exactly how many of "our children" might be intermarrying. The *American Jewish Yearbook* published its first article on the subject in 1963. After the mid-1960s it reported almost annually on studies, trends, and communal reactions. A National Jewish Population Survey conducted in 1971 opened the floodgate of research, analysis, and communal commentary on the subject. Initially published in the 1973 edition of the annual, the data in the report seemed grim indeed to many. Sociologists and demographers who conducted the research and interpreted the data noted that at that moment the percentage of Jews who had intermarried stood at 9.2 percent, a number that most considered disturbing but not threatening. But they also noted that the younger the respondents, the larger the percentage. Thus 17.4 percent of those who had married between 1956 and 1960 had wed non-Jewish partners, while of those Jews who had married between 1960 and 1965, 31.7 percent had chosen a non-Jewish spouse, amounting to an increase of 500 percent in a decade and for many serving as an ill omen of future trends.[2]

During the next two decades scholars from various disciplines, working with these and other data, sought to determine the factors that led to intermarriage. Among other issues, they looked at regional variations, marriage ages, community size, and geographic mobility to account for the phenomenon. Analysis of the subject continued unabated in the decades to come. Some sociologists emphasized Jewish continuity, in that many Jews who married non-Jews continued to consider themselves Jewish and made efforts to integrate their children into Jewish life. The optimists in the debate asserted that ultimate outcomes could not be predicted. With the right set of programs, they maintained, the children of the intermarried as well as the unaffiliated and uninvolved could be drawn into the Jewish orbit. The future of American Jews might not be so depressing after all.[3]

Others drew less sanguine conclusions from the data. They pointed to the lack of Judaic knowledge among the majority of American Jews and to the number of American Jews who made life decisions without regard to Jewish matters. Those who maintained no Jewish connections and felt no sense of responsibility to the Jewish community would in the end, they stated, contribute neither time nor money to keep the community alive. Sociologist Charles Liebman put the matter bluntly: "If the Jewish community is to survive, it must become more explicit and conscious about the incompatibility of integration and survival."[4] This succinct and pessimistic statement seemed correct in its negative assessment of both the present and future. In 1990 a second National Jewish Population Study by the Council of Jewish Federations was conducted. Some estimates from that survey put the rate of intermarriage at about 40 percent, while some communities, like that in Denver, registered even higher proportions.[5]

A debate over how accurately the statistics had been collected and tabulated raged. Scholars and community activists once again disagreed about how to read them. Their debates took place not just in Jewish publications but also in the pages of the *New York Times* and other general-market publications. Journalist J. J. Goldberg, for example, opined in a *Times* article that leaders of the Jewish community were going out of their way to overstate the problem, to point to the highest number, and to assume that intermarriage meant Jewish disappearance. Others, like Elliott Abrams in his book *Faith or Fear: How Jews Can Survive in a Christian America,* wrote with equal passion that the escalating numbers spelled the imminent doom of American Jews, and that only the embrace of traditional religious observance would forestall the inevitable. Not coincidentally the Goldberg-Abrams debate pivoted on a political dispute. Goldberg interpreted much of the lament over intermarriage as a sea change in the liberal political outlook of the American Jewish communal elite, while Abrams believed that only by aligning itself with political conservatives and their desire to breach the wall between church and state could Judaism indeed survive.[6]

Regardless of their opinions, all involved recognized the reality that large numbers of Jewish women and men no longer felt that they had to choose marriage partners from within the fold. They also agreed that spiraling rates of intermarriage threatened the Jewish future, though they disagreed over the severity of the problem. The phenomenon of intermarriage was discussed in historical terms. The image that surfaced most frequently was of the Holocaust. The Jewish people sustained the loss of 6 million people, a fact that was horrendous in and of itself. Of them, 2 million had been children, the girls and boys who should have grown up, married, and borne the next generation of Jews. Hitler had wiped them out and in the process destroyed the Jewish people's ability to regenerate naturally. By intermarrying, the sermons, speeches, pamphlets, conferences, and symposia noted, American Jews were compounding a tragedy whose demographic implications still reverberated.[7]

Denominations Respond

The various denominations of American Jewry debated within and among themselves over how best to respond to the issue, but the most dramatic change took place in Reform congregations. While the Reform movement made efforts to intensify Jewish education within its congregations and focused on deepening its commitment to traditional Jewish practice and ritual, it realized that the high rate of intermarriage pointed to a persisting problem that in particular needed to be addressed. Indeed, young people raised in Reform congregations showed the highest rate of intermarriage.

Reform rabbis and laypeople advocated outreach to the intermarried, devising programs that would make conversion to Judaism a positive option for the non-Jewish partner. Reform rabbis differed among themselves about the appropriateness of rabbis officiating at weddings between Jews and non-Jews. Some members of the Central Conference of American Rabbis (CCAR) considered it acceptable to participate in such ceremonies, while others refused to do so. Of those who approved of officiating at such weddings, some believed that the presence of a co-officiating Christian minister should not be thought of as an insurmountable obstacle to participating. Others disagreed, shunning the idea of blending religious symbols and motifs. Not only did these debates take place at the meetings of the Reform rabbinical body, but individual rabbis, congregation by congregation, had to decide what to do when congregants requested their involvement in the upcoming nuptials of their children.

Regardless of the stance individual rabbis took, they realized that the issue of intermarriage required drastic action. In 1983 the CCAR took a bold step. It decided, after intense debate, that it would accept as a Jew anyone who had a Jewish parent, either mother or father, and who had received a Jewish education. In taking this step, the Reform rabbis were deviating from a fundamental Jewish practice, in place since the early part of the Common Era, mandating that Jewishness descended from the mother alone. During the next two decades, after 1983, Reform congregations, recognizing the intractability of the issue, started allowing non-Jewish spouses to become synagogue members and to participate in congregational affairs. Their underlying rationale represented a profound confrontation with reality. Welcoming and building bridges rather than rejecting and constructing walls would, the Reform movement hoped, help to define intermarriage as a means to enrich Jewish life, rather than a trend perpetuating the damage of the Holocaust.

The Reform decision to accept patrilineal descent and to welcome rather than exclude the intermarried highlighted the divisions among contemporary American Jews. The Reconstructionists, a small but growing branch, stood with the Reform.[8] Ostracizing intermarried couples, they believed, drove Jews away and alienated them from Jewish life. After all, the "problem" involved matters of the heart. Many in the liberal movements feared that employing rhetoric comparing Jewish women and men who had met, fallen in love, and wanted to marry a non-Jew to the horrors of the Holocaust did no good, and indeed furthered the dissolution of American Jewish life. Finding ways to engage intermarried couples became the liberal project.

Conservative Judaism occupied a middle ground between the culture of welcome that evolved in Reform and Reconstructionism and Orthodoxy's clearly drawn prohibition. Committed as it remained to Jewish law, the Conservative movement could not go as far as the other liberal denominations in renegotiating Jewish status. Rabbis and committed laypeople in Conservative congregations worried that welcoming the intermarried could be misinterpreted as condoning the practice. The Rabbinical Assembly remained committed to the proposition that none from its ranks could solemnize an intermarriage or co-officiate with a priest or minister. The non-Jewish partner in an interfaith marriage could not belong to a Conservative congregation, let alone hold office and participate in decision making. Yet many Conservative Jews keenly understood that intermarriage did not grow out of rebellion against Judaism. Many Conservative congregations and rabbis have dedicated themselves to *kiruv*—drawing near—to intermarried families, without sanctioning intermarriage as a legitimate option. Like their more liberal coreligionists, they understood that because of the openness of American society Jews will invariably fall in love with non-Jews and that the interests of the Jewish people would be best served by extending a hand of welcome to such families rather than by promoting either unconditional acceptance or outright rejection.

ORTHODOXY: A WORLD APART

No contrast of the late twentieth century loomed larger than that dividing liberal Judaism, in all its manifestations, from the world of the Orthodox. For the Orthodox, who constituted about 7 to 9 percent of the American Jewish population by the end of the twentieth century, details of observance became increasingly more significant and unswerving. They built their lives not only on all-Jewish institutions but on all-Orthodox ones. As they saw it, intermarriage had become a burden carried by those Jews who had chosen to live outside the intricate system of strict halakic observance.[9]

Post-1960s Orthodoxy represented a new phenomenon in American and Jewish history in a number of telling ways. Never before in the United States had the Orthodox been as comfortable using public spaces to further their religious agenda. That they could assemble twenty thousand men in September 1997 in Madison Square Garden to celebrate the end of a seven-and-a-half-year project of daily Talmud study could not have been imagined in earlier decades. That by the end of the twentieth century restaurants bearing the words "glatt kosher"—a hyperstandard of observance not known before the 1970s—served Indian, Chinese, and haute cuisine reflected the simultaneous pursuit of meticulous standards and of worldly pleasure among the Orthodox. Some sociologists also noted that in the last three decades of the twentieth century, the children of Orthodox parents had become more punctilious in their traditional behavior than their fathers and mothers. The son, more often than the father, kept his head covered at all times, including at the workplace, while the fringes of his ritual undergarment—the *tzitzit*—hung out for all to see. The married daughter of an Orthodox woman, more often than her mother, refrained from showing her hair in public and stood out from other American women for her hat or wig, her long sleeves and skirt. The growth of a population of *ba'alei teshuva,* the newly observant, added to the prominence and vigor in the Orthodox world.[10]

Among American Orthodox Jews, the most observant set the standard, and others felt called on to react. The ultra-Orthodox—a term specific to the 1960s—challenged from the right those observant Jews who hoped to partake of middle-class American culture. The practices of late-twentieth-century Orthodoxy acquired their basic shape from the commonly articulated assertion that American culture had little to offer those who defined themselves as "Torah true." Although they used the apparatus of American politics to advance their communal objectives and relied on modern technology to spread their message, they focused on sustaining and even intensifying their separateness from Americans in general and from other Jews in particular. They believed with great certainty that the future of American Jewry lay with them, and they took on the project of constructing thicker and more impervious fences around themselves and their communities to shut out the corrosive influences of America.[11]

Orthodox Jews were divided over how thick those walls should be. Its left wing, the modern Orthodox, associated with Yeshiva University, believed it possible, albeit requiring great vigilance, to combine Western culture, secular learning, some increase in the public roles of women, and a measured degree of cooperation with the liberal denominations with a deep commitment to normative practice and Torah study. In the post-1960s age of confrontation, Orthodox Jews aligned with Yeshiva University, as well as the modern Orthodox in general, often found themselves accused from the right of being too lax and too involved in secular matters. In the late 1960s through the 1970s, the modern faction at times took stands that offended the right wing. In the 1970s, for example, Yeshiva University closed its High School for Girls in Brooklyn because it believed that the school had been captured by extremists who disdained modernity and secular learning.

But as the right wing, sometimes referred to as the Yeshiva World (not to be confused with Yeshiva University), grew bolder, larger, and more strident, modern Orthodoxy felt compelled to respond to its challenge by confirming its own traditionalism and strengthening its own reticence to change.[12] In 1996, for example, Yeshiva University banned gay student clubs. Though such clubs previously had not existed, some students were now demanding them. Administrators might have been willing to allow students to create these kinds of activities, regardless of the administrators' sensibilities. But voices in the ultra-Orthodox world, condemning even the possibility that an Orthodox Jewish institution would condone such a club, pushed university officials to refuse to sanction the organizations. These officials could not remain impervious to accusations from the right that the modern Orthodox were deviating from the true principles of the Torah and therefore differed little from the liberal denominations no longer practicing "real" Judaism.[13]

American Hasidim

The more traditional flank of Orthodoxy splintered into an intricate assortment of groups, factions, and institutions. The Hasidim divided into a number of sects—Bobover, Lubavitch, Satmar, Skver, and Ger—with names derived from their European hometowns. They clearly marked themselves by their clothing, their highly segregated communal patterns, their Yiddish speaking, and their avoidance of contact with the vast majority of American Jews. The ultra-Orthodox lived primarily in their own communities, maintaining their own synagogues, schools, stores, and even in some cases transportation systems. In communities like Boro Park, Crown Heights, and Williamsburg in Brooklyn, and Monsey and New Square in New York's Rockland County, Hasidic sects dwelled by themselves and because of their residential concentration became quite forceful in local politics. Since their leader, their rebbe, could deliver all the votes of the community, American politicians, including congressional representatives, city council members, mayors, even governors and senators, met with them and tried to meet their demands.

One of the events that boldly highlighted the vast internal divisions within the Jewish people pivoted around the life and death of Rabbi Menachem Mendel Schneerson, the seventh Lubavitcher rebbe. Schneerson, the scion of a long Hasidic dynasty, arrived in the United States in 1942 and immediately set about creating institutions to promote his particular brand of Judaism. By the 1970s, he and his energized followers began planting Chabad houses reaching out to the non–Torah true Jews all over America and indeed the world. By 1990 over three hundred existed in cities and on college campuses around the country. The next decade saw greater expansion to every imaginable kind of place where Jews lived. Lubavitcher Hasidim approached Jews on the streets of American cities, in vacation spots, and in remote outposts where no other Jewish institutions existed. In one city after another, including the nation's capital, across the street from the White House, the Lubavitch put up mammoth Hanukkah candelabra, Jewish religious markers in public squares. Lubavitcher "mitzvah-mobiles" made their way through traffic, replete with giant pictures of Rebbe Schneerson. This missionary quest involved engaging secular Jews, those who felt little, or no, commitment to Judaism, and giving them a taste of living by the mitzvoth, the complex of normative obligations of Judaism.

Chabad also created a vast enterprise of communication for those already part of its community. It published books and magazines. It transmitted the Rebbe's talks and lessons over cable television, radio, and the Internet. It sought to intensify the links between the Rebbe, his organization, and the believers. Both the public manifestations of Lubavitcher activity—the posters, signs, vans, and black-clad men stopping people on the street and asking if they were Jewish—revealed much about the fluid quality of post-1960s America. Such activities derived much of their character from the cultural relativism and freedom of American society that had little problem with women and men assertively manifesting their differences in public places. Yet ironically, the Lubavitcher message, like that of much of ultra-Orthodox Judaism, also emphasized the corrosive effects of that freedom.

When Schneerson died in 1994, some of his followers proclaimed him the messiah, the anointed one, in whose wake would follow the prophesied "end of days." Lubavitch billboards appeared all over America. Bumper stickers exalting Schneerson and proclaiming his eternal life sprouted up on cars. The Rebbe's death in fact intensified the activities of the Lubavitch missionaries. They now approached Jews on the street and begged them to return to the "real" Judaism to hasten the resurrection of the Rebbe.[14] The messianic fervor of the Lubavitch Hasidim con-

tributed to the disarray of American Orthodoxy. Many deeply observant
Orthodox Jews considered the veneration of the Rebbe and talk of his
messianic status a form of idolatry alien to Judaism.[15]

In addition, the zeal of other elements in the Orthodox world, not just
Hasidim, to avoid contact with liberal Jews exacerbated the general disarray of American Judaism. In 1996, for example, the executive vice president of Young Israel refused to participate in New York's community-
wide Warsaw Ghetto Memorial program being held at the Reform
Temple Emanu-El. He claimed that participating in a ceremony being held
in a Reform temple would desecrate the memory of the ghetto fighters,
"mostly Orthodox people." Although he had his history completely
wrong, he effectively brought a note of discord into a communal event
that involved the common fate of the Jewish people. That same year
Young Israel refused to participate in a memorial service for slain Israeli
Prime Minister Yitzhak Rabin. Such actions reflected the hardening of
lines separating the Orthodox and about 90 percent of American Jewry
and exacerbating the internal tensions within the observant world itself.[16]

REDEFINING JEWISHNESS

Of that overwhelming majority of American Jews, an untold number
maintained little sustained involvement with Judaism or Jewish life. Jewishness had ceased having much influence on how they led their lives.
They chose their mates and their places of residence independent of Jewish considerations. Their rapid movement to neighborhoods, towns, and
regions with no or few Jews showed how little living in a Jewish community meant to many.[17] Unlike the suburban-bound young families of
the previous era, they did not necessarily think about the presence, or
lack thereof, of other Jews as they chose where to live. Personal choice
dominated. Although they did not go so far as to convert to Christianity, Judaism and Jewish culture ceased to define how they lived and how
they understood themselves.

Yet below the surface a more complicated and nuanced picture than
simply a wholesale simple abandonment of Jewish commitment could be
seen. Surveys found, for example, that a majority of American Jews did
attend Passover seders every year. A majority lit Hanukkah candles. In
fact, even among those who intermarried, most wanted some Jewish element present at their wedding ceremonies, a *huppah* (a bridal canopy),
a rabbi, the breaking of a glass, a *kippah* (head covering) on the groom's
head. Intermarried couples often chose to have their infant sons circum-

cised. They may not have worried if a ritually trained *mohel* performed the ceremony. A Jewish physician made the event just as meaningful. From the parents' perspective the act itself mattered and not the specific halakic requirements. For many, then, the symbols resonated at the same time that they took on a new significance.

In the same years that communal leaders worried about spiraling intermarriage rates some American Jews invested deep meaning in the quality of their Jewish lives, even if they defined themselves as far removed from the world of the "Torah true." They, like the Orthodox, worried a great deal about the future of Jewish life in America. They wrote and read a stream of popular books examining the state of American Judaism.[18] Whether these writing were gloomy or upbeat, celebratory or alarmist, the sheer volume of commentary on the future of Jewish life in America demonstrated how much American Jews cared about the future of Judaism and Jewish culture in America. Rather than erecting fences to sustain Jewish life, their strategies involved building bridges.

As late-twentieth-century Jews, they wanted to incorporate into their lives the cultural forms of the society around them. If, for example, modern America increasingly determined that "biology was not destiny" and that men and women ought to play equal roles in the professions and the academy, in families and communities, then Judaism too, many believed, must embrace that same egalitarianism. In matters of liturgy, they chose from a wide array of options—American folk music, Eastern meditation chants, Hasidic melodies, Israeli popular songs, poetry from a variety of sources—to express Jewish ideas. Jewish women and men sought ways to manifest Jewish culture as it made sense to them, although many of their journeys took them outside organized communities, the established congregations, the historic denominations, or even normative practice. They experimented with a kind of niche Judaism, forms of expression that fit their particular sensibilities. In the last three decades of the twentieth century, American Jews have felt empowered to cobble together a bricolage of practices, old and new, that reflected the postmodernist multiculturalism of their era.[19]

Individual American Jews cared so deeply about their Jewishness that they demonstratively challenged existing institutions. Young people in the late 1960s, creators of a Jewish counterculture, confronted the Jewish "establishment," which had spent decades cultivating its image of respectability. In the age of Second-Wave feminism, Jewish women, rather than opting out of Jewishness because of its male-dominated structure, demanded the right to be included as equals in Judaic ritual practice and in its leadership ranks. Rather than demurring to the weight of history, women in the Conservative movement in particular called on Judaism to change and accommodate to a new reality. The feminist challenge, and subsequent demands of homosexuals, for an equal place in the Jewish community represented exactly how much Judaism meant to them. In an American culture where Jews could be anything—or nothing—their demands for rights reflected the depth of their Jewish commitment.[20]

In the late 1960s organizations and institutions that had once concerned themselves with the defense of the Jews became advocates for strengthening Jewish culture and religion. The American Jewish Committee provides an interesting case. In its first phase, in the early twentieth century, the Committee sought to protect the Jews at home and abroad from attacks from the outside. The Committee operated as a small group made up of highly successful elite men who relied on their personal contacts to represent the Jews in political matters. By the 1940s the AJC began to devote some of its attention to intergroup relations and emerged as a major player in the civil rights movement. Seeking to broaden the base of its leadership and to move away from being just a small committee, it organized local chapters and brought more individuals into its activities. Those activities still pivoted around the defense of the Jews largely through combating anti-Semitism and general antidiscrimination work.

But in the late 1960s it started to weigh in on internal issues particular to the Jews and entered into debates about the content of American Jewish life. It created task forces and launched various projects dealing with Jewish culture and education and the Jewish family, projects reflecting its anxiety about Jewish continuity. American Jewish Committee meetings, like those of federations, community centers, and other avowedly "secular" bodies, now opened with brief *divrei torah,* short discourses on Jewish learning. In the 1970s the American Jewish Committee, like other agencies, began to serve only kosher food at banquets and lunches, partly to attract a broader spectrum of participants and to emphasize distinctive Jewish practice. The Sabbath emerged as sacred time for these agencies, which previously did not care about it, except in as much as they fought in courts against the blue laws. This infusion of Jewish culture into the meetings of such organizations as the AJC represented a blurring of the long-established American Jewish separation of church and state and amounted to a conversion from taking a purely defensive stance against outside enemies into a positive embrace of Judaism.[21]

The Composition Changes: Conversion and Immigration

Other changes in the composition of the American Jewish world manifested themselves in this era. Ironically, in the last third of the twentieth century, as more Jews drifted away both from organized Jewish life and from the practice of Judaism than ever before, more non-Jews than ever were choosing to become Jewish, mostly, although not exclusively, as a result of marriage to Jewish partners. In 1954 about three thousand non-Jews converted. At the end of the 1970s the annual rate stood at ten thousand. By the 1980s about one hundred and fifty thousand non-Jews had chosen Judaism. Conversion not only lowered the number of intermarriages, but converts in congregations around the country started to take active roles in synagogue life. They added not just bodies but also enthusiasm for Jewish ritual, something they had just learned about. When Rachel Cowan, a product of a Congregational home, converted to Judaism, she inspired her husband, Paul, to spend time studying the religion he had known little about in his childhood and that had engaged none of his time or energy as a young adult. In the process they both became actively involved in New York's Ansche Chesed congregation and religiously observant in their home. As a newcomer to Judaism, Cowan found the tradition so meaningful that she enrolled in Hebrew Union College and received rabbinic ordination.[22]

At the beginning of this era in American Jewish history, no one could have predicted either the rise of the Lubavitcher movement or the numbers of converts to Judaism. Likewise no one foresaw that immigration would once again add both numbers and diversity to the ranks of American Jews. The single largest group came from the Soviet Union and its successor states. In 1967 a mere seventy-two Soviet Jews made their way to the United States. By 1973 the number jumped to 1,449, and in 1979 to nearly 30,000. In 1989, 36,738 Soviet Jews emigrated, while in the decade after the fall of the Soviet Union the numbers grew larger. The Jews from the Soviet Union, and those from the former Soviet states who migrated in the 1990s, added a new element to American Jewish life. They came from a place where Judaism had ceased to be a living force. Those Soviet citizens who defined themselves as Jews did so very differently from how American Jews, products of a fluid, voluntaristic, and democratic society, did. When Soviet immigration to the United States began, a complex meeting took place between the newcomers and American Jews, many of whose grandparents and great-grandparents had come from Russia. American Jews, particularly through the federations and the other social-service agencies, took on the project of "judaizing" the immigrants, who did not necessarily want to go through this process, and certainly not on the terms presented to them by American Jews. The immigrants sought access to housing, jobs, and education. They believed that they alone ought to shape and develop the communities in which they lived in, like Brooklyn's Brighton Beach "Little Odessa."[23]

Regardless of the differences between the expectations each had of the other, the arrival of Jews from eastern Europe to the United States coincided with the late-twentieth-century upsurge in general immigration. Made possible by the 1965 passage of the Hart-Cellar bill, massive immigration once again reshaped the social and cultural profile of the United States. Once again it complicated the definition of "American," and as it had in the earlier century of migration, it shook up the status quo. And, just as the previous era of migration had included Jews, so too the newest epoch in America's immigration history played itself out within the Jewish community as well. Not just Jews from the Soviet (and post-Soviet) state but also about thirty-five thousand Iranian Jews who fled to the United States after the Islamic revolution of 1979 and streams from South Africa and Israel helped to offset the low Jewish birth rate and added new cultural ingredients to the mix of American Jewish life.[24]

After the 1970s Jewish enclaves from Syria and Morocco also took root in the United States. The arrival of these immigrants, along with those from eastern Europe, fostered a degree of Jewish diversity as had never before existed. A hub of Syrian Jewish life, for example, primarily involving immigrants from Aleppo, developed in Brooklyn's Ocean Parkway and Kings Highway. Here Syrian Jewish stores, synagogues, day schools, and social clubs came into being. Likewise, in Los Angeles, Brooklyn, and Deal, New Jersey, Moroccan Jews settled near each other, carved out particular niches in the economy, and fashioned communal institutions.[25] Jews born in the United States and descended from immigrant ancestors viewed the arrival and settlement of these new Jews both with a sense of communal responsibility toward their coreligionists and with a fascination with the exotic. They evinced both a desire to acquaint themselves with the newcomers and their cultures and a strong sense that they controlled the community institutions and as such knew best how to structure Jewish life in America.

Jewish Education Shifts

Yet nowhere did the contradictory and unprecedented tendencies of late-twentieth-century American Jewish life manifest themselves more sharply than in the area of education. On the one hand, the percentage of Jewish children who received any Jewish education spiraled downward. Large numbers of parents who defined themselves as Jewish felt no obligation to provide their children with some exposure to Jewish learning. No more than half attended any kind of Jewish educational program, and of those who did, most dropped out at the magic age of thirteen, when they celebrated their bar or bat mitzvah. On the other hand, the amount of money spent on Jewish education spiraled upward. Between 1966 and 1974 federation spending on Jewish education went from $7 million to $20 million, as communal agencies fretted over the future and pinned their hopes for continuity on Jewish schools. But despite the millions spent on formal Jewish education, most involved lamented what they saw as the sad state of the field. They bemoaned the scant number of hours devoted to Jewish education, what they perceived of as the watering down of the curriculum, the fading away of Hebrew-language instruction, and the overemphasis on the affective element of the learning, which stressed identity and loyalty, as opposed to the actual study of key texts.

This shift in Jewish education reflected much about the contradictory trends at work in American Jewish life. While fewer and fewer Jewish children received a Jewish education and while supplementary—weekend or after-school—Jewish schools reduced both their hours and the rigor with which subjects were taught, more Jewish children than ever in American history received their education in an all-day setting, in Jewish schools offering both Judaic and general subjects. While Orthodox institutions sponsored most of the day schools, not necessarily all of the children enrolled came from Orthodox homes. In addition the non-Orthodox also began to focus on creating day schools in order to provide their children with an intensive Jewish education in the company of other Jewish children. By the 1990s nearly 40 percent of Jewish children enrolled in a Jewish educational program attended a Jewish day school. The day school population has tripled since the 1960s, and day schools have cropped up far from the major centers of Jewish life. Since the 1960s communities like St. Louis, Richmond, St. Petersburg, Pittsfield, and Syracuse opened day schools, as Jewish parents who had attended public schools began to send their own children to Jewish schools.

In the middle of the 1960s the Conservative movement began to create Solomon Schechter day schools, and the Reform movement, deeply committed as it long had been to integration and participation in American society, launched its day school movement in the following decade. In some communities nondenominational schools added another dimension to the Jewish educational landscape. These schools articulated an ethos celebrating Jewish pluralism and offering its pupils a variety of options for expressing Jewish identity, but within the context of rigorous Jewish learning. They tried to appeal to all Jews, although they had few or no Orthodox children in their classes.[26]

A Rise to Prominence

The last three decades of the twentieth century involved yet another dichotomous reality for American Jews. Never had Jews in America, or possibly in any place, been so secure, successful, and integrated as they found themselves in the years since 1967. Their soaring rates of intermarriage demonstrated their normalization, as did their diffusion into the American economy and their rise to prominence in many fields that had been previously off-limits to Jews. They found no positions closed to them, no options restricted, no neighborhood or school beyond their reach. In short, their Jewishness did not disable them. Colleges and universities that less than a half-century earlier had imposed quotas on Jews now had Jewish presidents. Jewish faculty members taught in nearly every discipline at all kinds of institutions, particularly the most elite. Many universities offered Judaic studies courses, and schools that once had disdained the presence of Jews among their students now offered kosher dining facilities and offered courses in such diverse subjects as Talmud, Yiddish, and Jewish history. At the beginning of this era defense organizations still felt compelled to track discrimination in the boardrooms of major corporations and in most Wall Street law firms. By the end of the era, Jews served as CEOs of many of the nation's largest and wealthiest corporations. The more prestigious the law firm, the more Jewish attorneys it had on its staff.[27]

Perhaps American politics provides the most dramatic illustration of the fading of anti-Semitism by the end of the twentieth century. In the first year of the new century, an observant Jew, Connecticut's Senator Joseph Lieberman, stood in front of the Democratic National Convention, accepted his party's nomination for the vice presidency, and publicly attested to the powerful and positive impact that being a Jew had made on his career in public service and on his vision of America. That he did not become vice president had nothing to do with American antipathy to Jews but rather to the malfunctioning of the Florida electoral system and the decision of five of the nine justices on the Supreme Court. Judging by the fact that Al Gore and Lieberman essentially had won the popular vote, the American electorate seemingly had no problem that the person second in line to the president, the one who stood "one heartbeat away" from the Oval office, would be a Sabbath-observing Jew who rather than hide his Jewishness made a point of referring to it. Lieberman's popularity and the decision of the Democratic Party that a religious Jew would help, rather than harm, the national ticket made 2000 a notable year in the Jewish encounter with America.

AMERICAN JEWS' RELATIONSHIP TO ISRAEL

These vast achievements and the Jews' almost universal upper-middle-class affluence notwithstanding, the rumblings of anti-Semites, from both the right and the left, filled the airwaves, clogged the information superhighway, and resounded from speakers' platforms to live, cheering audiences. That American Jews in the late twentieth century elevated the Holocaust to near iconic status reflected the discrepancy between the reality of total acceptance and the reality that even in America Jews had enemies who used centuries-old images and stinging words of hatred to accuse them of controlling and corrupting American society, or some segment of it.

The symbolism of the Holocaust to American Jews, enshrined so powerfully in the U.S. Holocaust Memorial Museum, which in 1993 opened its doors on American sacred space, the Mall in Washington, D.C., functioned as a kind of memento mori, a reminder that Jewish affluence and political prestige once before had been crushed by a demagogue who started off on the lunatic fringe. It mattered not that late-twentieth-century America bore little resemblance to Weimar Germany and that few analogies could be drawn between the two historic situations. Furthermore, in their minds the fact that Jews lived so securely in America contrasted sharply with the constant political stress of their "other land," Israel. Though the overwhelming majority of even deeply committed American Jews had no intention of moving to Israel, they had woven into their communal tapestry the images and motifs of Israel and Israeli culture. American Jews believed that in some way their fate and that of the Jewish state had been bound together by the Holocaust.

Israel faced wars in both 1967 and 1973. It launched an incursion into Lebanon in 1982, ostensibly to protect its citizens living on the northern border. It endured terrorist hostilities within its borders, particularly although not limited to the Palestinian *Intifadas* of 1988 and of 2000. In 1991 it endured months of bombardment from Iraqi missiles during the U.S. Gulf War. Israel suffered intense international isolation, and in 1975

American Jews reacted in horror to the news that the United Nations, a body they had supported passionately, declared, "Zionism is Racism." To complicate matters vastly, Israel itself was experiencing a deep internal struggle between the ultra-Orthodox minority and the more secular majority. The 1995 assassination of Prime Minister Yitzhak Rabin by an ultra-nationalist Orthodox Jew convulsed American Jews.

The Six-Day War Brings Jews Together

Each crisis as well as each promise of peace played itself out in American Jewish life. The struggles in Israel mirrored themselves in the political activities of American Jews with an intensity not seen before. American Jews identified with Israel, even when deeply critical of Israeli policies. Indeed, the events in the Middle East in the spring of 1967 and the Six-Day War of that year lent this era much of its distinctive character.

Throughout May of that year rumblings from the Arab capitals put Israel's supporters in America, which included most American Jews to one degree or another, on edge. Tension had indeed been high for several months on the Syrian border, with incessant shells hitting Israeli towns and kibbutzim. On May 14 the crisis spread as large numbers of Egyptian troops massed on the Sinai peninsula, followed two days later by a Cairo Radio broadcast, which declared, "The existence of Israel has continued too long. We welcome the Israeli aggression, we welcome the battle that we have long awaited. The great hour has come. The battle has come in which we shall destroy Israel."

To do so Egypt closed off the Straits of Tiran to ships sailing in and out of Israel. The United Nations withdrew its force, which had patrolled the international waters. Both France and Great Britain declared that they no longer stood by a 1957 agreement guaranteeing free passage through the crucial waterway. On May 30 King Hussein of Jordan, Israel's neighbor to the east, pledged to put his troops under the command of the Egyptian army, as forces from Iraq, Saudi Arabia, Algeria, Kuwait, and Egypt gathered in Jordan on the Israeli border. On June 3 Radio Cairo declared to its listeners in the Arab world that "the Holy War through which you will restore the rights of the Arabs which have been stolen from you in Palestine and reconquer the plundered soil of Palestine" had begun. Two days after that, beginning on June 5, the Israeli air force attacked the airfields of Jordan, Syria, Iraq, and Egypt. A war fought in the air, on land, and at sea had begun in earnest. It took only six days for Israel, considered by world Jewry to be weak, numerically inferior, and standing alone, to bring the war to a dramatic and lopsided victory. It conquered vast territories and defeated mighty armies, and its soldiers reunited Jerusalem, enshrined in Jewish canonical texts as the sacred center of the Jews' history.

While all of this took place thousands of miles from the United States, the war, its prelude and aftermath, shook American Jews deeply. Wherever they congregated they talked about the crisis, speculating on what it would mean if the Arab armies actually did what they had promised and destroyed the Jewish state and annihilated the Jews living there. To many American Jews the days leading up to the war, dominated by the rhetoric of bravado emanating from Cairo and Amman and heard in the chambers of the United Nations—which met around the clock and whose sessions were broadcast live on American television—a new Holocaust seemed to be in the works. In early May, before the war had officially begun, they experienced an "eerie awareness of once again being put to the ultimate test."[28]

American Jews, even those who previously had expressed only a passing interest in Israel, rallied to the support of the beleaguered state. The United Jewish Appeal, the premier fund-raising arm of American Jewry, raised $100 million in one month to send to Israel. At a lunch in New York, within fifteen minutes five people pledged, on the spot, a total of $5.5 million. College students held mass meetings on their campuses. Despite their overwhelming antagonism to the U.S. war in Vietnam, they identified with Israel and its need to wage what the students saw as a very different and just war. Thousands signed up to go to Israel to aid in the war effort. Teenagers collected money on street corners. Government officials found themselves inundated with delegations, letters, and telegrams urging American support. Much of the American Jewish outpouring happened spontaneously, and even individuals with no connection to Jewish organizations and institutions interpreted the frightening crisis and the jubilant victory as a drama in which they too played a role.[29]

The Yom Kippur War in 1973 provoked a similar American Jewish reaction. Once again Israel stood threatened. In this case the trauma dragged on longer, and the beginning proved more shocking, but the ending brought about the same euphoria and pride. American Jews again shared in the sense of doom. They reacted as they could, sending money—this time $107 million in the first week of the war alone and $675 million all together—rallied, petitioned those in power, and about thirty thousand volunteered to go to Israel and participate directly.[30]

This intense support for Israel helped shaped the contours of American Jewish life in the decades following 1967. The roller-coaster of seemingly imminent destruction followed by the joy of victory and salvation left its mark on American Jews and their cultural practices. Much of the tenor of American Jewry changed with the 1967 war and the emergence of a popular image of Jews as heroic and triumphant fighters. It gave American Jews a political cause to pursue with fervor. Concerns for Israel's safety could bring Jews together beyond denominational boundaries, as few other issues could. The victory in the Middle East seemed to have unleashed among American Jewry a new kind of assertiveness about themselves and their connection to the little country that stood up to its powerful neighbors. One Hillel rabbi observed that the Six-Day War had created "a new breed of Jewish students" energized by Israel's example.[31]

The image of a victorious Israel facing a seemingly unending chain of crises helped enable American Jews to talk openly about Jewish identity, concerns, and interests. They hid less often behind the veil of universalistic rhetoric, although their commitment to general causes did not diminish. Rather, they felt emboldened to highlight the Jewish element of their agenda, even as they advocated for and with others. In 1944 the umbrella organization of most Jewish communal agencies, the National Community Relations Advisory Committee (NCRAC), had formed in the darkest period of Jewish history. Its purpose became to articulate, in the face of the European catastrophe, a single American Jewish policy on the crucial issues of the day. It also took stands on all policy matters and in the 1950s and 1960s aligned itself with the civil rights effort. Notably, the organization carefully left out the crucial word "Jewish" in its name. In 1971, in a very different world, while it continued to define a Jewish position on such concerns as the environment, energy policy, abortion, and the like, the National Community Relations Advisory Committee changed its name to the National Jewish Community Relations Advisory Committee (NJCRAC), stating publicly what it had always been.

Institutions and organizations that previously had paid scant attention to Israel now turned to it as a source of inspiration. Hebrew schools, Jewish community centers, and Jewish social service agencies decorated their walls with posters of Israel's landscape and of its people. Except for the oldest and most traditional among them, most American Jews switched to using and teaching Israeli-style or Sephardic Hebrew, as opposed to the Ashkenazic Hebrew that had long been the language of American Jewish ritual. Hebrew first names rose in popularity. After 1967 observant Jewish men, who in the past did not appear in public with their heads covered, assertively donned *kippot,* no longer feeling the need to follow the Emancipation-era edict advising that one "be a man in the streets and a Jew at home." The era ushered in by the 1967 war allowed them to be Jews wherever they chose.[32]

Jewish institutions found ways to work Israel into their formal programming. Summer camps, for example, which were outside the traditional orbit of Zionist organizations, began to hire Israeli counselors to help American youngsters feel a connection to Israel. Synagogues, federations, and Jewish clubs of various kinds organized trips to Israel, often referred to as "missions," for every possible constituency: families, couples, teenagers, singles, non-Jewish public officials, college students, even the Christian clergy. In 1999 Jewish philanthropists Charles Bronfman and Michael Steinhardt organized "Operation Birthright." Every young American Jew, they declared, had a basic need to learn about Israel and therefore a basic right to receive a free trip to the only place where they could see Judaism thrive as an integral part of everyday life. Bronfman and Steinhardt and the organizers of many other programs asserted that through Israel, American Jews would feel their connection to the Jewish people as a whole.

Owing to the technological revolutions of the last part of the twentieth century, and the relatively low cost of airfare, Jewish students at every stage of their education—high school, college, and graduate school—could choose from a wide array of programs in Israel. They could go for a summer or a year. They could travel to Israel to work, to study, or just to tour. If they went to study, they could pursue religious learning at yeshivot, matriculate at one of the Israeli universities, or enroll in special programs in science, art, or ecology. Whether sponsored by Jewish community centers, Zionist organizations, more general Jewish organizations, or religious denominations, organized youth pilgrimages to Israel became a relatively common American Jewish experience. Young people came to view Israel as a close-by place that shaped their identities. American Jewish families staged their children's *b'nai mitzvah* at the hilltop fortress of Masada on the edge of the Judean wilderness, a reminder of the Jews' rebellion against the Romans in 73 C.E., and at the Western Wall in Jerusalem, the supporting wall of the Mount on which the Temple had once stood. The Wall had been taken by Israel from Jordan in the Six-Day War and by virtue of that victory represented both the newest and the oldest link in the Jews' historic connection to Jerusalem.

The 1967 war brought about a profound change in the lives of some. More American Jews felt called upon to make aliyah (literally, "to go up"), to move to Israel, in the immediate aftermath of the war than at any other time. The years from 1967 to 1970 represented a watershed of American aliyah. In the first years after the Six-Day War American immigrants to Israel tended to be secular Zionists, the products of the youth movements, women and men deeply influenced by the student activism of the 1960s. By the end of the 1970s the majority came from the ranks of the Orthodox, and many of them headed for settlements in the occupied territories of the West Bank.[33]

Support of Israel Complicates the Political Agenda

The "Israel-centeredness" of American Jewish culture and politics came with a price tag, however. It brought Israel close to the top of the communal agenda. In all political maneuvers over domestic matters, the leaders of the community calculated the impact of Israel on various positions. Since 1967, and particularly after 1973, Israel became highly dependent on U.S. military aid, and any threats to cut the size of the benefit package, any rumors that Israel might receive less, came to be defined as a threat to Israel's survival. The American Israel Public Affairs Committee (AIPAC) had grown out of an earlier body, the American Zionist Council, a World War II–era organization. In 1954 the AIPAC registered as a lobbying agency and coordinated most pro-Israel activity with the U.S. Congress. Considered by many one of the most powerful lobby groups in Washington, the AIPAC pursued a nonpartisan strategy that sought to win friends for Israel and advocated for support among the American Jewish public. AIPAC effectively developed ties to members of Congress, who in tandem with Jewish organizations ensured that Israel's cause got a thorough hearing.

But this support of Israel grew complicated in the ensuing years, particularly after the 1973 war. Beginning in the 1980s, the rise of a politically engaged Christian evangelical bloc put American Jews in a quandary. Politically the two groups shared precious little. American Jews arrayed themselves on the liberal side of nearly all issues of the day. They actively supported abortion rights, welfare rights, immigration policies, the separation of church and state, and equal rights for women—all anathema to the Christian right. Many Christian fundamentalists, whose voices increasingly could be heard in the U.S. House of Representatives and the Senate after the early 1980s, espoused an essentially evangelical worldview. They believed it their mission to bring the truth of the Gospel to the Jews, something that Jews obviously did not favor.

The two groups did, however, find common ground in the fact that the Christian right embraced Israel. Partly they viewed Israel as a bulwark against Communism, since until the fall of the Soviet Union Egypt received much support from the Communist regime. More important, they believed that the Jews' restoration to their land and to Jerusalem would trigger the Second Coming of Christ. Israeli government officials, particularly in the Likud administrations of Menachem Begin, Yitzhak Shamir, Benjamin Netanyahu, and Ariel Sharon, addressed gatherings of American fundamentalists, encouraged their political efforts on Israel's behalf, and welcomed them as tourists to Israel.[34] Many American Jews found the alliance uncomfortable. It did not serve their interests at home, yet Israel increasingly depended on it.

The issue of Israel complicated the pursuit of political goals by American Jews. At international feminist gatherings in Mexico City in 1975 and in Copenhagen in 1980, Jewish women like Representative Bella Abzug and journalist Letty Cottin Pogebrin found the strident anti-Israel rhetoric dominating the meeting deeply disturbing and profoundly alienating. As Jewish women they felt an obligation to defend Israel, to disprove statements about Israel as an imperialist state and about Zionism as a form of racism. To them, as to most active American Jews, Zionism represented a movement for liberation and Israel, the place that had gathered Jewish refugees from many lands, a haven for those who had no home. As they saw it, criticism of Israel made it impossible for them to focus on the project at hand: improving women's status around the world.

The power of Israel to shape American Jewish consciousness led to the stifling of dissent within American Jewry. For a community that historically had been open to debate and to differing approaches to common problems, the taboo on criticizing specific Israeli policies compromised communal democracy and shattered even the semblance of unity. In the early 1970s a number of highly committed Jews, many of whom had spent years in Israel and even longer working for Jewish institutions, believed that the time had come for a public discussion about Israel, in particular on the relationship between Israel, the one million Palestinians then under Israeli rule, and the growing number of Jewish settlements in land conquered from Jordan, on the river's West Bank. In 1973 they formed an organization called Breira, meaning "alternative" or "choice." By the spring of 1977 over twelve thousand people had joined, including a number of rabbis, and the group organized forums to discuss their concerns and to educate the Jewish community. The *breira* that they envi-

sioned involved dialogue and compromise with the Palestinians rather
than violence and occupation.

The organized Jewish community reacted swiftly and harshly. The
mainline Jewish organizations castigated Breira. The Jewish Community
Council of Washington, D.C., refused to give the group a seat in its Delegate Assembly, thereby asserting that the dissenting organization had
no Jewish legitimacy. Rabbi Arthur Lelyveld, who a decade earlier had
been the victim of a brutal attack by a racist mob in Mississippi, decried
Breira as a group that gave "aid and comfort . . . to those who would cut
aid to Israel and leave it defenseless before murderers and terrorists."
Arthur Hertzberg, the president of the American Jewish Congress, would
not speak at a conference because a Breira member also had been invited.[35] The Jewish press demonized the members of Breira as self-haters
and enemies of Israel, lumping it together with the American Council for
Judaism, which had been formed in 1942 to oppose the creation of a
Jewish state. Breira members with long and warm ties to Israel found
themselves blacklisted in the American Jewish world, with speaking invitations canceled and longtime colleagues refusing to sit down with
them.[36]

The veterans of Breira, along with new recruits to the cause of progressive Jewish politics, reconvened in 1980 as the New Jewish Agenda.
While Agenda adopted a much broader platform than Breira, it also
hoped to stem what it saw as the movement of many American Jewish
organizations away from liberalism and social justice issues. But at the
heart of New Jewish Agenda lay the hope for a new kind of Israel, one
that would find a way to recognize Palestinian rights. Notably, by the
time Agenda captured the attention of American Jews, movements like
Peace Now had coalesced in Israel, and members of the Knesset were articulating positions strikingly similar to those of the American organization. But like Breira before it, New Jewish Agenda as well as the American Friends of Peace Now inspired loathing in much of organized
American Jewry. As it had with Breira, the Jewish press abounded with
articles condemning Agenda. Jewish community councils in various
cities refused to allow Agenda to be represented as a legitimate organization under the community umbrella.

Over time, as the peace movement in Israel grew, the American Jewish community opened itself up to these kinds of discussions. As Israel
began to participate formally in meetings with Palestinian officials, it became possible for rabbis, community activists, and employees of Jewish
organizations to discuss the needs of the Palestinians and the problems

posed by West Bank settlements. Yet American Jewish communities and organizations remained splintered over the issue of Israel, and for some a commitment to a particular stance toward Israel became a communal litmus test of trustworthiness.

The bitter division of American Jewry over Israel manifested itself in at least two significant ways. First, a core of American Jews remained steadfast in their belief that Israel ought never to compromise, particularly territorially, with the Palestine Liberation Organization (later the Palestinian Authority). The Jewish press resounded with bitter arguments over Israel, with editorials and letters to the editor bristling with recrimination and harsh language. Individuals and organizations alike threatened the viability of broad-based communal events by bickering over what should or should not be considered "anti-Israel" and over who hated Israel and who did not. In 1997, for example, the Anti-Defamation League invited *New York Times* columnist Thomas Friedman to give a speech at its annual dinner in Los Angeles. Morton Klein, president of the Zionist Organization of America, a body that saw the 1993 accords reached by then–prime minister Yitzhak Rabin in Oslo with the P.L.O. as harmful to Israel, launched a vigorous protest. He considered Friedman, who had written numerous columns in support of the Oslo Accords and about the need for Israel to recognize Palestinian claims, an enemy of Israel, someone who should not be honored at a Jewish event. Klein organized a mass protest against Friedman's appearance at the dinner. This in turn set in motion a barrage of hostile rhetoric between Klein and Abraham Foxman, the ADL's national director, who defended inviting the respected journalist. In the end Foxman won and Friedman spoke, but hard feelings lingered.[37] Similar stories repeated themselves regularly, at the local and national level, demonstrating how much Israel divided rather than united American Jews.

American Religious Tensions Intensify

Debates over the nature of Israeli society also exacerbated religious tensions among American Jews. Israel, unlike the United States, did not separate religion from civil society. Orthodox rabbis, and Orthodox rabbis alone, determined policies about personal status and life-cycle issues. The state recognized as valid only Orthodox marriages, burials, and conversions to Judaism. Only Orthodox religious institutions received direct state subsidy, and despite the numerical majority of nonreligious Jews in Israel, Orthodox rabbis alone functioned with state authority. Additionally, the Orthodox establishment in Israel did not recognize the validity of any other form of Jewish practice. The liberal branches did not count, plain and simple, as Judaism. The men and women who belonged might be Jews, but the religion they practiced fell outside the category of Judaism.

Since Orthodox Judaism was the only recognized branch, American Jews, the vast majority of whom did not identify as Orthodox, found themselves repeatedly and painfully at odds with Israeli policy. In most cases they had few reasons to interact with Orthodox Jews, particularly in religious matters at home, and American Orthodox opinions about Reform, Conservative, and Reconstructionist Judaism had few implications in their American communities. But when it came to Israel, the denominational divide proved to be powerful, divisive, and painful.

A war of words raged between the liberal branches in America and the Orthodox rabbinate in Israel. Particularly in the late 1990s, leaders of the Reform and Conservative movements, like Eric Yoffie of the Union of American Hebrew Congregations and Ismar Schorsch, chancellor of the Jewish Theological Seminary, demanded that their rabbis be allowed to perform weddings in Israel, that conversions to Judaism performed by their clergy be considered valid, and that their institutions be recognized as legitimate sites for the practice of Judaism. When American Jewish women and men traveling and studying in Israel organized egalitarian religious services at the Wailing Wall, they endured physical attacks and vicious verbal assaults by mobs of ultra-Orthodox men, who believed that the behavior of the Americans amounted to heresy. The war of words then became a war of brickbats.[38]

POST-1967 AMERICA

Israel had emerged in 1967 as a powerful symbol of Jewishness. It inspired much of the creativity and assertiveness of American Jews in their communities and in their interactions with other Americans. It symbolized for many, as the 1985 Conservative Prayer book, *Sim Shalom*, phrased it, *"raysheet tzimachat ge'ulatenu,"* "the first flowering of our redemption."[39] Federations raised money for Israel with the stirring slogan "We Are One." Yet the realities of politics, both international and internal to Israel, complicated such lofty rhetoric. The year 1967 symbolized not just the beginning of an era because of the euphoria of the victory, but because it unleashed a series of communal crises that at the beginning of the twenty-first century still rock American Jewry.

Renewed Holocaust Consciousness

Although the 1967 war left its mark on the lives of America's Jews, independent of the war, the late 1960s can be seen as a point of departure for American Jews in numerous other ways. In the late 1960s, and with increasing intensity in subsequent decades, the Holocaust emerged as a central element in American Jewish public life. Since the late 1940s, the calamity of World War II had been remembered, performed, and ritualized in a series of internal Jewish settings. But after 1967 Holocaust consciousness started to show itself in highly demonstrative ways, directed at non-Jewish audiences as often as Jewish ones. Post-1967 American Jewish public culture derived much from the telling and retelling of the details of the Holocaust. In the late 1960s survivors of the Holocaust who had settled in the United States began to organize as a way to share their memories with their children and with other American Jews. That they began to speak out at a time when Israel seemed so beleaguered cannot have been accidental.

The American Federation of Jewish Fighters, Camp Inmates, and Nazi Victims organized after the first conference of survivors was held in Israel in 1971. They devoted their attention first to having the twenty-seventh day of the Hebrew month of Nisan recognized by American Jewry as a day of remembrance, Yom HaShoah. The Federation distributed educational materials and sent lecturers to schools and community groups to bear witness to what its members had endured. On the state level the group played a key role in formulating Holocaust curricula for public schools. It lobbied with officials in a number of states, including New York, to make the Holocaust a mandatory subject in public schools.

By the middle of the 1970s hundreds of American communities conducted memorial observances for the Holocaust, at which survivors spoke, with public officials also offering some words. The press covered these events extensively. So widespread had local Holocaust memorialization become that in 1974 the NJCRAC issued guidelines to communities on how best to conduct such events. During the last quarter of the twentieth century, the pace of Holocaust-related activity quickened so much that the tragedy emerged as a major element in American Jewish consciousness and in the public enactments of Jewishness.

The NBC television series *Holocaust,* which aired in 1978, captured the attention of millions of viewers, while Stephen Spielberg's 1993 film

Schindler's List drew an even bigger audience, making it possible for the filmmaker to create the Shoah Foundation, which set out to interview as many survivors of the Holocaust as possible. Books, conferences, documentary films, and lectures about the Holocaust became standard fare throughout the country. Publishers produced a seemingly ceaseless flow of fiction and nonfiction, memoir and analysis of the Holocaust. Communities of all sizes—Boston and Charleston, South Carolina, as two examples—built Holocaust memorials, turning markers of the events of Europe of the 1930s and 1940s into permanent features of the American landscape. Holocaust resource centers sprouted around the country, and cities and counties set aside space to build local memorials.

In their history, literature, and religion departments, universities started offering courses on the Holocaust. "Holocaust Studies" became part of the curriculum in the academy. Artists, musicians, documentary filmmakers, dancers, and even cartoonists turned to the Holocaust to explore questions of good and evil and the complex ways human beings respond to trauma. References to the Holocaust abounded as American Jews searched for ways to think about the horrific event and its connection to their lives. A book on the state of the Jewish family in America, published in 1970, opened with a dedication "For the Six Million who exemplified the fine values in the Jewish family." In essence invocations of the Holocaust and the "six million" revealed more about late-twentieth-century American Jews than about the ordinary women and men who perished in Europe.[40]

Starting in the 1980s with the easing of entry into eastern Europe, American Jews organized visits to the former concentration camps and to sites associated with Jewish suffering, in Poland in particular. Thousands of American Jewish teenagers participated yearly in the March of the Living, a solemn procession from Auschwitz to Birkenau on Yom HaShoah. Once they reenacted the death march, the teenagers flew to Israel, where they arrived just in time to mark Yom Hazikaron—Israel's memorial day—followed immediately by the boisterous celebration of Yom Ha'Atzmaut, independence day. The symbolism of the march left little to the imagination.

In 1979 the federal government became an active partner in the Jews' desire to see the Holocaust remembered. President Jimmy Carter, in response to Jewish criticism of his Middle East policies, created a national Holocaust commission, later renamed the United States Holocaust Memorial Council. This group set in motion a process that resulted in the dedication of the Holocaust Museum in Washington, D.C., in 1993, an edifice that testified to American Jews' success in imposing their aspirations and anxieties on the American consciousness. In 1979 an Office of Special Investigations in the Department of Justice started tracking down former Nazis living in the United States.

The public displays of bravado by Nazi, or neo-Nazi, groups in the United States in the last quarter of the twentieth century played a role in the mushrooming of Holocaust imagery. Right-wing anti-Semitic groups with Nazi leanings had been part of the American scene since the 1930s. Through the war years and into the mid-1960s American Jewish organizations had advocated that the worst policy would be to engage the extremists since it gave them the press attention they so craved. Jewish organizations and communities refused to engage in debate with hate mongers, preferring to extend the silent treatment to them.

But in the post-1967 era, such reticence seemed outdated, and a Jewish public willingness to confront manifestations of Nazism took its place. In 1978 the National Socialist White Workers Party of America requested a permit to parade through the streets of Skokie, Illinois, a Chicago suburb of sixty-nine thousand of whom seven thousand had survived the Holocaust. The town refused the permit, so the Nazi group turned to the American Civil Liberties Union for assistance. The ACLU, which counted many Jews among its members and leaders, agreed to take the case, consistent with its seventy-year history of defending free speech, however repellant. In protest some Jews resigned from the ACLU, and Chicago-area Jewish organizations sponsored meetings to discuss the appropriate Jewish stance to take toward the Nazis. These events all served to generate national coverage of the Jews, the Nazis, and the survivors, and the Holocaust itself.[41]

Since the end of the 1970s an array of organizations and individuals have captured public attention by denying that the Holocaust ever happened. These "revisionists" used print media and the Internet to broadcast their position, claiming that Jewish assertions about the 6 million victims, the crematoria, and the gas chambers should be considered propaganda. An immeasurable portion of Jewish Holocaust discourse and activity grew out of a concern that the public would believe the lies of the deniers.[42]

Further, in 1991 a Holocaust survivor in New Orleans, Anne Skorecki Levy, decided that she had a particular responsibility to confront David Duke, a Nazi then running for governor of Louisiana. Levy, who until then had never spoken publicly about her experiences in Treblinka, considered Duke's popularity too great a threat to allow her to continue her silence. As a result she mounted a concerted campaign to record her memories of the horrors of the concentration camp and those of others to impress on the voters where Duke's views could lead.[43] The message delivered by all of these rituals and events was that Jews had in the very recent past stood on the brink of extermination. They had had no homeland to provide them with a place of refuge, and the rest of the world had turned its back on them.[44]

Most likely the explosion of Holocaust-related activities would have taken place without the momentous events in Israel having occurred. The passage of time, the aging of the survivors, the increased comfort of American Jews to talk about experiences that set them apart from other Americans, and the general culture of the 1970s, which valorized group difference and privileged suffering, functioned independently of the turbulence in the Middle East. Yet the 1967 war cannot be taken out of the equation in explaining the emergence of the Holocaust as an icon of American Jewish identity. American Jews, in the spring of 1967, had felt a kind of imaginary engagement with the events of the 1930s and 1940s. They seemed to have experienced viscerally a sense of looming disaster, and in that context, the years of the Nazi triumph over Europe's Jews served as their analogy and their emotional touchstone.

Jewish-Black Tensions

From the late 1960s onward the public life of American Jews also took much of its tone from a constant and highly charged discussion about tensions between Jews and blacks. A series of events beginning in the late 1960s seemed repeatedly to pit Jews and African Americans against each other, and newspapers, magazines, conferences, and books described in detail the many ways in which Jews and blacks saw the world differently, had little in common, and indeed, functioned as each other's antagonists. As did Holocaust consciousness, the much-publicized conflict between American Jews and blacks owed its origins to factors far more complicated than the 1967 war in Israel. But the war, the passion of American Jews for Israel, and the identification of black nationalists with the cause of the Palestinians intensified a seemingly inevitable social drama.

In the summer of 1967, while American Jews basked in the glory of the recent Israeli victory, a small conference of about two thousand people took place in Chicago's Palmer House Hotel. Antiwar and civil rights activists from different campuses and communities convened at the Conference for a New Politics, dedicated to creating a viable, radical, alternative to both the Republican and Democratic parties in the upcoming presidential election. That many Jews attended surprised no one, since Jewish students and activists had played an inordinately prominent role in the New Left turbulence of the 1960s and beyond.[45]

That the conference attacked Israel may also not have been surprising. In the late 1960s, nationalism emerged as a potent force among African Americans, college students, and young activists in general. They drew a good deal of their inspiration from the freedom struggles in Africa and rejected the idea of politics through compromise, respectability, and slow bridge building. Many African and other newly liberated third world countries considered Israel a European entity, imposed on the Palestinian people by imperialists, the British and the Americans, and now itself engaged in imperialism. Furthermore, just two years earlier in 1965, Stokely Carmichael of the Student Non-Violent Co-ordinating Committee, one of the key players in the militant civil rights effort, had told whites—Jews included or perhaps Jews in particular—to "get off the bandwagon," that they had no place in the civil rights struggle.

When the conference's Black Caucus spearheaded a resolution declaring that the Six-Day War had been an "imperialist Zionist war" and that Israel, a white nation, had expropriated land from dark-skinned Arabs, many Jews in attendance were dismayed. Jewish activists like Arthur Waskow and Martin Peretz, longtime participants in radical politics, experienced deep anguish over the need to choose between their long-standing commitment to a "new politics," which would achieve racial equity and social justice, and their Jewishness, which had become so deeply wrapped up with Israel, the reunification of Jerusalem, and the inspiration engendered by the recent war. The Jewish delegates left. While the event involved only a handful of American Jews and a small number of African Americans, it heralded the beginning of three decades of public anguish and debate over the relationship between African Americans and Jews.

These conflicts notwithstanding, there were also many glimmers of hope. During the next thirty years much continued as it had in the political arena. In Congress members of the Black Caucus and Jewish senators and representatives tended to vote almost exactly the same on nearly every issue. Black newspapers often condemned terrorist attacks against Israel, and many blacks and Jews, veterans of the civil rights movement, found ways to cooperate with each other. Jewish organizations sponsored dialogue groups, black-Jewish Passover seders, joint youth projects, and a range of other programs allowing women and men of the two communities to meet and share their differences and similarities. In the 1980s a Jewish woman in Washington, D.C., Karen Kalish, founded Operation Understanding, a project that brought Jewish and black teenagers together for a year-long program where they shared their thoughts and ideas about group identity with each other. Even when they differed among themselves, the high school students who went through Operation Understanding found that they shared much.

With regard to public policy, more remained the same than changed. While Jewish organizations opposed racial quotas in hiring and university admissions, they supported affirmative action and the vigorous enforcement of antidiscrimination legislation. They supported liberal immigration policy, even as the source of immigration after the 1970s shifted to the Caribbean, South America, Asia, and other parts of the decolonializing world, and they opposed cuts in government spending on welfare and education. In 1983 the American Jewish Congress took out a full-page advertisement in major American newspapers pointing out that the policies of the Reagan administration hurt the poor. The advertisement exhorted the readers, "America Must Not Quit on Social Justice." The Reform movement's Rabbi Alexander Schindler blasted the weakening of the country's social welfare commitment, commenting sarcastically, "[T]he war against poverty has become a war against the poor."[46] In 1997 the American Jewish Committee along with Howard University announced the inauguration of a new publication, *CommonQuest: The Magazine of Black-Jewish Relations,* as a forum for discussion and as evidence that the two groups could still be seen as entwined with each other, just as they had in the past.

In national and local elections, Jews voted more like African Americans than like any other identifiable group of white voters. Certainly the number of Jews who voted for Republican candidates grew from earlier years when they voted almost universally Democratic. In 1972 as black-Jewish tension brewed, as "the Jewish people found itself arrayed against enemies and difficulties, old and new," 35 percent voted for Richard Nixon, as opposed to the 17 percent who had supported him four years earlier. Polling data revealed that the highest level of Jewish support of the Republican party could be found in areas with the most racial tension. In that election, class mattered. The poorer Jews felt abandoned by the Democratic party and voted accordingly.[47]

Yet taking this era as a whole, American Jews, despite their widespread upper-middle-class status, voted as liberals, along with African Americans. Even Jewish conservatives, known collectively as the "neoconservatives" and including such prominent figures as Norman Podhoretz, Irving Kristol, Gertrude Himmelfarb, and Milton Himmelfarb, commented with frustration that the Jewish community persisted in behaving against its own interests. In 1967 Milton Himmelfarb wrote an article entitled "Are Jews Still Liberals?" To his chagrin, his answer to his own question was in the affirmative.[48] Himmelfarb's conclusion continued to prove true. In the 1998 congressional elections, 78 percent of the votes cast by Jews went to Democratic candidates.[49] Indeed, Jewish voting patterns and the positions enunciated by the whole spectrum of Jewish religious and defense organizations, Orthodox groups excepted, stood in stark contrast to the rightward drift of much of white America. Many Catholics, for example, the grandchildren and great-grandchildren of the immigrants who had come to America during the same century as had Jewish immigrants, could be counted on, by the end of the twentieth century, to vote Republican more often than Democratic.

Despite the solid commitment of American Jews to liberalism, the constant flaring of tension in the years after the 1967 conference did in fact create a great deal of dissonance between Jews and blacks. One episode after another highlighted clear areas of tension and dispute. In 1968, for example, New York City schoolteachers, mostly Jews, supported by their union, with its heavily Jewish leadership, went on strike in opposition to the actions of the independent school district in Brooklyn's Ocean Hills-Brownsville section, a largely black neighborhood. A number of teachers, all of them Jews, had received notice of transfer out of the schools. To the teachers, this amounted to a violation of their union contract. To the community leaders, it seemed a necessary measure, since they felt the teachers and their union showed no sensitivity to the African American children in their classes.

The strike went from being a routine labor action or even a debate over educational policy to a full-blown conflict between the two groups that played itself out in the media. Both sides, the teachers and the supporters of the experimental, community-controlled schools, resorted to inflammatory language to make their case. Probably the most shocking moment was when an African American radio commentator, Julius Lester, read the following poem, written by a student in one of the schools, over the airwaves of WBAI:

Hey, Jew boy, with that yarmulka on your head
You pale-faced Jew boy—I wish you were dead;
I can see you Jew boy—no you can't hide,
I got a scoop on you—yeh you gonna die.

I'm sick of seeing in everything I do
About the murder of six million Jews.
Hitler's reign lasted only fifteen years,
My suffering last over 400 years, Jew boy. . . .
I hated you, Jew boy, because your hang-up was the Torah,
And my only hang-up was my color.[50]

Incidents that brought public attention to the seeming irreconcilability of Jews and African Americans erupted with frequency and provided one of the leitmotifs of this era. In 1967 and 1968 riots in American cities, the product of anger and frustration of young, black men, while not directed at Jews, destroyed the last of the Jewish shops in the city centers. The last Jews, the remnant of what had been a few decades before thriving and institution-rich communities like Newark, New Jersey, and Detroit, Michigan, left in the wake of the conflagrations.

The episodes continued. In 1979 members of a black Islamic group, the Hanafis, invaded the B'nai B'rith headquarters in Washington, D.C., holding the staff hostage for days. In the 1974 *DeFunis v. Odegaard* case and the 1978 *Regents of the University of California v. Bakke,* argued before the U.S. Supreme Court, Jewish organizations filed amicus briefs against the use of explicit racial quotas in law and medical school admissions. Jews had long before crafted a political position maintaining that antidiscrimination legislation offered the best way to redress the inequities in society. They considered affirmative action "vitally essential."[51] But at the same time they believed that in the university admissions process and in hiring practices, individual merit should continue to be the chief criterion for making decisions. To Jewish defense organizations setting numerical quotas on the basis of race seemed essentially racist. For a group of people who in the past had been the victims of quotas instituted to keep them out and to restrict their numbers in universities, hospitals, law firms, and corporations, a social policy that legalized and validated group membership seemed anathema. The decision by the ADL, the American Jewish Congress, and the American Jewish Committee, among other organizations, to side with the white applicants who claimed to have been denied their rights because of race focused attention on the rift between Jews and blacks, groups that had long seen social policy issues through a single lens.[52]

Episodes in which Jews and African Americans aligned on opposite sides of a painful political divide went on through the 1970s, 1980s, and 1990s. A few suffice to demonstrate the heat of the rhetoric and the degree to which it seemed that an era of alliance between the two groups had come to an end. In 1979 sources revealed that Andrew Young, an African American veteran of the civil rights movement and at the time ambassador to the United Nations, met in secret with officials of the Palestine Liberation Organization. Jewish organizations protested, and while they did not call for his resignation, they criticized him publicly for seeming to grant legitimacy to the sworn enemy of the Jewish state, and as such, the Jewish people. President Carter removed Young from his post, which in turn unleashed angry protests in the African American press, which blamed the Jews for Young's dismissal. At that point Young had held the highest rank ever held by an African American in the foreign service and the foreign policy community. Then in 1984 civil rights leader Jesse Jackson ran for the presidential nomination for the Democratic party. Earlier in the decade he had profoundly irritated American Jews by publicly linking arms with Yasser Arafat and singing, amid the flashing of cameras, "We Shall Overcome," a song many Jews had learned as participants in the civil rights movement. When in 1984 Jackson referred to Jews, off the record, as "Hymies" and to New York City as "Hymietown," Jewish newspapers and community leaders strongly objected, linking the offensive language to Jackson's earlier embrace of the PLO leader.

Into the fray entered a relatively little-known figure, Louis Farrakhan, a leader of the Nation of Islam, who threatened the Jews for hampering Jackson's candidacy. Indeed, from that point on most Jewish rage and fear focused on Farrakhan. The spellbinding speaker who called Jews "bloodsuckers" and described Judaism as a "gutter religion" drew enormous crowds. In 1987 he brought out six thousand cheering admirers in Detroit, seven thousand in Atlanta, fifteen thousand in Los Angeles, and a massive twenty-five thousand at New York's Madison Square Garden.[53] On college campuses black students thronged in the thousands to hear him speak. While Jews had no way of knowing why Farrakhan commanded such audiences, they could not disassociate the venom of his anti-Jewish rhetoric from the rest of his words and from the wildly enthusiastic crowds that greeted him.

At times words escalated into violence. In the summer of 1991 a young black child, Daren Cato, was accidentally hit and killed in Brooklyn's Crown Heights neighborhood by a car driven by a member of the Lubavitch Hasidic community. The Lubavitch rescue squad, Hatzalloh, tried to enter the area to bring medical attention to the child, but the massing crowd on the street had gotten too large and angry to allow it in. The crowd soon became a mob, and the long-simmering tension brewing between the two very different groups living in Crown Heights exploded into a riot. Roving bands of African American youngsters attacked Hasidism in the streets and in their homes. A mob beat to death a visiting yeshiva student from Australia, Yankel Rosenbaum. To the Jews of Crown Heights, many of who were the children of Holocaust survivors, and to those who watched film clips of the spectacle on television and read about it in the newspaper, a seemingly full-scale pogrom had broken out in an American city.[54]

It may have not been coincidental that this "pogrom" erupted in Brooklyn. One of New York's outer boroughs, not only had it attracted a large number of Hasidim, but it also housed some of America's poorest Jews. Elderly Jews left in the neighborhood had missed the Jewish exodus to suburbia and had not experienced the Jewish ride into the upper middle class. Altogether in New York about one hundred thousand Jews, mostly older people, the last of the immigrant generation, lived in poverty in high-crime neighborhoods, and as they saw it had been abandoned by the Jewish agencies.[55]

The Birth of the Jewish Defense League

From the fertile soil of black-Jewish tension, heightened awareness of the thousands of poor Jews left behind, and the 1960s culture, which generated social militancy, sprang Rabbi Meir Kahane and his Jewish Defense League. Kahane, an Orthodox rabbi, founded the JDL early in 1968. Dedicated to using force, if necessary, to protect Jews and Jewish interests, the JDL started out with thirty members in Brooklyn. By 1972 it had grown to ten thousand in New York and to about fifteen thousand nationally, with supporters forming branches in a number of other cities.[56] The Jewish Defense League first came to public attention in October 1968 when it thwarted an act of vandalism at Brooklyn's Montefiore cemetery. JDL members organized themselves into "citizen patrols," walking the tough streets of a number of Brooklyn neighborhoods, claiming that the police provided no protection for poor elderly Jews, often the victims of street crimes. It used language previously unheard in American Jewish political discourse. In September 1970 one JDL official told a reporter for the *Christian Science Monitor,* "We do whatever is necessary to protect the life and property of little Jews. Whatever is necessary may mean a speech on a troubled college campus, or a court injunction. It also may mean a raw show of force—including the use of arms."[57]

The rhetoric and actions of the JDL struck fear in the heart of the organized Jewish community. In these same years Jewish leaders spoke out against this kind of rhetoric when used by New Left student militants. It also opposed such behavior on the part of black nationalists. The fact that Jews adopted such a stance hardly pleased community leaders. The Jewish establishment made no distinction between militants bent on acting outside the boundaries of civil society, whether they were Jews or non-Jews. The behavior of the JDL put others in the community in an awkward position. In May 1968, for example, James Forman, leader of a group called Black Manifesto, began a national campaign demanding that reparations be paid to the descendants of America's slaves, people whose labor, freedom, and lives had been forcibly taken from them. He threatened to interrupt synagogue services in a number of cities and specified that he would be at New York's elegant and prestigious Temple Emanu-El on Fifth Avenue on Yom Kippur. Kahane, neither a fan of Reform Judaism nor an admirer of the temple, vowed that the JDL would meet Forman on the steps of the synagogue armed with lead pipes. A JDL advertisement appeared in the *New York Times* admonishing Forman, "the extremist, that the Jew is not quite the patsy some think he is." This strident and blaring notice went on to criticize other Jews, "people and organizations [that are] too nice. Maybe in time of crisis Jewish boys should not be that nice. Maybe—just maybe—nice people build their own road to Auschwitz." The Reform movement, whose house of worship stood at the center of the controversy, had no intention of giving Forman a forum or of accepting Kahane's promise of protection. Rabbi Maurice Eisendrath of the Union of American Hebrew Congregations responded:

> Jews carrying baseball bats and chains, standing in phalanxes, like goon squads, in front of synagogues, led by rabbis, are no less offensive, and, in essence, no different from whites carrying robes and hoods, led by self-styled ministers of the Gospel, standing in front of burning crosses. . . . This so-called "Jewish" Defense League violates every ethic and tradition of Judaism and every concept of civil liberties and democratic process in American life.

Likewise, in November 1970 the NCRAC issued a statement, that the Council and its constituent members stand "opposed to vigilantism, whatever its auspices and firmly rejects the paramilitary operations of the Jewish Defense League as destructive of public order and contributory to divisiveness and terror."[58]

Jewish organizational leaders sought to distance themselves as much as possible from the extremist organization. Yet the JDL did have an impact. In 1972 the National Jewish Community Security Committee came together in New York, founded by such communal luminaries as Abraham Joshua Heschel, Wolfe Kelman of the Rabbinical Assembly, Seymour Siegel of the Jewish Theological Seminary, and novelist Elie Wiesel. The group hoped to overcome the "crisis in confidence" experienced by some American Jews with regard to the classic community organizations. Jews, particularly the poor and the elderly in the central cities, had "legitimate fears," which to that point had been in fact ignored.[59] Jewish social-service agencies took a second look at the decaying neighborhoods of America's cities and discovered the plight of poor Jews. Agencies began to redirect some of their energy and resources to the care of Jews who supposedly no longer existed.[60]

"Never Again": Rescuing Soviet Jewry

The Jewish Defense League also played a role in focusing American Jewish attention on the plight of Soviet Jews. Since the 1950s American Jews had been demonstrating and lobbying on behalf of Soviet Jews. One of the key organizations to do so, the American Jewish Conference on Soviet Jewry, initially adopted only conventional, low-key, and diplomatic means. An umbrella organization of all the major Jewish groups, the Conference had been founded in 1964, before the assertive paradigm ushered in by the late 1960's turmoil.[61] Likewise, in 1966 Elie Wiesel, who brought the Holocaust to the attention of the American public through his highly personal book, *Night,* wrote another work, *The Jews of Silence,* an exposé of the conditions of Soviet Jewry. In it he demanded that world Jewry, among them those in America, who constituted the largest, richest, and freest community, do more than mutely tolerate such repression, as, he claimed, they had in standing by idly during the Nazi era.[62] In the late 1960s, in the aftermath of the Six-Day War, and in part owing to the self-proclaimed "outrageous" behavior of the JDL, American Jews heeded that call. The entire array of American Jewish organizations, and the vast majority of American Jews, converged in their concern for Soviet Jewry. The distress of Soviet Jews, unable to practice any form of Judaism and unable to leave, inspired the support of American Jews. As a cause it became second only to Israel in emotional intensity.

The JDL captured much of the press coverage of the movement, at least in the early years of the struggle. It staged noisy demonstrations outside the Soviet mission to the United Nations. Its members got arrested. It sent bomb threats to Soviet consulates and disrupted performances by Soviet ballet and opera companies. In 1971 the JDL staged a sit-in at the offices of Sol Hurok, the impresario who booked many of the artistic groups coming from the Soviet Union. In May 1971, in a curious twist, the JDL occupied the Park East Synagogue, which stood opposite the Soviet's U.N. mission. Though the rabbi demanded that they leave, the militants refused and persisted in shouting demands and blaring music at the diplomatic mission across the street. In October 1972 the JDL claimed responsibility for firing four shots into the mission, and Kahane claimed that such violence constituted a key element in "our Soviet-Southern strategy," referring to the civil rights movement, which had directed its militancy against the American South in the early part of the 1960s. Indeed, Rabbi Yahudi Leib Levin, the chief rabbi of the Soviet Union, who understood the precariousness of Jewish life in Moscow, Leningrad, and the other Soviet cities, condemned the JDL, warning Kahane, "You cannot talk to the Soviet Union that way. It is too strong a country."[63]

Although Kahane and his group clearly represented the far extreme of the movement to aid the Jews of the Soviet Union, their motto, "Never Again," struck a responsive chord among American Jews. In the culture of this era, in which consciousness of the Holocaust rose to great prominence in the Jewish community's rhetorical repertoire, the phrase had deep meaning. American Jews began quite forcefully to discuss not just the events of the World War II era but also what they saw as the impotence of the Jews of the United States when European Jewry had stood on the brink of destruction. Kahane, among others, declared that such weakness would never again mark the behavior of Jews when their coreligionists found themselves in peril.

The movement contained a kind of microcosm of the American, and American Jewish, political cultures of the late 1960s and beyond. It divided along establishment and anti-establishment lines, with the latter position articulated most forcefully by Student Struggle for Soviet Jewry, a group founded in 1964. Student Struggle staged a march through Brooklyn in 1966, handing out leaflets claiming that "History Shall Not Be Repeated." To highlight their concerns the group staged special events and created liturgical texts to coincide with Jewish holidays such as Passover, Simhat Torah, and Tisha B'Av as highly charged ways to demonstrate that once again Jews found themselves in peril. They hung banners across buildings demanding "Let My People Go." During the early 1970s the SSSJ style won out, and even establishment organizations began to adopt the confrontational posture associated with the student group. Jewish civil servants and rabbis used to endless meetings now found themselves marching with placards, even getting arrested if need be.

A good deal of the movement's effort went into public protests. Signs appeared in front of synagogues across America with the pictures of refuseniks, Jews like Ida Nudel and Anatoly Sharansky who had been refused permission to emigrate, some of whom then ended up in the Soviet Union's prisons or mental hospitals. Activists began to visit Jews in the Soviet Union, bringing them Hebrew books, matzo, Jewish ritual objects, and medical supplies. Jewish lawyers, physicians, academicians, and rabbis organized within their professional communities to bring the condition of Soviet Jewry to the attention of the American people. Synagogues began to incorporate the issues of the Soviet Jewry movement into ritual life. It became common in the 1980s for American Jewish youngsters celebrating their b'nai and b'not mitzvah to be "twinned" to a boy or girl in the Soviet Union who had no real chance of experiencing Jewish life. A placard with the name of the "twin" appeared on a chair draped with a prayer shawl on the *bimah* next to the ark with the Torah scrolls. The rabbi, or the thirteen-year-old celebrating her entry into Jewish adulthood, read a description of the twin's life, emphasizing how much the Soviet family wanted to leave and how many obstacles the Soviet government had placed in its path. The family of the American twin typically made a financial contribution to the Soviet Jewry movement.

An even larger share of the movement's effort went into supporting the passage of the Jackson-Vanick Amendment, which linked the granting of trade privileges, much sought after by the Soviet Union, to its human rights policies, particularly with regard to allowing those who so desired the right to emigrate. The fate of the legislation rested on the ability of American Jews to work with Congress and to use the media to air their opinions. They needed to bring delegations to Washington and crowds to rallies. They did both with great success, and the bill passed in 1975. The number of Jews allowed to leave increased, and Soviet authorities began to ease restrictions on the practice and teaching of Judaism. By the time the Soviet Union, as well as the Communist regimes in much of eastern Europe, fell in the early 1990s, much had been accomplished by American Jews. The movement had played a role in the loosening of emigration restrictions in the U.S.S.R., with the immigration of Soviet Jews to the United States an unintended consequence of a political project to direct the emigrants to Israel.[64]

The movement had some other important implications for American Jews. It demonstrated their political clout and their ability to move world politics. The Soviet Jewry movement owed its origins to the activism of American Jews inspired by the 1967 war. It owed its energy to the example of the civil rights struggle, which had so captured the sympathy and imagination of American Jews. It also grew out of the rupture between activist Jews and African Americans, engaged in a nationalist phase of their struggle. The high energy of the Soviet Jewry movement also can be attributed to the emergence on American campuses of a cohort of "new Jews."

THE *HAVURAH* MOVEMENT

Jewish students and other young people who sought to bring the energy and passion of the turbulent decade into their lives, had lit the fire under the Soviet Jewry movement. They also began to place demands on the Jewish establishment. A group of students staged a noisy protest at the 1969 meeting of the General Assembly of the National Council of Jewish Federations and Welfare Funds, the national umbrella organization of local Jewish community social-service and funding agencies. The activists charged that CJF and Hillel, its campus arm, paid scant attention to Jewish education, Jewish identity, Soviet Jewry, feminism, the war in Vietnam, and the needs of the Jewish poor. The new Jews looked askance at what they saw as the conservative, compromising, and utterly respectable profile of American Jewry and at the blandness of Jewish ritual practice.[65]

The *havurah* movement may be the best place to locate these young activist Jews, particularly as they sought to create new kinds of Jewish worship. Spontaneous groupings of Jews, the members of the *havurot*— literally, fellowship groups—sprang up in the late 1960s on campuses and in a few cities. Boston's Havurat Shalom, New York's Minyan Me'at, and Washington, D.C.'s Farbrangen proved to be among the most durable of the *havurot*. Those young Jews attracted to the *havurot* emphasized the equality of all who belonged, a disdain for decorum, and a commitment to experimentation. Many of the young Jews who created the movement had been the products of large postwar suburban synagogues, particularly of the Reform and Conservative denominations. In the *havurot* they sought to negate as much as possible what they had known in their previous congregations. As they saw it, those synagogues valued form over substance, bourgeois respectability over spiritual intensity, and hierarchy over active participation. While the Jewish students attracted to the *havurot* also sympathized with and participated in the other major causes of the day—the civil rights, feminist, and peace movements—they also demonstrated high levels of commitment to their Jewishness. Essentially they wanted to bring to Judaism the inventiveness and assertiveness associated with the youth culture of their era.

The groups they founded purposely remained relatively small, had no rabbis, and affiliated with no denominations. Often meeting in rented space or in members' homes, worshipers took off their shoes when they prayed and felt free to experiment with new forms of worship, mixing dance, poetry, and meditation with the words of the prayer book and the Torah. When disputes arose over matters of ritual practice, since they had no clergy, *havurah* members resolved problems themselves. They stressed creativity and consensus.[66]

The *havurah* movement never grew very large. That had never been its goal. Nonetheless, it had a powerful effect on many American Jews. Many synagogues, the very places that *havurah* Jews had rejected, picked up some of the style and mode of worship pioneered by the *havurot*. Rabbis and laypeople in large congregations decided to split up the large, relatively impersonal membership into smaller, more congenial groups. Pioneered by Rabbi Harold Schulweis of Encino, California, in 1970, these synagogue-based fellowships catered to the specific needs and interests of particular constituencies: study-oriented *havurot*, liturgically experimental *havurot*, social-action *havurot*, and *havurot* for singles, families, or couples. Even when conventional synagogues did not break down into more intimate groups, the *havurah* movement pushed rabbis and lay leaders to lessen the formality and de-emphasize their previous concern with decorum.[67]

In congregations around the country the spirit of innovation and experimentation inspired by the *havurah* movement led to the recovery of ritual practices that had fallen into disuse during the evolution of Judaism into a middle-class, respectable American religion. Congregations, for example, examined their own funeral practices and realized how much the for-profit funeral homes had taken over what traditionally had been a solemn obligation of individuals toward each other, in the process abandoning Jewish law. Congregants began to learn about *taharah*, the ritual washing of the dead, and *shimirah*, the obligation of sitting with the dead until burial, and in communities around the country they started performing these holy acts. In part inspired by the consumers movement that swept middle-class America in the 1960s and 1970s, Jewish funeral practice committees sprang up, and the women and men who taught themselves these rites revived Jewish rituals from centuries past. One Minneapolis congregation created a documentary film in 1977 called *A Plain Pine Box*, which demonstrated how groups of women and men could reclaim Judaic tradition.[68]

By 1978 some 350 *havurah* Jews attended the first National Havurah Conference. At that event, and at the subsequent annual National Havurah Summer Institutes, attendees studied texts, prayed, danced, sang, and explored ways to bring the intensity of the *havurah* experience to the growing number of Jews who had not found a place for themselves within existing institutions. In the years to come the summer conference continued to offer Jews a chance to experiment with ritual and to discuss the meaning of Jewish life.

An Impact on Literature and Art

The movement's impact did not stop with synagogue reform. In 1973 three members of Boston's Havurat Shalom published an immensely popular book, *The Jewish Catalog*, subtitled, "A Do-It-Yourself Kit." Two more volumes appeared in 1976 and 1980. Widely used, and frequently given as bar and bat mitzvah gifts even in the most established congregations, the three-volume *The Jewish Catalog* offered Jews advice on how to "plug in" and on how to create a Jewish life with or without the formal apparatus of a community. It did not shy away from criticizing Jewish institutions. The *Catalog*, in essence, represented the age of communal criticism and creativity. That synagogues endorsed it and that venerable institution like the Jewish Publication Society published it demonstrated both the *Catalog's* appeal and the degree to which the counterculture came to infuse important parts of the American Jewish world.[69]

Some Jews "plugged in" through the realm of the arts, and in the spirit of the time, the new Jewish arts blended traditional and modern, Jewish and non-Jewish modes of expression. The *havurah* movement, broadly defined, unleashed a new kind of Jewish creativity. In a variety of media—music, dance, weaving and tapestry, photography, filmmaking, paper-cutting, calligraphy—the late 1960s saw the birth of explicitly Jewish arts, which derived much of their inspiration from traditional texts, from the tropes of the Jewish past, and from many others sources of world culture.

Nothing demonstrates this better than the revival of klezmer music. Jewish musicians took the marginalized, indeed almost forgotten, musical style of eastern European Jewry, which itself was a mélange of Romanian, Gypsy, and Jewish idioms, and fused it with American sounds.

They brought klezmer music into worship. They used it to celebrate family and community events, and by the 1980s commercially successful groups like the New England Conservatory Klezmer Band, the Klezmatics, and the Klezmorim, along with numerous others, attracted a broader, more mixed audience.[70]

From the 1980s this burgeoning of the Jewish arts scene also included the phenomenon of the Jewish film festival. San Francisco, New York, Chicago, Washington, D.C., even Raleigh-Durham, North Carolina, and Portland, Maine, blocked off time to screen Jewish films produced in the United States, Israel, and Europe. Likewise, Jewish museums grew and offered American Jews a way to engage with Judaism through exhibitions. In 1950 only two museums in America focused on the Jewish experience. In 1977 enough museums existed to lead to the creation of the Council of American Jewish Museums, which by 1991 listed thirty-five affiliated institutions, divided between those that displayed art, those that focused on history, and others that displayed both.[71]

The *havurah* movement's emphasis on spirituality migrated from the limited, relatively private domain of these small fellowship groups into the larger Jewish world. Both Jews and non-Jews, inspired by the call for deeper spiritual striving, discovered the lore and knowledge of Kabbalah, a form of Jewish mysticism born in the Middle Ages. Jews interested in exploring and practicing new forms of spiritual engagement, influenced by Kabbalah, founded the retreat center of Elat Hayim in Pennsylvania and P'nai Or Religious Fellowship, created by Zalman Schachter-Shalomi, which sought to renew Judaism through a pastiche of forms new and old, intrinsic and extrinsic to Judaism. In 1995 the National Center for Jewish Healing brought together Jews, both clergy and laypeople, from around the country interested in bringing matters of the spirit to matters of the flesh and emphasizing the power of prayer in coping with illness.[72] Jewish Lights Publishing Company offered readers an array of books on Jewish spirituality: Tamar Frankiel's *The Gift of Kabbalah: Discovering the Secrets of Heaven, Renewing Your Life on Earth,* Elie Kaplan Spitz's *Does the Soul Survive? A Jewish Journey to Belief in Afterlife, Past Life & Living with Purpose,* Alan Lew and Sherril Jaffe's *One God Clapping: The Spiritual Path of a Zen Rabbi,* and a string of others that "focus on the issue of the quest for the self, seeking meaning in life. They are books that help you to understand who you are and who you might become as a Jewish person."[73] The incorporation of Buddhist forms and ideas into Jewish practice became particularly prominent in the late 1990s after writer

Rodger Kamenetz lead a group of Jews to a meeting with the Dalai Lama. American Jews read about Kamenetz's experience with the spiritual leader of Tibetan Buddhism in the widely read book *The Jew in the Lotus*. Kamenetz spoke to Jewish community groups around the country, and rather than being viewed as the importer of an alien tradition in conflict with Judaism, he and his book received acclaim from rabbis and other communal leaders eager to breathe fresh life into American Judaism.[74]

Student activism, articulated in explicitly Jewish terms, had yet another transformative impact on Jewish life. Until the late 1960's very little, save a handful of courses, in the way of Jewish studies existed in American universities. The professors who taught them, like Harvard's Harry Wolfson, secured their positions in these universities not because of the subject matter, but because of their scholarly stature. The fact that they taught courses on various aspects of Jewish culture had not been the reason for their appointment. Until the late 1960s students had little chance of seriously studying Jewish history, culture, literature, or philosophy in an American university, with the exceptions of those attending either Brandeis or Yeshiva University.

All this changed dramatically in the late 1960s, when Jewish students began to demand Jewish studies courses. Professors with an interest in the subject began to teach classes, although by definition few had any formal training. Most important, individuals in Jewish communities with financial means provided gifts to colleges and universities, both public and private, to hire professors to teach Judaic subjects. The demand for faculty to teach Jewish history, Jewish literature, and Jewish philosophy led students to pursue Jewish studies at the graduate level, in turn fostering the growth of the field and producing a massive increase in the number of Jewish studies courses, programs, departments, conferences, scholarly books, and journals.

Building on this emerging interest, in 1969 a few dozen academics met to create the Association for Jewish Studies. By the beginning of the twenty-first century, nearly a thousand professors and students were coming together annually to explore the many facets of the Jewish experience. The founding of the AJS and its growth over the next three decades demonstrated the increased sophistication of the field, the student demand for it, and the concern of American Jews, both at the leadership and lay level, about their future. Many of the shareholders in the Jewish studies enterprise hoped that through university-based learning, young Jews would anchor themselves to Jewish life.[75]

JEWISH FEMINISM

Of all the transformations launched by the student movements of the 1960s, none had as revolutionary an impact on American Judaism as Jewish feminism. Jewish feminism made possible the admission of women into rabbinical and cantorial school, the emergence of women as lay leaders in their synagogues, and the transformation of the liturgy in reflecting the era's regnant idea that women had an equal share in the history and destiny of the Jewish people. It was in the *havurot,* which were unburdened by the decision-making process of rabbinical and congregational bodies, that women first assumed full and equal roles. From the *havurot* the movement spread into the synagogues, giving Jewish women the idea that they had the right to demand an equal voice in the practice of Judaism. *Havurah* Jews launched the first Jewish feminist publication in 1971, *Brooklyn Bridge.* A group of women from the Conservative movement who assertively demanded changes in women's status formed Ezrat Nashim, also in 1971. They met in 1973 in New York and founded the National Jewish Women's Conference. In 1974 those who had been inspired by the small, experimental, and egalitarian fellowships created the Jewish Feminist Organization.

Like all the other late-twentieth-century changes in Jewish life, the demand for gender equality reflected two trends. The influence of the larger society could not be clearer. Second-Wave feminism, launched by Betty Friedan's 1963 book, *The Feminine Mystique,* and the founding of the National Organization for Women unleashed a movement that engulfed American society. Jewish women had played a role in American feminism since the middle of the nineteenth century, when Ernestine Rose, a Polish-born daughter of a rabbi, became a leader in the struggle over women's right to inherit property. An associate of Elizabeth Cady Stanton and Susan B. Anthony, Rose spoke out against anti-Semitism, even as she devoted the bulk of her energy to the cause of women's rights. In the early twentieth century Maud Nathan served, unofficially to be sure, as the Jewish voice in the upper echelons of the suffrage struggle. But the women's liberation movement of the last part of the twentieth century saw an exceptional growth in the number of Jewish women who functioned as leaders as well as the rank-and-file membership of the movement. Bella Abzug, Vivian Gornick, Gloria Steinem, Robin Morgan, Shulamith Firestone, Meredith Tax, Letty Cottin Pogebrin, along with Friedan, emerged as the political and intellectual mainstays of the movement. Florence Howe founded the Feminist Press, and nine Jewish women counted themselves among the twelve who constituted the Boston Women's Health Collective, the group that put together the enduring *Our Bodies, Ourselves,* a guidebook helping women to take charge of their own health. Jewish women played a powerful and formative role in that movement, not a surprising development, given how powerfully feminism spoke to them. Jewish women attended college at the same rate as Jewish men, and they, like other educated middle-class women, wanted access to the professions, equal pay for equal work, and the right to be viewed as full-fledged human beings, not as the appendages of fathers or husbands.

But Jewish feminism had a history of its own, related to, yet distinct from, the general movement. On some level it developed as the culmination of a process that had been building since the early nineteenth century, when synagogues increasingly became the domain of women. In the 1950s suburban synagogues existed in large measure because of women. In recognition of that support, rabbis increasingly gave women the chance to participate on a limited basis in public ritual. The 1955 decision of the Conservative movement's Committee on Jewish Law and Standards to grant women the right to have aliyah, the privilege of being called to recite the blessings over the Torah, had been barely taken advantage of by congregations. A 1962 study found that 196 Conservative congregations still did not allow women to be called to the Torah, despite the ruling. Some fifty allowed it, but with restrictions, and only in eight did gender not encumber the women as they ascended the *bimah* to bless the Torah.[76]

Likewise, the fact that in the 1950s and beyond Jewish women became the major consumers of adult Jewish education no doubt played a role in the growth of Jewish feminism. These women came to realize that they knew so little simply because of their anatomy and not owing to any lack of intellectual ability. Historically, American Jewish parents had felt that only boys needed, or deserved, a Jewish education. Therefore, for the women in the Reform and Conservative congregations, attending classes on Jewish history, religion, and philosophy amounted to acts of consciousness raising. In 1972, despite the amount of organizing taking place and the new practices developing in the *havurot,* most American Jews still saw Judaism as a religion in which men had most—if not all—the public roles.

They must have been quite shocked in the spring of 1972 to read in newspapers around the country that among the graduates of the Hebrew Union College who stood up to receive their rabbinic ordination that year was a woman named Sally Priesand. Perhaps they should not have been surprised. The issue had been in the air for decades. When in 1968 the Reconstructionist Rabbinical College opened in Philadelphia, it immediately welcomed women as rabbinical students and announced that their ordination as rabbis would not be a matter of debate or discussion. The RRC's bold decision as well as Priesand's ordination opened the floodgates of women applying to rabbinical schools. From those schools, the newly ordained female rabbis moved on to the pulpits of American congregations and to the organizations that in this era of emphasizing Jewish values in communal institutions increasingly began to hire rabbis to staff positions. The entry of women into the rabbinate, be it at a Hillel on a college campus, a congregation, a hospital, or an organization, changed the public face of Judaism.

For Reform and Reconstructionism the issue of women's ordination had been resolved with relative ease and little fanfare. Since neither movement considered itself bound to halakah, each could respond to the demands of women and accommodate the dictates of the culture with little anguish. Indeed, the ordination of women helped Reform Judaism as it sought to "retraditionalize." The women who received Reform ordination generally expressed a greater commitment to traditional practice than did their male colleagues. In fact, some of these women would have chosen to become Conservative rabbis, had that option existed for them. For more than a decade after the first women enrolled at Hebrew Union College, the Conservative movement remained closed to them. So the women who aspired to the rabbinate broke the first barrier in Reform, pushing their congregants and fellow rabbis to re-embrace practices long discarded. For Reconstructionism, which had achieved its denominational status in this era, the ordination of women constituted tradition. Mordecai Kaplan, the movement's visionary, had long been an advocate of equal rights for women, and the rabbinical college that he and his followers established made women's equality a fundamental principle.

For the Orthodox the question of women's ordination also posed no problem, although for very different reasons. At the turn of the twenty-first century, Orthodox institutions remain as firmly committed to their belief that rabbis must be men, plain and simple. Only men could fulfill the tasks associated with the rabbinate. Women surely played roles in fulfilling the obligations of kashrut, strict Sabbath observance, and the myriad other details of Jewish law that informed their lives. Yet even within Orthodoxy change crept in. The most salient factor that ushered in this change involved the rising levels of Judaic education of Orthodox girls. By the 1970s several generations of Orthodox girls had gone through the Bais Yaakov schools as well as other Orthodox institutions like the Ramaz School in New York City, which provided girls with in-depth Jewish learning. With the passage of time, the number of Judaically educated women grew, creating a cohort that was new in the history of the Jews. Some of them, like Blu Greenberg, an Orthodox feminist, took her newfound knowledge and began to write and lecture about the possibility of reconciling traditional Judaism with feminism's call for expanding human rights to encompass all women.[77]

Some Orthodox rabbis endorsed broadening women's participation in public religious practice. The rabbi of Manhattan's Lincoln Square Synagogue, Shlomo Riskin, declared that women could hold their own celebration of Simhat Torah, the joyous fall holiday that marks the completion of the annual cycle of reading the Torah. No longer did they have to watch the spectacle of men rejoicing in the Torah. They too could share in the reading and the veneration of the text itself, in the company of other women. Other Orthodox rabbis sanctioned the formation of women's prayer groups, allowing women on their own, in a separate space, to perform the rituals previously restricted to men.

In the late 1990s Orthodox Jewish feminists, many of whom had received educations quite similar in depth and content to that of their brothers, began to organize for greater rights, although they barely raised the ordination issue. The Jewish Orthodox Feminist Alliance offers an illustrative example of feminism's impact on the tradition. Called together by Orthodox women at the end of the twentieth century, JOFA took up the call to "[e]xpand the spiritual, ritual, intellectual, and political opportunities for women in the framework of halakha." It advocated "meaningful participation and equality for women in family life, synagogues, houses of learning and Jewish communal organizations to the full extent possible within halakha."[78]

The Jewish Orthodox Feminist Alliance held both national conferences and local meetings and created a variety of projects to realize its declaration of principles. It took on advocacy for *agunot,* women whose recalcitrant husbands would not grant them a divorce, thereby making it impossible for the women to remarry. These *agunot* often found themselves blackmailed by their husbands, who used their power to withhold the *get,* or divorce, until their wives had made substantial financial concessions. JOFA made resources available to *agunot,* helping these women in distress negotiate and to look for recourse within the rabbinic process. In a manner typical of its era, JOFA created new prayers for *agunot*. One by Shelley Frier List beseeched the Creator to free these captive wives:

> Creator of heaven and earth, may it be
> Your will to free the captive wives of
> Israel when love and sanctity have fled
> the home, but their husbands bind them . . . Grant
> wisdom to the judges of Israel: teach them to
> recognize oppression and rule against it . . .
> Blessed are you, Creator of heaven and
> earth, who frees the captives.

Rabbi Mordechai Tendler wrote a similar prayer:

> He who Blessed our Patriarchs Abraham, Isaac
> and Jacob . . . and our Matriarchs Sarah, Rebecca,
> Rachel and Leah, may He release and deliver all
> the *agunot* from the bonds of their plight.[79]

JOFA and other Orthodox Jewish feminists functioned in a legal and cultural context in which only the rabbis in their communities could make changes. By definition, controversies could not be confrontational, and those yearning for change had no alternative to deferring both to long-established procedures and to male rabbinic prerogatives.

Therefore the controversy over women's equality, focused particularly on the question of women's ordination, flared primarily in the Conservative movement. Here the demand of women to receive ordination became a source of pain and divisiveness. As a denomination Conservatism had always asserted that it followed halakah. Yet it had always maintained that Judaism must accommodate itself—as much as possible—to the demands of modernity. The issue of women's ordination reminded them of the potential disjunction between these two principles and challenged them to determine where the boundary between accommodation and the law ought to be.

The call for admitting women to the rabbinical program at the Jewish Theological Seminary, as well as truly equalizing the roles of men and women within Conservative synagogue practice, came from the women themselves, through Ezrat Nashim. This group, which consisted of graduate students, Jewish professionals, and highly educated women committed to Judaism, demanded that Conservative Judaism come to terms with their quest for equality. Their use of the term *ezrat nashim* reflected both their commitment to Judaism and their feminist agenda. Meaning literally "women's help," *ezrat nashim,* in traditional congregations, referred to the women's section of the synagogue, the separate and decidedly unequal space given to women. The feminist challenge to Conservative Judaism came from a group of women bent both on preserving tradition and pushing the movement to help women achieve basic rights.

The struggle within the Conservative movement lasted a little longer than a decade. Ezrat Nashim brought its first demand to the 1972 meeting of the Rabbinical Assembly, presenting a paper entitled "Jewish Women Call for Change," which challenged the all-male membership of the Assembly: "The social position and self-image of women have changed in recent years. It is now universally accepted that women are equal to men in intellectual capacity, leadership ability and spiritual depth. . . . To educate women and deny them the opportunity to act from this knowledge is an affront to their intelligence, talents and integrity."[80]

These were strong words for an organization long committed to finding the middle way between divergent positions but words with which some men agreed. The newly appointed chancellor of the Jewish Theological Seminary, Gerson Cohen, suggested strongly to the law committee of the Rabbinical Assembly to take heed of the women's demands. The rabbinical body responded piecemeal. First it allowed women to be counted in the minyan, the prayer quorum that traditionally called for ten men for public worship. In 1973 it ruled favorably on women's equal participation in synagogue life. But it was not until 1983, after years of hearings held around the country, pressure by women, articles and manifestos, that women were admitted to the Jewish Theological Seminary on an equal footing with men. Traditionalists in the movement believed that ordaining women as rabbis could not be squared with Jewish law. Supporters of women's ordination made a two-pronged argument in defense of their position. In scouring the sources they found justifications for ordaining women, and at the same time they declared that at the end of the twentieth century the stakes had become too high for Judaism to remain committed to the practices of the past.

In May 1985, Amy Eilberg became the first woman to become ordained at the Jewish Theological Seminary. Yet the Conservative movement's stormy encounter with feminism had hardly come to a peaceable end. An even longer struggle took place as women in the movement expressed their desire to become cantors. By 1990 the Cantor's Assembly turned down the women's demands a third time, maintaining that Jewish law and tradition made no room for a woman to be a *shaliach tzibbur,* a messenger of the community. To circumvent the opposition of the rank-and-file membership, the executive committee itself of the Cantor's Assembly made the decision to allow women to be ordained as cantors.[81]

The Conservative movement's decision to choose gender equality over strict interpretation of Jewish law did not take place without internal consequences. The outcome of the decade-long debate so appalled some of the Seminary's staunchest traditionalists that in 1984 they broke off to form the Union for Traditional Conservative Judaism. They interpreted halakah very differently than did their former colleagues at J.T.S. However much they might sympathize with the fervor of the women who wanted to become rabbis, they believed that the law simply did not permit it. In 1989 some of the dissidents, including talmudist David Weiss Halivni and Jewish Theological Seminary scholars David Feldman and David Novak, founded the Institute of Traditional Judaism committed to "Genuine Faith and Intellectual Honesty."[82]

New Rituals

The influence of feminism on American Jewry neither began nor ended with the ordination issue. Since the movement's birth, Jewish women around the country, in and out of the synagogue setting, have created new rituals and crafted new texts to express their sense of themselves as Jews and as women. In the early 1970s they began to stage public ceremonies to mark the birth of daughters, challenging the centuries-old dichotomy in which the birth of sons provided the occasion for a public ritual—the *brit millah*—replete with feasting, while a daughter's birth afforded little ceremonial expression. Many women have adopted Rosh Hodesh, the beginning of the new month, as a special women's ritual and formed Rosh Hodesh groups for prayer and study. Jewish women have added to the Passover ritual by placing on the seder table a goblet of water, a Miriam's cup, to bring the sister of Moses into what they see as her rightful place in the narrative of the exodus from Egypt.

Many Jewish women who as children received no Jewish education have decided to make up for that deficiency. They have started to learn, and many, through their congregations, have marked the completion of their course of study with an adult bat mitzvah, one of the new rituals created by Jews, women in particular, in this age of creativity. Feminist Passover seders, complete with feminist Haggadoth, have cropped up around the country, as thousands of Jewish women have decided to mark Jewish sacred time with a rite they could shape and enjoy. The magazine *Lilith*, founded in 1973, served as a voice for Jewish feminism and as a showcase for Jewish feminists who described in its pages their feelings, their creative works, and their struggles. Additionally, in the late twentieth century a cadre of novelists captured the Jewish—and American—literary scene. The immense success of novels by Jewish women like Rebecca Goldstein, Allegra Maud Goodman, Nessa Rappaport, Tova Mirvis, and Pearl Abraham, among others, showed how women's activism and their exploration of Judaism inspired a new zest for Jewish themes.

Probably no book represented this tendency more powerfully than Anita Diamant's *The Red Tent*. A retelling of the biblical story of Dinah, the only daughter of Jacob, Diamant's novel harkens back to the Midrashic tradition, but with a decidedly feminist edge. She tells the story from the perspective of Dinah, a character who in the Bible functions as an object of men's actions rather than as an actor with feelings, thoughts, and control over her own destiny. *The Red Tent* initially received little publicity, but Jewish women read it, passing it on to friends and family. They formed reading groups to discuss it, and the novel became the Jewish women's classic of the century's end.[83]

Those Jewish women who have struggled with the texts and demanded that the institutions of Jewish life take their concerns seriously in some way represent the essence of late-twentieth-century American Jewish history. As educated, affluent, integrated citizens of the nation—like most American Jews—they had a seemingly endless array of choices from which to choose. That they stayed anchored in Judaism but sought to change it indicated the depth of their concerns and the centrality of Jewishness to their lives.

Their actions made it possible for other groups, previously silent, to assert their right to participate. By the end of the twentieth century, the rights and roles of homosexuals within Judaism became the emerging issue, particularly in the realm of ritual practice. In the 1980s separate gay congregations formed in San Francisco, New York, Washington, D.C., and elsewhere. Beth Mishpacha, the Washington congregation, saw itself as relatively conservative liturgically, but by its very nature it challenged the conventional face of American Judaism. Liberal rabbis and rabbinical bodies faced the question about the participation of homosexuals in congregations and the ordination of gays into the rabbinate. Should rabbis perform commitment ceremonies? Where should congregations draw the line?

In congregation after congregation, rabbis and laity differed, as did different constituencies within congregations. Individual congregations in turn disagreed with the policies of the denominational bodies. In 1999, for example, members of New York's Conservative B'nai Jeshurun directed the synagogue's board not to send any congregational dues to the Jewish Theological Seminary because it refused to admit and ordain homosexuals.[84] While the resolution of the issue lies in the future, if the women's revolution can provide a model, most American Jews will choose inclusion rather than a rigid reading of ancient canonical texts.

Like the earlier feminist challenge, the decision by gay Jews to assert their right to be part of the formal apparatus of American Judaism offers a way of seeing the salience of Jewishness in a world of multiple possibilities. These Jews of the late twentieth century desperately wanted to be included and recognized within the Jewish world. In an era when so many Jews seemed not to care about Jewish life, that they wanted inclusion says much.

The choices these—and indeed most—Jews made involved highly personal and idiosyncratic concerns. Jewish women, along with men, mostly do not feel bound to operate within conventional and inherited institutions. They do not feel compelled to behave as their parents or grandparents did. In a postmodern age, with its intense focus on personal choice, they look for ways and places to function as Jews. The solutions they produce do not necessarily reflect the weight of tradition or the continuity of past practice. By the beginning of the twenty-first century, on some level all American Jews, not just the growing number of converts, had become Jews by choice. While those communal leaders who worry about continuity can hardly be dismissed, and their apprehension about what the future of the Jewish people in America may be well justified, they might take solace from the reality that large numbers of American Jews, whether or not they affiliate, continue to invest their Jewishness with meaning. Definitions of Jewishness may be more elastic than they have been at any time in the modern past. But that elasticity, a hallmark of American culture, may indeed hold the key to the continuance of the "eternal people" in a new and uncharted age.

NOTES

CHAPTER 1. AMERICAN JEWISH ORIGINS

1. Quoted in Morris U. Schappes, *A Documentary History of The Jews in the United States, 1654–1875*, 3rd ed. (New York: Schocken, 1971), 1–2.

2. Schappes, *Documentary History,* 2–4.

3. Quoted in Jacob Rader Marcus, *Early American Jewry: The Jews of New York, New England, and Canada, 1649–1794* (Philadelphia: Jewish Publication Society of America, 1961), 26.

4. Schappes, *Documentary History,* 4–5.

5. Stanley F. Chyet, *Lopez of Newport: Colonial American Merchant Prince* (Detroit: Wayne State University Press, 1970).

6. Joyce D. Goodfriend, *Before the Melting Pot: Society and Culture in Colonial New York City, 1664–1730* (Princeton: Princeton University Press, 1992), 11.

7. Schappes, *Documentary History,* 4–5.

8. Quoted in Karla Goldman, *Beyond the Synagogue Gallery: Finding a Place for Women in American Judaism* (Cambridge, Mass.: Harvard University Press, 2000), 69.

9. Saul J. Rubin, *Third to None: The Saga of Savannah Jewry, 1733–1893* (Savannah: S. J. Rubin, 1983), 2–13.

10. B. H. Levy, "The Early History of Georgia's Jews," in *Forty Years of Diversity: Essays on Colonial Georgia,* ed. Harvey H. Jackson and Phinizy Spalding (Athens: University of Georgia Press, 1984), 163–78.

11. Miriam Bodian, *Hebrews of the Portuguese Nation: Conversos and Community in Early Modern Amsterdam* (Bloomington: Indiana University Press, 1997).

12. Goodfriend, *Before the Melting Pot,* 67, 156.

13. Irene Neu, "The Jewish Businesswoman in America," *American Jewish Historical Quarterly* 66, no. 1 (September 1976): 137.

14. David Sorkin, "The Port Jew: Notes Toward a Social Type," *Journal of Jewish Studies* 50, no. 1 (Spring 1999): 87–97.

15. Jacob Rader Marcus, "Light on Early Connecticut Jewry," *American Jewish Archives* 1, no. 1 (January 1949): 3–52.

16. Quoted in Eli Faber, *A Time for Planting: The First Migration, 1654–1820,* Jewish People in America 1 (Baltimore: Johns Hopkins University Press, 1992), 37.

17. James William Hagy, *This Happy Land: The Jews of Colonial and Antebellum Charleston* (Tuscaloosa: University of Alabama Press, 1993), 6.

18. See Frances D. Cogliano, *No King, No Popery: Anti-Catholicism in Revolutionary New England* (Westport, Conn.: Greenwood Press, 1995); Charles P. Hanson, *Necessary Virtue: The Pragmatic Origins of Religious Liberty in New England* (Charlottesville: University of Virginia Press, 1998); Ray Allen Billington, *The Protestant Crusade, 1800–1860: A Study in the Origins of American Nativism* (New York: Macmillan, 1938), 1–25, on the colonial background of American anti-Catholicism.

19. Abbot E. Smith, *Colonists in Bondage: White Servitude and Convict Labor in America, 1607–1776* (1947; reprint, Gloucester, Mass: P. Smith, 1965).

20. Naomi Cohen, *Jews in Christian America: The Pursuit of Religious Equality* (New York: Oxford University Press, 1992), 19.

21. Ira Berlin, *Many Thousands Gone: The First Two Centuries of Slavery in North America* (Cambridge, Mass.: Belknap Press of Harvard University Press, 1998).

22. Goodfriend, *Before the Melting Pot,* 76.

23. Chyet, *Lopez of Newport;* Eli Faber, *Jews, Slaves, and the Slave Trade: Setting the Record Straight* (New York: New York University Press, 1998); Seymour Drescher, *From Slavery to Freedom: Comparative Studies in the Rise and Fall of Atlantic Slavery* (New York: New York University Press, 1999), 339–54.

24. Ira Rosenwaike, "An Estimate and Analysis of the Jewish Population of the United States in 1790," *Publications of the American Jewish Historical Society* 50, no. 1 (September 1960): 31.

25. Morris Gutstein, *The Story of the Jews of Newport: Two and a Half Centuries of Judaism, 1658–1908* (New York: Bloch, 1936).

26. Leo Hershkowitz, *Wills of Early New York Jews, 1704–1799* (New York: American Jewish Historical Society, 1967), xii.

27. Hyman Grinstein, *The Rise of the Jewish Community of New York, 1654–1860* (Philadelphia: Jewish Publication Society of America, 1947), 30.

28. Hershkowitz, *Wills,* xii, 865.

29. Neu, "Jewish Businesswoman," 139.

30. Grinstein, *Rise of the Jewish Community,* 166; David de Sola Pool, *Portraits Etched in Stone: Early Jewish Settlers, 1682–1831* (New York: Columbia University Press, 1953), 170–73.

31. Bernard Weinryb, *The Jews of Poland: A Social and Economic History of the Jewish Community in Poland from 1100 to 1800* (Philadelphia: Jewish Publication Society of America, 1973), 181–205.

32. Bodian, *Hebrews of the Portuguese Nation,* 126–31.

33. Abigail Franks, *The Lee Max Friedman Collection of American Jewish Colonial Correspondence: Letters of the Franks Family, 1733–1748*, ed. Leo Hershkowitz and Isidore S. Meyer (Waltham, Mass.: American Jewish Historical Society, 1968), 66–67.

34. R. D. Barnett, "Dr. Samuel Nunes Ribiero and the Settlement of Georgia," in *Migration and Settlement: Proceedings of the Anglo-American Jewish Historical Conference Held in London Jointly by the Jewish Historical Society of England and the American Jewish Historical Society, July 1970* (London: Jewish Historical Society of England, 1971), 87, 94.

35. Pool, *Portraits Etched in Stone*, 170–73.

36. Quoted in Hagy, *This Happy Land*, 60.

37. Quoted in Goldman, *Beyond the Synagogue Gallery*, 52.

38. "The Earliest Extant Minute Books of the Spanish and Portuguese Congregation Shearith Israel in New York, 1728–1786," *Publications of the American Jewish Historical Society* 21 (1913): 74–75.

39. Quoted in Faber, *Time for Planting*, 69.

40. John Demos, *A Little Commonwealth: Family Life in Plymouth Colony* (New York: Oxford University Press, 1970).

41. Mary Beth Norton, *Founding Mothers and Fathers: Gendered Power and the Forming of American Society* (New York: Knopf, 1996), 5–14.

42. Mark Slobin, *Chosen Voices: The History of the American Cantorate* (Urbana: University of Illinois Press, 1989), 30–34.

43. "Earliest Extant Minute Book," 14.

44. Jeremiah Berman, *Shehitah: A Study in the Cultural and Social Life of the Jewish People* (New York: Bloch, 1941), 274–87.

45. "Earliest Extant Minute Book," 35–36.

46. Leo Hershkowitz, "Some Aspects of the New York Jewish Merchant and Community, 1654–1820," *American Jewish Historical Quarterly* 67, no. 1 (September 1976): 24.

47. Rachel Wischnitzer, *Synagogue Architecture in the United States: History and Interpretation* (Philadelphia: Jewish Publication Society of America, 1955), 11–22.

48. Gutstein, *Story of the Jews of Newport*, 93–94.

49. Jacob Rader Marcus, *The Colonial American Jew, 1492–1776* (Detroit: Wayne State University Press, 1970), 1: 508.

50. Leo Hershkowitz, "Asser Levy and the Inventories of Early New York Jews," *American Jewish History* 80, no. 1 (Autumn 1990): 56–73.

51. Franks, *Lee Max Friedman Collection*.

52. Malcolm Stern, "The Function of Genealogy in American Jewish History," in *Essays in American Jewish History to Commemorate the Tenth Anniversary of the Founding of the American Jewish Archives under the Direction of Jacob Rader Marcus* (Cincinnati: American Jewish Archives, 1958), 83–86.

53. Carl Becker, in *The Declaration of Independence: A Study in the History of Political Ideas* (New York: Knopf, 1942), made the point that the American Revolution involved a struggle for both home rule and who should rule at home.

CHAPTER 2. BECOMING AMERICAN

1. Jacob Rader Marcus, *Early American Jewry: The Jews of New York, New England, and Canada, 1649–1794* (Philadelphia: Jewish Publication Society of America, 1961), 100–101.

2. Werner Sollors, *Beyond Ethnicity: Consent and Descent in American Culture* (New York: Oxford University Press, 1986).

3. Quoted in Eli Faber, *A Time for Planting: The First Migration, 1654–1820,* Jewish People in America 1 (Baltimore: Johns Hopkins University Press, 1992), 105.

4. James William Hagy, *This Happy Land: The Jews of Colonial and Antebellum Charleston* (Tuscaloosa: University of Alabama Press, 1993), 116.

5. Cecil Roth, "Some Jewish Loyalists in the War of American Independence," *Publications of the American Jewish Historical Society* 35, pt. 1 (December 1948): 81–107.

6. Samuel Rezneck, *Unrecognized Patriots: The Jews in the American Revolution* (Westport, Conn.: Greenwood Press, 1975), 23–24.

7. "Items Relating to Congregation Shearith Israel, New York," *Publications of the American Jewish Historical Society* 27 (1920): 31.

8. Hasia R. Diner and Beryl Lieff Benderly, *Her Works Praise Her: A History of Jewish Women in America from Colonial Times to the Present* (New York: Basic Books, 2002), 48–49.

9. Nathan Kaganoff, "The Business Career of Haym Salomon as Reflected in His Newspaper Advertisements," *American Jewish Historical Quarterly* 66, no. 1 (September 1976): 35–49; Charles Edward Russell, *Haym Salomon and the Revolution* (New York: Cosmopolitan Books, 1930).

10. Edwin Wolf and Maxwell Whiteman, *History of the Jews of Philadelphia from Colonial Times to the Age of Jackson* (Philadelphia: Jewish Publication Society of America, 1957), 32, 58.

11. Sidney M. Fish, *Barnard and Michael Gratz: Their Lives and Times* (Lanham, Md.: University Press of America, 1994).

12. Richard Morris, "The Role of the Jews in the American Revolution in Historical Perspective," in *Jewish Life in America: Historical Perspectives,* ed. Gladys Rosen (New York: KTAV Publishing House, 1978), 11.

13. Hyman Grinstein, *The Rise of the Jewish Community of New York, 1654–1860* (Philadelphia: Jewish Publication Society of America, 1947), 69.

14. Reprinted in Jonathan Sarna and David Dalin, *Religion and State in the American Jewish Experience* (Notre Dame, Ind.: University of Notre Dame Press, 1992), 65, emphasis mine; see also Morton Borden, *Jews, Turks, and Infidels* (Chapel Hill: University of North Carolina Press, 1984).

15. Morris, "Role of the Jews," 21–22.

16. Isaac M. Fein, *The Making of an American Jewish Community: The History of Baltimore Jewry from 1773 to 1920* (Philadelphia: Jewish Publication Society of America, 1971).

17. E. Milton Altfeld, *The Jew's Struggle for Religious and Civil Liberty in Maryland* (Baltimore: M. Curlander, 1924).

18. Leonard Rogoff, *Homelands: Southern Jewish Identity in Durham and*

Chapel Hill, North Carolina (Tuscaloosa: University of Alabama Press, 2001), 6–14; Emily Bingham, *Mordecai: An Early American Family* (New York: Hill and Wang, 2003).

19. Joseph L. Blau and Salo Baron, eds., *The Jews of the United States, 1790–1840: A Documentary History,* vol. 1 (New York: Columbia University Press, 1963).

20. Naomi W. Cohen, *Jews in Christian America: The Pursuit of Religious Equality* (New York: Oxford University Press, 1992), 22–28.

21. Leonard W. Levy, *Treason against God: A History of the Offense of Blasphemy* (New York: Schocken Books, 1981), 333–34.

22. Jon Butler, *Awash in a Sea of Faith: Christianizing the American People* (Cambridge, Mass.: Harvard University Press, 1990).

23. Morris, "Role of the Jews," 63.

24. Morris U. Schappes, *A Documentary History of the Jews of the United States, 1654–1875,* 3rd ed. (New York: Schocken, 1971), 65.

25. Quoted in Faber, *Time for Planting,* 136.

26. Quoted in Schappes, *Documentary History,* 92–96.

27. Quoted in Hagy, *This Happy Land,* 119.

28. Edward Eitches, "Maryland's Jew Bill," *American Jewish Historical Quarterly* 60, no. 3 (March 1971): 258–79.

29. Butler, *Awash in a Sea of Faith.*

30. Frederick D. Williams, ed., *The Northwest Ordinance: Essays on Its Formulation, Provisions, and Legacy* (East Lansing: Michigan State University Press, 1989).

31. Reprinted in Sarna and Dalin, *Religion and State,* 72–74.

32. Quoted in Cohen, *Jews in Christian America,* 32.

33. "The Federal Parade of 1788," *American Jewish Archives* 7 (January 1955): 65–67.

34. For the full exchange of letters between four congregations and George Washington, see Schappes, *Documentary History,* 77–83.

35. Quoted in Faber, *Time for Planting,* 132.

36. David Eichhorn, *Evangelizing the American Jew* (Middle Village, N.Y.: Jonathan David, 1978).

37. Diane Ravitch, *The Great School Wars: A History of the New York City Public Schools* (New York: Basic Books, 1974), 7.

38. Ravitch, *Great School Wars,* 9–11.

39. George Paul Jacoby, *Catholic Child Care in Nineteenth Century New York* (1941; reprint, New York: Arno Press, 1974).

40. Quoted in Jonathan Sarna, *Jacksonian Jew: The Two Worlds of Mordecai Noah* (New York: Holmes and Meier, 1981), 26.

41. Jacob Katz, *Jews and Freemasons in Europe* (Cambridge, Mass.: Harvard University Press, 1970); no historian has yet studied the involvement of Jews with Freemasonry in America. Yet the individual histories of Jewish communities as well as the primary biographical and journalistic accounts of the late eighteenth and nineteenth centuries point to an important link between Jews and Freemasons. See, for example, Barnett A. Elzas, *The Jews of South Carolina from the Earliest Times to the Present Day* (Philadelphia: Lippincott, 1905), 144–45.

Elzas declared, "In Freemasonry the Jews of South Carolina have always taken a prominent part" (144).

42. Myron Berman, *Richmond's Jewry, 1769–1976* (Charlottesville: University Press of Virginia, 1979), 36.

43. Grinstein, *Rise of the Jewish Community of New York*, 175.

44. Quoted in Hagy, *This Happy Land*, 43.

45. Faber, *Time for Planting*, 119.

46. David de Sola Pool, *An Old Faith in the New World: Portrait of Shearith Israel, 1654–1954* (New York: Columbia University Press, 1955), 260–64.

47. Rachel Wischnitzer, *Synagogue Architecture in the United States: History and Interpretation* (Philadelphia: Jewish Publication Society of America, 1955), 12.

48. Karla Goldman, *Beyond the Synagogue Gallery: Finding a Place for Women in American Judaism* (Cambridge, Mass.: Harvard University Press, 2000), 51.

49. Daniel J. Elazar, Jonathan D. Sarna, and Rela G. Monson, eds., *A Double Bond: The Constitutional Documents of American Jewry* (Lanham, Md.: University Press of America, 1992), 103–13.

50. Berman, *Richmond Jewry*, 36–63.

51. Wolf and Whiteman, *History of the Jews of Philadelphia*, 225.

52. Hagy, *This Happy Land*, 68–69.

53. Diane Ashton, *Rebecca Gratz: Women and Judaism in Antebellum America* (Detroit: Wayne State University Press, 1997).

54. Faber, *Time for Planting*, 123.

55. Quoted in Faber, *Time for Planting*, 133.

CHAPTER 3. A CENTURY OF MIGRATION

1. Steven Lowenstein, *The Jews of Oregon, 1850–1950* (Portland: Jewish Historical Society of Oregon, 1987), 9–16.

2. Ted Gostin, *The Katsiv Chronicles: A Genealogy of the Kite, Kaciff, Weprin, Wander, and Dorfman Families* (n.p., 1991), 55–59, 71–73.

3. Arthur Ruppin, *The Jews in the Modern World* (London: Macmillan, 1934), 43; Moses Shulvass, *From East to West: The Westward Migration of Jews from Eastern Europe during the Seventeenth and Eighteenth Centuries* (Detroit: Wayne State University Press, 1971).

4. Jacob Katz, *Out of the Ghetto: The Social Background of Jewish Emancipation, 1770–1870* (Cambridge, Mass.: Harvard University Press, 1973).

5. Gerald Sorin, *A Time for Building: The Third Migration, 1880–1920*, Jewish People in America 3 (John Hopkins University Press, 1992), 1–2.

6. Roger Daniels, *Coming to America: A History of Immigration and Ethnicity in American Life* (New York: HarperCollins, 1990), coined the phrase "a century of migration" and is an important corrective to the scholarship.

7. Carol Sheriff, *The Artificial River: The Erie Canal and the Paradox of Progress, 1817–1860* (New York: Hill and Wang, 1996); Stuart W. Bruchey, *Growth of the Modern American Economy* (New York: Dodd, Mead, 1975);

Thomas Dublin, *Transforming Women's Work: New England Lives in the Industrial Revolution* (Ithaca, N.Y.: Cornell University Press, 1994).

8. Maldwyn Allen Jones, *American Immigration,* 2nd ed. (Chicago: University of Chicago Press, 1992); Allen Kraut, *The Huddled Masses: The Immigrant in American Society, 1880–1921* (Arlington Heights, Ill.: Harlan Davidson, 1982).

9. Walter T. K. Nugent, *Crossings: The Great Transatlantic Migrations, 1870–1914* (Bloomington: Indiana University Press, 1992).

10. Jones, *American Immigration,* 153.

11. Barbara Miller Solomon, *Ancestors and Immigrants: A Changing New England Tradition* (Cambridge, Mass.: Harvard University Press, 1956); John Higham, *Strangers in the Land: Patterns of American Nativism, 1860–1925* (New York: Atheneum, 1963).

12. Michael Stanislawski, *Tsar Nicholas I and the Jews: The Transformation of Jewish Society in Russia, 1825–1855* (Philadelphia: Jewish Publication Society of America, 1983).

13. Sorin, *Time for Building,* 1–2.

14. Quoted in Mark Wischnitzer, *To Dwell in Safety: The Story of Jewish Migration Since 1800* (Philadelphia: Jewish Publication Society of America, 1948), 29; Max J. Kohler and Simon Wolf, "Jewish Disabilities in the Balkan States," *Publications of the American Jewish Historical Society* 24 (1916): 1–153.

15. Hasia R. Diner, "Before the Promised City: Eastern European Jews in America Before 1880," in *An Inventory of Promises: Essays on American Jewish History in Honor of Moses Rischin,* ed. Jeffrey S. Gurock and Marc Lee Raphael (Brooklyn: Carlson, 1995), 43–62; Carol Kruckoff, *Rodfei Zedek: The First Hundred Years* (Chicago: Congregation Rodfei Zedek, 1976), 2–9.

16. Marc Angel, "The Sephardim of the United States: An Exploratory Study," *American Jewish Yearbook* 74 (1973): 77–138.

17. David Sorkin, *The Transformation of German Jewry, 1780–1840* (New York: Oxford University Press, 1980); Werner Mosse, Arnold Paucker, and Reinhard Rurup, *Revolution and Evolution: 1848 in German-Jewish History* (Tübingen: J. C. B. Mohr, 1981).

18. Marion Kaplan, *The Making of the Jewish Middle Class: Women, Family, and Identity in Imperial Germany* (New York: Oxford University Press, 1991).

19. Quoted in Hasia R. Diner, *A Time for Gathering: The Second Migration, 1820–1880,* Jewish People in America 2 (Baltimore: Johns Hopkins University Press, 1992), 46.

20. Wischnitzer, *To Dwell in Safety,* 6.

21. Diner, *Time for Gathering,* 6–59.

22. Guido Kisch, *In Search of Freedom: A History of American Jews from Czechoslovakia* (London: E. Goldston, 1949); Hillel Kieval, *The Making of Czech Jewry: National Conflict and Jewish Society in Bohemia, 1870–1918* (New York: Oxford University Press, 1988).

23. Quoted in Wischnitzer, *To Dwell in Safety,* 22.

24. Paula Hyman, *The Emancipation of the Jews of Alsace: Acculturation*

and Tradition in the Nineteenth Century (New Haven: Yale University Press, 1991).

25. Zosa Szajkowski, "A Bintel Fakten Vegen Elsasser Yiden in America," *YIVO Bleter* 20, no. 2 (November–December 1942): 312–16.

26. Guido Kisch, "The Revolution of 1848 and the Jewish 'On to America Movement'" *Publications of the American Jewish Historical Society* 38 (March 1949): 185–208.

27. One explanation offered by some historians for the phrase "hep, hep" is that it was an acronym for the Latin *Hierosolyma est perdita,* or "Jerusalem is destroyed." Others, like Lloyd Gartner in *History of the Jews in Modern Times* (New York: Oxford University Press, 2001), are convinced that it was an imitation of the sound of goats, "mocking . . . Jews who wore traditional beards" (135).

28. Jacob Katz, "Pera'ot hep-hep shel shenat 1819 be-germaniya 'al rik'an ha-histori," *Zion* 38, nos. 1–4 (1973): 62–115.

29. Hyman, *Emancipation of the Jews of Alsace,* 20–27.

30. Gunther Moltmann, "American-German Return Migration in the Nineteenth and Early Twentieth Centuries," *Central European History* 13, no. 4 (December 1980): 378–92; Frank Trommler and Joseph McVeigh, eds., *America and the Germans: As Assessment of a Three-Hundred-Year History: Immigration, Language, Ethnicity* (Philadelphia: University of Pennsylvania Press, 1985), vol. 1; Mack Walker, *Germany and the Emigration, 1816–1885* (Cambridge, Mass.: Harvard University Press, 1964).

31. Avraham Barkai, *Branching Out: German-Jewish Immigration to the United States, 1820–1914* (New York: Holmes and Meier, 1994).

32. Diner, *Time for Gathering,* 43.

33. Quoted in Lothar Kahn, "Early German-Jewish Writers and the Image of America (1820–1840)," *Leo Baeck Institute Yearbook* 31 (1986): 407–39.

34. Vital, *People Apart,* 298–99.

35. Jack Wertheimer, *Unwelcome Strangers: East European Jews in Imperial Germany* (New York: Oxford University Press, 1987); Marsha Rozenblit, *The Jews of Vienna: Assimilation and Identity* (Albany: State University of New York Press, 1983); Nancy Green, *The Pletzl of Paris: Jewish Immigrant Workers in the Belle Epoque* (New York: Holmes and Meier, 1986); Lloyd Gartner, *The Jewish Immigrant in England, 1870–1914* (Detroit: Wayne State University Press, 1960).

36. Israel Cohen, *Vilna* (Philadelphia: Jewish Publication Society of America, 1943); Steven J. Zipperstein, *The Jews of Odessa: A Cultural History, 1794–1881* (Stanford: Stanford University Press, 1985).

37. Vital, *People Apart,* 289.

38. Edward H. Judge, *Easter in Kishinev: Anatomy of a Pogrom* (New York: New York University Press, 1992).

39. Stephen M. Berk, *Year of Crisis, Year of Hope: Russian Jewry and the Pogroms of 1881–1882* (Westport, Conn.: Greenwood Press, 1985); Michael I. Aronson, *Troubled Waters: The Origins of the 1881 Anti-Jewish Pogroms in Russia* (Pittsburgh: University of Pittsburgh Press, 1990); Robert Weinberg, "Anti-Jewish Violence and Revolution in Late Imperial Russia," in *Riots and Pogroms,* ed. Paul R. Bass (New York: New York University Press, 1996), 56–88.

40. John D. Klier and Shlomo Lambroza, *Pogroms: Anti-Jewish Violence in Modern Russian History* (New York: Cambridge University Press, 1992); Henry Abramson, *A Prayer for the Government: Ukrainians and Jews in Revolutionary Times, 1917–1920* (Cambridge, Mass.: Harvard University Press, 1999).

41. Ezra Mendelsohn, *Class Struggle in the Pale: The Formative Years of the Jewish Workers' Movement in Tsarist Russia* (Cambridge: Cambridge University Press, 1970); Henry J. Tobias, *The Jewish Bund in Russia: From Its Origins to 1905* (Stanford: Stanford University Press, 1972).

42. Emma Lazarus, *Songs of a Semite: The Dance to Death, and Other Poems* (New York: Office of *The American Hebrew*, 1882).

43. Cyrus Adler, ed., *The Voice of America on Kishineff* (Philadelphia: Jewish Publication Society of America, 1904); Gary Dean Best, *To Free a People: American Jewish Leaders and the Jewish Problem in Eastern Europe, 1890–1914* (Westport, Conn.: Greenwood Press, 1982).

44. Naomi W. Cohen, *Not Free to Desist: The American Jewish Committee, 1906–1966* (Philadelphia: Jewish Publication Society of America, 1972). There is to date no scholarly history of the American Jewish Congress.

45. Michael Davitt, *Within the Pale: The True Story of Anti-Semitic Persecutions in Russia* (Philadelphia: Jewish Publication Society of America, 1906).

46. Hasia R. Diner, *In the Almost Promised Land: American Jews and Blacks, 1915–1935* (Baltimore: Johns Hopkins University Press, 1992), 118–28.

47. Ruppin, *Jews in the Modern World*, 114.

48. Zosa Szajkowski, "How the Mass Migration to America Began," *Jewish Social Studies* 4, no. 4 (October 1942): 291–310.

49. Gartner, *Jewish Immigrant in England*; Nancy Green, *Pletzl of Paris*.

50. Robert M. Levine, *Tropical Diaspora: The Jewish Experience in Cuba* (Gainesville: University of Florida Press, 1993); Haim Avni, *Mi-bitul ha-Inkvizitsyah ve-'ad "Hok ha-shvut": Toldot ha-hagirah ha-yehudit le-Argentinah* (Jerusalem: Hebrew University, 1982); Gerald Tulchinsky, *Taking Root: The Origins of the Canadian Jewish Community* (Hanover, N.H.: University Press of New England, 1993).

51. Zipperstein, *Jews of Odessa*.

52. Simon Kuznets, "Immigration of Russian Jews to the United States: Background and Structure," *Perspectives in American History* 9 (1975): 35–124.

53. Ruppin, *Jews in the Modern World*, 68–82.

54. Nancy Green, *Ready-to-Wear and Ready-to-Work: A Century of Industry and Immigrants in Paris and New York* (Durham, N.C.: Duke University Press, 1997).

55. Jonathan Sarna, "The Myth of No Return: Migration to Eastern Europe, 1881–1914," *American Jewish History* 71, no. 2 (December 1981): 169–81.

56. Samuel Joseph, *Jewish Immigration to the United States from 1881 to 1910* (New York: Arno, 1969), 89–120.

57. John Klier, "The Concept of 'Jewish Emancipation' in a Russian Context," in *Civil Rights in Imperial Russia,* ed. Olga Crisp and Linda Edmonson (Oxford: Clarendon Press, 1989), 121–44; Michael Stanislawski, "Russian Jewry, the Russian State, and the Dynamics of Jewish Emancipation," in *Paths*

of Emancipation: Jews, States, and Citizenship, ed. Pierre Birnbaum and Ira Katznelson (Princeton: Princeton University Press, 1995), 262–83.

58. Carol B. Bailin, *To Reveal Our Hearts: Jewish Women Writers in Tsarist Russia* (Cincinnati: Hebrew Union College Press, 2000).

59. John D. Klier, *Russia Gathers Her Jews: The Origins of the "Jewish Question" in Russia, 1772–1825* (Dekalb: Northern Illinois University Press, 1986); John D. Klier, *Imperial Russia's Jewish Question, 1855–1881* (New York: Cambridge University Press, 1995).

60. Salo W. Baron, *The Russian Jew under Tsars and Soviets* (New York: Macmillan, 1964), 50.

61. Celia Heller, *On the Edge of Destruction: Jews of Poland between the Two World Wars* (New York: Columbia University Press, 1977); Wischnitzer, *To Dwell in Safety,* 141–70.

62. The term comes from Nancy Green, ed., *Jewish Workers in the Modern Diaspora* (Berkeley and Los Angeles: University of California Press, 1998), 2.

63. Joshua Trachtenberg, *Consider the Years: The Story of the Jewish Community of Easton, 1752–1942* (Easton, Penn.: Centennial Committee of Temple Brith Shalom, 1944), 113; Jonathan Mesinger, "The Jewish Community in Syracuse, 1850–1880: The Growth and Structure of an Urban Ethnic Region" (Ph. D. diss., Syracuse University, 1977), 99–100; Diner, *Time for Gathering,* 68.

64. Rudolph Glanz, "Where the Jewish Press Was Distributed in Pre–Civil War America," *Western States Jewish Historical Quarterly* 5, no. 1 (1972): 1–14.

65. Judah David Eisenstein, "The History of the First Russian-American Jewish Congregation," *Publications of the American Jewish Historical Society* 9 (1901): 68; Samuel P. Abelow, *History of Brooklyn Jewry* (Brooklyn, N.Y.: Sheba Publishing, 1937), 11.

66. Bernard Weinstein, *Di Idishe yunyons in Amerika: bleter geshikhte un Erinnerungen* (New York: Fareinigten Yiddishe Geverkshaftn, 1929), 79, 82.

67. Quoted in Diner, *Time for Gathering,* 74.

68. Harriet and Fred Rochlin, *Pioneer Jews: A New Life in the Far West* (Boston: Houghton Mifflin, 1984).

69. Ewa Morawska, *Insecure Prosperity: Small-Town Jews in Industrial America, 1890–1940* (Princeton: Princeton University Press, 1996).

70. Lee Shai Weissbach, "The Jewish Communities of the United States on the Eve of Mass Migration," *American Jewish History* 78, no. 1 (September 1988): 79–108.

71. Hasia R. Diner, *Lower East Side Memories: The Jewish Place in America* (Princeton: Princeton University Press, 2000); Stanley Nadell, *Little Germany: Ethnicity, Religion, and Class in New York City, 1843–1880* (Urbana: University of Illinois Press, 1990).

72. Deborah Dash Moore, *B'nai B'rith and the Challenge of Ethnic Leadership* (Albany: State University of New York Press, 1981).

73. The same process was going on in Chicago in and around the Maxwell Street Market; see Louis Wirth, *The Ghetto* (Chicago: University of Chicago Press, 1929).

74. Sam Bass Warner, *Streetcar Suburbs: The Process of Growth in Boston, 1870–1900* (Cambridge, Mass.: Harvard University Press, 1978).

75. Quoted in Green, ed., *Jewish Workers*, 16-17.

76. Alter F. Landesman, *Brownsville: The Birth, Development, and Passing of a Jewish Community in New York* (New York: Bloch, 1969); Jeffrey Gurock, *When Harlem Was Jewish, 1870-1930* (New York: Columbia University Press, 1979).

77. Quoted in Green, *Ready-to-Wear*, 33.

78. Lynn Weiner, *From Working Girl to Working Mother: The Female Labor Force in the United States, 1820-1980* (Chapel Hill: University of North Carolina Press, 1985).

79. Thomas Kessner, "Jobs, Ghettoes, and the Urban Economy, 1880-1935," *American Jewish History* 71, no. 2 (December 1981): 224.

80. Sorin, *Time for Building*, 74.

81. On the preference of Jewish women for the big, modern factories, which paid better and where they felt less vulnerable to sexual harassment, see Susan Glenn, *Daughters of the Shtetl: Life and Labor in the Immigrant Generation* (Ithaca, N.Y.: Cornell University Press, 1990).

82. This pattern played itself out in the Jewish baking industry, for example, and in butchering, which saw some of the most explosive strikes in the Jewish immigrant communities. See Hasia R. Diner, *Hungering for America: Italian, Irish, and Jewish Foodways in the Age of Immigration* (Cambridge, Mass.: Harvard University Press, 2001).

CHAPTER 4. A CENTURY OF JEWISH LIFE IN AMERICA

1. Quoted in Hasia R. Diner, *A Time for Gathering: The Second Migration, 1820-1880,* Jewish People in America 2 (Baltimore: Johns Hopkins University Press, 1992), 207.

2. Mordecai Soltes, "The Yiddish Press: An Americanizing Agency," *American Jewish Yearbook* 26 (1924-25): 165-372.

3. David Max Eichhorn, *Evangelizing the American Jew* (Middle Village, N.Y.: Jonathan David, 1978).

4. Morton Borden, *Jews, Turks, and Infidels* (Chapel Hill: University of North Carolina Press, 1984).

5. Eleanor Flexner, *Century of Struggle* (Cambridge, Mass.: Belknap Press of Harvard University Press, 1959); Nancy F. Cott, *The Grounding of Modern Feminism* (New Haven: Yale University Press, 1987).

6. Quoted in Barbara Miller Solomon, *Ancestors and Immigrants: A Changing New England Tradition* (New York: John Wiley and Sons, 1956), 103.

7. The phrase comes from the formative study by John Higham, *Strangers in the Land: Patterns of American Nativism, 1860-1925* (New Brunswick, N.J.: Rutgers University Press, 1955), 264.

8. No scholar has yet written a history of Jewish conversion to Christianity in America. Hints in the literature, however, indicate that it did not compare to the rate or scope of conversion in Europe.

9. The phrase "resisters and accommodators" was coined by Jeffrey S. Gurock, "Resisters and Accommodators: Varieties of Orthodox Rabbis in Amer-

ica, 1886–1983," *American Jewish Archives* 35, no. 2 (November 1983): 120–30.

10. I. Harold Sharfman, *The First Rabbi: Origins of Conflict between Orthodox and Reform: Jewish Polemic Warfare in Pre–Civil War America: A Biographical History* (Malibu, Calif.: Pangloss Press, 1988).

11. Lance Sussman, *Isaac Leeser and the Making of American Judaism* (Detroit: Wayne State University Press, 1995).

12. Hyman Grinstein, *The Rise of the Jewish Community of New York, 1654–1860* (Philadelphia: Jewish Publication Society of America, 1947), 225–59.

13. Sussman, *Isaac Leeser.*

14. Michael Meyer, *Response to Modernity: A History of Reform Judaism* (New York: Oxford University Press, 1988), 225–95.

15. Alan Silverstein, *Alternatives to Assimilation: The Response of Reform Judaism to American Culture, 1840–1930* (Hanover, N.H.: University Press of New England, 1994); Isaac Fein, *The Making of an American Jewish Community: The History of Baltimore Jewry, 1773–1920* (Philadelphia: Jewish Publication Society of America, 1971), 56–57, 98.

16. Peter N. Williams, *Popular Religion in America: Symbolic Change and the Modernization Process in Historical Perspective* (Urbana: University of Illinois Press, 1989).

17. Moshe Davis, *The Emergence of Conservative Judaism* (Philadelphia: Jewish Publication Society of America, 1963), 53–59.

18. Stanley Rabinowitz, *The Assembly: A Century in the Life of the Adas Israel Hebrew Congregation of Washington, D.C.* (Hoboken, N.J.: KTAV, 1993).

19. Davis, *Emergence of Conservative Judaism.*

20. Walter Jacob, ed., *The Changing World of Reform Judaism: The Pittsburgh Platform in Retrospect* (Pittsburgh: Rodef Shalom Congregation, 1985).

21. Hasia R. Diner, " 'Like the Antelope and the Badger': The Founding and Early Years of the Jewish Theological Seminary, 1886–1902," in *Tradition Renewed: A History of the Jewish Theological Seminary of America,* ed. Jack Wertheimer (New York: Jewish Theological Seminary, 1997), 1: 1–42.

22. Abraham J. Karp, "New York Chooses a Chief Rabbi," *Publications of the American Jewish Historical Society* 44, no. 3 (March 1954): 129–98.

23. Mordecai Kaplan, "The Future of Judaism," *Menorah Journal* 2, no. 3 (June 1916): 160–72; Kaplan, "How May Judaism Be Saved?" *Menorah Journal* 2, no. 1 (February 1916): 34–44; Kaplan, "A Program for the Reconstruction of Judaism," *Menorah Journal* 6, no. 4 (August 1920): 181–96.

24. Robert Liberles, "Conflict over Reforms: The Case of Congregation Beth Elohim, Charleston, South Carolina," in *The American Synagogue: A Sanctuary Transformed,* ed. Jack Wertheimer (Hanover, N.H.: University Press of New England, 1987), 274–96.

25. Barnett Elzas, *The Jews of South Carolina from the Earliest Times to the Present Day* (Philadelphia: Jewish Publication Society of America, 1905); Charles Reznikoff and Uriah Z. Engelman, *The Jews of Charleston* (Philadelphia: Jewish Publication Society of America, 1950).

26. Quoted in Diner, *Time for Gathering,* 122.

27. Isaac Fein, *Making of an American;* Earl Pruce, *Synagogues, Temples, and Congregations of Maryland, Past and Present, 1830–1990* (Baltimore: Jewish Historical Society of Maryland, 1990).

28. Moses Rischin, *The Promised City: New York's Jews, 1870–1914* (Cambridge, Mass.: Harvard University Press, 1962), 146–47.

29. Karla Goldman, *Beyond the Synagogue Gallery: Finding a Place for Women in American Judaism* (Cambridge, Mass.: Harvard University Press, 2000).

30. Hutchins Hapgood, *Spirit of the Ghetto: Studies of the Jewish Quarter in New York* (New York: Funk and Wagnalls, 1902), 125–26; Andrew Heinze, *Adapting to Abundance: Jewish Immigrants, Mass Consumption, and the Search for American Identity* (New York: Columbia University Press, 1990).

31. Yaakov Ariel, *Evangelizing the Chosen People: Missions to the Jews in America, 1880–1920* (Chapel Hill: University of North Carolina Press, 2001).

32. See Hyman Grinstein, *The Rise of the Jewish Community of New York, 1654–1860* (Philadelphia: Jewish Publication Society of America, 1947), 404–5.

33. Grinstein, *Rise of the Jewish Community,* 145–47.

34. Quoted in Diner, *Time for Gathering,* 102.

35. Reena Friedman Sigmund, *These Are Our Children: Jewish Orphanages in the United States, 1880–1925* (Hanover, N.H.: University Press of New England, 1994).

36. Hasia R. Diner, *Hungering for America: Italian, Irish, and Jewish Foodways in the Age of Migration* (Cambridge, Mass.: Harvard University Press, 2001).

37. Rischin, *Promised City,* 101–3.

38. Adam Bellow and Bill Keens, *The Educational Alliance: A Centennial Celebration* (New York: Educational Alliance, 1990).

39. Quoted in Diner, *Time for Gathering,* 103.

40. Diner, *Time for Gathering,* 96–97.

41. Shelly Tenenbaum, *A Credit to Their Community: Jewish Loan Societies in the United States, 1880–1945* (Detroit: Wayne State University Press, 1993).

42. Daniel Soyer, *Jewish Immigrant Associations and American Identity in New York, 1880–1939* (Cambridge, Mass.: Harvard University Press, 1997).

43. Susan Ebert, "Community and Philanthropy," in *The Jews of Boston: Essays on the Occasion of the Centenary (1895–1995) of the Combined Jewish Philanthropies of Greater Boston,* ed. Jonathan Sarna and Ellen Smith (Boston: The Philanthropies, 1995), 224–25.

44. May Weisser Hartman, *I Gave My Heart* (New York: Citadel, 1960), 28–29.

45. Deborah Dash Moore, *The B'nai B'rith and the Challenge of Ethnic Leadership* (Albany: State University of New York Press, 1981).

46. Diner, *Time for Gathering,* 201–2.

47. On the Young Men's Hebrew Associations see Benjamin Rabinowitz, "The Young Men's Hebrew Associations (1854–1913)," *Publications of the American Jewish Historical Society* 37 (1947): 221–326.

48. Ruth Miller Elson, *Guardians of Tradition: American Schoolbooks of the Nineteenth Century* (Lincoln: University of Nebraska Press, 1964).

49. Diane Ashton, *Rebecca Gratz: Women and Judaism in Antebellum America* (Detroit: Wayne State University Press, 1997).

50. Linda Kerber, *Women of the Republic: Intellect and Ideology in Revolutionary America* (Chapel Hill: University of North Carolina Press, 1980).

51. Polly W. Kaufman, *Women as Teachers on the Frontier* (New Haven: Yale University Press, 1994).

52. Simon Litman, *Ray Frank Litman: A Memoir* (New York: American Jewish Historical Society, 1957).

53. Stephan F. Brumberg, *Going to America, Going to School: The Jewish Immigrant Public School Encounter in Turn-of-the-Century New York City* (New York: Praeger, 1986).

54. Selma C. Berrol, *Julia Richman: A Notable Woman* (Philadelphia: Balch Institute Press, 1993), 72.

55. Abram Simon, "The Jewish Child and the American Public School," *Religious Education* 6 (1911–1912): 527–28.

56. Quoted in Nathan H. Winter, *Jewish Education in a Pluralist Society: Samson Benderly and Jewish Education in the United States* (New York: New York University Press, 1966), 48.

57. Jeremiah H. Berman, "Jewish Education in New York City, 1860–1900," *YIVO Annual of the Jewish Social Science* 9 (1954): 247–45; Jeffrey S. Gurock, *The Men and Women of Yeshiva: Higher Education, Orthodoxy, and American Judaism* (New York: Columbia University Press, 1988), 12–13; Gilbert Klaperman, *The Story of Yeshiva University, the First Jewish University in America* (New York: Macmillan, 1969).

58. Confirmation also developed as a religious rite of passage in Germany, starting in the early nineteenth century; see Michael A. Meyer, *Response to Modernity: A History of the Reform Movement in Judaism* (New York: Oxford University Press, 1988), 46.

59. Jenna Weissman Joselit, *Aspiring Women: A History of the Jewish Foundation for Education of Women* (New York: Jewish Foundation for Education of Women, 1996).

60. Shmuel Niger, *The Struggle for a New Education* (New York: Education Department of the Workmen's Circle, 1940).

61. Ezra Mendelsohn, *On Modern Jewish Politics* (New York: Oxford University Press, 1993).

62. C. Bezalel Sherman, *Labor Zionism in America: Its History, Growth, and Programs* (New York: Farband-Labor Zionist Order, 1957); Mark Raider, *The Emergence of American Zionism* (New York: New York University Press, 1998).

63. Robert Wiebe, *The Search for Order, 1877–1920* (New York: Hill and Wang, 1967).

64. Quoted in Winter, *Jewish Education*, 199–200.

65. Isaac B. Berkson, *Theories of Americanization* (New York: Teachers College, Columbia University Press, 1920); Alexander M. Dushkin, *Jewish Education in New York City* (New York: Columbia University Press, 1918); Winter, *Jewish Education*.

66. Nahma Sandrow, *Vagabond Stars: A World History of Yiddish Theater* (New York: Harper & Row, 1977).

CHAPTER 5. A CENTURY OF JEWISH POLITICS

1. *Occident and American Jewish Advocate* 12 (February 1855): 561.

2. Bertram Wallace Korn, *American Jewry and the Civil War* (Philadelphia: Jewish Publication Society of America, 1951).

3. Richard Hofstadter, *The Idea of a Party System: The Rise of Legitimate Opposition in the United States, 1780–1840* (Berkeley and Los Angeles: University of California Press, 1969); Lawrence Fuchs, *The Political Behavior of American Jews* (Glencoe, Ill.: Free Press, 1956).

4. Theodore Lowi, *A Republic of Parties? Debating the Two-Party System* (Lanham, Md.: Rowman and Littlefield, 1998).

5. Quoted in Hasia R. Diner, *A Time for Gathering: The Second Migration, 1820–1880,* Jewish People in America 2 (Baltimore: Johns Hopkins University Press, 1992), 151–52.

6. Steven Lowenstein, *The Jews of Oregon, 1850–1950* (Portland: Jewish Historical Society of Oregon, 1987), 66–67.

7. William F. Holmes, "Whitecapping: Anti-Semitism in the Populist Era," *American Jewish Historical Quarterly* 63, no. 3 (March 1974): 244–61; C. Vann Woodward, *Tom Watson, Agrarian Rebel* (New York: Macmillan, 1938).

8. "Secretary Hay's Note and the Jewish Question," *Harper's Weekly,* October 11, 1902, 1447.

9. Cyrus Adler, *The Voice of America on Kishineff* (Philadelphia: Jewish Publication Society of America, 1904).

10. Naomi Cohen, *A Dual Heritage: The Public Career of Oscar S. Straus* (Philadelphia: Jewish Publication Society of America, 1969).

11. Robert Burt, *Two Jewish Justices: Outcasts in the Promised Land* (Berkeley and Los Angeles: University of California Press, 1988); Philippa Strum, *Louis D. Brandeis: Justice for the People* (Cambridge, Mass.: Harvard University Press, 1984).

12. Diner, *Time for Gathering,* 144.

13. Samuel Koenig, *An American Jewish Community: Fifty Years, 1889–1939* (Stamford: Works Projects Administration, Federal Writers Project for the State of Connecticut, 1940), 145.

14. H. L. Meites, *History of the Jews of Chicago* (Chicago: Jewish Historical Society of Illinois, 1924), 45.

15. Gerald Sorin, *The Prophetic Minority: American Jewish Immigrant Radicals, 1880–1920* (Bloomington: Indiana University Press, 1985).

16. Sorin, *Prophetic Minority.*

17. The most significant statement about Jewish politics as related to culture and the way a group sees itself is by Ezra Mendelsohn, *On Modern Jewish Politics* (New York: Oxford University Press, 1993).

18. Stephen V. Ash, "Civil War Exodus: The Jews and Grant's General Order No. 11," *The Historian* 44, no. 4 (1982): 505–23.

19. Quoted in Joakim Isaacs, "Candidate Grant and the Jews," *American Jewish Archives* 17, no. 1 (September 1965): 12–13.

20. Quoted in Diner, *Time for Gathering*, 159.

21. Naomi Cohen, *Jews in Christian America: The Pursuit of Religious Equality* (New York: Oxford University Press, 1992), 65–92.

22. Lloyd P. Gartner, "Roumania, America, and World Jewry: Consul Peixotto in Bucharest, 1870–1876," *American Jewish Historical Quarterly* 58, no. 1 (September 1968): 52.

23. Cohen, in *Jews in Christian America*, 93–94, mentions a 1929 lower court ruling in Georgia that disqualified Jews from jury service.

24. Scholars like Karen Brodkin, *How the Jews Became White Folks and What That Says about Race in America* (New Brunswick, N.J.: Rutgers University Press, 1998), and Matthew Frye Jacobson, *Whiteness of a Different Color: European Immigrants and the Alchemy of Race* (Cambridge, Mass.: Harvard University Press, 1998), have worked on the assumption that Jews had to construct a white identity for themselves in America, a fact that I am here contesting.

25. Abraham Simon, *A History of the Washington Hebrew Congregation: In Commemoration of Its Jubilee* (Washington, D.C.: Lippman Printing, 1905).

26. Diner, *Time for Gathering*, 148.

27. Cited in Louis Barish, "The American Jewish Chaplaincy," *American Jewish Historical Quarterly* 52, no. 1 (September 1962): 9–11.

28. Jonathan D. Sarna and David G. Dalin, *Religion and State in the American Jewish Experience* (Notre Dame, Ind.: Notre Dame University Press, 1997), 183.

29. Leonard Bloom, "A Successful Jewish Boycott of the New York City Public Schools," *American Jewish History* 70, no. 2 (December 1980): 180–85.

30. Cohen, *Jews in Christian America*, 112–15.

31. On the origins of the term *anti-Semitism*, with its racialized underpinnings, see Moshe Zimmerman, *Wilhelm Marr: The Patriarch of Antisemitism* (New York: Oxford University Press, 1986).

32. Leonard Dinnerstein, *Antisemitism in America* (New York: Oxford University Press, 1994), 61–63.

33. E. A. Ross, *The Old World in the New: The Significance of Past and Present Immigration to the American People* (New York: Century, 1914).

34. Walter T. K. Nugent, *The Tolerant Populists: Kansas, Populism, and Nativism* (Chicago: University of Chicago Press, 1963), sought to prove in this important work that Populism was actually much more complicated. Some Populists, he showed, were indeed notable for their religious and ethnic tolerance.

35. Quoted in Dinnerstein, *Antisemitism*, 179.

36. Leonard Dinnerstein, *The Leo Frank Case* (New York: Columbia University Press, 1968); Albert S. Lindemann, *The Jew Accused: Three Anti-Semitic Affairs (Dreyfus, Beilis, Frank), 1894–1915* (Cambridge: Cambridge University Press, 1991). The Reconstruction-era Klan had ceased operation when the U.S. Army left. The Klan no longer needed to intimidate black citizens since the legal system did that.

37. George Kibbe Turner, "The Daughters of the Poor," *McClures* 34 (November 1909): 45–61.

38. Quoted in Arthur Goren, *New York Jews and the Quest for Community: The Kehillah Experiment, 1908–1922* (New York: Columbia University Press, 1970), 25.

39. Eric Goldstein, "Race and the Construction of Jewish Identity in America, 1875–1945" (Ph.D. diss., University of Michigan, 2000).

40. Quoted in Diner, *Time for Gathering*, 228.

41. Jeffrey S. Gurock, "From *Publications* to *American Jewish History:* The *Journal of the American Jewish Historical Society* and the Writing of American Jewish History," *American Jewish History* 81, no. 2 (Winter 1993–1994): 155–270; quote in Nathan M. Kaganoff, "AJHS at 90: Reflections on the History of the Oldest Ethnic Historical Society in America," *American Jewish History* 71 (June 1982): 466–85.

42. Barbara Miller Solomon, *Ancestors and Immigrants: A Changing New England Tradition* (New York: Wiley, 1956), 105.

43. Quoted in Abraham J. Karp, *Haven and Home: A History of the Jews in America* (New York: Schocken, 1985), 44.

44. Jonathan Frankel, *The Damascus Affair: "Ritual Murder," Politics, and the Jews in 1840* (Cambridge: Cambridge University Press, 1997).

45. Bertram Wallace Korn, *The American Reaction to the Mortara Case, 1858–1859* (Cincinnati: American Jewish Archives, 1957).

46. Cohen, *Jews in Christian America,* 255.

47. Allen Tarshish, "The Board of Delegates of American Israelites (1859–1878)," *Publications of the American Jewish Historical Society* 49, no. 1 (September 1959): 16–32.

48. Gerald Sorin, *A Time for Building: The Third Migration, 1880–1920,* Jewish People in America 3 (Baltimore: Johns Hopkins University Press, 1992), 202.

49. Cyrus Adler, *The Voice of America on Kishineff* (Philadelphia: Jewish Publication Society of America, 1904); Taylor Stults, "Roosevelt, Russian Persecution of Jews, and American Public Opinion," *Jewish Social Studies* 30, no. 1 (January 1971): 13–22; Philip E. Schoenberg, "The American Jewish Reaction to the Kishinev Pogrom of 1903," *American Jewish Historical Quarterly* 63, no. 3 (March 1974): 262–83; Naomi W. Cohen, *Jacob H. Schiff: A Study in American Jewish Leadership* (Hanover, N.H.: University Press of New England, 1999).

50. Quoted in Gary Dean Best, *To Free a People: American Jewish Leaders and the Jewish Problem in Eastern Europe, 1890–1914* (Westport, Conn.: Greenwood Press, 1982), 91.

51. Sidney Lewis Gulick, *The White Peril in the Far East: An Interpretation of the Significance of the Russo-Japanese War* (New York: F. H. Revell, 1905).

52. Cyrus Adler and Aaron M. Margalith, *With Firmness in the Right: American Diplomatic Action Affecting Jews, 1840–1945* (New York: American Jewish Committee, 1946).

53. Charles Reznikoff, ed., *Louis Marshall, Champion of Liberty: Selected Papers and Addresses* (Philadelphia: Jewish Publication Society of America, 1957).

54. Salo Baron, *The Russian Jew under Tsars and Soviets,* 2nd ed. (New York: Macmillan, 1976), 158–62.

55. David Vital, *A People Apart: The Jews in Europe, 1789–1939* (New York: Oxford University Press, 2000), 654.

56. Daniel Soyer, *Jewish Immigrant Associations and American Identity in New York, 1880–1939* (Cambridge, Mass.: Harvard University Press, 1997), 172.

57. *American Jewish Yearbook* 41 (1939–40): 141–79.

58. Salo Baron, "Palestinian Messengers in America, 1849–1879: A Record of Four Journeys," in *Steeled by Adversity: Essays and Addresses on American Jewish Life* (Philadelphia: Jewish Publication Society of America, 1971), 158–266.

59. *American Jewish Yearbook* 16 (1916): 360.

60. Quoted in Karp, *Haven and Home,* 173–74.

61. Sheldon M. Neuringer, "American Jewry and United States Immigration Policy, 1881–1953" (Ph.D. dissertation, University of Wisconsin, 1969), 20–25.

62. Simon Wolf, *The Jew as Patriot, Soldier, and Citizen* (New York: Brentano's, 1895).

63. Robert Hunter, *Poverty* (New York: Macmillan, 1905), 279.

64. Schiff, *A Study in American Jewish Leadership,* 34.

65. Best, *To Free a People.*

66. Jack Wertheimer, *Unwelcome Stranger: East European Jews in Imperial Germany* (New York: Oxford, 1987); Nancy Green, *The Pletzl of Paris: Jewish Immigrant Workers in the Belle Epoque* (New York: Holmes and Meier, 1986); William Fishman, *Jewish Radicals: From Czarist Shtetl to London Ghetto* (New York: Pantheon, 1974).

67. The Simon Wolf quote can be found in Abraham Karp, *Haven and Home,* 173; see also Esther Panitz, "In Defense of the Jewish Immigrant," *American Jewish Historical Quarterly* 55, no. 1 (September 1965): 57–97.

68. Lance Sussman, *Isaac Leeser and the Making of American Judaism* (Detroit: Wayne State University Press, 1995).

69. Gary Michael Brown, "All, All Alone: The Hebrew Press in America from 1914 to 1924," *American Jewish Historical Quarterly* 59, no. 2 (December 1969/70): 139–63; Alan Mintz, ed., *Hebrew in America: Perspectives and Prospects* (Detroit: Wayne State University Press, 1993).

70. Victor Greene, *American Immigrant Leaders, 1800–1910: Marginality and Identity* (Baltimore: Johns Hopkins University Press, 1987), 83–104.

71. To date no one has treated the *Forverts* and its impact on the eastern European immigrant Jewish community more extensively than Irving Howe, *World of Our Fathers* (New York: Harcourt Brace Jovanovich, 1976).

72. Alan Tarshish, "The Board of Delegates of American Israelites (1859–1878)," *Publications of the American Jewish Historical Society* 49, no. 1 (September 1959): 16–33.

73. Deborah Dash Moore, *B'nai B'rith and the Challenge of Ethnic Leadership* (Albany: State University of New York Press, 1981); Robert Rockaway, *Words of the Uprooted: Jewish Immigrants in Early Twentieth-Century America* (Ithaca, N.Y.: Cornell University Press, 1998); Jack Glazier, *Dispersing the Ghetto: The Relocation of Jewish Immigrants* (Ithaca, N.Y.: Cornell University Press, 1998).

74. On the Anti-Defamation League, see Cohen, *Jews in Christian America,* 99.

75. There is to date no scholarly history of the Anti-Defamation League. See, however, Dinnerstein, *Antisemitism,* 74.

76. Faith Rogoff, *Gone to Another Meeting: The National Council of Jewish Women, 1893–1993* (Tuscaloosa: University of Alabama Press, 1993).

77. Edward Bristow, *Prostitution and Prejudice: The Jewish Fight against White Slavery, 1870–1939* (New York: Schocken, 1983).

78. Lowenstein, *Jews of Oregon,* 169.

79. Goren, *New York Jews,* 26.

80. Naomi Cohen, *Not Free to Desist: The American Jewish Committee, 1906–1966* (Philadelphia: Jewish Publication Society of America, 1972).

81. Zosa Szajkowski, "Private and Organized American Jewish Overseas Relief (1914–1938)," *American Jewish Historical Quarterly* 62, no. 1 (September 1967): 52–106.

82. Oscar Handlin, *A Continuing Task: The American Jewish Joint Distribution Committee, 1914–1964* (New York: Random House, 1964).

83. Merle Curti, *American Philanthropy Abroad* (New Brunswick, N.J.: Rutgers University Press, 1963).

84. See Martin Sicker, *Reshaping the Palestine: From Muhammad Ali to the British Mandate, 1831–1922* (Westport, Conn.: Praeger, 1999), 113–39.

85. Melvin Urofsky, *American Zionism from Herzl to the Holocaust* (Garden City, N.Y.: Doubleday, 1975).

86. Joseph Fulford Folsom, ed., *The Municipalities of Essex County, New Jersey, 1666–1924,* vol. 3 (New York: Lewis Historical Publishing Company, 1925), 106–7.

87. Quoted in "Hadassah," in *Jewish Women in America: An Historical Encyclopedia,* ed. Paula Hyman and Deborah Dash Moore (New York: Routledge, 1997), 1: 571.

88. Allon Gal, "Hadassah and the American Jewish Political Tradition," in *An Inventory of Promises: Essays on American Jewish History in Honor of Moses Rischin,* ed. Jeffrey S. Gurock and Marc Lee Raphael (Brooklyn, N.Y.: Carlson, 1995), 89–114.

CHAPTER 6. AT HOME AND BEYOND

1. *American Jewish Yearbook* 47 (1945–46).

2. Stuart Svonkin, *Jews against Prejudice: American Jews and the Fight for Civil Liberties* (New York: Columbia University Press, 1997), 89.

3. *American Jewish Yearbook* 50 (1948–49): 115.

4. Stephen J. Gould, *The Mismeasure of Man* (New York: Norton, 1981).

5. Leo Ribuffo, *The Old Christian Right: The Protestant Far Right from the Great Depression to the Cold War* (Philadelphia: Temple University Press, 1983).

6. On Artie Shaw and his involvement with black music, see Jeffrey Melnick,

A Right to Sing the Blues: African Americans, Jews, and American Popular Song (Cambridge, Mass.: Harvard University Press, 1999), 50, 95, 134–37.

7. James Lincoln Collier, *Benny Goodman and the Swing Era* (New York: Oxford University Press, 1989).

8. Neal Gabler, *An Empire of Their Own: How the Jews Invented Hollywood* (New York: Crown, 1988); Kenneth Kanter, *The Jews on Tin Pan Alley: The Jewish Contribution to American Popular Music, 1830–1940* (New York: KTAV, 1982); Ann Douglas, *Terrible Honesty: Mongrel Manhattan in the 1920s* (New York: Farrar, Straus, and Giroux, 1995).

9. David M. Chalmers, *Hooded Americanism: The First Century of the Ku Klux Klan, 1865–1965* (Garden City, N.Y.: Doubleday, 1965).

10. David Levering Lewis, "Henry Ford's Anti-Semitism and Its Repercussions," *Michigan History* 24 (1984): 3–10; Leo P. Ribuffo, "Henry Ford and the International Jew," *American Jewish History* 69 (June 1980): 437–77. See also Neil Baldwin, *Henry Ford and the Jews: The Mass Production of Hate* (New York: Public Affairs, 2001).

11. Marcia Graham Synnott, *The Half-Opened Door: Discrimination and Admissions at Harvard, Yale, and Princeton, 1900–1970* (Westport, Conn.: Greenwood Press, 1979); Harold Wechsler, *The Qualified Student: A History of Selective College Admission in America* (New York: John Wiley, 1977); quoted in Hasia R. Diner and Beryl Lieff Benderly, *Her Works Praise Her: A History of Jewish Women in America from Colonial Times to the Present* (New York: Basic Books, 2002), 282.

12. Quoted in Ann Douglas, "Siblings and Mongrels," *CommonQuest* 2, no. 1 (Summer 1997): 12; emphasis added.

13. Leonard Dinnerstein, *Antisemitism in America* (New York: Oxford University Press, 1994), 88–93.

14. Quoted in Dinnerstein, *Antisemitism*, 110.

15. Dominic Pacyga, *Polish Immigrants and Industrial Chicago: Workers on the South Side, 1880–1922* (Columbus: Ohio State University Press, 1991), 115–224.

16. Cheryl L. Greenberg, *"Or Does It Explode?": Black Harlem in the Great Depression* (New York: Oxford University Press, 1991).

17. Alan Brinkley, *Voices of Protest: Huey Long, Father Coughlin, and the Great Depression* (New York: Knopf, 1982).

18. Dinnerstein, *Antisemitism*, 147, 151.

19. Anti-Defamation League of B'nai B'rith, *Anti-Semitism in the United States in 1947* (New York: Anti-Defamation League, 1947), 5.

20. Jerold S. Auerbach, *Rabbis and Lawyers: The Journey from Torah to Constitution* (Bloomington: Indiana University Press, 1990), 159.

21. George Wolfskill and John A. Hudson, *All but the People: Franklin D. Roosevelt and His Critics, 1933–1939* (New York: Macmillan, 1969), 87.

22. Edward Renehan, *The Kennedys at War, 1937–1945* (New York: Doubleday, 2002).

23. Sander Diamond, *The Nazi Movement in the United States, 1924–1941* (Ithaca, N.Y.: Cornell University Press, 1974); Ronald Bayor, *Neighbors in Conflict: The Irish, Germans, Jews, and Italians of New York City, 1920–1941*, 2nd

ed. (Urbana: University of Illinois Press, 1988); Susan Canedy, *America's Nazis, a Democratic Dilemma: A History of the German-American Bund* (Menlo Park, Calif.: Markgraf Publications, 1990).

24. Emanuel Celler, *You Never Leave Brooklyn: The Autobiography of Emanuel Celler* (New York: Day, 1953), 81.

25. Hasia R. Diner, *In the Almost Promised Land: American Jews and Blacks, 1915–1935,* 2nd ed. (Baltimore: Johns Hopkins University Press, 1995).

26. Charles Reznikoff, ed., *Louis Marshall, Champion of Liberty: Selected Papers and Addresses* (Philadelphia: Jewish Publication Society of America, 1957), 1: 392.

27. Deborah Lipstadt, *Beyond Belief: The American Press and the Coming of the Holocaust* (New York: Free Press, 1986); Ruth Gruber, *Haven: The Unknown Story of 1,000 World War II Refugees* (New York: Coward, McCann, and Geoghegan, 1983).

28. Barbara M. Stewart, *United States Government Policy on Refugees from Nazism, 1933–1940* (New York: Garland, 1984).

29. Robert Weinberg, *Stalin's Forgotten Zion: Birobidzhan and the Making of the Soviet Jewish Homeland* (Berkeley and Los Angeles: University of California Press, 1998).

30. *American Jewish Yearbook* 47 (1945–46): 293.

31. Efraim Zuroff, *The Response of Orthodox Jewry in the United States to the Holocaust: The Activities of the Vaad ha-Hatzala Rescue Committee, 1939–1945* (New York: Michael Scharf Publication Trust of the Yeshiva University Press, 2002).

32. David S. Wyman, *The Abandonment of the Jews: America and the Holocaust, 1941–1945* (New York: Pantheon, 1984), 25–26.

33. Monty Penkower, "In Dramatic Dissent: The Bergson Boys," *American Jewish History* 70 (March 1981): 281–309; Rafael Medoff, "Shooting for a Jewish State: College Basketball Players and the 1947 U.S. Fundraising Campaign for the Jewish Revolt against the British," *American Jewish History* 89, no. 1 (September 2001): 284–85.

34. Mark A. Raider, Jonathan D. Sarna, and Ronald W. Zweig, "Abba Hillel Silver and American Zionism," *Journal of Israeli History* 17, no. 1 (Spring 1966).

35. *American Jewish Yearbook* 40 (1938–39): 189.

36. *American Jewish Yearbook* 41 (1939–40): 261–68.

37. Edward S. Shapiro, *A Time for Healing: American Jewry since World War II,* Jewish People in America 5 (Baltimore: Johns Hopkins University Press, 1992), 62–63.

38. *American Jewish Yearbook* 47 (1945–46): 304–5.

39. Gruber, *Haven.*

40. Henry Feingold, *The Politics of Rescue: The Roosevelt Administration and the Holocaust, 1938–1945* (New Brunswick, N.J.: Rutgers University Press, 1970).

41. Henry Feingold, *Bearing Witness: How America and Its Jews Responded to the Holocaust* (Syracuse: Syracuse University Press, 1995).

42. David S. Wyman, *Paper Walls: America and the Refugee Crisis, 1938–1941* (Amherst: University of Massachusetts Press, 1968).

43. The most analytically sophisticated and historically valid statement of this can be found in Gulie Ne'eman Arad, *America, Its Jews, and the Rise of the Nazis* (Bloomington: Indiana University Press, 2000).

44. *American Jewish Yearbook* 40 (1938–39): 87.

45. Feingold, *Politics of Rescue;* Feingold, *Bearing Witness.*

46. Abba Hillel Silver, *The World Crisis and Jewish Survival: A Group of Essays* (New York: R. R. Smith, 1941), 46.

47. Diner and Benderly, *Her Works Praise Her,* 271–75.

48. Allon Gal, ed., *Envisioning Israel: The Changing Ideals and Images of North American Jews* (Detroit: Wayne State University Press, 1996); Thomas A. Kolsky, *Jews against Zionism: The American Council for Judaism* (Philadelphia: Temple University Press, 1983).

49. Yaakov Ariel, *Evangelizing the Chosen People: Missions to the Jews of America, 1880–2000* (Chapel Hill: University of North Carolina Press, 2000).

50. Quoted in Seymour Lainoff, "Trilling, Lionel," in *Jewish-American History and Culture: An Encyclopedia,* ed. Jack Fischel and Sanford Pinsker (New York: Garland, 1992), 618.

51. Susanne Klingenstein, *Jews in the American Academy, 1900–1940: The Dynamics of Intellectual Assimilation* (New Haven: Yale University Press, 1991), 137–98.

52. Non-Jews with "Jewish"-sounding names found obstacles in their paths. Wallace Notestein and Frederick Nussbaum had to prove their Gentile origins. See Peter Novick, *That Noble Dream: The "Objectivity Question" and the American Historical Profession* (New York: Cambridge University Press, 1988).

53. Edward Alexander, *Irving Howe: Socialist, Critic, Jew* (Bloomington: Indiana University Press, 1998), 17–19.

54. Riv-Ellen Prell, *Fighting to Become Americans: Jews, Gender, and the Anxiety of Assimilation* (Boston: Beacon, 1999), 50–52; Sander Gilman, *The Jew's Body* (New York: Routledge, 1991). A scholarly analysis of the "nose job" as an American Jewish cultural phenomenon is long overdue.

55. Alfred Jospe, *The Test of Time* (Washington, D.C.: B'nai B'rith Hillel Foundation, 1974).

56. Jonathan Z. Pollack, "Jewish Problems: Eastern and Western Jewish Identities in Conflict at the University of Wisconsin, 1919–1941," *American Jewish History* 89, no. 2 (June 2001): 161.

57. Myrna Katz Frommer and Harvey Frommer, comps., *It Happened in the Catskills: An Oral History in the Words of Busboys, Bellhops, Guests, Proprietors, Comedians, Agents, and Others Who Lived It* (San Diego: Harcourt Brace Jovanovich, 1991).

58. Samuel Halperin, *The Political World of American Zionism* (Detroit: Wayne State University Press, 1961).

59. Melvin Urofsky, *American Zionism from Herzl to the Holocaust* (New York: Doubleday, 1975); Naomi Cohen, *American Jews and the Zionist Idea* (Hoboken, N.J.: KTAV, 1975); Mark Raider, *The Emergence of American Zionism* (New York: New York University Press, 1998).

60. There is no scholarly history of Hadassah or biography of Henrietta Szold; see Joan Dash, *Summoned to Jerusalem: The Life of Henrietta Szold* (New York: Harper & Row, 1979).

61. Harry A. Wolfson, "Escaping Judaism," *Menorah Journal* 7, no. 2 (June 1921): 71–83; Leo W. Schwarz, *Wolfson of Harvard* (Philadelphia: Jewish Publication Society of America, 1978).

62. Kurt Lewin, "Bringing Up the Jewish Child," *Menorah Journal* 28 (1940): 29–45; Lewin, "Self-Hatred Among Jews," *Contemporary Jewish Record* 4 (1941): 219–32.

63. Nathan Reich, "The Role of the Jews in the American Economy," *YIVO Annual of Jewish Social Science* 5 (1930): 198–202; Nathan Goldberg, "Economic Trends among American Jews," *Jewish Affairs* 1, no. 1 (October 1946): 11–16.

64. Maurice J. Karpf, "Jewish Community Organization in the United States," *American Jewish Yearbook* 39 (1937–38): 53.

65. Samuel Koenig, *An American Jewish Community: The Sociology of the Jewish Community in Stamford, Ct.* (Stamford: Works Projects Administration Federal Writers Project for the State of Connecticut, 1940), 56–57.

66. Barry Chiswick and June O'Neill, eds., *Human Resources and Income Distribution* (New York: Norton, 1977), 313–34; Joel Perlmann, *Ethnic Differences: Schooling and Social Structure among the Irish, Italians, Jews, and Blacks in an American City, 1880–1935* (New York: Cambridge University Press, 1988), 122–39, 154–62.

67. Beth Wenger, *New York Jews and the Great Depression: Uncertain Promise* (New Haven: Yale University Press, 1996), 20.

68. Henry Feingold, *A Time for Searching: Entering the Mainstream, 1920–1945*, Jewish People in America 4 (Baltimore: Johns Hopkins University Press, 1992), 146.

69. Feingold, *Time for Searching*, 147.

70. Hasia R. Diner, *Hungering for America: Italian, Irish, and Jewish Foodways in the Age of Migration* (Cambridge, Mass.: Harvard University Press, 2001), 178–219.

71. Annelise Orleck, *Common Sense and a Little Fire: Women and Working-Class Politics in the United States, 1900–1965* (Chapel Hill: University of North Carolina Press, 1995), 215–49.

72. Irving Howe, *A Margin of Hope: An Intellectual Biography* (New York: Harcourt Brace Jovanovich, 1982), 6.

73. Michael Gold, *Jews without Money* (New York: Horace Liveright, 1930).

74. Harry Lurie, *A Heritage Affirmed* (Philadelphia: Jewish Publication Society of America, 1961).

75. Wenger, *New York Jews*, 29.

76. Howard Goldstein, *The Home on Gorham Street and the Voices of Its Children* (Tuscaloosa: University of Alabama Press, 1996), 91.

77. Hyman Bogen, *The Luckiest Orphans: A History of the Hebrew Orphan Asylum of New York* (Urbana: University of Illinois Press, 1992), 221.

78. Karpf, "Jewish Community Organization," 90.

79. Quoted in Jenna Weissman Joselit, *Our Gang: Jewish Crime and the New York Jewish Community, 1900–1940* (Bloomington: Indiana University Press, 1983), 157.

80. Feingold, *Time for Searching*, 148.

81. William B. Helmreich, *The Enduring Community: The Jews of Newark and Metrowest* (New Brunswick, N.J.: Transaction Publishers, 1999), 207.

82. Lurie, *Heritage Affirmed*, 41–45.

83. Helmreich, *Enduring Community*, 187; Karpf, "Jewish Community Organization," 113.

84. Karpf, "Jewish Community Organization," 90.

85. I. M. Rubinow, "The Economic and Industrial Status of American Jewry," in *Trends and Issues in Jewish Social Welfare in the United States, 1899–1952,* ed. Robert Morris and Michael Freund (1930; reprint, Philadelphia: Jewish Publication Society of America, 1966), 329–43, in particular 342.

86. Wenger, *New York Jews,* 29, 16; Selig Adler and Thomas E. Connolly, *From Ararat to Suburbia: The History of the Jewish Community of Buffalo* (Philadelphia: Jewish Publication Society of America, 1960), 264.

87. Robert McElvaine, *The Great Depression: America, 1929–1941* (New York: New York Times Books, 1984), 173; on American men, in particular, blaming themselves for their own economic misfortunes, see E. Wight Bakke, *The Unemployed Man: A Social Study* (New York: E. P. Dutton, 1934); Mirra Kamorovsky, *The Unemployed Man and His Family: The Effect of Unemployment upon the Status of the Man in Fifty-Nine Families* (New York: Dryden Press, 1940).

88. Daniel Walkowitz, *Working with Class: Social Workers and the Politics of Class Identity* (Chapel Hill: University of North Carolina Press, 1999).

89. Jerold S. Auerbach, *Rabbis and Lawyers: The Journey from Torah to Constitution* (Bloomington: Indiana University Press, 1990), 159–60.

90. Paula Hyman and Deborah Dash Moore, eds., *Jewish Women in America: An Historical Encyclopedia* (New York: Routledge, 1997), s.v. "Bellanca, Dorothy Jacobs," 1: 133–35; "Newman, Pauline," 2: 993–96; "Rosenberg, Anna," 2: 1171–74, "Schneiderman, Rose," 2: 1209–12.

91. See *American Jewish Yearbook* 32 (1930–31) and 49 (1947–48).

92. Abraham Epstein, *Insecurity, a Challenge to America,* 2nd rev. ed. (New York: Random House, 1938).

93. Marc Lee Raphael, *Abba Hillel Silver: A Profile in American Judaism* (New York: Holmes and Meier, 1989).

94. Nathaniel Weyl, *The Jew in American Politics* (New York: Arlington House, 1968), 158.

95. Quoted in Feingold, *Time for Searching*, 214.

96. Lawrence Fuchs, *The Political Behavior of American Jews* (Glencoe, Ill.: Free Press, 1956).

97. Wenger, *New York Jews.*

98. Louis Wirth, *The Ghetto* (Chicago: University of Chicago Press, 1927), 241–61.

99. Deborah Dash Moore, *At Home in America: Second Generation New York Jews* (New York: Columbia University Press, 1981), 30.

100. Adler and Connolly, *From Ararat to Suburbia,* 320–27.

101. Suzanne R. Wasserman, "The Good Old Days of Poverty: The Battle over the Fate of New York's Lower East Side During the Depression," Ph.D. diss. (New York University, 1990).

102. Moore, *At Home in America,* 30.

103. Arnold Hirsch, *Making the Second Ghetto: Race and Housing in Chicago, 1940–1960* (Cambridge: Cambridge University Press, 1983), 4–5; Hillel Levine and Lawrence Harmon, *The Death of an American Jewish Community: A Tragedy of Good Intentions* (New York: Free Press, 1992), 33, 37, 53.

104. Daniel Soyer, *Jewish Immigrant Associations and American Identity in New York, 1880–1939* (Cambridge, Mass.: Harvard University Press, 1997), 191.

105. Mordecai Soltes, "The Yiddish Press: An Americanizing Agency," *American Jewish Yearbook* 26 (1924–25): 165–372.

106. Mordecai Soltes, *The Yiddish Press: An Americanizing Agency* (New York: Teachers College, Columbia University, 1925); Arthur Goren, "The Jewish Press," in *The Ethnic Press in the United States,* ed. Sally M. Miller (Westport, Conn.: Greenwood Press, 1987), 203–28.

107. Nahma Sandrow, *Vagabond Stars: A World History of Yiddish Theater* (Syracuse, N.Y.: Syracuse University Press, 1977), 251–302.

108. David S. Lifson, *The Yiddish Theatre in America* (New York: Thomas Yoseloff, 1965).

109. Donald P. Kent, *The Refugee Intellectual: The Americanization of the Immigrants of 1933–1941* (New York: Columbia University Press, 1953); Gabrielle Simon Edgcomb, *From Swastika to Jim Crow: Refugee Scholars at Black Colleges* (Malabar, Fla.: Krieger, 1993).

110. Kerry M. Olitzky, *The American Synagogue: A Historical Dictionary and Sourcebook* (Westport, Conn.: Greenwood Press, 1996), 245–46.

111. Hasia R. Diner, *Fifty Years of Jewish Self-Governance: The Jewish Community Council of Greater Washington, 1938–1988* (Washington, D.C.: Jewish Community Council of Greater Washington, 1989).

112. Steven Lowenstein, *Frankfurt on the Hudson: The German Jewish Community of Washington Heights, 1933–1983: Its Structure and Culture* (Detroit: Wayne State University Press, 1989).

113. Steven Lowenstein, foreword to *We Were So Beloved: Autobiography of a German Jewish Community,* by Gloria DaVidas Kirchheimer and Manfred Kirchheimer (Pittsburgh: University of Pittsburgh Press, 1997), xi.

114. Leonard Dinnerstein, *America and the Survivors of the Holocaust* (New York: Columbia University Press, 1982).

115. Wenger, *New York Jews.*

116. Raymond Pearl, *The Natural History of Population* (New York: Oxford, 1939), 242–43.

117. Ellen Chesler, *Women of Valor: Margaret Sanger and the Birth Control Movement in America* (New York: Simon & Schuster, 1992).

118. Hyman and Moore, eds., *Jewish Women in America,* s.v. "Simon, Caroline Klein," 2: 1258–60.

119. Benjamin Rabinowitz, "The Young Men's Hebrew Associations," *Publications of the American Jewish Historical Society* 37 (1947): 221–326.

120. "Fanny Goldstein, Obituary," *American Jewish Yearbook* 64 (1963): 493.

121. David Breslau, *Adventures in Pioneering: The Story of 25 Years of Habonim Camping* (New York: Chay Commission of the Labor Zionist Movement of New York, 1957).

122. Union of American Hebrew Congregations, *Reform Judaism in the Large Cities* (New York: UAHC, 1931), 10.

123. Ellen Umansky, "Reform Judaism's Lost Woman Rabbi: An Interview with Paula Ackerman," *Genesis* 2, no. 17 (June/July 1986): 3–20.

124. Leon Jick, "The Reform Synagogue," in *The American Synagogue: A Sanctuary Transformed,* ed. Jack Wertheimer (Hanover, N.H.: University Press of New England, 1987), 98–99.

125. For a text of the Columbus Platform, see Mark Lee Raphael, *Jews and Judaism in the United States: A Documentary History* (New York: Behrman House, 1983), 205–7.

126. David Kaufman, *Shul with a Pool: The "Synagogue-Center" in American Jewish History* (Hanover, N.H.: University Press of New England, 1999).

127. Deborah Melamed, *Three Pillars: Thought, Worship, and Prayer for the Jewish Woman* (New York: Women's League of the United Synagogue of America, 1927); Betty D. Greenberg and Althea O. Silverman, *The Jewish Home Beautiful* (New York: Women's League of the United Synagogue of America, 1941).

128. Quoted in Jack Wertheimer, "The Conservative Synagogue," in *The American Synagogue,* ed. Wertheimer, 121.

129. Mordecai Kaplan, *Judaism as a Civilization: Toward a Reconstruction of American-Jewish Life* (New York: Macmillan, 1934).

130. Mel Scult, *Judaism Faces the Twentieth Century: A Biography of Mordecai M. Kaplan* (Detroit: Wayne State University Press, 1993); Emmanuel S. Goldsmith, Mel Scult, and Robert M. Seltzer, *The American Judaism of Mordecai M. Kaplan* (New York: New York University Press, 1990).

131. Jeffrey S. Gurock, *From Fluidity to Rigidity: The Religious Worlds of Conservative and Orthodox Jews in Twentieth Century America* (Ann Arbor, Mich.: Jean and Samuel Frankel Center for Judaic Studies, 1998), 5–11.

132. Jeffrey S. Gurock, "The Orthodox Synagogue," in *American Synagogue,* ed. Wertheimer, 64.

133. Jenna Weissman Joselit, *New York's "Jewish Jews": The Orthodox Community in the Interwar Years* (Bloomington: Indiana University Press, 1990).

134. Jeffrey S. Gurock, "Resisters and Accommodators: Varieties of Orthodox Rabbis in America, 1886–1983," *American Jewish Archives* 35, no. 2 (November 1983): 100–187; Gershon Kranzler, *Williamsburg* (New York: Feldheim, 1961); Charles Liebman, "Orthodoxy in American Jewish Life," *American Jewish Yearbook* 66 (1965): 21–92.

135. Oscar Handlin and Mary Handlin, "A Century of Jewish Immigration to the United States," *American Jewish Yearbook* 50 (1948–49): 1–84.

136. Handlin and Handlin, "Century of Jewish Immigration."

CHAPTER 7. A GOLDEN AGE?

1. Will Herberg, *Protestant, Catholic, Jew: An Essay in American Religious Sociology* (Garden City, N.Y.: Doubleday, 1955).

2. Kenneth T. Jackson, *Crabgrass Frontier: The Suburbanization of the United States* (New York: Oxford University Press, 1985).

3. Michael J. Bennett, *When Dreams Come True: The GI Bill and the Making of Modern America* (Washington, D.C.: Brassey's, 1996). The history of the Jews' relationship to this transformative piece of legislation still needs to be written.

4. *American Jewish Yearbook* 59 (1958): 116.

5. Stuart E. Rosenberg, *America Is Different: The Search for Jewish Identity* (New York: Thomas Nelson, 1964), xi.

6. Peter Novick, *The Holocaust in American Life* (Boston: Houghton Mifflin, 1999).

7. "Lest We Forget," in possession of the author.

8. *High Holiday Prayer Book* (New York: Jewish Reconstructionist Foundation, 1948), 387–96.

9. *American Jewish Yearbook* 52 (1951): 91.

10. Menachen M. Kasher, *The Israel Passover Haggadah: Supplemented by One Hundred Chapters* (New York: Schulsinger Brothers, 1950), 93.

11. Quoted in Albert I. Gordon, *The Jews in Suburbia* (Boston: Beacon Press, 1959), 101.

12. *American Jewish Yearbook* 53 (1952): 161.

13. *World Over* 19, no. 14 (May 2, 1958): 5.

14. Eli Lederhendler, *New York Jews and the Decline of Urban Ethnicity, 1950–1970* (Syracuse, N.Y.: Syracuse University Press, 2001), 37.

15. For an excellent summation of the Eichmann Trial, see *American Jewish Yearbook* 63 (1962): 3–135.

16. *American Jewish Yearbook* 54 (1953): 156.

17. *American Jewish Yearbook* 64 (1963): 121.

18. *American Jewish Yearbook* 56 (1955): 86; Oscar Handlin, *Adventures in Freedom* (New York: McGraw-Hill, 1954), vii–viii; *American Jewish Yearbook* 52 (1951): 176.

19. *American Jewish Yearbook* 65 (1964): 18.

20. See the entry on Bella Abzug in *Jewish Women in America: An Historical Encyclopedia,* ed. Paula Hyman and Deborah Dash Moore (New York: Routledge, 1998), 1: 5–10.

21. Quoted in Hasia R. Diner, *Fifty Years of Jewish Self-Governance: The Jewish Community Council of Greater Washington, 1938–1988* (Washington, D.C.: Jewish Community Council of Greater Washington, 1988), 68.

22. Gerald E. Markowitz, *Children, Race, and Power: Kenneth and Mamie Clark's Northside Center* (Charlottesville: University Press of Virginia, 1996).

23. *American Jewish Yearbook* 56 (1955): 241–42.

24. Quoted in Marc Dollinger, *Quest for Inclusion: Jews and Liberalism in Modern America* (Princeton: Princeton University Press, 2000), 178.

25. *American Jewish Yearbook* 54 (1953): 107.

26. *American Jewish Yearbook* 56 (1955): 241.

27. *American Jewish Yearbook* 66 (1965): 175.

28. *American Jewish Yearbook* 65 (1964): 77.

29. Susannah Heschel, "Theological Affinities in the Writings of Abraham Joshua Heschel and Martin Luther King," in *Black Zion: African American Religious Encounters with Judaism*, ed. Yvonne Chireau and Nathaniel Deutsch (New York: Oxford University Press, 2000), 177.

30. *American Jewish Yearbook* 66 (1965): 163.

31. *American Jewish Yearbook* 62 (1961): 134.

32. Arnold Jacob Wolf, "The Negro Revolution and Jewish Theology," *Conservative Judaism* 12, no. 4 (Fall 1964): 479, 483.

33. Seth Forman, *Blacks in the Jewish Mind: A Crisis in Liberalism* (New York: New York University Press, 1998), 67–68.

34. Individuals within organized Jewish institutions at times expressed discordant and decidedly different ideas about the increasingly militant thrust of the civil rights movement. Some did not think the assertiveness on the streets bode well for the Jews. See Michael E. Staub, *Torn at the Roots: The Crisis of Jewish Liberalism in Postwar America* (New York: Columbia University Press, 2002).

35. Clive Webb, *Fight against Fear: Southern Jews and Black Civil Rights* (Athens: University of Georgia Press, 2001), 158.

36. Webb, *Fight against Fear,* 43–44; Eli Evans, *The Provincials* (New York: Free Press, 1973), 96.

37. Melissa F. Greene, *Temple Bombing* (Reading, Mass.: Addison-Wesley, 1996).

38. Quoted in Dollinger, *Quest for Inclusion,* 167.

39. Gary P. Zola, "What Price Amos? Perry Nussbaum's Career in Jackson, Mississippi," in *The Quiet Voices: Southern Rabbis and Black Civil Rights, 1880s to 1990s,* ed. Mark K. Bauman and Berkley Kalin (Tuscaloosa: University of Alabama Press, 1997), 230–57.

40. William Malev, "The Jew of the South in the Conflict on Segregation," *Conservative Judaism* 13, no. 1 (Fall 1958): 35–46.

41. *American Jewish Yearbook* 58 (1957): 164–65.

42. *American Jewish Yearbook* 56 (1955): 223.

43. *American Jewish Yearbook* 60 (1959): 44–45.

44. Nationally the overwhelming majority of Jewish youth attended college. As of 1963 between 70 and 80 percent of young Jews, aged eighteen to twenty-four, were enrolled in institutions of higher education. See "Jewish College Students in the United States," *American Jewish Yearbook* 65 (1964): 133.

45. Quoted in Dollinger, *Quest for Inclusion,* 188.

46. *American Jewish Yearbook* 64 (1963): 93.

47. *American Jewish Yearbook* 66 (1965): 180. For a discussion of a single school integration episode in New York, see Adina Back, "Blacks, Jews, and the Struggle to Integrate Brooklyn's Junior High School 258: A Cold War Story," *Journal of American Ethnic History* 20, no. 2 (Winter 2001): 38–69.

48. Forman, *Blacks in the Jewish Mind,* 72.

49. *American Jewish Yearbook* 66 (1965): 187–88.

50. Cited in C. Bezalel Sherman, *The Jew within American Society* (Detroit: Wayne State University Press, 1960).

51. See, for example, Robert Levy, *Ana Pauker: The Rise and Fall of a Jewish Communist* (Berkeley and Los Angeles: University of California Press, 2001). Pauker was a high official in the Communist government in Romania. In 1948 her photograph appeared on the cover of *Time* magazine, which described her as "the most powerful woman alive." The magazine article referred to her Jewishness and her unswerving loyalty to Stalinism.

52. *American Jewish Yearbook* 55 (1954): 146. See also *American Jewish Yearbook* 56 (1955): 615, 620.

53. Deborah Dash Moore, "Reconsidering the Rosenbergs: Symbol and Substance in Second-Generation American Jewish Consciousness," *Journal of American Ethnic History* 8 (Fall 1988): 21–37; Jeffrey M. Marker, "The Jewish Community and the Case of Julius and Ethel Rosenberg," *Maryland Historian* 3 (Fall 1972): 106–17.

54. Dollinger, *Quest for Inclusion,* 136.

55. Quoted in Dollinger, *Quest for Inclusion,* 138.

56. *American Jewish Yearbook* 56 (1955): 241–42.

57. *American Jewish Yearbook* 53 (1952): 77.

58. Leo Pfeffer, *Creeds in Competition* (New York: Harper and Brothers, 1958); Gregg Ivers, *To Build a Wall: American Jews and the Separation of Church and State* (Charlottesville: University of Virginia Press, 1995).

59. Stuart Svonkin, *Jews against Prejudice: American Jews and the Fight for Civil Liberties* (New York: Columbia University Press, 1997).

60. Theodore W. Adorno, Else Frenkel-Brunswick, Daniel J. Levison, and R. Nevitt Sanford, *The Authoritarian Personality* (New York: Harper, 1950); Bruno Bettelheim and Morris Janowitz, *Dynamics of Prejudice: A Psychological and Sociological Study of Veterans* (New York: Harper, 1950); Nathan Ackerman and Marie Jahoda, *Anti-Semitism and Emotional Disorder: A Psychoanalytic Interpretation* (New York: Harper, 1950).

61. Abram Sachar, *A Host at Last* (Boston: Little, Brown, 1976).

62. Edward Shapiro, *A Time for Healing: American Jewry since World War II,* Jewish People in America 5 (Baltimore: Johns Hopkins University Press, 1992), 28–44.

63. *American Jewish Yearbook* 53 (1952): 53, 91.

64. Gordon, *Jews in Suburbia,* 6.

65. Deborah Dash Moore, *To the Golden Cities: Pursuing the American Jewish Dream in Miami and L.A.* (New York: Free Press, 1994), 23.

66. *American Jewish Yearbook* 52 (1951): 142–43; *American Jewish Yearbook* 59 (1958): 98–99; *American Jewish Yearbook* 60 (1959): 19; *American Jewish Yearbook* 61 (1960): 11; *American Jewish Yearbook* 63 (1962): 146.

67. Gerald Gamm, *Urban Exodus: Why the Jews Left Boston and the Catholics Stayed* (Cambridge, Mass.: Harvard University Press, 1999).

68. *American Jewish Yearbook* 56 (1955): 26–27.

69. Nathan Glazer, "Social Characteristics of American Jews, 1654–1954," *American Jewish Yearbook* 56 (1955): 27.

70. Alfred Kazin, *A Walker in the City* (New York: Harcourt, Brace, 1951); Meyer Levin, *My Father's House* (New York: Viking, 1947).

71. Sydney Taylor, *All-of-a-Kind Family* (Chicago: Follett's, 1951).

72. Hasia R. Diner, *Lower East Side Memories: A Jewish Place in America* (Princeton, N.J.: Princeton University Press, 2000).

73. Elaine Tyler May, *Homeward Bound: American Families in the Cold War* (New York: Basic Books, 1988).

74. Gordon, *Jews in Suburbia,* 41.

75. Shapiro, *Time for Healing,* 159.

76. Sherman, *Jew within American Society,* 90.

77. *American Jewish Yearbook* 58 (1957): 75.

78. *American Jewish Yearbook* 52 (1951): 97–109.

79. For one list of such organizations and their membership numbers, see *American Jewish Yearbook* 53 (1952): 198–200; on the perceived problems of teenagers in this era, see James B. Gilbert, *A Cycle of Outrage: America's Reaction to the Juvenile Delinquent of the 1950s* (New York: Oxford University Press, 1986); Edgar Z. Friedenberg, *The Vanishing Adolescent* (Boston: Beacon, 1958).

80. *American Jewish Yearbook* 65 (1964): 75.

81. *American Jewish Yearbook* 54 (1953): 23.

82. Quoted in Jenna Weissman Joselit, *The Wonders of America: Reinventing Jewish Culture, 1880–1950* (New York: Hill and Wang, 1994), 105.

83. Quoted in Lederhendler, *New York Jews,* 108.

84. The most probing historical critique of the Judaism of this era has been offered by Lederhendler, *New York Jews.*

85. Nathan Glazer, *American Judaism,* 2nd ed. (Chicago: University of Chicago Press, 1989).

86. *American Jewish Yearbook* 60 (1959): 55.

87. *American Jewish Yearbook* 53 (1952): 153.

88. *American Jewish Yearbook* 56 (1955): 235.

89. Seth Farber, "Reproach, Recognition, and Respect: Rabbi Joseph B. Soloveitchik and Orthodoxy's Mid-Century Attitude toward Non-Orthodox Denominations," *American Jewish History* 89, no. 2 (June 2001): 194.

90. *American Jewish Yearbook* 63 (1962): 205–6.

91. *American Jewish Yearbook* 63 (1962): 176.

92. *American Jewish Yearbook* 64 (1963): 80.

93. *American Jewish Yearbook* 65 (1964): 62.

94. *American Jewish Yearbook* 58 (1957): 153.

95. The phrase obviously comes from Daniel Bell, *End of Ideology: On the Exhaustion of Political Ideas in the Fifties* (Glencoe, Ill.: Free Press, 1960). Americans, Bell wrote, had become "fearful of censure" and rejected positions not representing the lowest common denominator (13).

96. David Riesman, *The Lonely Crowd: A Study of the Changing American Character* (New Haven: Yale University Press, 1950); Vance Packard, *The Status Seekers* (New York: D. McKay, 1959).

97. Charles Liebman, "Orthodoxy in American Life," *American Jewish Yearbook* 66 (1965): 21–98.

98. Quoted in Joselit, *Wonders of America*, 115.

99. Leon Jick, "The Reform Synagogue," in *The American Synagogue: A Sanctuary Transformed*, ed. Jack Wertheimer (Hanover, N.H.: University Press of New England, 1987), 102–4.

100. Eugene Lipman and Albert Vorspan, *A Tale of Ten Cities* (New York: Union of American Hebrew Congregations, 1962), 298.

101. *American Jewish Yearbook* 62 (1961): 129.

102. *American Jewish Yearbook* 60 (1959): 54.

103. *Sabbath and Festival Prayer Book* (New York: Rabbinical Assembly and United Synagogue of America, 1948), vii, viii, x, 45.

104. Gordon, *Jews in Suburbia*, 78–79, 125.

105. *American Jewish Yearbook* 56 (1955): 247.

106. Pamela S. Nadell, *Women Who Would Be Rabbis: A History of Women's Ordination, 1889–1985* (Boston: Beacon Press, 1998), 165–67.

107. Philip Roth, *Goodbye, Columbus, and Five Short Stories* (New York: Houghton Mifflin, 1959). For a discussion of the internal Jewish intellectual critique of 1950s life see Lederhendler, *New York Jews*.

108. Riv-Ellen Prell, *Fighting to Become Americans: Jews, Gender, and the Anxiety of Assimilation* (Boston: Beacon Press, 1999), 170.

109. Quoted in Lederhendler, *New York Jews*, 183.

CHAPTER 8. IN SEARCH OF CONTINUITY

1. Robert Gordis, *Judaism in a Christian World* (New York: McGraw-Hill, 1966); *American Jewish Yearbook* 71 (1970): 101.

2. Peter Y. Medding, Gary A. Tobin, Sylvia Barack Fishman, and Mordechai Rimor, "Jewish Identity in Conversionary and Mixed Marriages," *American Jewish Yearbook* 93 (1992): 3–76.

3. Egon Mayer and Carl Sheingold, *Intermarriage and the Jewish Future* (New York: American Jewish Committee, 1979).

4. Charles Liebman, *The Ambivalent American Jew: Politics, Religion, and Family in American Jewish Life* (Philadelphia: Jewish Publication Society of America, 1973), viii.

5. For an excellent summary of the 1990 National Jewish Population Survey, see Sidney Goldstein, "Profile of American Jewry: Insights from the 1990 National Jewish Population Survey," *American Jewish Yearbook* 92 (1991): 77–173. See also Barry A. Kosmin, *Highlights of the CJF 1990 National Jewish Population Survey* (New York: Council of Jewish Federations, 1991).

6. *American Jewish Yearbook* 99 (1998): 139; Elliott Abrams, *Faith and Fear: How Jews Can Survive in Christian America* (New York: Free Press, 1997).

7. Egon Mayer, *Love and Tradition: Marriage between Jews and Christians*

(New York: Plenum Press, 1985); Egon Mayer and Carl Sheingold, *Intermarriage and the Jewish Future* (New York: American Jewish Committee, 1979); Robert Gordis, *Love and Sex: A Modern Jewish Perspective* (New York: Farrar, Straus, and Giroux, 1978).

8. On the denominalization of Reconstruction after 1968, see Charles Liebman, "Reconstructionism in American Life," *American Jewish Yearbook* 71 (1970): 3–99.

9. *American Jewish Yearbook* 99 (1999): 54.

10. Samuel C. Heilman, *Portrait of American Jews: The Last Half of the Twentieth Century* (Seattle: University of Washington Press, 1995), 149.

11. Jerome Mintz, *Hasidic People: A Place in the New World* (Cambridge, Mass.: Harvard University Press, 1992).

12. Samuel Heilman and Steven Cohen, *Cosmopolitans and Parochials: Modern Orthodox Jews in America* (Chicago: University of Chicago Press, 1989); Samuel Heilman, *Defenders of the Faith: Inside Ultra-Orthodox Jewry* (New York: Schocken, 1992).

13. *American Jewish Yearbook* 97 (1997): 195.

14. Shaul Shimon Deutsch, *Larger than Life: The Life and Times of the Lubavitch Rebbe Rabbi Menachem Mendel Schneerson* (New York: Chasidic Historical Productions, 1995); the harshest critic to date of the veneration of Schneerson is David Berger, *The Rebbe, the Messiah, and the Scandal of Orthodox Indifference* (London: Littman Library of Jewish Civilization, 2001).

15. Berger, *The Rebbe*.

16. *American Jewish Yearbook* 97 (1997): 194–95.

17. Sidney Goldstein and Alice Goldstein, *Jews on the Move: Implications for Jewish Identity* (Albany: State University of New York Press, 1995).

18. Charles Silberman, *A Certain People: American Jews and Their Lives Today* (New York: Summit Books, 1985); Leonard Fein, *Where Are We? The Inner Life of America's Jews* (New York: Harper & Row, 1988); Heilman, *Portrait of American Jews;* Samuel Freedman, *Jew versus Jew: The Struggle for the Soul of American Jewry* (New York: Simon & Schuster, 2000); J. J. Goldberg, *Jewish Power: Inside the American Jewish Establishment* (Reading, Mass.: Addison-Wesley, 1996); Jack Wertheimer, *A People Divided: Judaism in Contemporary America* (New York: Basic Books, 1993).

19. For a well-developed statement of this, see Chaim I. Waxman, *Jewish Baby Boomers: A Communal Perspective* (Albany: State University of New York Press, 2001).

20. Sylvia Barack Fishman, *A Breath of Life: Feminism in the American Jewish Community* (New York: Free Press, 1993).

21. See Milton Himmelfarb and Victor Baras, eds., *Zero Population Growth—For Whom? Differential Fertility and Minority Group Survival* (Westport, Conn.: Greenwood Press, 1978).

22. Joseph Rosenbloom, *Conversion to Judaism: From the Biblical Period to the Present* (New York: Behrman House, 1978); Paul and Rachel Cowan, *Mixed Blessings: Marriage between Jews and Christians* (New York: Doubleday, 1987).

23. Fran Markowitz, *A Community in Spite of Itself: Soviet Jewish Emigres in New York* (Washington, D.C.: Smithsonian Institution Press, 1993).

24. Murray Friedman and Albert Chernin, *A Second Exodus* (Hanover, N.H.: University Press of New England, 1999).

25. Walter Zenner, *A Global Community: The Jews from Aleppo, Syria* (Detroit: Wayne State University Press, 2000), 127–77; David Bibas, *Immigrants and the Formation of Community: A Case Study of Moroccan Jewish Immigration to America* (New York: AMS Press, 1998).

26. Jonathan Sarna, "American Jewish Education in Historical Perspective," *Journal of Jewish Education* 64, nos. 1, 2 (Winter/Spring 1998): 8–21; Jack Wertheimer, "Jewish Education in the United States: Recent Trends and Issues," *American Jewish Yearbook* 99 (1999): 3–115.

27. Samuel Z. Klausner, "Anti-Semitism in the Executive Suite: Yesterday, Today, and Tomorrow," *Moment* 13 (September 1988): 33–39, 55.

28. *American Jewish Yearbook* 69 (1968): 203–5.

29. *American Jewish Yearbook* 69 (1968). The *Yearbook* devoted no fewer than 115 pages to the war and its impact on American Jewry.

30. Daniel J. Elazar, "United States of America: Overview," in *The Yom Kippur War: Israel and the Jewish People,* ed. Moshe Davis (New York: Arno Press, 1974), 1–35; Stephen D. Isaacs, *Jews and American Politics* (Garden, City, N.Y.: Doubleday, 1974), 267.

31. *American Jewish Yearbook* 72 (1971): 141–42.

32. The quote is from Y. L. Gordon's 1869 poem. See Michael Stanislawski, *For Whom Shall I Toil: Judah Leib Gordon and the Crisis of Russian Jewry* (New York: Oxford University Press, 1988), 49–50.

33. Chaim Waxman, *American Aliya: Portrait of an Innovative Migration Movement* (Detroit: Wayne State University Press, 1989); Kevin Avruch, *American Immigrants in Israel: Social Identities and Change* (Chicago: University of Chicago Press, 1981).

34. See, for example, *American Jewish Yearbook* 83 (1983): 70–71, 102; *American Jewish Yearbook* 85 (1985): 113; *American Jewish Yearbook* 98 (1998): 98.

35. Goldberg, *Jewish Power,* 208.

36. William Novak, "Dynamics of American Jewish Dissent: The Breira Story," *Genesis* 2 (March 16, 1977): 1–8; Rael J. Isaac and Erich Isaac, "The Rabbis of Breira," *Midstream* 23, no. 4 (April 1977): 3–17.

37. *American Jewish Yearbook* 98 (1998): 110–11.

38. *American Jewish Yearbook* 99 (1999): 179.

39. Jules Harlow, ed., *Siddur Sim Shalom: A Prayerbook for Shabbat, Festivals, and Weekdays* (New York: Rabbinical Assembly, 1985), 416.

40. Gilbert S. Rosenthal, ed., *The Jewish Family in a Changing World* (Cranbury, N.J.: Thomas Yoseloff, 1970).

41. Donald A. Downs, *Nazis in Skokie: Freedom, Community, and the First Amendment* (Notre Dame, Ind.: University of Notre Dame Press, 1985).

42. Deborah E. Lipstadt, *Denying the Holocaust: The Growing Assault on Truth and Memory* (New York: Free Press, 1993).

43. Lawrence N. Powell, *Troubled Memory: Anne Levy, the Holocaust, and David Duke's Louisiana* (Chapel Hill: University of North Carolina Press, 2000).

44. Peter Novick, *The Holocaust in American Life* (Boston: Houghton Mifflin, 1999).

45. For one statement on Jewish participation in the New Left, see Seymour Martin Lipset, " 'The Socialism of Fools': The Left, the Jews, and Israel," *Encounter* (December 1969), 24–35.

46. *American Jewish Yearbook* 83 (1983): 70–71.

47. *American Jewish Yearbook* 74 (1973): 158; quote, *American Jewish Yearbook* 73 (1972): 301.

48. Milton Himmelfarb, "Are Jews Still Liberals?" *Commentary* 43 (April 1967): 67–72.

49. *American Jewish Yearbook* 99 (1999): 120.

50. *American Jewish Yearbook* 70 (1969): 84.

51. *American Jewish Yearbook* 74 (1973): 175.

52. Nathan Glazer, *Affirmative Discrimination: Ethnic Inequality and Public Policy* (New York: Basic Books, 1975).

53. Arthur Magida, *Prophet of Rage: A Life of Louis Farrakhan and His Nation* (New York: Basic Books, 1996).

54. Richard H. Girgenti, *A Report to the Governor on the Disturbances in Crown Heights* (Albany: New York State Division of Criminal Justice Services, Office of Justice Systems Analysis, 1993).

55. Sharon Strassfeld and Michael Strassfeld, *The Third Jewish Catalog: Creating Community* (Philadelphia: Jewish Publication Society of America, 1980), 78–91.

56. *American Jewish Yearbook* 73 (1972): 116.

57. *American Jewish Yearbook* 72 (1971): 151.

58. *American Jewish Yearbook* 71 (1970): 226.

59. Janet Dolgin, *Jewish Identity and the JDL* (Princeton, N.J.: Princeton University Press, 1977).

60. Dolgin, *Jewish Identity*.

61. According to Paul S. Applebaum, "The Soviet Jewry Movement in the United States," in *Jewish American Voluntary Organizations,* ed. Michael Dobkowski (Westport, Conn.: Greenwood Press, 1986), 613–38, the Lubavitch Hasidim and a number of the other Hasidic communities "opposed the new movement for fear of jeopardizing their existing clandestine links with members in the Soviet Union, contacts that were apparently winked at to some degree by the Soviet government" (620).

62. Elie Wiesel, *Night* (New York: Hill and Wang, 1960); Wiesel, *The Jews of Silence* (New York: Holt, Rinehart and Winston, 1966).

63. *American Jewish Yearbook* 71 (1970): 228; *American Jewish Yearbook* 73 (1972): 115–16; *American Jewish Yearbook* 72 (1971): 151.

64. *American Jewish Yearbook* 94 (1994): 3.

65. Michael E. Staub, *Torn at the Roots: The Crisis of Jewish Liberalism in Postwar America* (New York: Columbia University Press, 2002), analyzes the intensely negative reaction of the "Jewish establishment" to the political demands of the Jewish student movement.

66. Riv-Ellen Prell, *Prayer and Community: The Havurah in American Judaism* (Detroit: Wayne State University Press, 1989).

67. Bernard Reisman, *The Chavurah: A Contemporary Jewish Experience* (New York: Union of American Hebrew Congregations, 1977); Jacob Neusner, ed., *Contemporary Judaic Fellowship in Theory and Practice* (New York: KTAV, 1972).

68. "Kavod n'Nichum," program of the First North American Chevra Kadisha Conference, June 22–24, 2003, Rockville, Maryland.

69. Richard Siegel, Michael Strassfeld, and Sharon Strassfeld, *The First Jewish Catalog: A Do-It-Yourself Kit* (Philadelphia: Jewish Publication Society of America, 1970); Sharon Strassfeld and Michael Strassfeld, *The Second Jewish Catalog: Sources and Resources* (Philadelphia: Jewish Publication Society of America, 1976); Strassfeld and Strassfeld, *Third Jewish Catalog.*

70. Henry Sapoznik, *Klezmer! Jewish Music from Old World to Our World* (New York: Schirmer, 1999); Mark Slobin, *Fiddler on the Move: Exploring the Klezmer World* (New York: Oxford University Press, 2000).

71. *American Jewish Yearbook* 91 (1991).

72. *American Jewish Yearbook* 97 (1997): 206.

73. From the spring/summer 2001 catalog for Jewish Lights; P.O. Box 237 Sunset Farm Offices, Rt. 4 Woodstock, Vermont 05091.

74. Rodger Kamenetz, *The Jew in the Lotus: A Poet's Rediscovery of Jewish Ideas in Buddhist India* (San Francisco: HarperCollins, 1994).

75. Leon Jick, ed., *The Teaching of Judaica in American Universities: The Proceedings of a Colloquium* (Waltham, Mass.: Association for Jewish Studies, 1970).

76. Anne Lapidus Lerner, " 'Who Hast Not Made Me a Man': The Movement for Equal Rights for Women in American Jewry," *American Jewish Yearbook* 77 (1977): 20–21.

77. Blu Greenberg, *On Women and Judaism: A View from Tradition* (Philadelphia: Jewish Publication Society of America, 1981).

78. See JOFA's website, www.jofa.org.

79. See www.jofa.org.

80. Quoted in Reena Sigman Friedman, "The Jewish Feminist Movement," in *Jewish American Voluntary Organizations,* ed. Dobkowski, 580.

81. *American Jewish Yearbook* 92 (1992).

82. Quoted in Edward Shapiro, *A Time for Healing: American Jewry since World War II,* Jewish People in America 5 (Baltimore: Johns Hopkins University Press, 1992), 178–79.

83. Allegra Goodman, *Kaaterskill Falls* (New York: Dial, 1998); Rebecca Goldstein, *The Mind-Body Problem* (New York: Random House, 1983); Rebecca Goldstein, *Mazel* (New York: Penguin, 1995); Pearl Abraham, *The Romance Reader* (New York: Riverhead, 1995); Nessa Rappaport, *Preparing for Sabbath* (New York: Morrow, 1981); Tova Mirvis, *The Ladies Auxiliary* (New York: Norton, 1999).

84. *American Jewish Yearbook* 99 (1999): 186.

BIBLIOGRAPHY

Abelow, Samuel P. *History of Brooklyn Jewry*. Brooklyn, N.Y.: Scheba Publishing, 1937.

Adler, Selig, and Thomas E. Connolly. *From Ararat to Suburbia: The History of the Jewish Community of Buffalo*. Philadelphia: Jewish Publication Society of America, 1960.

Alexander, Edward. *Irving Howe: Socialist, Critic, Jew*. Bloomington: Indiana University Press, 1998.

Alexander, Michael. *Jazz Age Jews*. Princeton: Princeton University Press, 2001.

Antler, Joyce. *The Journey Home: Jewish Women and the American Century*. New York: Free Press, 1997.

———, ed. *Talking Back: Images of Jewish Women in American Popular Culture*. Hanover, N.H.: University Press of New England, 1998.

Arad, Gulie Ne'eman. *America, Its Jews, and the Rise of the Nazism*. Bloomington: Indiana University Press, 2000.

Ariel, Yaakov. *Evangelizing the Chosen People: Missions to the Jews in America, 1880–2000*. Chapel Hill: University of North Carolina Press, 2001.

Ashton, Dianne. *Rebecca Gratz: Women and Judaism in Antebellum America*. Detroit: Wayne State University Press, 1997.

Auerbach, Jerold S. *Rabbis and Lawyers: The Journey from Torah to Constitution*. Bloomington: Indiana University Press, 1990.

Back, Adina. "Blacks, Jews, and the Struggle to Integrate Brooklyn's Junior High School 258: A Cold War Story." *Journal of American Ethnic History* 20, no. 2 (Winter 2001): 38–69.

Baldwin, Neil. *Henry Ford and the Jews: The Mass Production of Hate*. New York: Public Affairs, 2001.

Barkai, Avraham. *Branching Out: German-Jewish Immigration to the United States, 1820–1914*. New York: Holmes and Meier, 1994.

Barnett, R. D. "Dr. Samuel Nunes Ribiero and the Settlement of Georgia." In

Migration and Settlement: Proceedings of the Anglo-American Jewish Historical Conference Held in London Jointly by the Jewish Historical Society of England and the American Jewish Historical Society, July 1970. London: Jewish Historical Society, 1968.

Baron, Salo, and Jeannette Meisel Baron, eds. *Steeled by Adversity: Essays and Addresses on American Jewish Life.* Philadelphia: Jewish Publication Society, 1971.

Bauer, Yehuda. *My Brother's Keeper: A History of the American Jewish Joint Distribution Committee, 1929–1939.* Philadelphia: Jewish Publication Society of America, 1974.

Baum, Charlotte, Paula Hyman, and Sonya Michel. *The Jewish Woman in America.* New York: Dial Press, 1976.

Bauman, Mark K., and Berkley Kalin, eds. *The Quiet Voices: Southern Rabbis and Black Civil Rights, 1880s to 1990s.* Tuscaloosa: University of Alabama Press, 1997.

Bayor, Ronald. *Neighbors in Conflict: The Irish, Germans, Jews, and Italians of New York City, 1929–1941.* 2nd ed. Urbana: University of Illinois Press, 1988.

Berman, Jeremiah. *Shehitah: A Study in the Cultural and Social Life of the Jewish People.* New York: Bloch, 1941.

Berman, Myron. *Richmond's Jewry, 1769–1976.* Charlottesville: University Press of Virginia, 1979.

Berrol, Selma C. *Julia Richman: A Notable Woman.* Philadelphia: Balch Institute Press, 1993.

Best, Gary Dean. *To Free a People: American Jewish Leaders and the Jewish Problem in Eastern Europe, 1890–1914.* Westport, Conn.: Greenwood Press, 1982.

Bingham, Emily. *Mordecai: An Early American Family.* New York: Hill and Wang, 2003.

Bogen, Hyman. *The Luckiest Orphans: A History of the Hebrew Orphan Asylum of New York.* Urbana: University of Illinois Press, 1992.

Borden, Morton. *Jews, Turks, and Infidels.* Chapel Hill: University of North Carolina Press, 1984.

Brandes, Joseph. *Immigrants to Freedom: Jewish Communities in Rural New Jersey since 1882.* Philadelphia: University of Pennsylvania Press, 1971.

Braunstein, Susan L., and Jenna Weisman Joselit, eds. *Getting Comfortable in New York: The American Jewish Home, 1880–1950.* Bloomington: Indiana University Press, 1991.

Brumberg, Stephan F. *Going to America, Going to School: The Jewish Immigrant Public School Encounter in Turn-of-the-Century New York City.* New York: Praeger, 1986.

Burt, Robert. *Two Jewish Justices: Outcasts in the Promised Land.* Berkeley and Los Angeles: University of California Press, 1988.

Chyet, Stanley F. *Lopez of Newport: Colonial American Merchant Prince.* Detroit: Wayne State University Press, 1970.

Cohen, Naomi. *American Jews and the Zionist Idea.* Hoboken, N.J.: KTAV, 1975.

———. *A Dual Heritage: The Public Career of Oscar S. Straus.* Philadelphia: Jewish Publication Society of America, 1969.

————. *Encounter with Emancipation: The German Jews in the United States, 1830–1914*. Philadelphia: Jewish Publication Society of America, 1984.

————. *Jacob H. Schiff: A Study in American Jewish Leadership*. Hanover, N.H.: University Press of New England, 1999.

————. *Jews in Christian America: The Pursuit of Religious Equality*. New York: Oxford University Press, 1992.

————. *Not Free to Desist: The American Jewish Committee, 1906–1966*. Philadelphia: Jewish Publication Society of America, 1972.

Cutler, Irving. *The Jews of Chicago: From Shtetl to Suburb*. Urbana: University of Illinois Press, 1995.

Davis, Moshe. *The Emergence of Conservative Judaism*. Philadelphia: Jewish Publication Society of America, 1963.

Dawidowicz, Lucy S. *On Equal Terms: Jews in America, 1881–1981*. New York: Holt, Rinehart and Winston, 1982.

Diner, Hasia R. "Before the Promised City: Eastern European Jews in America before 1880." In *An Inventory of Promises: Essays on American Jewish History in Honor of Moses Rischin*, ed. Jeffrey S. Gurock and Marc Lee Raphael, 43–62. Brooklyn, NY: Carlson Publishing, 1995.

————. *Hungering for America: Italian, Irish, and Jewish Foodways in the Age of Immigration*. Cambridge, Mass.: Harvard University Press, 2001.

————. *In the Almost Promised Land: American Jews and Blacks, 1915–1935*. Baltimore: Johns Hopkins University Press, 1992.

————. *Lower East Side Memories: The Jewish Place in America*. Princeton: Princeton University Press, 2000.

————. *A Time for Gathering: The Second Migration, 1820–1880*. Jewish People in America, vol. 2. Baltimore: Johns Hopkins University Press, 1992.

Diner, Hasia R., and Beryl Lieff Benderly. *Her Works Praise Her: A History of Jewish Women in America from Colonial Times to the Present*. New York: Basic Books, 2002.

Dinnerstein, Leonard. *America and the Survivors of the Holocaust*. New York: Columbia University Press, 1982.

————. *Antisemitism in America*. New York: Oxford University Press, 1994.

————. *The Leo Frank Case*. New York: Columbia University Press, 1968.

————. *Uneasy at Home: Antisemitism and the American Jewish Experience*. New York: Columbia University Press, 1987.

Dinnerstein, Leonard, and Mary Dale Palsson, eds. *Jews in the South*. Baton Rouge: Louisiana State University Press, 1973.

Dollinger, Marc. *Quest for Inclusion: Jews and Liberalism in Modern America*. Princeton: Princeton University Press, 2000.

Drescher, Seymour. "The Role of the Jews in the Transatlantic Slave Trade." In *From Slavery to Freedom: Comparative Studies in the Rise and Fall of Atlantic Slavery*, 339–54. New York: New York University Press, 1999.

Edgcomb, Gabrielle Simon. *From Swastika to Jim Crow: Refugee Scholars at Black Colleges*. Malabar, Fla.: Krieger, 1993.

Eichhorn, David. *Evangelizing the American Jew*. Middle Village, N.Y.: Jonathan David, 1978.

Eisen, Arnold M. *The Chosen People in America: A Study in Jewish Religious Ideology.* Bloomington: Indiana University Press, 1983.

Eitches, Edward. "Maryland's Jew Bill." *American Jewish Historical Quarterly* 60, no. 3 (March 1971): 258–79.

Elazar, Daniel J. *Community and Polity: The Organizational Dynamics of American Jewry.* Philadelphia: Jewish Publication Society of America, 1976.

Elazar, Daniel J., Jonathan D. Sarna, and Rela G. Monson, eds. *A Double Bond: The Constitutional Documents of American Jewry.* Lanham, Md.: University Press of America, 1992.

Endelman, Judith. *The Jewish Community of Indianapolis, 1849 to the Present.* Bloomington: University of Indiana Press, 1984.

Erdman, Harley. *Staging the Jew: The Performance of an American Ethnicity, 1860–1920.* New Brunswick, N.J.: Rutgers University Press, 1997.

Evans, Eli. *The Provincials: A Personal History of Jews in the South.* New York: Atheneum, 1973.

Ewen, Elizabeth. *Immigrant Women in the Land of Dollars: Life and Culture on the Lower East Side, 1890–1925.* New York: Monthly Review Press, 1985.

Faber, Eli. *Jews, Slaves, and the Slave Trade: Setting the Record Straight.* New York: New York University Press, 1998.

———. *A Time for Planting: The First Migration, 1654–1820.* Jewish People in America, vol. 1. Baltimore: Johns Hopkins University Press, 1992.

Farber, Seth. "Reproach, Recognition, and Respect: Rabbi Joseph B. Soloveitchik and Orthodoxy's Mid-Century Attitude toward Non-Orthodox Denominations." *American Jewish History* 89, no. 2 (June 2001): 193–214.

Fein, Isaac M. *The Making of an American Jewish Community: The History of Baltimore Jewry from 1773 to 1920.* Philadelphia: Jewish Publication Society of America, 1971.

Feingold, Henry. *Bearing Witness: How America and Its Jews Responded to the Holocaust.* Syracuse: Syracuse University Press, 1995.

———. *The Politics of Rescue: The Roosevelt Administration and the Holocaust, 1938–1945.* New Brunswick, N.J.: Rutgers University Press, 1970.

———. *A Time for Searching: Entering the Mainstream, 1920–1945.* Jewish People in America, vol. 4. Baltimore: Johns Hopkins University Press, 1992.

Fischel, Jack, and Sanford Pinsker, eds. *Jewish-American History and Culture: An Encyclopedia.* New York: Garland, 1992.

Fish, Sidney M. *Barnard and Michael Gratz: Their Lives and Times.* Lanham, Md: University Press of America, 1994.

Forman, Seth. *Blacks in the Jewish Mind: A Crisis in Liberalism.* New York: New York University Press, 1998.

Fried, Albert. *The Rise of the Jewish Gangster in America.* Rev. ed. New York: Columbia University Press, 1995.

Friedman, Murray, ed. *Jewish Life in Philadelphia, 1830–1940.* Philadelphia: Jewish Publication Society of America, 1983.

Friedman, Reena Sigmund. *These Are Our Children: Jewish Orphanages in the United States, 1880–1925.* Hanover, N.H.: University Press of New England, 1994.

Fuchs, Lawrence. *The Political Behavior of American Jews*. Glencoe, Ill.: Free Press, 1956.

Gabler, Neal *An Empire of Their Own: How the Jews Invented Hollywood*. New York: Crown, 1988.

Gal, Allon, ed. *Envisioning Israel: The Changing Ideals and Images of North American Jews*. Detroit: Wayne State University Press, 1996.

Gamm, Gerald. *Urban Exodus: Why the Jews Left Boston and the Catholics Stayed*. Cambridge, Mass.: Harvard University Press, 1999.

Gelin, James A. *Starting Over: The Formation of the Jewish Community of Springfield, Massachusetts, 1840–1905*. Lanham, Md.: University Press of America, 1984.

Gerber, David, ed. *Anti-Semitism in American History*. Urbana: University of Illinois Press, 1986.

Glanz, Rudolf. *The German Jew in America: An Annotated Bibliography*. Cincinnati: Hebrew Union College Press, 1969.

———. "The German-Jewish Mass Emigration, 1820–1880." *American Jewish Archives* 22, no. 1 (April 1970): 49–66.

Glazer, Nathan. *American Judaism*. 2nd ed., rev. Chicago: University of Chicago Press, 1989.

Glazier, Jack. *Dispersing the Ghetto: The Relocation of Jewish Immigrants across America*. Ithaca, N.Y.: Cornell University Press, 1998.

Glenn, Susan. *Daughters of the Shtetl: Life and Labor in the Immigrant Generation*. Ithaca, N.Y.: Cornell University Press, 1990.

Goldman, Karla. *Beyond the Synagogue Gallery: Finding a Place for Women in American Judaism*. Cambridge, Mass.: Harvard University Press, 2000.

Goldsmith, Emanuel S., Mel Scult, and Robert M. Seltzer, eds. *The American Judaism of Mordecai M. Kaplan*. New York: New York University Press, 1990.

Goldstein, Eric. "Race and the Construction of Jewish Identity in America, 1875–1945." Ph.D. diss., University of Michigan, 2000.

Goldstein, Howard. *The Home on Gorham Street and the Voices of Its Children*. Tuscaloosa: University of Alabama Press, 1996.

Goodfriend, Joyce D. *Before the Melting Pot: Society and Culture in Colonial New York City, 1664–1730*. Princeton: Princeton University Press, 1992.

Gordon, Albert I. *The Jews in Suburbia*. Boston: Beacon Press, 1959.

Goren, Arthur. *The American Jews*. Cambridge, Mass.: Harvard University Press, 1982.

———. "The Jewish Press." In *The Ethnic Press in the United States*, edited by Sally M. Miller, 203–28. Westport, Conn.: Greenwood Press, 1987.

———. *New York Jews and the Quest for Community: The Kehillah Experiment, 1908–1922*. New York: Columbia University Press, 1970.

———. *The Politics and Public Culture of American Jews*. Bloomington: Indiana University Press, 1999.

Greene, Melissa F. *Temple Bombing*. Reading, Mass: Addison-Wesley, 1996.

Grinstein, Hyman. *The Rise of the Jewish Community of New York, 1654–1860*. Philadelphia: Jewish Publication Society of America, 1945.

Gruber, Ruth. *Haven: The Unknown Story of 1,000 World War II Refugees*. New York: Coward, McCann, and Geoghegan, 1983.

Gurock, Jeffrey S. *From Fluidity to Rigidity: The Religious Worlds of Conservative and Orthodox Jews in Twentieth Century America.* Ann Arbor, Mich.: Jean and Samuel Frankel Center for Judaic Studies, 1998.

————. *The Men and Women of Yeshiva: Higher Education, Orthodoxy, and American Judaism.* New York: Columbia University Press, 1988.

————. "Resisters and Accommodators: Varieties of Orthodox Rabbis in America, 1886–1983." *American Jewish Archives* 35, no. 2 (November 1983): 100–187.

————. *When Harlem Was Jewish, 1870–1930.* New York: Columbia University Press, 1979.

Gurock, Jeffrey S., and Marc Lee Raphael, eds. *An Inventory of Promises: Essays on American Jewish History in Honor of Moses Rischin.* Brooklyn, N.Y.: Carlson, 1995.

Gutstein, Morris. *The Story of the Jews of Newport: Two and a Half Centuries of Judaism, 1658–1908.* New York: Bloch, 1936.

Hagy, William James. *This Happy Land: The Jews of Colonial and Antebellum Charleston.* Tuscaloosa: University of Alabama Press, 1993.

Halperin, Samuel. *The Political World of American Zionism.* Detroit: Wayne State University Press, 1961.

Handlin, Oscar. *A Continuing Task: The American Joint Distribution Committee, 1914–1964.* New York: Random House, 1964.

Heinze, Andrew. *Adapting to Abundance: Jewish Immigrants, Mass Consumption, and the Search for American Identity.* New York: Columbia University Press, 1990.

Helmreich, William B. *The Enduring Community: The Jews of Newark and MetroWest.* New Brunswick, N.J.: Transaction Publishers, 1999.

Hershkowitz, Leo. "Asser Levy and the Inventories of Early New York Jews." *American Jewish History* 80, no. 1 (Autumn 1990): 56–73.

————. "Some Aspects of the New York Jewish Merchant and Community, 1654–1820." *American Jewish Historical Quarterly* 67, no. 1 (September 1976): 10–34.

Hertzberg, Steven. *Strangers within the Gate City: The Jews of Atlanta, 1845–1915.* Philadelphia: Jewish Publication Society of America, 1978.

Higham, John. "Social Discrimination against Jews, 1830–1939." In *Send These to Me: Jews and Other Immigrants in Urban America.* New York: Atheneum, 1975.

Howe, Irving. *World of Our Fathers.* New York: Harcourt Brace Jovanovich, 1976.

Hyman, Paula, and Deborah Dash Moore, eds. *Jewish Women in America: An Historical Encyclopedia.* New York: Routledge, 1997.

Ivers, Gregg. *To Build a Wall: American Jews and the Separation of Church and State.* Charlottesville: University of Virginia Press, 1995.

Jacob, Walter, ed. *The Changing World of Reform Judaism: The Pittsburgh Platform in Retrospect.* Pittsburgh: Rodef Shalom Congregation, 1985.

Jacobson, Matthew Frye. *Special Sorrows: The Diasporic Imagination of Irish, Polish, and Jewish Immigrants in the United States.* Cambridge, Mass.: Harvard University Press, 1995.

——. *Whiteness of a Different Color: European Immigrants and the Alchemy of Race.* Cambridge, Mass.: Harvard University Press, 1998.

Jick, Leon. *The Americanization of the Synagogue, 1820–1870.* Hanover, N.H.: University Press of New England, 1992.

Joselit, Jenna Weissman. *Aspiring Women: A History of the Jewish Foundation for Education of Women.* New York: Jewish Foundation for Education of Women, 1996.

——. *New York's Jewish Jews: The Orthodox Community in the Interwar Years.* Bloomington: Indiana University Press, 1990.

——. *Our Gang: Jewish Crime and the New York Jewish Community, 1900–1940.* Bloomington: Indiana University Press, 1983.

——. *The Wonders of America: Reinventing Jewish Culture, 1880–1950.* New York: Hill and Wang, 1994.

Joseph, Samuel. *Jewish Immigration to the United States from 1881 to 1910.* New York: Arno, 1969.

Kaganoff, Nathan. "The Business Career of Haym Salomon as Reflected in His Newspaper Advertisements." *American Jewish Historical Quarterly* 66, no. 1 (September 1976): 35–49.

Kaganoff, Nathan, and Melvin Urofsky, eds. *"Turn to the South": Essays on Southern Jewry.* Charlottesville: University Press of Virginia, 1979.

Kahn, Lothar. "Early German-Jewish Writers and the Image of America (1820–1840)." *Leo Baeck Institute Yearbook* 31 (1986): 407–39.

Kanter, Kenneth. *The Jews on Tin Pan Alley: The Jewish Contribution to American Popular Music, 1830–1940.* New York: KTAV, 1982.

Karp, Abraham J. *Haven and Home: A History of the Jews in America.* New York: Schocken, 1985.

——, ed. *The Jewish Experience in America.* Waltham, Mass.: American Jewish Historical Society, 1969.

Kaufman, David. *Shul with a Pool: The "Synagogue-Center" in American Jewish History.* Hanover, N.H.: University Press of New England, 1999.

Kessner, Thomas. *The Golden Door: Italian and Jewish Immigrant Mobility in New York City, 1880–1915.* New York: Oxford University Press, 1977.

Kisch, Guido. *In Search of Freedom: A History of American Jews from Czechoslovakia.* London: E. Goldston, 1949.

Klaperman, Gilbert. *The Story of Yeshiva University, the First Jewish University in America.* New York: Macmillan, 1969.

Klingenstein, Susanne. *Jews in the American Academy, 1900–1940: The Dynamics of Intellectual Assimilation.* New Haven: Yale University Press, 1991.

Kolsky, Thomas A. *Jews against Zionism: The American Council for Judaism.* Philadelphia: Temple University Press, 1983.

Korn, Bertram Wallace. *American Jewry and the Civil War.* Philadelphia: Jewish Publication Society of America, 1951.

Kosak, Hadassa. *Cultures of Opposition: Jewish Immigrant Workers, New York City, 1881–1905.* Albany: State University of New York Press, 2000.

Landesman, Alter F. *Brownsville: The Birth, Development, and Passing of a Jewish Community in New York.* New York: Bloch, 1969.

Lederhendler, Eli. *Jewish Responses to Modernity: New Voices in America and Eastern Europe*. New York: New York University Press, 1994.

———. *New York Jews and the Decline of Urban Ethnicity, 1950–1970*. Syracuse, N.Y.: Syracuse University Press, 2001.

Lee, Albert. *Henry Ford and the Jews*. New York: Stein and Day, 1980.

Levine, Hillel, and Lawrence Harmon. *The Death of an American Jewish Community: A Tragedy of Good Intentions*. New York: Free Press, 1992.

Levine, Peter. *Ellis Island to Ebbet's Field: Sport and the American Jewish Experience*. New York: Oxford University Press, 1992.

Levy, B. H. "The Early History of Georgia's Jews." In *Forty Years of Diversity: Essays on Colonial Georgia*, edited by Harvey H. Jackson and Phinizy Spalding, 163–78. Athens: University of Georgia Press, 1984.

Lifson, David S. *The Yiddish Theatre in America*. New York: Thomas Yoseloff, 1965.

Lipstadt, Deborah. *Beyond Belief: The American Press and the Coming of the Holocaust, 1933–1945*. New York: Free Press, 1986.

Lowenstein, Steven. *Frankfurt on the Hudson: The German-Jewish Community of Washington Heights, 1933–1983, Its Structure and Culture*. Detroit: Wayne State University Press, 1989.

———. *The Jews of Oregon, 1850–1950*. Portland: Jewish Historical Society of Oregon, 1987.

Marcus, Jacob Rader. *The Colonial American Jew, 1492–1776*. 3 vols. Detroit: Wayne State University Press, 1970.

———. *Early American Jewry: The Jews of New York, New England, and Canada, 1649–1794*. 2 vols. Philadelphia: Jewish Publication Society of America, 1961.

———. "Light on Early Connecticut Jewry." *American Jewish Archives* 1, no.1 (January 1949): 3–52.

———. *United States Jewry, 1776–1985*. 4 vols. Detroit: Wayne State University Press, 1989.

Marinbach, Bernard. *Galveston: Ellis Island of the West*. Albany: State University of New York Press, 1983.

Marker, Jeffrey M. "The Jewish Community and the Case of Julius and Ethel Rosenberg." *Maryland Historian* 3, no. 2 (Fall 1972): 104–21.

Markowitz, Ruth Jacknow. *My Daughter, the Teacher: Jewish Teachers in the New York City Schools*. New Brunswick, N.J.: Rutgers University Press, 1993.

May, Lary, and Elaine Tyler May. "Why Jewish Movie Moguls: An Exploration in American Culture." *American Jewish History* 72, no. 1 (September 1982): 6–25.

Mayo, Louise A. *The Ambivalent Image: Nineteenth-Century America's Perception of the Jew*. Rutherford, N.J.: Fairleigh Dickinson University Press, 1988.

Melnick, Jeffrey. *A Right to Sing the Blues: African Americans, Jews, and American Popular Song*. Cambridge, Mass.: Harvard University Press, 1999.

Meyer, Michael. *Response to Modernity: A History of the Reform Movement in Judaism*. New York: Oxford University Press, 1988.

Mintz, Alan, ed. *Hebrew in America: Perspectives and Prospects*. Detroit: Wayne State University Press, 1993.

Moore, Deborah Dash. *At Home in America: Second Generation New York Jews*. New York: Columbia University Press, 1981.

———. *B'nai B'rith and the Challenge of Ethnic Leadership*. Albany: State University of New York Press, 1981.

———. "Reconsidering the Rosenbergs: Symbol and Substance in Second-Generation American Jewish Consciousness." *Journal of American Ethnic History* 8, no. 1 (Fall 1988): 21–37.

———. *To the Golden Cities: Pursuing the American Jewish Dream in Miami and L.A.* New York: Free Press, 1994.

Morawksa, Ewa. *Insecure Prosperity: Small-Town Jews in Industrial America, 1890–1940*. Princeton: Princeton University Press, 1996.

Morris, Richard. "The Role of the Jews in the American Revolution in Historical Perspective." In *Jewish Life in America*, edited by Gladys Rosen, 8–27. New York: American Jewish Committee, 1978.

Nadell, Pamela S. "The Journey to America by Steam: The Jews of Eastern Europe in Transition." *American Jewish History* 71, no. 2 (December 1981): 269–84.

———. *Women Who Would Be Rabbis: A History of Women's Ordination, 1889–1985*. Boston: Beacon Press, 1998.

Nadell, Pamela S., and Jonathan D. Sarna, eds. *Women and American Judaism: Historical Perspectives*. Hanover, N.H.: University Press of New England, 2001.

Novick, Peter. *The Holocaust in American Life*. Boston: Houghton Mifflin, 1999.

Oren, Dan A. *Joining the Club: A History of Jews and Yale*. New Haven: Yale University Press, 1985.

Orleck, Annelise. *Common Sense and a Little Fire: Women and Working-Class Politics in the United States, 1900–1965*. Chapel Hill: University of North Carolina Press, 1995.

Panitz, Esther L. *Simon Wolf: Private Conscience and Public Image*. Rutherford, N.J.: Farleigh Dickinson University Press, 1982.

Papo, Joseph M. *Sephardim in Twentieth Century America: In Search of Unity*. San Jose, Calif.: Pele Yoetz Books, 1987.

Penkower, Monty. "In Dramatic Dissent: The Bergson Boys." *American Jewish History* 70, no. 3 (March 1981): 281–309.

Perlmann, Joel. "Beyond New York: The Occupations of Russian Jewish Immigrants in Providence, Rhode Island, and in Other Small Jewish Communities, 1900–1915." *American Jewish History* 72, no. 3 (March 1983): 369–94.

———. *Ethnic Differences: Schooling and Social Structure among the Irish, Italian, Jews, and Blacks in an American City, 1880–1935*. New York: Cambridge University Press, 1988.

Pool, David de Sola. *An Old Faith in the New World: Portrait of Shearith Israel, 1654–1954*. New York: Columbia University Press, 1955.

———. *Portraits Etched in Stone: Early Jewish Settlers, 1682–1831*. New York: Columbia University Press, 1953.

Pratt, Norma Fain. *Morris Hillquit: A Political History of an American Jewish Socialist*. Westport, Conn.: Greenwood Press, 1987.

Prell, Riv-Ellen. *Fighting to Become Americans: Jews, Gender, and the Anxiety of Assimilation*. Boston: Beacon, 1999.

Raider, Mark. *The Emergence of American Zionism*. New York: New York University Press, 1998.

Raphael, Marc Lee. *Abba Hillel Silver: A Profile in American Judaism*. New York: Holmes and Meier, 1989.

————. *Jews and Judaism in a Midwestern Community: Columbus, Ohio, 1840–1975*. Columbus: Ohio Historical Society, 1979.

————. *Profiles in American Judaism: The Reform, Conservative, Orthodox, and Reconstructionist Traditions in Historical Perspectives*. New York: Harper and Row, 1988.

Rezneck, Samuel. *Unrecognized Patriots: The Jews in the American Revolution*. Westport, Conn.: Greenwood Press, 1975.

Reznikoff, Charles, and Uriah Z. Engelman. *The Jews of Charleston*. Philadelphia: Jewish Publication Society of America, 1950.

Ribuffo, Leo P. "Henry Ford and the International Jew." *American Jewish History* 69, no. 4 (June 1980): 437–77.

Rischin, Moses. *The Promised City: New York's Jews, 1870–1914*. Cambridge, Mass.: Harvard University Press, 1962.

————, ed. *The Jews of North America*. Detroit: Wayne State University Press, 1987.

Rochlin, Harriet, and Fred Rochlin. *Pioneer Jews: A New Life in the Far West*. Boston: Houghton Mifflin, 1984.

Rockaway, Robert. *The Jews of Detroit: From the Beginning, 1762–1914*. Detroit: Wayne State University Press, 1986.

Rogin, Michael. *Blackface, White Noise: Jewish Immigrants in the Hollywood Melting Pot*. Berkeley and Los Angeles: University of California Press, 1996.

Rogoff, Leonard. *Homelands: Southern Jewish Identity in Durham and Chapel Hill, North Carolina*. Tuscaloosa: University of Alabama Press, 2001.

Rogow, Faith. *Gone to Another Meeting: The National Council of Jewish Women, 1893–1993*. Tuscaloosa: University of Alabama Press, 1993.

Rosenberg, Stuart E. *America Is Different: The Search for Jewish Identity*. New York: Thomas Nelson, 1964.

Rosenwaike, Ira. "An Estimate and Analysis of the Jewish Population of the United States in 1790." *Publications of the American Jewish Historical Society* 50, no. 1 (September 1960): 23–67.

Roth, Cecil. "Some Jewish Loyalists in the War of American Independence." *Publications of the American Jewish Historical Society* 35, pt. 1 (December 1948): 81–107.

Russell, Charles Edward. *Haym Salomon and the Revolution*. New York: Cosmopolitan Books, 1930.

Sachar, Howard. *A History of the Jews in America*. New York: Knopf, 1992.

Sandrow, Nahma. *Vagabond Stars: A World History of Yiddish Theater*. Syracuse, N.Y.: Syracuse University Press, 1996.

Sarna, Jonathan. *Jacksonian Jew: The Two Worlds of Mordecai Noah*. New York: Holmes and Meier, 1981.

———. *Jews and the Founding of the Republic*. New York: Markus Weiner, 1985.

———. "The Myth of No Return: Migration to Eastern Europe, 1881–1914." *American Jewish History* 71, no. 2 (December 1981): 169–81.

———, ed. *The American Jewish Experience*. New York: Holmes and Meier, 1986.

Sarna, Jonathan, and David Dalin. *Religion and State in the American Jewish Experience*. Notre Dame, Ind.: Notre Dame University Press, 1992.

Sarna, Jonathan, and Ellen Smith, eds. *The Jews of Boston: Essays on the Occasion of the Centenary (1895–1995) of the Combined Jewish Philanthropies of Greater Boston*. Boston: Combined Jewish Philanthropies of Greater Boston, 1995.

Schultz, Debra L. *Going South: Jewish Women in the Civil Rights Movement*. New York: New York University Press, 2001.

Scult, Mel. *Judaism Faces the Twentieth Century: A Biography of Mordecai M. Kaplan*. Detroit: Wayne State University Press, 1993.

Shapiro, Edward S. *A Time for Healing: American Jewry since World War II*. Jewish People in America, vol. 5. Baltimore: Johns Hopkins University Press, 1992.

Sharfman, I. Harold. *The First Rabbi: Origins of Conflict between Orthodox and Reform: Jewish Polemic Warfare in Pre–Civil War America*. Malibu, Calif.: Pangloss Press, 1988.

Sherman, C. Bezalel. *The Jew within American Society*. Detroit: Wayne State University Press, 1960.

———. *Labor Zionism in America: Its History, Growth, and Programs*. New York: Farband-Labor Zionist Order, 1957.

Silverstein, Alan. *Alternatives to Assimilation: The Response of Reform Judaism to American Culture, 1840–1930*. Hanover, N.H.: University Press of New England, 1994.

Slobin, Mark. *Chosen Voices: The Story of the American Cantorate*. Urbana: University of Illinois Press, 1989.

Sorin, Gerald. *Irving Howe: A Life of Passionate Dissent*. New York: New York University Press, 2002.

———. "Mutual Contempt, Mutual Benefit: The Strained Encounter Between German and Eastern European Jews in the United States." *American Jewish History* 81, no. 1 (Autumn 1993): 34–59.

———. *The Nurturing Neighborhood: The Brownsville Boys Club and Jewish Community in Urban America, 1940–1990*. New York: New York University Press, 1990.

———. *The Prophetic Minority: American Jewish Immigrant Radicals, 1880–1920*. Bloomington: Indiana University Press, 1985.

———. *A Time for Building: The Third Migration, 1880–1920*. Jewish People in America, vol. 3. Baltimore: Johns Hopkins University Press, 1992.

———. *Tradition Transformed: The Jewish Experience in America*. Baltimore: Johns Hopkins University Press, 1997.

Sorkin, David. "The Port Jew: Notes toward a Social Type." *Journal of Jewish Studies* 50, no. 1 (Spring 1999): 87–97.

Soyer, Daniel. *Jewish Immigrant Associations and American Identity in New York, 1880–1939.* Cambridge, Mass.: Harvard University Press, 1997.

Staub, Michael E. *Torn at the Roots: The Crisis of Jewish Liberalism in Postwar America.* New York: Columbia University Press, 2002.

Sterba, Christopher M. *Good Americans: Italian and Jewish Immigrants during the First World War.* New York: Oxford University Press, 2003.

Stern, Malcolm. "The Function of Genealogy in American Jewish History." In *Essays in American Jewish History: To Commemorate the Tenth Anniversary of the Founding of the American Jewish Archives under the Direction of Jacob Rader Marcus,* 69–97. Cincinnati: American Jewish Archives, 1958.

Strum, Philippa. *Louis D. Brandeis: Justice for the People.* Cambridge, Mass.: Harvard University Press, 1984.

Sussman, Lance. *Isaac Leeser and the Making of American Judaism.* Detroit: Wayne State University Press, 1995.

Svonkin, Stuart. *Jews against Prejudice: American Jews and the Fight for Civil Liberties.* New York: Columbia University Press, 1997.

Temkin, Sefton D. *Isaac Mayer Wise: Shaping American Judaism.* Albany: State University of New York Press, 1992.

Tenenbaum, Shelly. *A Credit to Their Community: Jewish Loan Societies in the United States, 1880–1945.* Detroit: Wayne State University Press, 1993.

Toll, William. *The Making of an Ethnic Middle Class: Portland Jewry over Four Generations.* Albany: State University of New York Press, 1982.

Urofsky, Melvin. *American Zionism from Herzl to the Holocaust.* Garden City, N.Y.: Anchor, 1975.

Webb, Clive. *Fight against Fear: Southern Jews and Black Civil Rights.* Athens: University of Georgia Press, 2001.

Weinberg, Sydney Stahl. *The World of Our Mothers.* New York: Schocken, 1990.

Weissbach, Lee Shai. "The Jewish Communities of the United States on the Eve of Mass Migration." *American Jewish History* 78, no.1 (September 1988): 79–108.

Wenger, Beth. *New York Jews and the Great Depression: Uncertain Promise.* New Haven: Yale University Press, 1996.

Wertheimer, Jack, ed. *The American Synagogue: A Sanctuary Transformed.* Hanover, N.H.: University Press of New England, 1987.

———, ed. *Tradition Renewed: A History of the Jewish Theological Seminary of America.* New York: Jewish Theological Seminary, 1997.

Weyl, Nathaniel. *The Jew in American Politics.* New York: Arlington House, 1968.

Whitfield, Stephen J. *In Search of American Jewish Culture.* Hanover, N.H.: University Press of New England, 1999.

Winter, Nathan H. *Jewish Education in a Pluralist Society: Samson Benderly and Jewish Education in the United States.* New York: New York University Press, 1966.

Wischnitzer, Rachel. *Synagogue Architecture in the United States: History and Interpretation*. Philadelphia: Jewish Publication Society of America, 1955.

Wolf, Edwin, and Maxwell Whiteman. *History of the Jews of Philadelphia from Colonial Times to the Age of Jackson*. Philadelphia: Jewish Publication Society of America, 1957.

Woocher, Jonathan. *Sacred Survival: The Civil Religion of American Jews*. Bloomington: University of Indiana Press, 1987.

Wyman, David S. *The Abandonment of the Jews: America and the Holocaust, 1941–1945*. New York: Pantheon, 1984.

———. *Paper Walls: America and the Refugee Crisis, 1938–1941*. Amherst: University of Massachusetts Press, 1968.

Zuroff, Efraim. *The Response of Orthodox Jewry in the United States to the Holocaust: The Activities of the Vaad ha-Hatzala Rescue Committee, 1939–1945*. New York: Michael Scharf Publication Trust of the Yeshiva University Press, 2000.

INDEX

abolitionists, 155–56. *See also* slavery
Abraham, Pearl, 357
Abrams, Elliott, 308
Abzug, Bella, 266, 327, 350
Ackerman, William, 249–50
adjunta, 32
Adler, Cyrus, 173, 195
Adler, Felix, 122
Adler, Samuel, 120, 156
Adventures in Freedom (Handlins), 265
The Adventures of K'tonton, 253
affirmative action, 336, 338
African Americans, 208, 211, 243, 374n36; anti-Semitism, 211, 276; black nationalism, 334, 335, 341, 345; civil rights, 165, 259, 265–76, 282–83; discrimination vs., 165, 238, 265–70, 274–75, 285, 336; Jews joining rights struggle with, 259, 265–70, 273–75, 282–83, 298, 304, 316; moving into old Jewish enclaves, 240, 285, 288; NAACP, 92, 115, 267; slaves, 25, 26, 165, 341; tension between Jews and, 211, 274–76, 334–40, 341, 345. *See also* civil rights movement
Agricultural Adjustment Administration (AAA), 212–13
agriculture. *See* farmers
Aguilar Free Library Society, 136
Aleichem, Sholom, 287
Alexander II, 89, 96–97
Allen, Michael, 167

Allgemeine Zeitung des Judentums, 83
Amalgamated Clothing Workers' Union, 110, 161
America: colonies, 3, 13–40; early Republic, 41–67, 73, 143–44. *See also* American Revolution; government, U.S.; immigration era (1820–1924)
America fever, 83, 119. *See also* immigration era
American Association of University Professors, 115
American Civil Liberties Union (ACLU), 115, 333
American Council for Judaism, 222, 328
American Federation of Jewish Fighters, Camp Inmates, and Nazi Victims, 331
American Federation of Labor, 103, 217
American Friends of Peace Now, 328
American Hebrew, 158, 178–79
American Israel Public Affairs Committee (AIPAC), 326
Americanization: Conservative, 251, 300; cosmetic surgery, 224, 380n54; German refugees, 245; immigration restrictions and, 183–84; as Jewish defense, 173–75, 223–24, 229; Jewish economy advanced by, 154; of Jewish families, 241; middle class, 206; in popular culture, 224–25. *See also* Jewish American identity
American Jewish Committee (AJC), 113, 198, 281–82, 316; and anti-

409

Text:	10/13 Sabon
Display:	Filosofia Grand Bold
Indexer:	Barbara Roos
Compositor:	Binghamton Valley Composition, LLC
Printer:	Maple-Vail Manufacturing Group